THE MOST GRACIOUS SPEECHES TO PARLIAMENT 1900–1974

Statements of Government Policy and Achievements

OTHER BOOKS IN THIS SERIES

THE MOST GRACIOUS SPEECHES TO PARLIAMENT
1900-1974

Statements of Government Policy and Achievements

Compiled and Edited by
F. W. S. Craig

M

ISBN 978-1-349-02726-2   ISBN 978-1-349-02724-8 (eBook)
DOI 10.1007/978-1-349-02724-8

First published 1975 by
THE MACMILLAN PRESS LTD
London and Basingstoke
Associated companies in New York
Dublin Melbourne Johannesburg and Madras

SBN 333 18820 9

Typeset by
LITHOSET
Chichester

Contents

To the extreme left and right in British politics
of the mid-1970's this book is dedicated

O wad some Pow'r the giftie gie us
To see oursels as others see us!
It wad frae manie a blunder free us
An' foolish notion

(From "To a Louse" by Robert Burns, 1759-1796)

Preface

The Sovereign's Speech at the opening of each Parliamentary session has its origins in the address made by the Lord Chancellor in medieval times which explained to Parliament the reasons for its summons. With the emergence of a Cabinet system in the seventeenth and eighteenth centuries the Speech (formally referred to as the Most Gracious Speech from the Throne) has been used to announce the policy which the Government intend to pursue and the legislation which they hope to introduce. A somewhat similar speech at the end of the session summarizes the legislation which has been carried through.

In presenting a collection of the Speeches at the opening and prorogation of the eighty sessions of the twenty-one Parliaments since 1900, my aim has been to provide a convenient reference source to the policy and major legislation of the Conservative, Labour, Liberal and Coalition Governments of Britain during the past seventy-five years. The book is intended as a companion volume to my *British General Election Manifestos 1900–1974*.

The Speeches have been reproduced verbatim (a few obvious typographical errors were noticed and corrected) from the *Parliamentary Debates (Hansard), 4th and 5th series, House of Commons*, with the permission of the Controller, Her Majesty's Stationery Office.

The index to a book such as this raises numerous problems of length, style and cross-references and I would like to thank John Prince for the excellent index he has compiled.

At a time when the Parliamentary system in Britain is under increasing attack from the extremists of both left and right, and politicians are all too often being associated with greed, graft and incompetence, it is encouraging to be reminded by the Speeches that a great deal of worthwhile and moderate legislation has been enacted during this century.

The British Parliamentary system has its defects and shortcomings but it is still the envy of millions of less fortunate people throughout the world.

F.W.S. CRAIG

Parliamentary Research Services
Chichester

September 1975

FIRST SESSION OF THE TWENTY-SEVENTH PARLIAMENT

1900

OPENING (3 December 1900)

My Lords and Members of the House of Commons:
It has become necessary to make further provision for the expenses incurred by the operation of My Armies in South Africa and China.

I have summoned you to hold a Special Session in order that you may give your sanction to the enactments required for that purpose. I will not enter upon other public matters requiring your attention until the ordinary meeting of Parliament in the Spring.

PROROGATION (15 December 1900)

My Lords and Members of the House of Commons:
I thank you for the liberal provision which you have made for the expenses incurred by the operations of My Armies in South Africa and China.

SECOND SESSION OF THE TWENTY-SEVENTH PARLIAMENT

1901

OPENING (14 February 1901)

My Lords and Members of the House of Commons:

I address you for the first time at a moment of National sorrow, when the whole Country is mourning the irreparable loss which we have so recently sustained, and which has fallen with peculiar severity upon Myself. My beloved Mother, during Her long and glorious reign, has set an example before the world of what a Monarch should be. It is My earnest desire to walk in Her footsteps.

Amid this public and private grief it is satisfactory to Me to be able to assure you that My relations with other Powers continue to be friendly.

The war in South Africa has not yet entirely terminated; but the capitals of the enemy and his principal lines of communication are in My possession, and measures have been taken which will, I trust, enable My troops to deal effectually with the forces by which they are still opposed. I greatly regret the loss of life and the expenditure of treasure due to the fruitless guerilla warfare maintained by Boer partisans in the former territories of the two Republics. Their early submission is much to be desired in their own interests, as, until it takes place, it will be impossible for Me to establish in those Colonies institutions which will secure equal rights to all the white inhabitants, and protection and justice to the Native population.

The capture of Peking by the allied forces, and the happy release of those who were besieged in the Legations, results to which My Indian troops and My Naval forces largely contributed, have been followed by the submission of the Chinese Government to the demands insisted on by the Powers. Negotiations are proceeding as to the manner in which compliance with these conditions is to be effected.

The establishment of the Australian Commonwealth was proclaimed at Sydney on the 1st January with many manifestations of popular enthusiasm and rejoicing.

My deeply beloved and lamented Mother had assented to the visit of the Duke of Cornwall and York to open the first Parliament of the new Commonwealth in Her name.

A separation from My Son, especially at such a moment, cannot be otherwise than deeply painful; but I still desire to give effect to Her late Majesty's wishes, and as an evidence of Her interests, as well as of My own, in all that concerns the welfare of My subjects beyond the seas, I have decided that the visit to Australia shall not be abandoned, and shall be extended to New Zealand and to the Dominion of Canada.

The prolongation of hostitities in South Africa has led Me to make a further call upon the patriotism and devotion of Canada and Australasia. I rejoice that My request has met with a prompt and loyal response, and that large additional contingents from those Colonies will embark for the seat of war at an early date.

The expedition organised for the supression of the rebellion in Ashanti has been crowned with signal success. The endurance and gallantry of My Native troops, ably commanded by Sir James Willcocks, and led by British officers, have overcome both the stubborn resistance of the most warlike tribes in West Africa and the exceptional difficulties of the climate, the season, and the country in which the operations have been conducted.

The garrison of Coomassie, which was besieged by the enemy, has been relieved after a prolonged and gallant defence; the principal Kings have surrendered, and the chief impediment to the progress and development of this rich portion of My West African possessions has now, I hope, been finally removed.

The suffering and mortality caused by a prolonged drought over a large portion of My Indian Empire has been greatly alleviated by a seasonable rainfall; but I regret to add that in parts of the Bombay Presidency distress of a serious character still continues, which my officers are using every endeavour to mitigate.

Members of the House of Commons:

The Estimates for the year will be laid before you. Every care has been taken to limit their amount, but the Naval and Military requirements of the Country, and especially the outlay consequent on the South African war, have involved an inevitable increase.

The demise of the Crown renders it necessary that a renewed provision shall be made for the Civil List. I place unreservedly at your disposal those hereditary revenues which were so placed by My predecessor: and I have commanded that the Papers necessary for a full consideration of the subject shall be laid before you.

My Lords and Members of the House of Commons:

Proposals will be submitted to your judgment for increasing the efficiency of My Military forces.

Certain changes in the constitution of the Court of Final Appeal are rendered necessary in consequence of the increased resort to it, which has resulted from the expansion of the Empire during the last two generations.

Legislation will be proposed to you for the amendment of the Law relating to Education.

Legislation has been prepared, and, if the time at your disposal shall prove to be adequate, will be laid before you, for the purpose of regulating the Voluntary Sale by Landlords to Occupying Tenants in Ireland, for amending and consolidating the Factory and Workshops Acts, for the better administration of the Law respecting Lunatics, for amending the Public Health Acts in regard to Water Supply, for the prevention of drunkenness in Licensed Houses or Public Places, and for amending the Law of Literary Copyright.

PROROGATION (17 August 1901)

My Lords and Members of the House of Commons:

It is satisfactory to be able to close the first Parliament of My reign with the assurance that the cordiality of the relations between Great Britain and other Powers remains undiminished.

The nature and extent of the reparations to be given by China for the unexampled outrages committed last summer have been the subject of protracted discussion among the Powers. I am glad to be able to inform you that, by a general agreement, in which China has concurred the extent of the indemnity to be provided by that Government and the security for its payment to the various Powers have been determined; and the punishment of the guiltiest of the offenders has also been insisted on.

The progress of My forces in the conquest of the two Republics by whom My South African Colonies have been invaded has been steady and continuous; but, owing to the difficulty and extent of the country to be traversed, the length of the Military operations has been protracted.

The signal success which has attended the visit of the Duke and Duchess of Cornwall and York to the Colonies has afforded Me the greatest gratification, which, I am convinced, is shared by all classes of My subjects throughout the Empire. The opening of the first Parliament of the Australian Commonwealth by the Heir to the Throne is an event of wide significance and deep interest, and the enthusiastic welcome which has been given to My son and his wife in every Colony they have visited is an additional proof of the patriotism, loyalty, and devotion of the people of My Dominions oversea.

In My Indian Empire the recovery of agriculture and trade from the depression caused by the famine has been somewhat retarded by the lateness of the rainfall. The most recent information is,

however, reassuring, and prospects are reported to be much improved. Should these favourable conditions continue, a rapid reduction in the present area of distress and the restoration to the population of their usual means of livelihood may confidently be expected.

Members of the House of Commons:

I have to note with great satisfaction the liberal provision which you have made for the Naval and Military Services during the current year.

I thank you for the arrangements you have made for the maintenance of the honour and dignity of the Crown; and especially for those which affect the state and comfort of My Royal Consort.

My Lords and Members of the House of Commons:

Your attention has been directed during the past Session mainly to the legislative provisions required by the special circumstances of the year. Unusual demands have been made upon the time at the disposal of Parliament by the demise of the Crown, by the continuance of an arduous war, and the necessity of raising fresh revenue by a wider range of taxation. While providing for the heavy expenditure of the war, you have further made provision for the increase in many important respects of the efficiency of the Naval and Military Forces of the Empire.

I have observed with great satisfaction, that you have passed a Bill to amend and consolidate that code of Factory Law from which so much benefit has already been derived by the working classes of this Country; and that the Law relating to youthful offenders has been amended in such a manner as will prevent the imprisonment of young children.

The measure which you have adopted for vesting in local authorities the superintendence of certain important departments of education will in itself be of great benefit to them, and will prepare the way for further reforms.

I am gratified to see that you have given effect to a widely expressed desire on the part of My subjects beyond the sea by authorising Me to make such additions to the Royal Title as may seem to Me expedient.

THIRD SESSION OF THE TWENTY-SEVENTH PARLIAMENT

1902

OPENING (16 January 1902)

My Lords and Members of the House of Commons:

Since the close of the last Session of Parliament I have had the happiness to welcome back the Prince and Princess of Wales on their return from their lengthened voyage to various parts of My Empire. They have everywhere been received with demonstrations of the liveliest affection, and I am convinced that their presence has served to rivet more closely the bonds of mutual regard and loyalty by which the vigour of the Empire is maintained.

My relations with other Powers continue to be of a friendly character.

I regret that the war in South Africa has not yet been concluded, though the course of the operations has been favourable to our arms.

The area of the war has been largely reduced, and industries are being resumed in My new Colonies. In spite of the tedious character of the campaign, My soldiers have throughout displayed a cheerfulness in the endurance of the hardships incident to guerilla warfare, and a humanity, even to their own detriment, in the treatment of the enemy, which is deserving of the highest praise.

The necessity of relieving those of My troops who have most felt the strain of the war has afforded Me an opportunity of again availing myself of the loyal and patriotic offers of My Colonies, and further contingents will shortly reach South Africa from the Dominion of Canada, the Commonwealth of Australia, and from New Zealand.

On the invitation of the King of the Belgians, an International Conference on Sugar Bounties has recently reassembled at Brussels. I trust that its decision may lead to the abandonment of a system by which the sugar-producing Colonies, and the home manufactures of sugar, have been unfairly weighted in the prosecution of this most important industry.

I have concluded with the President of the United States a Treaty, the provisions of which will facilitate the construction of an interoceanic canal under guarantees that its neutrality will be maintained, and that it will be open to the commerce and shipping of all nations.

I have concluded a Treaty with the President of the United States of Brazil referring to arbitration questions relative to the frontier between My Colony of British Guiana and Brazil. I have much pleasure in stating that the King of Italy has consented to act as Arbitrator.

In My Indian Empire the rainfall has been less abundant than was desired, and the continuance of relief measures, though on a less extensive scale than in the past year, will be necessary in certain parts of the Bombay Presidency and of the adjoining Native States. I anticipate a further improvement in the methods and efficiency of famine relief in the future from the labours of the Commission who have recently reported.

The death of Abdur Rahman, the Ameer of Afghanistan, has been followed by the accession of his son and appointed heir, the Ameer Habibulla, who has expressed his earnest desire to maintain the friendly relations of Afghanistan with my Indian Empire.

Members of the House of Commons:

The Estimates for the service of the year will be laid before you. They have been framed as economically as a due regard to efficiency renders possible, in the special circumstances of the present exigency.

My Lords and Members of the House of Commons:

Proposals for the co-ordination and improvement of primary and secondary education will be laid before you.

A measure will be introduced for amending the administration of the water supply in the area at present controlled by the London Water Companies.

A Bill for facilitating the sale and purchase of Land in Ireland will be submitted for your consideration.

Measures will be proposed to you for improving the Law of Valuation; for amending the Law relating to the Sale of Intoxicating Liquors and for the Registration of Clubs; for amending the Patent Law; and for sundry reforms in the Law of Lunacy.

PROROGATION (18 December 1902)

My Lords and Members of the House of Commons:

The period since the meeting of Parliament last January has been fruitful in events of public importance and interest. The war in South Africa, after lasting for two years and a half, has been brought to a successful and honourable conclusion; the new Colonies of the Transvaal and the Orange River have been incorporated in My Empire, and, in spite of the inevitable difficulties consequent on a long and destructive war, there seems every reason to hope that material prosperity, greater than any they have yet experienced, may visit these regions, and that all sections of the population may live together in friendship with each other and loyalty to the Crown.

The ceremony of the Coronation had of necessity to be postponed through the dangerous illness, from which, by the blessing of Almighty God, I have been granted a complete recovery. But the sympathy and affection manifested by all classes of the community have caused Me deep gratification, and have rendered even more memorable an occasion which differed from every preceding event of a like character in respect of the numbers and the importance of those who visited this Kingdom from the most distant portions of My Empire.

The great Indian Feudatory Princes showed by their presence at a ceremony of Imperial significance their devotion to the King-Emperor; while the Prime Ministers of the self-governing Colonies gave by their attendance yet another proof of the strong feeling of attachment binding these free communities to the Crown and to the Mother Country which was so strikingly manifested during the recent war.

Advantage was taken of the presence of these representative statesmen to discuss many questions closely affecting the relations between the various portions of My Empire, and I am confident that these personal communications, followed as they have been by the visit of the Secretary of State for the Colonies to South Africa for the purpose of investigating on the spot the difficult problems which there await solution, will be of the utmost value both in respect of their immediate effects and as precedents for the future.

Operations have been undertaken in Eastern Africa for the purpose of checking the depredations committed by the Mullah Abdullah against the tribes under My protection. These operations have been conducted in the face of difficulties which have hitherto stood in the way of their complete success. My forces are receiving valuable facilities from the Italian Government, whose African Possessions are also affected by the Mullah's aggression. I hail with satisfaction the co-operation of the two countries in a matter which concerns them both.

The Chilean and Argentine Governments accepted the good offices of My reverend Mother for the purpose of obtaining a settlement of a long-standing difference regarding the frontiers of the two Republics. After a careful examination of the documentary evidence and a survey of the localities in dispute by a Commission of experts, I have pronounced an arbitral Award, which has been readily accepted by both parties, and which may be expected to prevent the recurrence of misunderstandings between them. It has given Me cordial satisfaction to have been able to contribute in this way to the establishment of good relations between the two Republics.

In concert with other Governments interested in the sugar trade, I have entered into a Convention for the purpose of putting an end to the grave inconveniences resulting from the grant of excessive bounties on the production of sugar.

I regret that the constant complaints which My Government have found it necessary to address to the Government of Venezuela in regard to unjustifiable and arbitrary acts against British subjects and property during the last two years have been persistently disregarded. It has become necessary for My Government acting in concert with that of His Imperial Majesty the German Emperor, which has also serious causes of complaint against the Republic, to insist upon measures of redress.

An Agreement was concluded early in the present year between My Government and that of His Imperial Majesty the Emperor of Japan, under which the two Governments have bound themselves to assist one another in certain eventualities for the defence of their respective interests. This Agreement will, I believe, be for the advantage of both countries, and will contribute towards the maintenance of the general peace in the extreme East.

I have concluded with His Imperial Majesty the Emperor of China a Commercial Treaty which promises to secure, not only for this Country, but for the commerce of the world, valuable facilities and advantages. Portions of this Treaty will not become operative unless the same engagements be entered into with China by other Powers; it contains, however, provisions of great value which do not depend upon their assent. Arrangements have been made for the withdrawal of the International Forces which have been in occupation of Shanghae.

I have also concluded with His Imperial Majesty the Emperor of Ethiopia a Treaty defining the frontier between that country and the Soudan.

In My Indian Dominions, which, during the last few years have suffered so severely from famine, much anxiety was caused by the anticipation of another year of drought; but I rejoice to say that this danger has now been averted by a plentiful fall of rain, and that the prospects of the agricultural population throughout the country are generally good.

The Governer General is about to hold a great assembly at Delhi for the purpose of proclaiming My succession to the Imperial Crown of India, and it gives me the highest satisfaction to reflect that this important ceremony will be associated with a period of unusual commercial and financial prosperity.

Members of the House of Commons:
I thank you for the liberal provision which you have made for the services of the year.

My Lords and Members of the House of Commons:
During a Session of unusual length you have

passed measures dealing with the Supply of Water to
the Metropolis, with the Sale of Intoxicating Liquors,
and the Registration of Clubs, and with a much
needed reform of the Patent Laws. These subjects
have long called for legislative treatment, and I rejoice
that time has been found to pass the necessary Acts.
The heaviest portion, however, of your labours has
been devoted to the Bill for the co-ordination and
improvement of primary, secondary, and higher
Education in England and Wales. It was impossible, in
the public interest, to defer any longer dealing with
this great subject; nor could it be touched without
raising issues which all would desire to see left
outside the region of political discussion. I trust that
the controversies which have been aroused during
the passing of the Measure will not be of long
duration, and that it will greatly contribute to the
solution of what is perhaps the most difficult, and is
certainly not the least important, of all the questions
of domestic legislation which can engage your
attention.

FOURTH SESSION OF THE TWENTY-SEVENTH PARLIAMENT

1903

OPENING (17 February 1903)

My Lords and Members of the House of Commons:

My relations with all the Foreign Powers continue to be friendly.

The blockade of Venezuelan ports, rendered necessary by outrages on the British flag and wrongs inflicted on the persons and property of British subjects by the Venezuelan Government, has led to negotiations for the adjustment of all the matters in dispute. I rejoice that a settlement has now been arrived at which has justified the blockading Powers in bringing all hostile naval operations to an immediate close. Papers on the subject have been laid before you.

Negotiations have taken place for the adjustment of the questions which have arisen with regard to the boundary between My possessions in North America and the territory of Alaska. A treaty providing for the reference of these questions to an Arbitral Tribunal has been signed and ratified.

The condition of the European provinces of Turkey gives cause for serious anxiety. I have used My best efforts to impress upon the Sultan and his Ministers the urgent need for practical and well-considered measures of reform. The Governments of Austria-Hungary and Russia have had under their consideration what reforms it would be desirable that the Powers who were parties to the Treaty of Berlin should recommend to the Sultan for immediate adoption. I trust that the proposals made will prove to be sufficient for the purpose, and that I shall find it possible to give them My hearty support. Papers on the subject will be laid before you.

I regret that the efforts which My Government have been making to arrive to a joint delimitation with the Turkish Government of the boundaries of the tribal country adjoining Aden have hitherto failed to bring about a settlement. Negotiations upon this subject are being urgently pressed forward.

A body of My troops, including a small corps of mounted infantry raised from the inhabitants of the Transvaal and Orange River Colony, has been disembarked at Obbia, in Italian Somaliland, to operate against the Mullah Abdullah, and an advance inland is about to be made. The co-operation of the Italian Government in this undertaking has been most cordial, and I trust that as a result of these operations the tribes of both Protectorates may be secured from further molestation.

The progress of events in South Africa has been satisfactory. The visit of the Secretary of State for the Colonies to that portion of My dominions has already been productive of the happiest results; and the opportunity which it has provided for personal conference with Lord Milner, with the Ministers of the self-governing Colonies, and with the representatives of all interests and opinions, has greatly conduced to the smooth adjustment of many difficult questions, and to the removal of many occasions of misunderstanding.

It has been found necessary to send an expedition to Kano in consequence of the hostile action of the Emir of that place. My troops have successfully occupied his capital, and I trust that it will now become possible to proceed in safety with the delimitation of the boundary between My territory of Northern Nigeria and the adjoining possessions of the French Republic. Papers upon this subject will at once be presented.

My succession to the Imperial Crown of India has been proclaimed and celebrated in an assembly of unexampled splendour at Delhi. I there received from the fuedatory Princes and Chiefs, and from all classes of the peoples within My Indian dominions, gratifying marks of their loyalty and devotion to My Throne and family. I am glad to be able to state that this imposing ceremony has coincided, in point of time, with the disappearance of drought and agricultural distress in Western India, and that the prospects both of agriculture and commerce throughout My Indian Empire are more encouraging and satisfactory than they have been for some years past.

Members of the House of Commons:

The Estimates for the coming year will be laid before you. Although they have been framed with due regard to economy, the needs of the Country and of the Empire make a large expenditure inevitable.

My Lords and Members of the House of Commons:

A Bill will be laid before you which will, I trust, complete the series of measures which have already done much to substitute single ownership for the costly and unsatisfactory conditions still attaching to the Tenure of Agricultural Land over a large portion of Ireland.

Proposals will be submitted to you for completing the scheme of Educational Reform passed last session by extending and adapting it to the Metropolitan area.

Measures will be introduced for the purpose of carrying into effect engagements arising out of the Convention for the Abolition of Bounties on Sugar which has recently been ratified at Brussels; and for guaranteeing a Loan to be raised for the Development of My new Colonies in South Africa.

A Bill will be laid before you for Improving the Administration of the Port and Docks of London, the condition of which is a matter of National concern.

A measure Amending and Consolidating the Licensing Laws in Scotland is greatly desired in that country, and I trust will pass into Law.

Measures will also be proposed to you for Improving the Law of Valuation and Assessment; for Regulating the Employment of Children; for dealing with the Sale of Adulterated Dairy Produce; for Amending the Law relating to Savings Banks; and for Reconstituting the Royal Patriotic Fund Commission.

PROROGATION (14 August 1903)

My Lords and Members of the House of Commons:
The visit which I was able to pay during the spring to the capitals of Portugal, Italy and France, has, I trust, produced good results. Nothing could have exceeded the cordiality of the reception which I experienced throughout my journey.

More recently the President of the French Republic has been My guest. His visit has given rise to a striking exhibition of the feelings of mutual good-will which prevail between the two countries.

The situation in the European provinces of Turkey continues to be a subject of general anxiety. My Government, acting in concert with those of Austria-Hungary and Russia and the other Signatories of the Treaty of Berlin, have used their best efforts to restrict the area of disturbance, and to impress upon those concerned the necessity of self-restraint and moderation.

I earnestly hope that the scheme of reforms pressed on the Porte by the two Powers most nearly concerned, and strongly supported by My Government, may effect some improvement in the condition of all classes of the population in Macedonia.

The ratifications of the Treaty of Commerce and Navigation concluded with China in September, 1902, have now been exchanged, and portions of the Treaty will come into immediate operation.

I have also concluded with His Imperial Majesty the Shah of Persia a Convention which will place the commercial relations of the two countries on a more secure amd satisfactory basis in the future.

In the Transvaal and Orange River Colonies the work of resettlement and pacification has made great progress. The recently constituted Legislative Councils, containing unofficial members representing the various interests and sections of the community,

have held their first session, and have rendered valuable services in preparing and passing the measures necessary for the good Government of My new Colonies. A Customs Convention, which includes preferential treatment for imports from the mother country, has been ratified by the Legislatures of all the Colonies of British South Africa, the union of which, for fiscal purposes, is an important and necessary step in the direction of their ultimate political federation.

In My Indian Empire the return of favourable seasons and the improvement of the finances have enabled important reductions of taxation to be given, which, I trust, will perceptibly ameliorate the condition of the people. Agriculture and trade continue to exhibit signs of sustained progress, while the most recent information as to the present season's rainfall and the promise of the crops is generally reassuring.

The operations conducted by My forces in Somaliland for the protection of certain tribes who had suffered from the depredations of the Mullah Abdullah have not yet been concluded; but the flight of the enemy's forces from his original position in a north-easterly direction will enable a further movement to be undertaken against him under more favourable conditions.

I am glad to have been able, within the last few months, to visit My people both in Scotland and Ireland. The warm expressions of goodwill with which I was everywhere received have greatly touched Me.

In Ireland My visit to the Capital, to Belfast, the chief centre of industrial enterprise, to Londonderry, through Connemara to Galway, and to Cork, enabled Me to realise how much is being attempted, and by how many agencies, to improve the housing accommodation of the working population, to stimulate commercial activity, to advance the methods of agriculture, to develop technical education, and to provide for the sick and infirm. Much remains to be done, but it was with feelings of the deepest gratification that I noticed signs of increasing concord between all classes in Ireland, presaging, as I hope, a new era of united efforts for the general welfare.

Members of the House of Commons:
I thank you for the liberality with which you have made provision for the services for the year.

My Lords and Members of the House of Commons:
A measure to expedite the conversion of agricultural tenancies into occupation ownerships throughout Ireland has been passed in a form which offers inducements towards the continued residence of landowners among their countrymen, and provides facilities for improving the conditions of life in the poorer districts of the West. This reform, by removing ancient causes of social dissension, will, I heartily trust,

conduce to the common benefit of all My Irish subjects.

The scheme for co-ordinating and improving our system of secondary and elementary education, which was applied to the rest of England and Wales by the enactment of last year, has now been completed by its extension to London. I am hopeful that great advantage will be derived from this far-reaching educational reform.

Although the measure for making the Port of London adequate, under modern conditions, to the commercial needs of the Metropolis, has not passed through all its stages, the time expended on it has not been lost; and I trust it will become law at an early period of next session.

I congratulate you on passing an Act enabling My Government to carry into effect My engagement to co-operate with other Powers in bringing about the abolition of bounties on sugar.

The law relating to the sale of intoxicating liquors in Scotland has been consolidated and greatly improved.

I have gladly given My assent to legislation for regulating the employment of children, for controlling the use of motor-cars, and for reorganising the administration of the Patriotic Fund.

FIFTH SESSION OF THE TWENTY-SEVENTH PARLIAMENT

1904

OPENING (2 February 1904)

My Lords and Members of the House of Commons:

My relations with Foreign Powers continue to be of a satisfactory character.

My Government has concluded with that of the French Republic an Agreement which will, I trust, do much to promote the recourse to arbitration in cases of international dispute. Apart from its intrinsic value, the Agreement affords a happy illustration of the friendly feelings prevailing between the two Countries, of which striking proofs were given during My visit to France and that of the President of the French Republic to Great Britain, and of which further evidence has been furnished by a recent exchange of international courtesies.

Similar Agreements are in process of negotiation with the Governments of Italy and the Netherlands.

An Agreement has been concluded between My Government and that of Portugal for the settlement by arbitration of the frontier line between the possessions of Portugal in South-West Africa and the territory of the Barotse Kingdom. His Majesty the King of Italy has been pleased to accept the office of Arbitrator.

The Tribunal appointed under the Convention concluded on the 3rd March last between My Government and that of the United States has given a decision on the points referred to it. On some of these the verdict has been favourable to British claims; on others it has been adverse. Much as this last circumstance is to be deplored, it must, nevertheless, be a matter of congratulation that the misunderstandings, in which ancient Boundary Treaties, made in ignorance of geographical facts, are so fertile, have in this case been finally removed from the field of controversy.

The military operations in Somaliland are being pushed forward as rapidly as difficulties of climate and transport will permit. The successes recently obtained by My troops under General Egerton will materially contribute to the destruction of the Mullah's power and the consequent pacification of the country. I have received cordial co-operation from the Italian Government, and from the Emperor Menelik of Abyssinia, who has organised a force which, by advancing from the west, will, it is hoped, materially assist the movement now in progress.

I have watched with concern the course of the negotiations between the Governments of Japan and Russia in regard to their respective interests in China and Corea. A disturbance of the peace in those regions could not but have deplorable consequences. Any assistance which My Government can usefully render towards the promotion of a pacific solution will be gladly afforded.

The scheme of Macedonian reforms proposed in February last by the Russian and Austro-Hungarian Governments, with the concurrence of the other Powers Signatories of the Treaty of Berlin, has been improved and strengthened in several important particulars. The revised scheme has been concurred in by the other Powers and accepted, after a regrettable delay, by the Porte. The winter has brought a cessation in the disturbances which prevailed throughout Macedonia during the greater part of last year; and it is to be earnestly hoped that advantage will be taken of this respite in order to carry out those practical measures of amelioration which are so sorely needed in these unhappy regions.

Amongst these measures the organisation of the Macedonian Gendarmerie deserves a prominent place. I note with satisfaction that His Majesty the Sultan has appointed a distinguished General Officer of the Italian Army to take charge of this reform. He is to be assisted in the discharge of his task by other officers appointed by the Powers, and I have authorised the employment of a Staff Officer of My Army, aided by other British Officers, for this purpose.

I am gratified to observe that the Legislatures of the Commonwealth of Australia and the Colony of New Zealand have passed laws giving effect to the Naval Agreements entered into at the Colonial Conference of 1902, under which they assume a larger share than heretofore in the general Scheme of Imperial Defence. The New Zealand Legislature has also sanctioned a Tariff which gives a preference in its markets to the produce of this Country.

The insufficiency of the supply of the raw material upon which the great cotton industry of this Country depends has inspired Me with deep concern. I trust that the efforts which are being made in various parts of My Empire to increase the area under cultivation may be attended with a large measure of success.

With the concurrence of the Chinese Government, a Political Mission has entered Thibetan territory in order to secure the due observance of the Convention of 1890 relating to Sikkim and Thibet. A Chinese official has been despatched from Pekin to meet it, and I trust that an arrangement may be arrived at with the Chinese and Thibetan authorities which will peacefully remove a constant source of difficulty and friction on the northern frontier of My Indian Empire. Papers on the subject will be laid before you.

Members of the House of Commons:

The Estimates for the year will be laid before you. Although they have been framed with the utmost desire for economy, the burden imposed on the resources of the Country by the necessities of Naval and Military Defence is undoubtedly serious. The possibility of diminishing this burden is being carefully considered in connection with the general problem of Army and War Office Reform.

My Lords and Members of the House of Commons:

A measure for the purpose of dealing with the evils consequent on the Immigration of Criminal and Destitute Aliens into the United Kingdom will be laid before you.

A Bill amending the Law with respect to Licences for the Sale of Intoxicating Liquors in England will be submitted to you.

A measure for the Amendment of the Law with respect to Valuation Authorities and the Preparation of Valuation Lists will be introduced.

A Bill to Amend the Laws relating to Education in Scotland has been prepared for your consideration.

A measure will be introduced to Amend the Labourers Acts and the Housing of the Working Classes Act in Ireland.

Proposals will be laid before you for Amending the Workmen's Compensation Acts, for Amending the Law relating to Public Health, for dealing with the Hours of Employment in Shops, for Consolidating the Enactments relating to Naval Prizes of War, for removing, after the termination of the present Parliament, the necessity for Re-election in the case of Acceptance of Office by Members of the House of Commons, for Supplementing the Powers of the Congested Districts Board in Scotland, and for Amending the Law relating to Sea Fisheries.

PROROGATION (15 August 1904)

My Lords and Members of the House of Commons:

My relations with Foreign Powers continue to be of a satisfactory character. I have paid visits to the King of Denmark at Copenhagen and to the German Emperor at Kiel. My reception was in each case of the most cordial description.

Agreements have been entered into between My Government and that of the French Republic for the settlement of a series of questions involving the interests of both countries in different parts of the world. These agreements will not only be advantageous in themselves to all concerned but will have the effect of materially strengthening the ties of friendship which now so happily unite My subjects and the citizens of the French Republic.

Agreements for referring certain classes of questions to Arbitration have been concluded between My Government and the Governments of Italy, Spain, and Germany.

The King of Italy has pronounced his Arbitral Award with regard to the Boundary between My Colony of British Guiana and the United States of Brazil, with the result that a long-standing cause of difficulty between the Colony and the neighbouring Republic has been satisfactorily removed. Arrangements will be made at once for putting the Award into effect.

The military operations in Somaliland have ended in the infliction of a severe defeat upon the Mullah's forces, and, with the exception of a temporary garrison to cover the work of organising the tribes with a view to their own defence, My troops and those of the Emperor Menelek, who were acting in co-operation with them, have been withdrawn.

Hostilities are, I regret to say, still in progress between Russia and Japan. Upon the outbreak of the war, I issued a Proclamation declaring My neutrality, and enjoining upon all My people the strict observance thereof. Important questions involving the treatment of neutral commerce at the hands of belligerents have arisen in connection with these operations. The issues involved, which are of the gravest moment to the trade of My Empire, will, I trust, be amicably settled, and without prejudice to the vast commercial interests of this Country. My Government will energetically support My subjects in the exercise of the rights recognised by international law as belonging to neutrals.

The scheme for the reorganisation of the Macedonian *gendarmerie* has been put into operation, and the Foreign Officers appointed by the Powers are now employed in the areas assigned to them. Their efforts under the able direction of General de Giorgis Pasha, promise satisfactory results. A scheme for the reform of the tithe system has been elaborated by the Civil Agents, and has been applied experimentally in certain districts.

On the advice of My Government, I have decided to sanction the introduction of an elective element into the Legislative Council of the Transvaal, and I trust that all classes of My subjects in that Colony will unite in rendering this step in the direction of ultimate self-government conducive to the welfare and development of this part of My Dominions.

The political mission which, with the concurrence of the Chinese Government, I found it necessary to dispatch into Tibetan territory, in order to secure the due observance of the Convention of 1890 relating to Sikkim and Tibet, has encountered some resistance in its advance. Its safe arrival at Lhasa affords Me the greatest satisfaction, and reflects the highest credit on the officers and men composing the small force employed. I trust that, by conference with the Tibetan authorities, in conjunction with the Chinese representative at Lhasa, terms may be arranged which will facilitate trade and put an end to the difficulty and friction which have arisen on the northern frontier of My Indian Empire.

Members of the House of Commons:

I thank you for the satisfactory provision which you made for the requirements of the public service.

My Lords and Members of the House of Commons:

I have been glad to note the attention which you have given to the important questions affecting the reorganisation of My Army and its central administration. I trust that these reforms will conduce to the defensive strength of My Empire.

The enactments contained in the measure for reducing the number of existing licences for the sale of intoxicating liquors, and for regulating new grants, constitute a sensible improvement of the present law, and, while calculated to further the cause of temperance and public order, avoid any injustice to those interests which have grown up under the prevailing system.

My assent has been given to a Bill for securing that the educational reforms embodied in the Act of 1902 shall be impartially applied for the benefit of all children attending public elementary schools in England and Wales.

A measure has been passed to give approval to the arrangements which are included in the Convention which I have entered into with the Government of the French Republic.

A Bill designed to facilitate the earlier closing of shops throughout the United Kingdom has received My assent.

SIXTH SESSION OF THE TWENTY-SEVENTH PARLIAMENT

1905

OPENING (14 February 1905)

My Lords and Members of the House of Commons:

My relations with Foreign Powers continue to be of a friendly description.

It gave Me particular satisfaction to receive as My guests during the past autumn the King and Queen of Portugal, a country which has for centuries been connected with Great Britain by ties of the closest friendship.

The war which has been in progress since February last between Russia and Japan unhappily continues. My Government have been careful to observe in the strictest manner the obligations incumbent upon a neutral Power.

The condition of the Balkan Peninsula continues to give cause for anxiety. The measures adopted at the instance of the Austro-Hungarian and Russian Governments have been instrumental in bringing about some amelioration of the state of the disturbed districts. Progress has notably been made in the reorganisation of the *gendarmerie,* to which officers belonging to My Army have contributed valuable assistance. These measures have still to be supplemented by radical reforms, especially of the financial system, before any permanent improvements can be effected in the administration of these provinces of the Turkish Empire. I note with satisfaction that the Austro-Hungarian and Russian Governments have lately addressed to the Porte proposals for this purpose. My Government is in communication with those of the other Powers mainly concerned upon this important ·subject.

The Convention entered into between My Government and that of the French Republic for the amicable settlement of questions involving the interests of both countries has been approved by the French Legislature and duly ratified. It will, I believe, operate in a manner advantageous to both countries, while it cannot fail to strengthen the friendly relations which so happily subsist between them.

Agreements, under which international questions of a certain class will be referred to arbitration, have been concluded between My Government and the Governments of Sweden and Norway, Portugal and Switzerland.

My Government has also come to an Agreement with that of Russia under which an International Commission of Inquiry, assembled in conformity with the principles of The Hague Convention of 1899, has been entrusted with the duty of investigating the circumstances connected with the disaster to British trawlers which resulted from the action of the Russian fleet in the North Sea; and of apportioning the responsibility for this deplorable incident.

The steps to be taken for establishing a Representative Constitution in the Transvaal are receiving the earnest consideration of My Government and of those administering the Colony, and will, I hope, result in substantial progress towards the ultimate goal of complete self-government.

An Agreement, the provisions of which are calculated to place the relations of the Tibetan Government and the Government of India on a satisfactory footing was concluded at Lhasa on the 7th September. The great difficulties which the Mission encountered were brilliantly surmounted by the civil and military authorities responsible for its conduct.

The Chinese Government have sent a Commissioner to Calcutta to negotiate a Convention of Adhesion on their part to the Agreement with the Tibetan Government. Papers on the subject have been laid before you.

The Amir of Afghanistan has sent his son, the Sirdar Inayatulla, to pay a complimentary visit to the Viceroy and Governor-General of India at Calcutta, and a high officer of the Government of India has been deputed to Cabul to discuss with His Highness the Amir questions affecting the relations of the two Governments.

A situation has arisen connected with the administration of the property belonging to certain ecclesiastical bodies in Scotland which requires legislative intervention. With a view to the wise consideration of such a measure I have appointed Commissioners, who are engaged in making an inquiry into all the circumstances of the case, and whose Report may enable you to frame such proposals as will, I trust, tend to the efficient administration of ecclesiastical funds, and the promotion of peace and goodwill.

Members of the House of Commons:

The Estimates for the service of the ensuing year will be laid before you. They have been framed with the utmost economy which the circumstances of the present time admit.

My Lords and Members of the House of Commons:

Your attention will be directed to proposals for diminishing the anomalies in the present arrangement of electoral areas which are largely due to the growth and movement of population in recent years.

A Bill to mitigate the evils arising out of alien immigration into the United Kindom will be laid before you.

Legislation will be submitted to you for the establishment of authorities to deal with the question of the unemployed. I have noticed, with profound regret and sympathy, the abnormal distress which has been caused by the want of employment during the present winter. Arrangements of a temporary character have been made to meet the difficulty, but it is expedient now to provide machinery for this purpose of a more permanent character.

You have already partially considered provisions for amending the laws relating to Education in Scotland. They will again be brought before you.

A Bill to amend and extend the Workmen's Compensation Acts will be submitted for your consideration.

Proposals for improving the *status* of the Local Government Board and the Board of Trade, and for establishing a Minister of Commerce and Industry, will be laid before you.

Bills will also be introduced for amending the law with respect to Valuation Authorities, and the procedure for making Valuations; for consolidating the enactments relating to Naval Prize of War; for amending the law relating to the notification of industrial accidents; for the renewal of the Agricultural Rates Acts and other temporary Acts affecting certain classes of ratepayers; for the prevention of the adulteration of butter; and for the amendment of the law with regard to cases stated for the Court of Crown Cases reserved.

PROROGATION (11 August 1905)

My Lords and Members of the House of Commons:

My relations with other Powers continues to be friendly. It gave Me great satisfaction to receive the King of Spain as My guest. His Majesty's stay in England will, I feel sure, serve to strengthen the cordial relations which have for so long subsisted between this country and the Spanish people.

Negotiations, due to the initiative of the President of the United States, are about to be entered into between the Russian and Japanese Governments for the purpose of terminating the deplorable conflict still proceeding in the Far East. It is My earnest hope that they may lead to a lasting and mutually honourable peace.

The Powers Signatories of the Madrid Convention of 1880 have been invited by the Sultan of Morocco to take part in a Conference for the purpose of considering the best means of introducing much-needed reforms into that country. The bases of such a Conference are under consideration.

The dissolution of the Union between Sweden and Norway is apparently imminent. I am confident that by the exercise of wise moderation on each side a settlement will be arrived at acceptable to both countries, and of such a nature as to enable My Government to maintain with the people of the Scandinavian Peninsula the same friendly relations which have prevailed in the past.

The condition of affairs in Macedonia and in Crete still gives cause for considerable anxiety, and continues to engage the attention of My Government and those of the other Powers concerned.

The King of Italy has delivered his Award in regard to the frontier between the possessions of Portugal in South-West Africa and the territory of the Barotse Kingdom, and a settlement of this difficult question has thus been effected.

I gladly accepted the invitation of His Majesty the King of Italy to send Delegates to the Conference called under his auspices to consider the question of establishing an International Institute for the collection and exchange of information bearing upon agriculture. I cordially hope that the outcome of the Conference will be of service to agriculturists both at home and abroad.

My Government has received from the Dominion of Canada a most patriotic offer to assume the entire administrative and financial responsibility for the defence of Halifax and Esquimalt, and that offer has been cordially accepted. The transfer of control will take place at an early date under arrangements in regard to which My Government have been fortunate enough to obtain the fullest and most appreciative co-operation of the Dominion Government.

In accordance with the expectation held out at the opening of this session, I have granted to the Transvaal representative institutions, which will be brought into operation as soon as the measures necessary for holding elections can be completed. I trust that all sections of the community will unite in exercising the large measure of political power thus conferred upon them for the advancement and welfare of the Colony.

I have concluded a Treaty with His Highness the Ameer of Afghanistan continuing the engagements which existed with the late Ameer, and which, during his lifetime, secured friendly relations between My Government in India and His Highness' Government.

The text of the Agreement has been laid before you.

Members of the House of Commons:

I thank you for the satisfactory provision which you have made for the services of the year.

My Lords and Members of the House of Commons:

I have given My assent with much pleasure to measures for renewing the legislation which lightens the local burdens which press upon the agricultural population, and for the mitigation of the evils which have arisen out of alien immigration into the United Kingdom.

I have gladly sanctioned a temporary Act for the establishment of authorities to deal with the question of the unemployed. I trust that the Commission which I have approved to investigate the operation of the existing Poor Law will materially assist the deliberations of a future Parliament in its examination of this difficult problem.

A Bill dealing with the Ecclesiastical difficulties in Scotland has been passed into law. I hope that its results may not only put an end to a serious controversy between two Presbyterian Churches in that country, but may ultimately conduce to the closest and most harmonious co-operation between all religious bodies who accept Presbyterian doctrine and discipline.

FIRST SESSION OF THE TWENTY-EIGHTH PARLIAMENT

1906

OPENING (19 February 1906)

My Lords and Members of the House of Commons:

The lamented death of the King of Denmark, to whom I was united by the closest ties of family and affection, has caused Me much sorrow, and I feel convinced that the sympathy of the country will be extended to Queen Alexandra, who, in consequence of Her severe bereavement, is prevented from accompanying Me on the important occasion of the opening of the new Parliament.

The Prince and Princess of Wales left last autumn for India, and are visiting as many portions of My vast Empire as time will admit of. The reception they have met with from all classes has been most gratifying to Me, and I trust that their visit will tend to strengthen, among My subjects in India, the feeling of loyalty to the Crown and attachment to this country.

It was with real satisfaction that I received the King of the Hellenes, who is so closely related to Me, as My guest during the autumn. His Majesty's visit will, I am confident, confirm the friendly ties which have so long governed the relations existing between the two countries.

My relations with Foreign Powers continue to be friendly.

I rejoice that the war between Russia and Japan has been brought to an end by the satisfactory conclusion of the negotiations commenced last August, and due to the initiative of the President of the United States, which resulted in an honourable peace.

An Agreement has been concluded with the Government of the Emperor of Japan prolonging and extending that which was made between the two Governments in January 1902. Its text has already been made public.

The Conference summoned by the Sultan of Morocco to consider the introduction of reforms into his Kingdom has assembled at Algeciras, and Delegates from the Powers Signatories of the Madrid Convention of 1880 are engaged in deliberations, which still continue. It is earnestly to be hoped that the result of these negotiations may be conducive to the maintenance of peace among all nations.

The dissolution of the union between Sweden and Norway has been peacefully accomplished, and, in accordance with the declared desire of the Norwegian people, My Son-in-law and Daughter, the Prince and Princess Charles of Denmark, have ascended the Throne of Norway as King and Queen.

The insurrectionary movement in Crete has subsided, and the four Protecting Powers have appointed Commissioners with a view to the introduction of reforms in the island.

The condition of the Macedonian vilayets, though in some respects improved, continues to give cause for anxiety. The Sultan has agreed to the appointment of an International Financial Commission to supervise the financial administration of these provinces, and I trust that this may lead to the introduction of salutary reforms and the improvement of the condition of the population.

Papers will be laid before you respecting Army administration in India.

In order to establish responsible government in the Transvaal Colony, I have decided to recall the Letters Patent which provided for the intermediate stage of representative government, and to direct that the new Constitution be drawn up with as much expedition as is consistent with due care and deliberation in all particulars. The elections to the first Legislative Assembly, which had been expected in July, must accordingly be postponed, but it is not anticipated that the additional delay need extend beyond a few months.

The directions which have been given that no further licences should be issued for the importation of Chinese coolies will continue in force during that period.

A Constitution granting responsible government will also be framed for the Orange River Colony.

It is my earnest hope that in these Colonies, as elsewhere throughout My dominions, the grant of free institutions will be followed by an increase of prosperity and of loyalty to the Empire.

The Colonial Conference, which, in existing circumstances, cannot be held this year, has been postponed until the early part of next year, with the concurrence of the Colonial Governments concerned.

Members of the House of Commons:

I note with satisfaction that the imports and exports of the country continue to show a steady and accelerating increase, and, together with the growing activity of trade at home, indicate that the industries of My people are, in general, in a sound and progressive condition.

The additions which have been made in recent years to the national expenditure and to the capital liabilities of the State are matters to which I invite your earnest attention.

The Estimates of charge which will be laid before you will be presented in as moderate a form as time and circumstances have allowed.

My Lords and Members of the House of Commons:

My Ministers have under consideration plans for improving and effecting economies in the system of government in Ireland and for introducing into it means for associating the people with the conduct of Irish affairs. It is my desire that the government of the country, in reliance upon the ordinary law, should be carried on, so far as existing circumstances permit, in a spirit regardful of the wishes and sentiments of the Irish people; and I trust that this may conduce to the maintenance of tranquility and of good feeling between different classes in the community.

The social and economic conditions of the rural districts in Great Britain require careful consideration. Inquiries are proceeding as to the means by which a larger number of the population may be attracted to and retained on the soil, and they will be completed at no distant date.

A Bill will be laid before you at the earliest possible moment for amending the existing law with regard to Education in England and Wales.

Bills will also be submitted to you for dealing with the law regulating Trade Disputes, and for amending the Workmen's Compensation Acts; for the further Equalisation of Rates in the Metropolis, and for amending the Unemployed Workmen Act.

Your attention will also be called to measures dealing with the Merchant Shipping Law, for amending and extending the Crofters' Holdings (Scotland) Act, for amending the Labourers (Ireland) Act, for checking commercial corruption, for improving the law regarding certain Colonial Marriages, for abolishing the property qualification required of County Justices in England, and for the prevention of plural voting in Parliamentary Elections.

PROROGATION (21 December 1906)

My Lords and Members of the House of Commons:

The marriage of My niece to the King of Spain took place last June in Madrid, and the ceremony was attended by the Prince and Princess of Wales. Happily, their Majesties the King and Queen of Spain were mercifully preserved from being injured by the outrage committed against them.

The recent visit of the King of Norway with the Queen, My daughter, has given Me sincere pleasure, and cannot fail to promote friendly relations between the two Countries.

My relations with Foreign Powers continue to be friendly.

The Conference which met at Algeciras, on the invitation of the Sultan, to consider the introduction of reforms into Morocco, concluded its labours by the signature of an International Act which should be conducive to an improvement of the situation in Morocco.

There has been a distinct improvement in the condition of affairs in Crete, and the Powers are still giving close attention to the reforms which are being gradually introduced into the administration of the Macedonian vilayets.

My Government have concluded Agreements with the French and Italian Governments for the maintenance of the *status quo* in the dominions of the Emperor Menelek in Abyssinia, and for the regulation of the traffic in arms on the Somali Coast.

In conformity with the Declaration of the 8th April, 1904, concerning the New Hebrides, a Convention with France has been signed for the purpose of putting an end to the difficulties arising from the absence of jurisdiction over the natives, and of settling land disputes in those islands.

My Government have concluded satisfactory arrangements with the German Government in regard to our respective frontiers in the neighbourhood of Lake Tchad and Lake Victoria Nyanza, and with the Government of the French Republic respecting the Anglo-French boundary between Lake Tchad and the Niger.

The boundaries between the Anglo-Egyptian Soudan and the Congo State have been satisfactorily settled by an Agreement which has been signed with The Sovereign of the Congo State, and the eastern administrative boundary of Egypt has been delimited by a Joint Commission with the Government of Turkey.

A Conference, in which my Plenipotentiaries took part, was held at Brussels in October to revise the Regulations instituted under the Brussels Act for the restriction of the liquor traffic in Africa, and a Convention was signed, which will shortly be laid before you.

The visits of friendship which the Amir of Afghanistan will shortly pay to the Governor-General of India is a gratifying indication of the amicable relations that exist between the Amir and my Government.

In pursuance of the promise given in my speech at the opening of Parliament, the arrangements for the establishment of Responsible Government in the Transvaal have now been completed, and I have caused Letters Patent to issue under the Great Seal. The Instruments providing for the grant of a similar Constitution to the Orange River Colony are in preparation.

I trust that during the coming year the new form of Government will come into full operation and will exert a powerful influence not only in securing the peace and prosperity of both Colonies, but in contributing to the unity and strength of my possessions in South Africa.

Members of the House of Commons:

I thank you for the liberality with which you

have made provision for the services of the year.

My Lords and Members of the House of Commons:

A measure for further extending and facilitating the provision of cottages and allotments of land by the Rural District Councils of Ireland for the use of labourers and for conferring other benefits on this deserving class of My subjects has passed into law. I am happy to say that the country continues tranquil and that the general improvement in the state of the peasantry makes the failure of the potato crop, which has in some districts been serious, a less grave misfortune than it would have been in former times.

A Bill relating to the Tenancy of certain classes of houses in Ireland, which has also been passed, will place the law on a more equitable footing and remove a long-standing sense of grievance.

Important measures have received My sanction for the Amendment of the existing Merchant Shipping Laws, having in view alike the well-being of the seamen and the interests of shipowners, and for taking a periodical census of the industrial production of the country.

A measure has been passed amending the Law in regard to Trade Disputes, which will, I hope, remove all legitimate cause of grievance, and I have also given My assent to an Act to amend and consolidate the Law of Workmen's Compensation, extending the benefits of the Law to over 6,000,000 persons not included under the provisions of preceding Acts.

I have assented to an Act for the amendment of the Law relating to Agricultural Holdings and to other measures affecting agriculture. I trust that the close attention which has been given to these questions will be of material benefit to that important industry.

I hope that the Public Trustee Act will afford, especially to the poorer classes of the population, valuable facilities for the safe and inexpensive management and distribution of Trust funds.

Further measures have been passed for placing the control of the National Galleries in Scotland on a better footing, for abolishing the property qualification previously required of County Justices, for more effectually dealing with the evils incident to the prevalence of street betting, and for making provision for the feeding of school children.

I regret that, notwithstanding the protracted consideration which you have given to the improvement of primary and secondary education, no settlement of the difficulties which surround this question has been arrived at.

SECOND SESSION OF THE TWENTY-EIGHTH PARLIAMENT

1907

OPENING (12 February 1907)

My Lords and Members of the House of Commons:

I am happy to say that my relations with foreign Powers continue to be friendly, and I have no occasion to add to the full statement which was laid before you in December reciting a number of satisfactory Agreements recently concluded.

The earthquake at Kingston adds one more to the series of calamities which Jamaica and my other Colonies in the West Indies have experienced. I regret the deplorable loss of life and destruction of property in an important city, and I have seen with satisfaction that the emergency has been met by the Governor and his officers with courage and devotion, and by the people with self-control.

The occasion has called forth many proofs of practical goodwill from all parts of my Empire; and I recognise with sincere gratitude the sympathy shown by the people of the United States of America, and the assistance promptly offered by their naval authorities.

The first visit of an Amir of Afghanistan to my Indian dominions for more than twenty years, and his active survey of leading features in Indian life, have been to me, and, as I understand, to the Amir himself, a source of much gratification, as tending to promote that right feeling, which is even more important than formal compacts.

In India, while firmly guarding the strength and unity of executive power unimpaired, I look forward to a steadfast effort to provide means of widening the base of peace, order, and good government among the vast populations committed to my charge.

Members of the House of Commons:

Estimates of the National Expenditure for the forthcoming financial year will in due course be laid before you. They have been framed with the object of effecting economies consistent with the efficient maintenance of the public service.

My Lords, and Members of the House of Commons:

Serious questions affecting the working of our Parliamentary system have arisen from unfortunate differences between the two Houses. My Ministers have this important subject under consideration with a view to a solution of the difficulty.

A measure of licensing reform will be introduced, with the object of effectively diminishing the evils which result from the sale and use of intoxicating liquors under present conditions.

Proposals will be laid before you for more clearly defining the functions of the military forces of the Crown, both regular and auxiliary, and for the improvement of their organisation.

Bills will be introduced dealing with the Holding and Valuation of land in Scotland.

Your attention will be called to measures for further associating the people of Ireland with the management of their domestic affairs, and for otherwise improving the system of government in its administrative and financial aspects. Proposals will also be submitted for effecting a reform of University education in Ireland, whereby I trust that the difficulties which have so long retarded the development of higher education in that country may be removed.

You will also be invited to consider proposals for the establishment of a Court of Criminal Appeal, for Regulating the Hours of Labour in Mines, for the Amendment of the Patent Laws, for improving the Law relating to the Valuation of Property in England and Wales, for enabling Women to serve on Local Bodies, for amending the Law affecting Small Holdings in England and Wales, and for the better Housing of the People.

PROROGATION (28 August 1907)

My Lords and Members of the House of Commons:

The recent visit of the King and Queen of Denmark, who are closely related to Me, gave great pleasure to the Queen and Myself, and cannot fail to improve the friendly relations existing between the two countries.

I was much gratified at receiving the visit of His Imperial Highness Prince Fushimi, who had been sent on a Special Mission by My Ally, the Emperor of Japan, to convey His Majesty's thanks for the Order of the Garter, bestowed upon him during the Mission of My nephew, Prince Arthur of Connaught, to Japan in 1906.

My relations with foreign Powers continue to be friendly.

My Government, animated by the desire to contribute in every possible way to the maintenance of peace, have concluded an Agreement with the Spanish Government for the preservation of their respective interests in that part of the Mediterranean and Atlantic with which both countries are concerned. The terms of this Agreement have been already laid before you. In response to an invitation from the Russian Government, I appointed Delegates to take part in the International Conference now sitting at the Hague. I trust that its deliberations may result in the conclusion of Agreements that will tend to mitigate the evils of war and secure the peace of the world.

In the great Dependency of India, certain passing difficulties have not discouraged My Government in framing plans for improving the machinery of administration. These plans have been laid before you, and practical steps have already been taken for securing the presence and advice of Indian Members in the Council of India.

The meeting of the Prime Ministers and other leading Statesmen of My dominions beyond the Seas with the Representatives of the Imperial Government was a source of deep satisfaction to Me, and I note with gratification the arrangement for future meetings at fixed intervals, under the title of "Imperial Conferences", for the free discussion of questions of common concern.

The grant of full self-government to the people of the Orange River Colony has been completed, and will, I trust, conduce to their welfare and contentment.

Members of the House of Commons:

I thank you for the liberality with which you have made provision for the needs of the public service and for the reduction of national indebtedness.

My Lords and Members of the House of Commons:

I have recently reviewed the newly-constituted Home Fleet, and was profoundly impressed by the efficient condition and admirable appearance of My ships, and the fine bearing and discipline of the officers and men of all ranks.

Attention has been directed to the problem of the reorganisation of the Forces of the Crown. The broad principles for the reorganisation of the Regular Forces at home into six great divisions have been successfully put into operation. The reorganisation of the Auxiliary Forces into a Home or Second Line Army has been provided for in the Territorial and Reserve Forces Act, which has received My assent. In this Act provision has further been made for filling up serious gaps in the Regular or Field Army of the First Line.

An important measure has received My sanction for facilitating the acquisition of Small Holdings and Allotments in England and Wales, which will afford opportunities of advancement to the rural population, and will, I hope, act as some check on migration to the towns.

I trust that the establishment of a Court of Criminal Appeal will confirm still further the confidence of the public in the administration of justice.

I have also given My assent to a measure for the amendment of the existing Law relating to Patents and Designs, with a view especially to restraining the abuse of monopolies and to strengthening the provisions in regard to the revocation of British patents which are worked abroad, but which are not adequately worked in this country.

A Bill has also been passed into law for the amendment of the Companies Acts, which, by affording fuller information concerning public companies and by other provisions, will secure a greater degree of protection to creditors, share-holders, and the public generally.

I have also sanctioned an Act which will secure certain administrative improvements in public education, and introduce a system of medical inspection of school children.

I have given My assent to a measure for the purpose of accelerating the process of providing farms for evicted tenants in Ireland.

I have assented to a measure for codifying and in several important particulars altering and improving the whole procedure of the Sheriff Courts in Scotland.

Important measures affecting the public health have been passed into law, providing, among other things, for the more efficient protection of the community against injurious food-stuffs, whether imported or home produced, and for the better notification of births.

A grievance of long standing is removed by the passing of the Act for legalising Marriage with a Deceased Wife's Sister.

Further measures have been passed for enabling women to serve on Local Bodies in England and Scotland, for giving My Courts a discretionary power to place offenders under the care of probation officers instead of committing them to prison, for the better regulation of the hours and conditions of labour of the women and girls employed in Laundries, for protecting the interests of the producers and consumers of butter, for amending the Vaccination Laws in England and Scotland, and for regulating Whale Fisheries in Scotland.

THIRD SESSION OF THE TWENTY-EIGHTH PARLIAMENT

1908

OPENING (29 January 1908)

My Lords and Members of the House of Commons:

The visit of the German Emperor with his Imperial Consort during the past autumn was a source of great pleasure to Me and to the Queen. The cordial reception given to their Majesties by My people was warmly appreciated, and cannot fail to confirm the friendly relations existing between the two nations.

The lamented death of the King of Sweden has caused Me much sorrow.

My relations with Foreign Powers continue to be friendly.

My Government, animated by the sincere desire to settle by mutual agreement certain questions concerning the interests of Great Britain and Russia on the Continent of Asia, have concluded with the Russian Government a Convention relating to their respective interests in Persia, Afghanistan, and Thibet. The terms of this Convention have already been laid before you, and, acting in its spirit, the two Governments have been able, notwithstanding disturbances and complications in Persia, to maintain a peaceful policy.

My Government have joined with the Governments of France, Germany, and Russia, in a Treaty for preserving the integrity of the Kingdom of Norway. The text of the Treaty will be published in due course.

The correspondence recently presented to you has placed you in possession of the results of the Second International Peace Conference at The Hague, which concluded its labours in October last. The various instruments annexed to the Final Act of that Conference show the progress that has been made, and they are receiving the attentive consideration of My Government. One of the most important of these instruments establishes the great principle of an International Court of Appeal in Prize cases. My Government are considering the question of inviting representatives of the leading maritime nations to attend a Conference in London in the course of next autumn, with a view of coming to an understanding on certain important points of International Law for the guidance of the Court.

The condition of the Christian and Mussulman population in the Macedonian vilayets shows no improvement: the bands of different nationalities continue to pursue a campaign of violence, and the situation gives serious cause for anxiety. The Great Powers of Europe have agreed to present to the Turkish Government a scheme for the improvement of the judiciary in that region, and My Government have made further proposals to the Sultan, and also to the Great Powers, for dealing effectually with the principal causes of disturbance.

My Goverment are fully aware of the great anxiety felt with regard to the treatment of the native population in the Congo State. Their sole desire is to see the government of that State humanely administered in accordance with the spirit of the Berlin Act, and I trust that the negotiations now proceeding berween the Sovereign of the Congo State and the Belgian Government will secure this object.

Negotiations are being conducted with the Government of the United States for an Agreement to refer to the International Court of Arbitration at the Hague questions pending between the two Governments which relate to the Newfoundland fisheries. It is hoped that by this friendly procedure a long-standing source of difficulty may be satisfactorily removed.

The difficulty which had arisen respecting Japanese immigration into Canada has been settled on terms agreed upon between the respective Governments.

I sincerely lament to have to inform you that, owing to failure of the rains over parts of India during last year, conditions of scarcity accompanied by much sickness have arisen. Prompt and well-considered measures of relief have been taken, and the situation is faced both by the stricken people and by My officers with courage and hope.

Members of the House of Commons:

Estimates for the expenditure of the year will in due course be laid before you.

In connection with the financial arrangements of the year, proposals will be brought forward for making better provision for old age, and legislation with that object will be submitted.

My Lords and Members of the House of Commons:

Bills will be laid before you for the following purposes:—

To amend the Law of Licensing in England and Wales; to amend the Law relating to Elementary Education in England and Wales; to regulate the hours of underground labour in Coal Mines; to amend the Acts relating to the Housing of the Working Classes, and to regulate the laying out of land needed for the development of growing urban centres; to amend the system of Valuation of property in England and Wales for the assessment of Imperial and Local charges; to improve and extend University Education in Ireland; to amend in various particulars the Land Purchase (Ireland) Act of 1903, especially with reference to the compulsory acquisition of untenanted land in connection with the relief of congestion; to establish an authority for the control and improvement of the Port and Waterway of London and to consolidate and amend the Law relating to the Protection of Children and to the treatment of Juvenile Offenders.

The Bills relating to Scottish Land and Valuation, which were introduced last session but failed to pass into law, will be again submitted to you.

PROROGATION (21 December 1908)

My Lords and Members of the House of Commons:
I was much gratified at receiving last May an official visit from the President of the French Republic on the occasion of the Franco-British Exhibition in London. The reception given to M. Fallieres by the citizens of London afforded a renewed proof of the cordial feelings entertained in this country towards the French nation.

The recent visit of the King and Queen of Sweden gave great pleasure to the Queen and myself, and will confirm the traditions of friendship which happily exist between the two countries.

My relations with foreign Powers continue to be friendly.

During the past year several important Agreements with foreign Governments have been concluded, which, by eliminating causes of contention, must tend to the consolidation of peace.

Amongst these may be mentioned Treaties with the United States of America for general arbitration, and for regulating certain questions between the United States of America and the Dominion of Canada; and the Agreement for the maintenance of the existing territorial status in the regions bordering on the North Sea.

A Convention has been signed by the Representatives of my Government and of the other States, parties to the International Union for the Protection of Literary and Artistic Works, consolidating and revising the Berne Convention and the Additional Act of Paris. The amended Convention, which will need legislation to give effect to it, will be examined by a Committee before I decide upon its ratification. Papers will be laid before you.

Certain events have recently occurred calculated to disturb the provisions of the Treaty of Berlin in the Balkan peninsula; but there is reason to hope that wise and conciliatory counsels will prevail, and that an amicable settlement will be reached with the consent of the Powers who are parties to the Treaty.

Since I last addressed you, the Belgian Government have notified the assumption by Belgium of the Sovereignty of the Independent State of the Congo. My Government are at present discussing with the Government of Belgium the conditions by which the provisions of the Treaties affecting the territory in question will be safeguarded, when the transfer has been recognised.

I have appointed Commissioners to attend the International Conference, which is to meet at Shanghai in February, to investigate the opium trade and opium habit in the Far East, and to offer suggestions for measures which the Powers concerned may adopt for the gradual suppression of the cultivation, traffic, and use of opium within their Eastern possessions, with a view to assisting China in her purpose of eradicating the opium trade in the Chinese Empire.

A Conference of the principal Naval Powers is at present sitting in London, on the invitation of my Government, with a view to declaring and formulating by common agreement such rules on certain questions affecting the conduct of naval warfare as will, it is hoped, command general assent.

The raids of certain tribes on the North-West Frontier of India rendered military operations necessary for the protection of my subjects and the punishment of the offenders. These operations were skilfully devised and successfully conducted by all concerned.

The famine that unhappily prevailed over parts of India was met by the people with great courage and self-reliance, and the efforts of my officers to relieve suffering and restore prosperity were effective and unremitting.

I deeply regret that the internal tranquillity of parts of my Indian Dominions has been disturbed by a conspiracy of evil-disposed persons against the lives of my officers and the continuance of British rule. But the actions of these persons, while they have necessitated deterrent legislation of an exceptional nature for the protection of life and property and the maintenance of order, have also called forth in all parts of India demonstrations of loyalty to my person and my Government. My Government have, therefore, felt justified in pressing forward the measures that have long been under their consideration for enlarging the share of the Indian peoples in the administration of the country. These measures have been laid before you, and I earnestly hope that they will be received in the spirit of mutual trust and goodwill in which they are proposed.

In the month of July my Son, the Prince of Wales, acting as my representative, paid a visit to the Dominion of Canada, and took part in the interesting celebrations which had been arranged under the auspices of the Governor-General to commemorate the founding of the city of Quebec by Samuel de Champlain. The affectionate reception given to my Son by all classes of my Canadian subjects touched me deeply, and I learned from him with great satisfaction of the loyalty and enthusiasm everywhere displayed upon that unique and historic occasion.

The visit of the American Fleet to Australasian waters evoked warm feelings of cordiality in my Dominions in that quarter of the globe, and was a source of gratification to myself and to my Government.

The important Convention of Statesmen formed to discuss proposals for the closer union of my South African Dominions still continues its deliberations. I am well assured that its labours will conduce to the abiding prosperity of the people of South Africa.

Members of the House of Commons:

I thank you for the provision which you have made for the services of the year.

My Lords. and Members of the House of Commons:

The Navy has been maintained in a high state of efficiency, and steady progress continues to be made with the reorganisation of the Military Forces of the Crown in accordance with the principles already sanctioned by Parliament.

It was with much satisfaction that I gave my assent to a measure for securing better provision for necessitous old age.

An Act has been passed establishing in Ireland two Universerities, to be called respectively the Queen's University of Belfast, and the National University of Ireland. I trust that both seats of learning may play an important and honourable part in the future education of the country.

I have assented to a measure for educational reform in Scotland which confers new powers of control over young persons up to the age of seventeen, improves the position of the teacher, and consolidates all Scottish funds available for the promotion of education, and simplifies their administration.

I regret that, in regard to the controversies connected with the subjects of licensing and national education in England, notwithstanding the time and labour which have been given to their consideration, no settlement has been attained.

Much-needed provision has been made for affording judicial assistance to the Judicial Committee of the Privy Council and to the Court of Appeal in England.

For the purpose of improving the conditions of labour, I have given my assent to a measure to limit the daily hours worked below ground by the men and boys employed in coal mines.

A measure has been passed largely extending in a variety of directions, the law for the protection of children from cruelty, danger, and neglect, and reforming the methods for dealing with juvenile offenders.

I have sanctioned an Act for the Prevention of Crime, through provision for the reformation of young offenders in Borstal Institutions, and through the detention, under new regulations, of habitual criminals.

My assent has been given to a measure for the improvement and better administration of the Port of London, which closes a long period of uncertainty detrimental to the commerce and shipping of the capital, and which will, I trust, afford a just and comprehensive settlement of this intricate and important question.

A large number of other measures of public utility have been added to the Statute-book, and amongst them several Acts of unusual scope and comprehensiveness for consolidating existing enactments in various branches of the law.

FOURTH SESSION OF THE TWENTY-EIGHTH PARLIAMENT

1909

OPENING (16 February 1909)

My Lords and Members of the House of Commons:

I was much impressed and gratified by the warmth of the public reception given to the Queen and myself during our recent visit to the German Emperor and Empress at Berlin by all classes of the community. It afforded us great pleasure to meet their Majesties again, and I feel confident that the expression of cordial welcome which there greeted us will tend to strengthen those amicable feelings between the two countries which are essential to their mutual welfare and to the maintenance of peace.

My relations with foreign Powers continue to be friendly.

Satisfactory progress has been made in the negotiation of outstanding questions with the United States of America. A treaty to regulate the use of the waterways adjacent to the international boundary between Canada and the United States has been arranged. The question being one of special Canadian interest, the advice of the Dominion Government was sought and followed throughout.

My Ambassador at Washington has also negotiated, with the co-operation of the Canadian and Newfoundland Ministers of Justice, an Agreement for the reference to arbitration of the North American Fisheries question. I trust that the Agreement will be the means of effecting a final and friendly settlement of matters which have been long under discussion between this country and the United States.

Arbitration Agreements concluded by my Government with those of France, Italy, and Spain, which were on the point of expiring, have been renewed for a further term of five years, and it is proposed to treat similar instruments in the same manner.

The situation in Persia continues to cause anxiety. My Government have no desire to depart from the principle of non-intervention in the internal affairs of that country. At the same time, they are of opinion that the state of affairs in Persia imperatively demands the introduction of representative institutions in a practical form, in order to assure the realisation of indispensable economic, financial, and administrative reforms, and to pacify the country. As the present troubles endanger numerous commercial and economic interests which Great Britain and Russia have in Persia, the two Governments are exchanging views on the subject.

I am happy to think that there is now an improved prospect of a solution of the difficulties which have arisen in the Balkans. It is my earnest hope that a settlement may be arrived at which will be satisfactory to all the States whose interests are concerned.

The news of the disastrous earthquake which occurred recently in Sicily and Calabria called forth the deepest feelings of compassion for the afflicted population. Assistance was rendered by the officers and men of my Fleet, and the naval and military stores in the Mediterranean were utilised for the relief of the sufferers. I am glad that my people have shown their sympathy with the friendly nation of Italy in this terrible calamity.

An International Conference, which is now sitting in London, will, I trust, soon reach an agreement on certain questions of maritime law. The conclusion arrived at will be laid before you, that there may be due opportunity of considering them when your assent is asked to such legislation as may be necessary to enable my Government to ratify the International Prize Court Convention.

The reception of the measures designed by my Government for improving Indian administration has given me deep satisfaction. A Bill will at once be laid before you, dealing with matters in which your sanction is required; and it is my strong desire that the steps to be taken for giving effect to the policy announced in my Message of last November to the Princes and people of India may impartially protect the interests and advance the welfare of all races, classes, and communities in my Indian dominions.

The work accomplished by the Convention for closer Union, which concluded its sittings at Cape Town in the present month, in framing the plan of a South African Constitution for submission to the constituent Colonies marks the achievement of the first stage in the consolidation of that important part of my Empire.

Members of the House of Commons:

Estimates for the expenditure of the year will in due course be laid before you.

Owing to various causes, including the new provision which was made last year for old age, and an increase which has become necessary in the cost of my Navy, the expenditure of the year will be considerably in excess of that of the past twelve months. In these circumstances, the provision necessary for the services of the State in the ensuing year will require very serious consideration, and, in consequence, less time than usual will, I fear, be available for the consideration of other legislative measures.

My Lords and Members of the House of Commons:

The Bills dealing with Irish Land and Housing

and Town Planning, to the discussion of which time and labour were given in your last Session, will be re-introduced.

A Bill will be laid before you for the Dis-establishment and Disendowment of the Church in Wales.

I have now received the Report of the Commission, which I appointed more than three years ago, to inquire into the working of the Poor Law, and into the provision for meeting distress arising from want of employment. The recommendations of the Commission are engaging the careful attention of my Government.

A measure will be proposed for the better organisation of the labour market through a system of co-ordinated labour exchanges, with which other schemes for dealing with unemployment may subsequently be associated.

A Bill will be introduced for the constitution of Trade Boards in certain branches of industry in which the evils known as "sweating" prevail.

A measure will be laid before you to alter the law affecting Parliamentary Elections and Registration in London.

In connection with the financial arrangements of the year, proposals will be brought forward for amending the Old-Age Pensions Act in certain particulars where, in practice, inequalities of treatment have been found to arise.

A Bill prohibiting the landing and selling in the United Kingdom of fish caught in prohibited areas of the sea adjoining Scotland will also be introduced.

Bills will be presented to amend the law in regard to inebriates, to the supply of milk, and to the hours of work in shops.

PROROGATION (3 December 1909)

My Lords and Members of the House of Commons:
The official visit which His Majesty the King of Portugal has paid to me, on the occasion of his accession, has afforded to the Queen and Myself great pleasure, and has consolidated and strengthened the bonds of friendship which have so long and happily united the two allied nations.

My relations with foreign Powers continue to be friendly.

The difficulties which unfortunately arose in South-Eastern Europe in the autumn of last year have happily resulted in a practical solution and in the maintenance of peace while the constitutional regime in the Turkish Empire continues to make satisfactory progress.

Subject to certain reservations made by My Plenipotentiaries at the time of signature, I have ratified such of the Conventions which resulted from the Peace Conference held at The Hague in 1907 as do not require municipal legislation in this country to give effect to their provisions.

Arbitration Conventions and Agreements with Germany, Sweden, Norway, Switzerland, and Portugal have been renewed for a further term of five years. Others which are about to expire, are in process of renewal.

A measure for improving Indian administration by enlarging the numbers and extending the functions of the various Legislative Councils has become law, duly supplemented by the necessary Regulations.

Early in the coming year the Councils will have been constituted, and will undertake the burden of their new responsibilities.

I look with confidence for their loyal co-operation with My appointed officers in the tasks of Government, thus furthering the moral and material progress of My Indian subjects, and strengthening the foundations of My Empire.

I have, with the greatest satisfaction, assented to the Act establishing the Union of South Africa, which embodies the united wishes of the Parliaments of the four constituent Colonies.

This fruit of the success which has attended the grant of free institutions to My new Colonies is, I am assured, a matter of cordial congratulation throughout My Dominions.

I cannot doubt that union will add to the strength of South Africa, and I pray that its people may be blessed in the years to come with growing prosperity and lasting concord.

The important Conference which met in July last for the exchange of views between My Government and the Governments of My self-governing Dominions beyond the seas upon the subject of naval and military defence has been of great mutual advantage, and as the outcome of its deliberations it may confidently be expected that the stability of My Dominions will be preserved and their unity promoted.

Members of the House of Commons:
I thank you for the liberality and care with which you provided for the heavy additions to the national expenditure due to the requirements of Imperial defence and social reform.

I regret that provision has proved unavailing.

My Lords and Members of the House of Commons:
An Irish Land Act has been passed which, by relieving local funds from liabilities arising under previous Purchase Acts and by increasing the administrative area and the resources of the Congested Districts Board, will, I sincerely hope, conduce both to the general welfare of the country and to a permanent improvement in the condition of the occupiers of small holdings in the West of Ireland.

I have watched with interest the progress of a

measure, which has now been placed upon the Statute Book, for facilitating the Housing of the Working Classes and for strengthening the law dealing with the sanitary conditions under which they live.

This measure also contains long-needed provisions for controlling the development of towns with a view to securing not only improved sanitary conditions, but also amenity and convenience.

I have given My assent to a Bill for the establishment of Labour Exchanges, which will, I trust, be an important step towards the better regulation of the Labour Market and a foundation for further measures for dealing effectively with some of the evils of unemployment.

The measure which has been passed for the constitution of Trade Boards in certain industries will, I hope, with judicious administration, prove a valuable boon to a specially helpless class of workers.

I anticipate beneficial results to agriculture and to the rural industries of the country from the measure for the economic development of the United Kingdom, and for the improvement of roads.

I have had pleasure in assenting to a Bill to give effect to a Treaty which secures the full benefits of the French law of Workmen's compensation to British workmen injured in the course of their employment in France.

Important Bills have also been passed dealing with Trawling in prohibited areas, the consolidation and amendment of the law relating to Assurance Companies, the suppression of gambling on loss by maritime perils, and the amendment of the Electric Lighting Acts.

FIRST SESSION OF THE TWENTY-NINTH PARLIAMENT

1910

OPENING (21 February 1910)

My Lords and Members of the House of Commons:

My relations with all foreign Powers continue to be friendly.

The establishment of the Union of South Africa has been fixed at the end of May, when its new Government will be constituted, and soon afterwards the first Parliament, representing a consolidated electorate, will be ready to assemble for its important deliberations.

I am sending My son, the Prince of Wales, to make an extended journey through My South African possessions in the autumn, before opening, in My name, the first Session of the new Legislature at Cape Town.

It is with peculiar interest and pleasure that I contemplate this visit, when My son will have the privilege, not for the first time, of inaugurating the Parliamentary life of a great united Dominion, and will convey to South Africa, on behalf of Myself and the Empire, our ardent prayers for the welfare and future progress of her people.

In conformity to the important Measure of last year for extending the functions of the Legislative Councils in India and increasing the number of their Members, those bodies have been elected, and have met. They have entered, with good promise, upon the enlarged duties and responsibilities entrusted to them.

Members of the House of Commons:

The Estimates for the service of the ensuing year will be laid before you in due course. They have been framed with the utmost desire for economy; but the requirements of the Naval Defence of the Empire have made it necessary to propose a substantial increase in the cost of My Navy.

You will also be asked to complete provision which was made in the last Session of Parliament for the year about the expire, but to which effect has not yet been given.

The expenditure authorised by the last Parliament is being duly incurred; but as the revenue required to meet it has not been provided by the imposition of taxation, recourse has been had, under Parliamentary sanction, to temporary borrowing. Arrangements must be made at the earliest possible moment to deal with the financial situation thus created.

My Lords and Members of the House of Commons:

Recent experience has disclosed serious difficulties, due to recurring differences of strong opinion between the two branches of the Legislature.

Proposals will be laid before you, with all convenient speed, to define the relations between the Houses of Parliament, so as to secure the undivided authority of the House of Commons over Finance, and its predominance in Legislation. These Measures, in the opinion of My advisers, should provide that this House should be so constituted and empowered as to exercise impartially, in regard to proposed legislation, the functions of initiation, revision, and, subject to proper safeguards of delay.

PROROGATION (28 November 1910)

My Lords and Members of the House of Commons:

I address you for the first time under the shadow of the great calamity occasioned by the death of My beloved Father. I have received abundant evidence from every part of My dominions that the irreparable loss which has befallen Me and My family is deeply lamented by My subjects. Their sympathy has fortified Me in My sorrow, and I have devoted Myself to the duties to which I have been called with the earnest desire to follow in My dear Father's footsteps.

My relations with Foreign Powers continue to be friendly.

I confidently hope that the questions connected with the North Atlantic Fisheries between Canada and Newfoundland on the one hand, and the United States of America on the other, which have been a subject of controversy for nearly a century, have been at last finally settled by the award of The Hague Tribunal. It is a cause of special satisfaction that it has been found possible to solve, by arbitration, problems of such an intricate and difficult nature, and that the award has been received on both sides in a spirit which must tend to increase good-will.

I recently entrusted to My Uncle, the Duke of Connaught, the mission of opening the first Parliament of the Union of South Africa—a ceremony which it was intended that I should Myself perform. It is my earnest hope that under the legislature which he has inaugurated South Africa will continue to advance in happiness and prosperity.

In My Indian Empire, further effect has been given to the scheme of administrative reform authorised

by the Indian Council Act of 1909, by the creation of
an Executive Council for the Province of Bengal.

Members of the House of Commons:

    I note with satisfaction the liberality with which
you have provided for the requirements of the year,
including the increased grants for the Navy and the
additional expenditure upon Old Age Pensions
consequent upon the removal of the pauper disqualifi-
cation at the close of the present year.

    I thank you for the arrangements you have made
for the maintenance of the honour and dignity of the
Crown.

My Lords and Members of the House of Commons:

    I regret that the Conference which took place
with a view to arriving at a solution of the recurring
difficulties between the two Houses of Parliament
has failed to come to an agreement.

    I am gratified that you have passed into law
the Acts dealing with the Regency, and the form of
the Declaration required to be made by the
Sovereign on his Accession.

FIRST SESSION OF THE THIRTIETH PARLIAMENT

1911

OPENING (6 February 1911)

My Lords and Members of the House of Commons:

In opening the first Parliament elected in My reign, the greivous loss which the Empire has sustained by the death of My beloved Father is uppermost in My thoughts. When, a year ago, He addressed you from the Throne no one could have forseen that His life of unceasing and devoted activity in the service of His subjects was so soon to be cut short. Bowing to the inscrutable decree of Providence, I take courage from His example, and I am sustained in My abiding sorrow by the sympathy extended to Me by My people in every part of My Dominion.

I have welcomed back My Uncle, the Duke of Connaught, on the completion of the Mission in South Africa, which I entrusted to him, and it has deeply gratified Me to learn that he was received with demonstrations of the utmost enthusiasm and loyalty in every part of My South African Dominions, and by every class of the community.

My relations with foreign Powers continue to be friendly.

The Japanese Government, having given notice of their intention to terminate the Treaty of Commerce and Navigation of 1894, negotiations, which it is hoped will result in a satisfactory arrangement, have been entered upon for the conclusion of a new Treaty.

Frequent complaints of the injury inflicted on British trade by the continued disorder on the trade routes in Southern Persia led My Government reluctantly to address strong representations to the Persian Government, who have since given attention to the subject. Some improvement has lately been shown in the condition of the routes, and My Ministers propose to await further developments before pressing for the adoption of their own proposals, which, in any case, would have no other object than to see the authority of the Persian Government restored and trade protected.

I look forward with much interest to the assembling in May next of the Imperial Conference, at which the Chief Ministers of My Self-Governing Dominions and of the Mother Country will unite in counsel regarding matters of importance submitted by My respective Governments.

It is My intention, when the solemnity of My Coronation has been celebrated, to revisit My Indian Dominions, and there to hold an Assemblage in order to make known in person to My subjects My succession to the Imperial Crown of India.

Members of the House of Commons:

The Estimates for the ensuing year will in due course be laid before you.

My Lords and Members of the House of Commons:

Proposals will be submitted to you without delay for settling the relations between the two Houses of Parliament, with the object of securing the more effective working of the Constitution.

Measures will be presented to you, in pursuance of intentions already declared, for carrying out and extending the policy initiated in previous Parliaments, by securing the permanent provision of Old Age Pensions to persons previously disqualified by reason of the receipt of Poor Relief; and by providing for the insurance of the industrial population against sickness and invalidity, and for the insurance against unemployment of those engaged in trades specially liable to it.

Bills dealing with other measures of importance will be introduced and proceeded with as time and opportunity allow.

PROROGATION (16 December 1911)

My Lords and Members of the House of Commons:

My relations with foreign Powers continue to be friendly.

I am happy to say that the negotiations which have taken place between the Governments of France and Germany in regard to Morocco—a matter in which My Government was concerned by its treaty engagements —have been brought to a conclusion.

In the state of war which unhappily exists between Italy and Turkey I have issued a proclamation declaring the strict neutrality of this country.

The deliberations of the Imperial Conference in May and June bore witness to the harmony of the relations subsisting between the Governments of the United Kingdom and of the self-governing Dominions beyond the Seas and to the growing consciousness of their common interests, as well as to the spirit of loyalty and kinship which pervades these Dominions and adds lustre to My Crown.

I trust that the labours of the Royal Commission which will shortly be appointed to inquire into the natural resources and the improvement of the trade of the Empire may be fruitful in showing means of ensuring the greater prosperity and promoting the mutual intercourse of My Dominions.

Members of the House of Commons:
I thank you for the liberality with which you have made provision for the services of the year.

My Lords and Members of the House of Commons:
The relations between the two Houses of Parliament have been adjusted by the passing of the Parliament Act.

I have given My assent to a Bill which will supplement the policy already sanctioned by Parliament by extending the benefit of Old Age Pensions to persons previously disqualified by reason of the receipt of poor-law relief.

It is with great satisfaction that I have assented to a Bill to provide for the insurance of the industrial population against loss of health and for the prevention and cure of sickness among them and for the insurance against unemployment of those engaged in trades specially liable to it.

I anticipate with confidence that the operation of this measure, while fortifying existing inducements to thrift and self-reliance, will do much to alleviate misery and to check disease among those whose social conditions it is designed to ameliorate; and to mitigate the hardships caused to workmen and their families by those depressions in the labour market which are especially felt in certain precarious trades.

An Act has been passed consolidating and amending the law relating to Copyright. This measure will enable Me to accede to the International Convention recently signed at Berlin; and when supplemented by corresponding legislation in My self-governing Dominions will, I trust, provide a comprehensive and equitable code of law regulating this important subject throughout My Empire.

The Act effecting modifications in the land system, and in the agricultural administration of Scotland will, I sincerely hope, confer benefit alike upon the agriculture and crofting population and upon the general community.

The measure for the consolidation and amendment of the Coal Mines Regulation Acts, which marks a great advance on previous legislation for the health and safety of persons employed in the mining industry, met with general acceptance on all sides, and its passage was made the easier by the mutual good-will with which it was received by the representatives of the owners and workmen.

The health and well-being of a large class in the community will be beneficially affected by the Act for securing a universal half-holiday to Shopkeepers and Shop Assistants.

SECOND SESSION OF THE THIRTIETH PARLIAMENT

1912–1913

OPENING (14 February 1912)

My Lords and Members of the House of Commons:

My relations with foreign Powers continue to be friendly.

The state of war between Italy and Turkey unfortunately still exists. My Government are ready, whenever a favourable opportunity may present itself, to associate themselves with other Powers in any mediation that may help to bring hostitities to an end.

The situation in Persia continues to engage the serious attention of My Ministers, who are in constant communication with the Russian Government in regard to the best means of enabling the Persian Government to re-establish order and tranquillity in the country. Papers will be laid as soon as possible before Parliament in connection with Persian affairs.

I trust that the crisis in China may soon be satisfactorily terminated by the establishment of a stable form of Government in conformity with the views of the Chinese people. My Government continue to observe an attitude of strict non-intervention, while taking all necessary steps to protect British life and property. I fully recognise that the leaders on both sides in China have shown every desire to safeguard the lives and interests of foreigners resident in the Empire. Papers regarding the affairs of China will be laid before you.

I am glad to be able to announce that at an International Conference which sat recently at The Hague and at which I was represented, an agreement was arrived at in regard to the regulation of the trade in opium and kindred drugs. A copy of the Convention, signed at The Hague on the 23rd January, will be presented to Parliament.

In My Indian dominions, the Durbar which I held with the Queen Empress, at Delhi, in order to make known in person My succession to the Imperial Crown of India, has furnished me with overwhelming proof of the devotion of the Princes, Nobles, and Peoples of My Indian Empire to Ourselves and of their loyalty to My rule. In the great Cities of Calcutta and Bombay the spontaneous manifestations of an enthusiastic affection and loyalty with which We were received by all classes of citizens touched Us most deeply.

We were not less moved by the welcome which has been accorded to Us on Our return home and by the sympathy shown to Us by all My subjects in the personal sorrow which has overtaken My family.

I trust that the transfer of the seat of the Government of India from Calcutta to the ancient capital Delhi, and the creation, in consequence of that transfer, of a Governorship for the Presidency of Bengal, of a new Lieutenant-Governorship in Council for Behar, Chota Nagpur and Orissa, and of a Chief Commissionership for Assam, may be fruitful in promoting the prosperity of My Indian Empire.

A Bill to provide for certain details required for the constitution of the new Provinces will be laid before you.

Members of the House of Commons:

The Estimates for the expenditure of the coming year will in due course be laid before you.

My Lords and Members of the House of Commons:

I view with grave concern the prospect of disputes between employers and workmen, and I firmly trust that a reasonable spirit may prevail on both sides and avoid developments that would seriously affect the trade of the country and the welfare of My people.

A measure for the better Government of Ireland will be submitted to you.

A Bill will be laid before you to terminate the Establishment of the Church in Wales and to make provision for its temporalities.

Proposals will be brought forward for the amendment of the law with respect to the Franchise and the Registration of Electors.

A Bill will be introduced to give effect to the unanimous recommendation of the last Imperial Conference, for the amendment and consolidation of the law relating to British nationality.

You will further be invited to consider proposals for dealing by legislation with certain social and industrial reforms.

PROROGATION (7 March 1913)

My Lords and Members of the House of Commons:

After a prolonged and exacting Session, I regret that you should enjoy only a nominal period of release from your labours. It is, however, necessary to call upon you again within a few days to consider the provision required for the service for the coming year, and to renew your deliberations upon public affairs.

I shall then have occasion again to address you in the ordinary course.

Members of the House of Commons:

I thank you for the liberal supplies which you have granted in order to maintain the full efficiency of the Public Service in its various branches.

My Lords and Members of the House of Commons:

I have assented to an Act which enables effect to be given to the administrative changes in India which I announced at my Coronation Durbar.

I have sanctioned a number of Statutes dealing with domestic reforms, from which I anticipate beneficial results.

THIRD SESSION OF THE THIRTIETH PARLIAMENT

1913

OPENING (10 March 1913)

My Lords and Members of the House of Commons:

To-day being the fiftieth anniversary of the marriage of My parents, I cannot forgo the opportunity of expressing for My dear Mother and Myself Our grateful sense of the devoted affection of the nation, which it has been Her happiness to enjoy for so many years, and which remains to support and console Her in Her abiding sorrow.

My relations with Foreign Powers continue to be friendly.

In December last an armistice was arranged between the belligerent Governments in South-East Europe. They chose London as the place in which to conduct their negotiations for a peace, and I welcomed the Delegates who were sent for that purpose, and gave to them every facility that was in My power. I much regret that, owing to their failure to come to an agreement, the war still continues.

The possible developments of the war and the changes that must result from it cannot be without interest for the Great Powers who are neutral and were parties to the Treaty of Berlin. All these Powers earnestly desire to prevent the war from spreading, and to see it terminated, as soon as possible.

My Government have, especially by means of the Ambassadors in London, kept in close touch and co-operation with the other Powers in the endeavours, in which all have shared, to preserve concerted view and action, and to establish agreement on all points on which differences might arise between any of them.

In this a large measure of success has been achieved. Agreement has been reached in principle on matters of the greatest importance, and though some points are still under discussion, I am hopeful that the consultations between the Powers will enable them not only to secure a complete understanding amongst themselves, but to exercise a beneficent influence in hastening the conclusion of the war.

My Government will continue to co-operate with the other Powers with the most earnest desire to secure the peace of Europe.

During last year the Prime Minister of My Dominion of Canada and several of his colleagues visited this country in order to confer with My Ministers here on matters of common interest, especially those relating to Naval Defence.

The Minister for Defence of My Dominion of New Zealand has lately arrived for a similar purpose.

I am confident that such an exchange of views between members of its responsible Governments will promote the solidarity of the Empire. The recent gift of a battleship by the Malay States, the ready consent of the New Zealand Government to the retention in the North Sea fleet of the battleship contributed by them, the steady progress towards the establishment of the Australian fleet, and the discussions now proceeding in the Canadian Parliament on matters of defence testify to the Universal desire within the Empire for the maintenance of common safety.

In My Indian Empire, on the 23rd December, at the ceremony of the State Entry into Delhi, a wicked attempt was made on the life of My Governor-General and Viceroy: Through the mercy of Divine Providence the plot failed in its full intent, but I deeply regret that innocent lives were sacrificed, and that the Viceroy was gravely wounded. The fortitude of the Viceroy and Lady Hardinge and the disciplined courage of all the officers of Government have My warmest admiration. I gratefully acknowledge the expressions of sympathetic loyalty which the crime has evoked from the Ruling Chiefs and from all classes of My Indian subjects.

My Commissioners appointed to report on the requirements of the public service in India have commenced their labours, and have taken evidence at various Provincial centres in India with regard to the Indian Civil Service and the Provincial Civil Services.

Members of the House of Commons:

The Estimates for the service of the ensuing year will be laid before you without delay. I commend them to your favourable consideration with the more confidence in view of the sustained prosperity which, as reflected in the statistics of trade and of employment, I rejoice to see that My people continue to enjoy.

My Lords and Members of the House of Commons:

The attention of Parliament will again be asked to the measures in regard to which there was disagreement between the two Houses last Session.

In view of your arduous labours during the past year the further legislation which you will be invited to consider will necessarily be restricted within narrow limits.

A measure will be brought forward to facilitate the progress and secure the completion of Land Purchase in Ireland.

You will be asked to authorise a guarantee from the Imperial Exchequer of a loan by the Government of the Soudan for ensuring the prosperity of that territory and the development therein of the industry of cotton-growing.

You will be invited to give renewed consideration to proposals for the better care and control of the feeble-minded, and for the further restriction of the industrial employment of children.

A Bill will be introduced for the prevention of plural voting at Parliamentary elections.

Proposals will be submitted to you for the development of a national system of education.

PROROGATION (15 August 1913)

My Lords and Members of the House of Commons:

The recent visit of the President of the French Republic to My Capital was a source of great gratification to me, and the manifestations of good-will to which it gave rise afford a fresh guarantee for the continuance of the cordial friendship which unites the two countries.

The Special Mission sent to this Country by the President of the Argentine Republic to convey to Me the thanks of the Argentine people and Government for the warm interest manifested by My beloved Father in the recent commemoration of the first centenary of the Argentine Republic cannot but strengthen the good relations which have happily existed so long.

The Conference of Delegates of the States at war in the Balkan Peninsula resumed its sittings in London earlier in the year, and agreed upon the terms of a Treaty of Peace. I much regret that hostilities between different nationalities again created a state of war accompanied by many deplorable incidents.

It is satisfactory that the Conference of belligerents at Bucharest has led to a cessation of hostilities, which I hope will be permanent.

It is a cause of great satisfaction that the Great Powers have kept constantly in touch with each other, and My Government has done all in its power to facilitate the interchange of views and co-operation in action through the Ambassadors in London.

Members of the House of Commons:

I thank you for the liberal supplies which you have granted in order to maintain the full efficiency of the Public Service in its various branches.

My Lords and Members of the House of Commons:

I view with satisfaction the passing, by agreement between the two Houses, of a Scottish Temperance Act, which will, I sincerely hope, advance the cause of Temperance in that Country, and thereby conduce to the general welfare of the community.

I have watched with sympathy the passage of Measures which have now been placed upon the Statute Book for making further and better provision for the care of Feeble-minded and other Mentally Defective Persons.

The National Insurance Act has been amended and supplemented in some of its provisions, where experience showed that alterations were desirable.

I have had pleasure in assenting to the Bill guaranteeing from the Imperial Exchequer a loan by the Government of the Soudan, which will, I confidently hope, not only add to the prosperity of that territory, but also afford increased sources of supply to the cotton industry of this country.

I have sanctioned the Appellate Jurisdiction Bill, which will ensure that the Supreme Tribunal of the Empire will be fully and adequately constituted so as to meet the growing requirements of My Indian Empire and of My Dominions Overseas.

Important measures have been passed dealing with the public health, the employment of children abroad, and other domestic reforms from which I anticipate beneficial results.

FOURTH SESSION OF THE THIRTIETH PARLIAMENT

1914

OPENING (10 February 1914)

My Lords and Members of the House of Commons:

My relations with Foreign Powers continue to be friendly.

It is a cause of much pleasure to Me that I shall be able, in the near future, to visit, with the Queen, the President of the French Republic, and that I shall thus be afforded an opportunity of testifying to the cordial relations which exist between Our two countries.

My Government has been in consultation with the other Powers respecting the settlement of Albania and of the Aegean Islands, with the view of giving effect to resolutions adopted by the Powers during the Conference held with Ambassadors in London last year. I hope that these consultations will contribute to the maintenance of peace in South-Eastern Europe.

Measures have been adopted by the International Commission of Control in Albania for the purpose of establishing order and security, and, on the arrival of the new Ruler, I trust that progress will be made towards the institution of an efficient and stable administration in that country.

I am happy to say that My negotiations, both with the German Government and the Ottoman Government, as regards matters of importance to the commercial and industrial interests of this country in Mesopotamia, are rapidly approaching a satisfactory issue, while questions which have long been pending with the Turkish Empire in respect to regions bordering on the Persian Gulf are in a fair way towards an amicable settlement.

It gives Me great gratification that the International Conference on Safety of Life at Sea, which recently met in London at the invitation of My Government, has resulted in the signature of an important Convention, which will, I trust, do much for the protection of life, especially on ocean-going passenger steamships. A Bill to enable Me to fulfil the obligations of the Convention will be laid before you.

I regret that in My Indian Dominions the early cessation of the seasonal rains last autumn has impaired the prospects of agriculture over considerable tracts. The area visited by severe drought is fortunately restricted, and in it timely measures have been taken by My officers for the relief of the distressed population.

Members of the House of Commons:

The Estimates for the service of the coming year will be laid before you in due course.

My Lords and Members of the House of Commons:

The measures in regard to which there were differences last Session between the two Houses will be again submitted for your consideration. I regret that the efforts which have been made to arrive at a solution by agreement of the problems connected with the Government of Ireland have, so far, not succeeded. In a matter in which the hopes and the fears of so many of My subjects are keenly concerned, and which, unless handled now with foresight, judgment, and in the spirit of mutual concession, threatens grave future difficulties, it is My most earnest wish that the good will and co-operation of men of all parties and creeds may heal dissension and lay the foundations of a lasting settlement.

Proposals will be laid before you for re-constituting the Second Chamber.

The Royal Commission which was appointed to enquire into the delay in the Administration of Justice in the King's Bench Division has now made its Report. Propositions will be made for you to carry into effect certain of the recommendations, which require the concurrence of Parliament. The consideration of other recommendations, which can be effected by administrative action, is already well advanced.

A Bill which has been prepared in consultation with the Governments of the Self-governing Dominions, relating to British nationality and providing for Imperial naturalisation, will be laid before you.

A Bill will be introduced to authorise the making of Loans to the Governments of the East African Protectorates to enable them to carry out certain public works which are urgently required for the better development of their territories.

Measures will be presented dealing with the Housing of the industrial and agricultural population; to give effect to the proposals, which were announced last Session, for the development of a National system of Education; to amend the Law with respect to the treatment and punishment of young offenders, and otherwise improve the Administration of Justice; and, if time and opportunity permit, for other purposes of social reform.

PROROGATION (18 September 1914)

My Lords and Members of the House of Commons:
    I address you in circumstances that call for action rather than for speech.
    After every endeavour had been made by My Government to preserve the peace of the world, I was compelled, in the assertion of treaty obligations deliberately set at nought, and for the protection of the public law of Europe and the vital interests of My Empire, to go to war.
    My Navy and Army have, with unceasing vigilance, courage, and skill, sustained, in association with gallant and faithful allies, a just and righteous cause.
    From every part of My Empire there has been a spontaneous and enthusiastic rally to our common flag.

Members of the House of Commons:
    I thank you for the liberality with which you have met a great emergency.

My Lords and Members of the House of Commons:
    We are fighting for a worthy purpose, and we shall not lay down our arms until that purpose has been fully achieved.

FIFTH SESSION OF THE THIRTIETH PARLIAMENT

1914—1916

OPENING (11 November 1914)

My Lords and Members of the House of Commons:

The energies and sympathies of My subjects in every part of the Empire are concentrated on the prosecution to a victorious issue of the War on which we are engaged. I have summoned you now in order that sharing, as I am aware you do, My conviction that this is a duty of paramount and supreme importance, you should take whatever steps are needed for its adequate discharge.

Since I last addressed you, the area of the War has been enlarged by the participation in the struggle of the Ottoman Empire. In conjunction with My Allies, and in spite of repeated and continuous provocations, I strove to preserve, in regard to Turkey, a friendly neutrality. Bad counsels, and alien influences, have driven her into a policy of wanton and defiant aggression, and a state of war now exists between us. My Mussulman subjects know well that a rupture with Turkey has been forced upon Me against My will, and I recognise with appreciation and gratitude the proofs, which they have hastened to give, of their loyal devotion and support.

My Navy and Army continue, throughout the area of conflict, to maintain in full measure their glorious traditions. We watch and follow their steadfastness and valour with thankfulness and pride, and there is, throughout My Empire, a fixed determination to secure, at whatever sacrifice, the triumph of our arms, and the vindication of our case.

Members of the House of Commons:

You will be asked to make due financial provision for the effective conduct of the War.

My Lords and Members of the House of Commons:

The only measures which will be submitted to you, at this stage of the Session, are such as seem necessary to My advisers for the attainment of the great purpose upon which the efforts of the Empire are set.

PROROGATION (27 January 1916)

My Lords and Members of the House of Commons:

For eighteen months My Navy and Army have been engaged, in concert with brave and steadfast Allies, in defending our common liberties and the public law of Europe against the unprovoked encroachments of the enemy. I am sustained by the determination of My people at home and overseas to carry our flag to a final and decisive victory.

Members of the House of Commons:

I thank you for the ungrudging liberality with which you have made provision for the heavy demands of the War.

My Lords and Members of the House of Commons:

In this struggle, forced upon us by those who hold in light esteem the liberties and covenants which we regard as sacred, we shall not lay down our arms until we have vindicated the cause which carries with it the future of civilisation.

SIXTH SESSION OF THE THIRTIETH PARLIAMENT

1916

OPENING (15 February 1916)

My Lords and Members of the House of Commons:
It has been My duty to summon you after a short recess to renew your deliberations.

The spirit of My Allies and of My people, who are united in this conflict by ever strengthening ties of sympathy and understanding, remains steadfast in the resolve to secure reparation for the victims of unprovoked and unjustifiable outrage and effectual safeguards for all nations against the aggression of a Power which mistakes force for right and expediency for honour.

With a proud and grateful confidence I look to the courage, tenacity, and resource of My Navy and Army, on whom we depend worthily to perform our part in the attainment of this goal.

Members of the House of Commons:
You will be asked to make due financial provision for the conduct of the War.

My Lords and Members of the House of Commons:
The only measures which will be submitted to you are such as in the opinion of My Advisers tend to the attainment of our common object.

PROROGATION (22 December 1916)

My Lords and Members of the House of Commons:
Throughout the months that have elapsed since I last addressed you My Navy and Army, in conjunction with those of our gallant and faithful Allies, have, by their unceasing vigilance and indomitable valour, justified the high trust I placed in them. I am confident that, however long the struggle, their efforts, supported by the inflexible determination of all My subjects throughout the Empire, will finally achieve the victorious consummation of those aims for which I entered into war. My Government has been reconstructed with the sole object of furthering those aims unaltered and unimpaired.

Members of the House of Commons:
I thank you for the unstinted liberality with which you continue to provide for the burdens of the War.

My Lords and Members of the House of Commons:
The vigorous prosecution of the War must be our single endeavour until we have vindicated the rights so ruthlessly violated by our enemies and established the security of Europe on a sure foundation.

In this sacred cause I am assured of the united support of all My peoples.

SEVENTH SESSION OF THE THIRTIETH PARLIAMENT

1917–1918

OPENING (7 February 1917)

My Lords and Members of the House of Commons:

For the third time in succession I summon you to your deliberations in the midst of war.

Certain overtures, of which you are aware, have been made by the enemy with a view to the opening of peace negotiations. Their tenour, however, indicated no possible basis for peace.

My people throughout the Empire and My faithful and heroic Allies remain steadfastly and unanimously resolved to secure the just demands for reparation and restitution in respect of the past and the guarantees for the future which we regard as essential to the progress of civilisation. In response to an invitation from the President of the United States of America, we have outlined, so far as can be done at present, the general objects necessarily implied by these aims. The threats of further outrages upon public law and the common rights of humanity will but serve to steel our determination.

During the winter months My Navy has maintained unchallenged its ceaseless watch on the Seas and has enforced with rigour the blockade of the enemy. My Armies have conducted successful operations not only in Europe but in Egypt, Mesopotamia, and East Africa, and they are fully prepared to renew the great struggle, in close and cordial co-operation with my Allies, on every field. I trust that their united efforts will carry the successes already won to a victorious conclusion.

I have invited representatives of My Dominions and of My Indian Empire, which have borne so glorious a share in the struggle, to confer with My Ministers on important questions of common interest relating to the war. The step so taken will, I trust, conduce to the establishment of closer relations between all parts of My Empire.

Members of the House of Commons:

You will be asked to make the necessary provision for the effective prosecution of the war.

My Lords and Members of the House of Commons:

The accomplishment of the task to which I have set My hand will entail unsparing demands on the energies and resources of all My subjects. I am assured, however, that My people will respond to every call necessary for the success of our cause with the same indomitable ardour and devotion that have filled Me with pride and gratitude since the war began.

PROROGATION (6 February 1918)

My Lords and Members of the House of Commons:

Since I last addressed you great events have happened. Within a few weeks of that occasion, the United States of America decided to take their stand by the side of this Country and Our Allies in defence of the principles of Liberty and Justice. Their entry into the War, followed by that of other neutral States, has united practically the whole civilised world in a League of Nations against unscrupulous aggression, has lent additional strength to Our arms, and inspires fresh confidence in the ultimate triumph of Our cause.

On the other hand, Russia, distracted by internal dissensions, has not been able to persevere in the struggle until the fruits of her great sacrifices could have been reaped: and for the present has ceased to bear her part in the Allied task. The negotiations opened by her with the enemy have, however, served but to prove that the ambitions which provoked this unhappy war are as yet unabated.

These tragic events have added to the burdens of the other Allies, but have not impaired the vigour and the loyalty with which one and all continue to pursue the common aim. Amid the confusion of changing events the determination of the democracies of the world to secure a just and enduring peace stands out ever more clearly.

In all the theatres of war, My Naval and Military Forces have displayed throughout the year a noble courage, a high constancy, and a fixed determination, which have won for them the admiration of My people. In France, the enemy has been repeatedly and successfully thrown back, and I await with assurance the further progress of the conflict. In Palestine and Mesopotamia the most revered and famous cities of the Orient have been wrested from the Turk; while in Africa the enemy has lost the last remnant of his Colonial possessions. In all of these fields, the forces of My Dominions and of the Indian Empire have borne their full share in the toil and in the glory of the day.

During the year the representatives of My Dominions and of the Indian Empire were summoned for the first time to the sessions of an Imperial War Cabinet.

Their deliberations have been of the utmost value, both in the prosecution of the War and in the promotion of Imperial Unity.

Members of the House of Commons:

I thank you for the liberality with which you

have made provision for the heavy expenditure of
the War.

My Lords and Members of the House of Commons:
I have been pleased to give My consent to your
proposals for the better Representation of the People.
I trust that this measure will ensure to a much larger
number of My subjects in the United Kingdom an
effective voice in the government of the country, and
will enable the National Unity, which has been so
marked a characteristic of the War, to continue in the
not less arduous work of reconstruction in times of
peace.

The settlement of this difficult question by
agreement leads me still to hope that, in spite of all
the complexities of the problem, a solution may be
possible in regard to the government of Ireland, upon
which a Convention of representatives of My Irish
people is now deliberating.

The successful prosecution of the War is still
our first aim and endeavour. I have watched with a
proud and grateful heart the unvarying enthusiasm
with which all sections of My people have responded
to every demand made upon them for this purpose,
and, as they face the final tests which may yet be
required to carry our efforts to fruition, I pray that
Almighty God may vouchsafe to us His Blessing.

EIGHTH SESSION OF THE THIRTIETH PARLIAMENT

1918

OPENING (12 February 1918)

My Lords and Members of the House of Commons:

The necessities of War render it imperative for Me, after but a brief interval, to summon you again to your deliberations.

The aims for which I and My Allies are contending were recently set forth by My Government in a statement which received the emphatic approval of My peoples throughout the Empire, and provided a fair basis for the settlement of the present struggle and the reestablishment of national rights and international peace in the future.

The German Government has, however, ignored our just demands that it should make restitution for the wrongs it has committed, and furnish guarantees against their unprovoked repitition. Its spokesmen refuse any obligations for themselves, while denying the rightful liberties of others.

Until a recognition is offered of the only principles on which an honourable peace can be concluded, it is Our duty to prosecute the War with all the vigour that we possess. I have full confidence that My forces in the field, in close co-operation with those of My faithful Allies, will continue to display the same heroic courage and My people at home the same unselfish devotion that have already frustrated so many of the enemy's designs and will ensure the ultimate triumph of a righteous cause.

Members of the House of Commons:

You will be asked to make suitable provision for the requirements of the combatant services and for the stability of Our national finance.

My Lords and Members of the House of Commons:

The struggle on which we are engaged has reached a critical stage, which demands more than ever Our united energies and resources.

PROROGATION (21 November 1918)

My Lords and Members of the House of Commons:

The occasion on which I address you marks the close of a period which will be for ever memorable in the history of our country.

The War, upon which all the energies of My Peoples throughout My Dominions have for more than four years been concentrated, has at length been brought to a triumphant issue. The conclusion of an Armistice with the last of the Powers that have been arrayed against us gives promise at no distant date of an honourable and enduring peace. I have already sought an opportunity of expressing publicly to My Peoples and to My Allies the sentiments of heartfelt admiration and gratitude with which I regard the supreme and self-sacrificing devotion that has led to this glorious result. Amidst our rejoicing let us not forget to render thanks to Almighty God for the success with which it has pleased Him to crown our arms.

Members of the House of Commons:

I thank you for the unfailing patriotism with which you have made provision for the requirements of the War.

My Lords and Members of the House of Commons:

The exertions which have carried us to victory in the field must in no wise be abated or slackened until the ravages of war have been repaired and the fabric of our national prosperity has been restored. Through the extension of the suffrage, which this Parliament has carried into effect, all classes of My People will have an opportunity of inspiring and guiding this beneficient undertaking. I trust that the spirit of unity which has enabled us to surmount the perils of war will not be wanting in the no less arduous task of establishing on the sure foundation of ordered liberty the common welfare of My People. In bidding you farewell, I pray that the blessing of Almighty God may rest upon your labours.

FIRST SESSION OF THE THIRTY-FIRST PARLIAMENT

1919

OPENING (11 February 1919)

My Lords and Members of the House of Commons:

The dissolution of the last Parliament followed almost immediately upon the collapse of Germany under the ceaseless blows of the Allied Armies. Since that date the terms of the Armistice, which have been more than once renewed, have been perseveringly enforced. The enemy forces have retired behind the Rhine, and have surrendered much of their armament. The Allied Armies have occupied the bridgeheads across that river, thus laying open the road into Germany should she attempt to renew the war. During the same period the might of the German Navy has been shattered by the surrender of the enemy's submarines and the internment of his main fleet in My ports.

These great results, which gave practical securities that the struggle between German tyranny and European freedom is at an end, and that a new era has dawned, has been achieved by the vigilance and disciplined efficiency of the British and Allied Fleets, and by the courage, the endurance, and the determination of My Armies and the Armies of the many Nations fighting with them. Among the resolutions to be submitted to you will be one asking you to give solemn expression to the gratitude of My People for the achievements and sacrifices of those who have suffered for the Country's cause by land, and sea, and air.

In order to reap the full fruits of victory and to safeguard the peace of the world an adequate Army must be maintained in the field, and proposals which will be necessary to secure the forces required will be submitted to you in due course.

For the last month a Conference of My Plenipotentiaries and of the Representatives of all the Allied and Associated Powers has been assembled in Paris to deliberate upon the terms of a just and lasting peace. Their discussions have been marked by the utmost cordiality and goodwill and by no disagreement. They have made good progress with the examination of the numerous and varied problems which will require settlement in the Terms of Peace, and I trust that before the Session is far advanced Preliminaries of Peace will be signed. I rejoice particularly that the Powers assembled in the Conference have agreed to accept the principle of a League of Nations, for it is by progress along that road that I see the only hope of saving mankind from a recurrence of the scourge of war.

I took an early opportunity to visit France and to convey to the President of the Republic the heartfelt enthusiasm with which My People acclaimed the final liberation of her territories and the vindication of the national unity of our faithful friend and ally. I was deeply moved by the demonstration of cordial affection which I received during My visit.

It has also given Me great pleasure to receive in this country the President of the United States of America. The enthusiastic welcome accorded him is a proof of the goodwill which all sections of My People feel towards the great Republic of the West, and an earnest of the increasing understanding with which I trust they will act together in the future.

For the last few months the Imperial War Cabinet has been in continuous session, and My counsels in regard to the War and external affairs have been both strengthened and enlightened by the presence of the leading Ministers of My self-governing Dominions, and of representatives of My Indian Empire. The inspiring sacrifice and the invaluable service which have been rendered by the Peoples of the Dominions and of India during the War have won for them an important place in the counsels of the world, and it has been a source of especial satisfaction to Me that their title to representation has been fully recognised in the Paris Conference.

I trust that the Reports of the Committees which are now enquiring into matters connected with Indian Constitutional Reform will be received in time to enable a Bill on the subject to the presented in the course of the Session.

The position in Ireland causes Me great anxiety, but I earnestly hope that conditions may soon sufficiently improve to make it possible to provide a durable settlement of this difficult problem.

Members of the House of Commons:

You will be asked to make further provision for meeting the permanent charges resulting from the War, and the new expenditure required for purposes of reconstruction.

My Lords and Members of the House of Commons:

The aspirations for a better social order which have been quickened in the hearts of My people by the experience of the War must be encouraged by prompt and comprehensive action. Before the War, poverty, unemployment, inadequate housing, and many remediable ills existed in our land, and these ills were aggravated by disunion. But since the outbreak of War every party and every class have worked and fought together for a great ideal. In the pursuit of this common aim they have shown a spirit of unity and self-sacrifice which has exalted the nation and has enabled it to play its full part in the winning of victory. The ravages of War and the wastage of War have not yet, however, been repaired. If we are to repair these losses and to build a better Britain, we must continue to manifest the same spirit. We must stop at no sacrifice of interest or prejudice to stamp out unmerited poverty, to diminish unemployment and mitigate its sufferings, to provide decent homes, to improve the nation's health, and to raise the standard of well-being throughout the community. We shall not achieve this end by undue tenderness towards acknowledged abuses, and it must necessarily be retarded by violence or even by disturbance. We shall succeed only by patient and untiring resolution in carrying through the legislation and the administrative action which are required. It is that resolute action which I now ask you to support.

A large number of measures affecting the social and economic well-being of the nation await your consideration, and it is of the utmost importance that their provisions should be examined and, if possible, agreed upon and carried into effect with all expedition. With this object in view, My Government will invite the consideration of the House of Commons to certain proposals for the simplification of the procedure of that House which, it is hoped, will enable delays to be avoided and give its Members an increasing opportunity of taking an effective part in the work of legislation. You will be asked to approve a Bill for the creation of a new Ministry to deal with public health, with a view to the establishment throughout the land of a scientific and enlightened health organisation to combat disease and to conserve the vigour of the race; also a Bill to establish a Ministry of Ways and Communications with a view to increasing and developing the industrial and agricultural resources of the country by improved means of transport. You will be asked to consider measures for effecting a speedy increase on a large scale in the housing accommodation of the country, for the fulfilment of the pledges given to Trade Unions, for the prevention of unfair competition by the sale of imported goods below their selling price in their country of origin, and for increasing industrial and agricultural output, without which a considerable and permanent betterment in the national condition cannot be effected. Proposals will also be laid before you for encouraging settlement on the land, particularly by those who have been in the fighting forces of the Crown, for providing suitable men with the necessary agricultural training and for enabling them to stock and equip their holdings, and for the reclamation of land and the promotion of a comprehensive scheme of afforestation.

Finally, I commend to your earnest consideration the industrial problems of the time. That the gifts of leisure and prosperity may be more generally shared throughout the community is My ardent desire. It is your duty, while firmly maintaining security for property and person, to spare no effort in healing the causes of the existing unrest, and I earnestly appeal to you to do all that in you lies to revive and foster a happier and more harmonious spirit in our national industrial life.

PROROGATION (23 December 1919)

My Lords and Members of the House of Commons:

After many months of arduous deliberation in Paris, the efforts of the Plenipotentiaries of the Allied and Associated Powers have been crowned with success, and Treaties of Peace with Germany, Austria and Bulgaria have been concluded. In the negotiations the Prime Ministers of all My Dominions and Representatives of India took an influential part. I have signified My approval of the Treaty of Peace with Germany and have ratified it. Peace still remains to be concluded with the Ottoman Empire and the Republic of Hungary, and I earnestly trust that the necessary negotiations for this purpose will shortly be brought to a satisfactory conclusion.

I regret that there is no improvement in the unhappy conditions prevailing in Russia, and that there is no immediate prospect in that country of the establishment of Constitutional Government, which alone can conduce to its permanent prosperity.

My relations with My Allies and Associates in the Great War remain of the most friendly character, and I have every expectation that the close and intimate co-operation which led to victory will be long continued to the benefit of all.

In August last My Government concluded with the Persian Government an Agreement tending to cement the ties of friendship between the two countries, which have so many interests in common, and to promote the welfare and progress of Persia. I have since had the pleasure of entertaining the Shah on his first visit to Europe.

The signal success which has attended the visit of the Prince of Wales to Canada and Newfoundland has filled My heart with feelings of pride and satisfaction. The overwhelming enthusiasm with which My son was everywhere welcomed affords a fresh proof of the affectionate loyalty which animates all My Peoples, and I rejoice that his visit has strengthened the ties of comradeship which unite the various countries of the Empire. He subsequently visited the United States of America, where he was greeted with a warmth and kindliness which will, I am confident, have the happiest effect on the relations between the British Empire and that great

Republic.

The whole Empire mourns the death of General Botha, one of the greatest and wisest of its Statesmen. The sagacity and far-sightedness which made him the trusted leader of the people of the Dominion of South Africa, and which contributed so much to the success of the Allies, won universal recognition at the recent deliberations in Paris.

A measure which marks the first stage in the development of responsible government in India has become law, and I rely on all My subjects to work together for its success. In a Proclamation which I am addressing to My Viceroy and to the Princes and People of India, I am expressing My hope that harmonious political life will be steadily built up on the foundations thus laid, and I am announcing My intention of sending My Son, the Prince of Wales, to India to inaugurate the new Constitution.

Members of the House of Commons:

I thank you for the provision that you have made for the service of a year in which public expenditure has necessarily continued on an abnormal scale largely exceeding both the permanent and temporary revenue. I trust that next year, with the return to more normal conditions, you will be able to take the first steps in the reduction of the National Debt. The condition of our finances and the state of our credit continue to occupy the serious attention of My Ministers. Only by strict economy in both public and private expenditure and by sustained increase of production can the country maintain its historic position in commerce and finance.

My Lords and Members of the House of Commons:

I cannot view without concern the grave economic position of a large part of Europe. The task of restoring credit and restarting industry in the countries whose economic life has been destroyed by five years of war is one of the first conditions of a return to settled peace, but it is too large a task for any nation to undertake unaided. I was enabled by the liberality of Parliament to place a large sum at the disposal of the Supreme Economic Council for the relief of immediate necessities, but that sum is now nearly exhausted. Further measures of relief and reconstruction can only be undertaken as the result of joint action by all nations interested in the restoration of international commerce. My Government would gladly co-operate with the Governments of other countries to this end if a suitable plan can be devised.

Great progress has been made during the past year in the gigantic task of demobilising My Navy, Army and Air Force, impeded as it has been by the uncertainties of the situation in large parts of Europe and Asia.

The lot of the men who have served in My Forces during the War, and especially of those who are disabled, has been the subject of anxious consideration. It is a source of great satisfaction to Me that it has been possible to increase the scales of pension paid to war veterans and to the dependants of those who gave their lives in the War. I am glad to know that very large numbers of men have been reabsorbed in peaceful industries, but it is important that employment should be within the reach of all who are able to take advantage of it. To this end I have made an appeal to the employers of the country which has received a large response. But more remains to be done, and I am hopeful that the measures which have been and are being taken for giving them training in skilled occupations and for placing them in employment will have the ready support of all My People.

Measures have also been passed to facilitate the settlement on the land of ex-Service men who have fought in the War, and for providing them with the necessary assistance in establishing themselves in agriculture.

The continued high cost of living, with all its evil consequences, has caused distress throughout the the world, though it is lower in the British Isles than elsewhere. The problem of reducing it has received your constant consideration, and measures have been taken which it is hoped may prevent the charging of unreasonable prices for necessary articles.

In the sphere of domestic legislation the Session has been marked by the passage of an unprecedented number of Bills dealing with reconstruction in all its aspects.

Important measures have been passed affecting the conditions of labour. There is no doubt that public opinion throughout the world is deeply interested in the manner in which Great Britain is dealing with its labour and industrial problem, and I am confident that though the difficult times are not yet passed our course is set fair towards a renewal of national strength and prosperity. I am glad to think that there has been a steady improvement in industrial conditions. Unemployment, which in the earlier part of the year was unexampled in extent, stands to-day at a figure which compares favourably with the years prior to the War. This is all the more remarkable considering the immense numbers of men and women discharged from the Services and from munition works at home. The Acts for restoring privileges surrendered during the War and for stabilising the conditions of employment have done much to avoid friction in the industrial life of the country. The establishment of an Industrial Court has provided the machinery for securing the peaceful settlement of disputes and promoting harmony among those engaged in industry. These measures form part of a programme which it has not been found possible to complete in the present Session. Proposals have been formulated for fixing a maximum number of hours of employment, for instituting a

minimum wage, and for making increased provision
against unemployment. I trust that at an early date
they may receive the assent of Parliament.

I have given My assent to an Act constituting a
Ministry of Agriculture, Agricultural Councils for England
and Wales, an Advisory Committee to assist the Minister,
and providing for the decentralisation of Agricultural
Administration to Committees of the County Councils.

I have also assented to Bills for the establishment
of the Ministry of Health in England, and a Board of
Health in Scotland, and a Council of Health in
Ireland. I anticipate that when they are in full working
order they will prove invaluable in co-ordinating and
improving the service of the health of the people.

The Housing and Town Planning Acts which
were passed in July, and the Housing (Additional
Powers) Act to which I have just given assent, mark a
new departure in housing legislation; and it is My
sincere hope that these measures will facilitate the
solution of the housing problem in the United
Kingdom by providing increased and better
accommodation and leading to the progressive
elimination of insanitary dwellings.

I view with satisfaction the passing of the Act
to establish a Ministry of Transport. The creation of
an effective system of transport will greatly
contribute to agricultural and industrial development,
to the solution of the housing problem, and to the
reparation of the immense losses inflicted on the
country by the War.

Upon these measures the future prosperity of
the country very largely depends.

The pressure on the time of Parliament has made
it impossible to enact in its entirety the Electricity
Supply Bill as passed by the House of Commons.
Provision has, however, been made which enables
the necessary Commissioners to be established and the
preliminary steps to be taken in the reorganisation of
this vital industry. A portion of this Bill was
temporarily postponed with the object of giving
adequate time to Parliament to deliberate fully upon
its terms. It is greatly hoped, however, that upon the
reassembly of Parliament consideration of the
remaining portion will be resumed.

In addition to these Bills, a number of other
Acts, relating to the Acquisition of Land, Patents and
Designs, Trademarks, Wireless Telegraphy, and other
matters of importance in the practical work of
reconstruction, have received My assent.

SECOND SESSION OF THE THIRTY-FIRST PARLIAMENT

1920

OPENING (10 February 1920)

My Lords and Members of the House of Commons:

I am thankful that since I last addressed you the final ratifications of the Peace Treaty with Germany have been exchanged in Paris, and that the state of war with that country which has lasted for more than five years has been finally brought to an end. I have accordingly despatched to Berlin a representative to act as Charge de Affaires at that capital, and I am about to receive a German representative at My Court of St. James's.

I intend shortly to accord My ratification to the Treaties for Peace which have been signed with Austria and Bulgaria, and proposals will be laid before you for giving effect to these Treaties.

I trust that it will be possible to conclude peace both with Hungary and Turkey at an early date. The negotiations concerning the Turkish peace which have already commenced are being pressed forward with all possible speed.

A number of Meetings between my Ministers and representatives of the Great Associated Powers have recently taken place in London and Paris and have confirmed the excellent relations which exist with all our Allies. I earnestly trust that, as the result of these meetings, a settlement of the long-continued Adriatic dispute will shortly be reached. In order, however, to assure the full blessings of peace and prosperity to Europe, it is essential that not only peace but normal conditions of economic life should be restored in Eastern Europe and in Russia. So long as these vast regions withold their full contribution to the stock of commodities available for general consumption, the cost of living can hardly be reduced nor general prosperity restored to the world.

I have had great pleasure in assenting to the proposal that the Prince of Wales should visit Australia and New Zealand and should take the opportunity on his return voyage of seeing some of My West Indian possessions. He will, I feel confident, receive a cordial welcome everywhere both from old comrades in arms and from all classes of the community.

Members of the House of Commons:

The estimates for the service in the coming year will be laid before you in due course.

My Lords and Members of the House of Commons:

The war has shaken to its foundations the economy of the national life, and the transition from war to peace has presented problems of unprecedented difficulty. I believe that Our country and the Empire are making rapid strides towards stability and prosperity. The price of foodstuffs and other necessary commodities is causing anxiety to all the peoples of the world, but I am glad to say that prices in these islands are appreciably lower than they are elsewhere. This fact and the condition of trade with the outside world, especially of the export trade, serve to show that My people are proving no less successful in dealing with the troubles which war has left behind it than they were in enduring the war itself.

If, however, we are to ensure lasting progress, prosperity and social peace, all classes must continue to throw themselves into the work of reconstruction with goodwill for others, with energy, and with patience, and legislation providing for large and far-reaching measures of reform must be passed into law.

The condition of Ireland causes Me grave concern, but a Bill will immediately be laid before you to give effect to the proposals for the better government of that country which were outlined at the end of the last Session. A Bill to make further provision for education in Ireland will also be submitted to you. The absence of facilities for education for a considerable part of the child population in certain districts makes the question one of urgency, but care will be taken to make the measure compatible with the Home Rule Bill.

It is imperative that the difficult problems which have arisen in connection with the coal-mining industry should be settled on an enduring basis. These problems will demand your anxious and early attention. In addition to an emergency measure to adjust the financial arrangements of the collieries to meet the abnormal economic conditions at present prevailing in the industry, you will be asked to consider proposals for the acquisition of coal royalties by the State, for the improvement of conditions in mining areas, and for the future ordering of the industry in the best interests of the community as a whole.

Experience during the war showed clearly the injurious effects upon national efficiency of the excessive consumption of strong drink and the amelioration both in health and efficiency which followed appropriate measures of regulation and control. A Bill will accordingly be presented to you providing for the development of a suitable system for the peace-time regulation of the sale and supply of alcoholic liquor.

Despite the increase of agricultural production during the war, the population of these islands is still dangerously dependent upon the supplies of food from Overseas, and the financial burden of purchasing such supplies in foreign markets against an adverse rate of exchange is very great. Uneasiness has also been caused by the unprecedented sale of landed property since the war. Measures will accordingly be proposed to mitigate any hardship which this operation may cause to the occupier, and to stimulate and develop the production of essential foodstuffs within the United Kingdom. A Bill will also be introduced to encourage and develop the Fishing Industry.

A Bill will also be submitted to you for the after-war organisation of the regular and territorial armies and for regulating the navigation of the air.

Among other important Bills which you will be invited to pass are measures dealing with Insurance against Unemployment, the regulation of hours of employment, and the establishment of a minimum rate of wage, and with the amendment of the Health Insurance Acts. Bills will also be introduced providing against the injury to national industries from dumping and for the creation of an adequate supply of cheap electrical and water power.

Proposals will also be laid before you during the present Session dealing with the Reform of the Second Chamber, and it is hoped that time will permit of their being passed into law.

PROROGATION (23 December 1920)

My Lords and Members of the House of Commons:

My relations with foreign Powers continue to be of a friendly nature, and throughout the year external policy has been conducted in close co-operation with the Allies. The general appeasement of the passions engendered by the War has been assisted by a Conference with our late enemies, at which certain matters in dispute were satisfactorily adjusted. The situation which has arisen with Greece will, however, require the earnest attention of My Government, who will, in conjection with the Allies, endeavour to reach a solution compatible with our joint responsibilities.

In Russia the situation is still unsettled and obscure. I trust that trade will shortly recommence with Russia, and that this may lead to an era of peace greatly needed by the suffering peoples of Eastern Europe. It is of the highest importance, however, that Poland and her neighbours should compose their political differences, and devote their undivided energies to producing internal stability and to the task of economic reconstruction.

I have accepted Mandates, under the Covenant of the League of Nations, in respect of Mesopotamia, Palestine, certain parts of Africa, and other German possessions in the Pacific Ocean south of the Equator.

The Mandates for German South-West Africa and the German possessions in the Pacific will be severally administered by the Governments of the Union of South Africa, of the Dominion of New Zealand, and of the Commonwealth of Australia. It will be the high task of all My Governments to superintend and assist the development of these countries, according to their varying degrees of advancement, for the benefit of the inhabitants and the general welfare of mankind.

During the past year the League of Nations has come into effective existence. A long series of important measures has been initiated by the Council of the League and the Labour Bureau. The first Assembly of the League has shown its sense of the importance of including all nations in its membership by admitting two of our late enemies. It is My earnest hope that the spirit of harmony and goodwill between nations manifested at the Assembly is an augury of the value of the League as a force making for conciliation and peace throughout the world.

Since I last addressed you I have had the happiness of welcoming My son the Prince of Wales, on his return from his visit to Australia, New Zealand, and the West Indies. The enthusiastic affection with which he has been everywhere received has afforded me the liveliest gratification, and I am confident that he has done much to strengthen the mutual sympathy and trust which cement the Empire.

The measures required to bring into operation the Government of India Act have been taken, and the new constitution will be in general effect within a few days. It is a matter of great regret to me that the Prince of Wales will not be able to inaugurate the new Councils. But the Duke of Connaught is now on his way to fulfil that duty, and I am confident that the people of India, to whom he is well-known as having filled the high office of Commander-in-Chief in Bombay, will accept his Royal Highness's visit on my behalf as proof of My earnest and unwavering hope that their Legislators will so fulfil the responsibilities entrusted to them as to bring increased prosperity and contentment to all My subjects in India.

Members of the House of Commons:

I thank you for the provision made for the public service and for the redemption of debt. Obligations arising out of the Great War, and the disturbed conditions still prevailing in a large part of the world, have made very heavy expenditure unavoidable. These difficulties are common to the whole world, and have been nowhere so successfully met as in this country. I am conscious of the great sacrifices entailed by this heavy draft upon the national resources, and of the vital need of economy in all Departments of the public service, and My Ministers will continue to make every effort to reduce expenditure.

My Lords and Members of the House of Commons:

The state of affairs in Ireland grieves Me profoundly. I deplore the campaign of violence and outrage by which a small section of My subjects seek to sever Ireland from the Empire, and I sympathise with the loyal servants of the Crown who are endeavouring to restore peace and maintain order under conditions of unexampled difficulty and danger. It is My most earnest hope that all sections of the people in Ireland will insist upon a return to constitutional methods, which alone can put an end to the terrible events which now threathen ruin to that country and make possible reconciliation and a lasting peace. I have given My assent to a Bill for the better government of Ireland. This Act, by setting up two Parliaments and a Council of Ireland gives self-government in Irish affairs to the whole of Ireland, and provides the means whereby the people of Ireland can of their own accord achieve unity. I sincerely hope that this Act, the fruit of more than thirty years of ceaseless controversy, will finally bring about unity and friendship between all the peoples of My Kingdom.

My Government are giving careful and anxious consideration to the question of Naval strength as affected by the latest developments of Naval warfare.

During the present Session I have been glad to give My assent to a number of measures for the promotion of the well-being of the people. Among other Acts, I may mention the Act providing old age pensions for blind persons at the age of fifty; the National Health Insurance Act, which increased the general rates of benefits to contributors; the Juvenile Courts Act, which secures an advance both in the treatment of children and in the co-operation of women in public affairs; the Mining Industry Act, which recognises the importance of mining in the industrial life of the country by the constitution of a Mines Department, in which all the powers and duties relating to the industry are now concentrated; the Act regulating the importation of dyestuffs in order securely to establish the dyestuffs industry in this country; the Agriculture Act, which will increase the production of food, promote good husbandry, and improve the legal position of agricultural tenants; and the Unemployment Insurance Act, which makes an important extension of the provisions against unemployment and enlarges the number of insurable workers from 4,000,000 to 12,000, 000.

A measure has also been passed whereby local authorities will be assisted in the maintenance and improvement of roads and bridges, thus facilitating the further development of the new methods of transport which are becoming every year of greater importance to the life of the community.

In the domestic sphere the past Session has seen a steady return to normal conditions. I am glad to believe that the weariness and exhaustion which beset the people after their sufferings and efforts during the War are passing away, and that the difficulties thus caused, especially in industrial affairs, are giving place to a better general understanding of the problems of industry and to better relations between employers and employed. The darkest cloud on the horizon, the growing amount of unemployment, now springs, not so much from internal causes, but from the contraction of the export trade due to the poverty of other nations and to their inability to secure credits for the purpose of placing orders in this country. All nations equally with ourselves are affected by these conditions. The problem of restoring trade and of providing for those left without employment has for some time been engaging the close and earnest attention of Ministers, and various schemes, of which some are already in operation, have been prepared to alleviate the distress arising therefrom. It will be the duty of My Ministers to continue to give unremitting attention to this problem with a view to mitigating, as far as is humanly possible, the hardships of unemployment.

As a direct consequence of the industrial depression, My hope that men who served in My forces during the War, and particularly those who are disabled, would by this time be absorbed in civil employment has been disappointed. No efforts have been spared by the Government to secure the resettlement of these men in civil life, but it has become more than ever necessary that these efforts should be supplemented by the active aid and co-operation of My people.

THIRD SESSION OF THE THIRTY-FIRST PARLIAMENT

1921

OPENING (15 February 1921)

My Lords and Members of the House of Commons:

My relations with Foreign Powers continue to be of a friendly nature. Conferences will be held at an early date in London, which will be attended by Our Allies in the late War, and also by representatives of Germany and Turkey. I earnestly trust that by this means further progress will be made in giving effect to the Treaties of Peace, in re-establishing concord in Europe and in restoring tranquillity in the Near East. It is My hope that the negotiations for a trade agreement with Russia will also be brought to a successful conclusion.

The Duke of Connaught has inaugurated the new Councils in India, and I pray that the assumption by My subjects in India of new political responsibilities may secure progress in administration and an early appeasement of political strife.

The policy of My Government in regard to Egypt, following upon the investigations of the Special Mission appointed in 1919, will be laid before you.

I am glad to say that arrangements have been made to renew that personal consultation between My Ministers here and their colleagues overseas, which produced such good results during the last two years of the War and during the Peace settlement. I hope that the Prime Ministers of Canada, Australia, New Zealand, the Union of South Africa and Newfoundland, as well as representatives of India, will be able to visit this country during the coming summer. I am confident that the discussions to take place during their visits will be of the utmost value in bringing about co-ordination both in the external and internal policy of the Empire.

Members of the House of Commons:

The Estimates for the Services in the coming year will be laid before you in due course, and these Estimates will reflect the determination of the Government to reduce expenditure to the lowest level consistent with the well-being of the Empire. The War has left upon the nation liabilities which can only be met by heavy taxation, but it is imperative in the interest of an early revival of trade and industry that this burden should be reduced to the utmost.

My Lords and Members of the House of Commons:

The situation in Ireland still causes me distress. A misguided section of the Irish people persist in resorting to methods of criminal violence with the object of establishing an independent Republic. Neither Irish unity nor Irish self-government can be attained by this means. The arrangements for bringing into force the Government of Ireland Act are now well advanced, and I earnestly trust that in the near future the majority of the people will show their determination to repudiate violence and to work an Act which confers upon them the responsibilities of self-government and provides the machinery whereby they can attain to Irish unity by constitutional means.

In view of the onerous programme of legislation which was set before you during last year, it is the intention of My Ministers to lighten as far as possible the business of the coming Session. The most pressing problem which confronts you is that of unemployment, consequent upon a world-wide restriction of trade, and this may be alleviated, but cannot be cured, by legislative means. This problem, with its acute and distressing consequences for hundreds of thousands of our fellow-citizens, is receiving the constant and anxious attention of My Ministers with the object both of reviving trade and prosperity and in the meantime of assisting those who are unfortunately unemployed. You will be invited to pass a Bill extending the provision which is made for the unemployed under the Unemployment Insurance Act. A Measure will also be introduced into the House of Commons to deal with the safe-guarding of essential key industries of the country and with certain aspects of unfair and abnormal industrial competition. I earnestly trust that these efforts will be seconded by loyal and frank co-oper-ation between employers and employed for it is through the co-operation of capital and labour in a spirit of mutual trust and confidence that an early solution of this grave problem is to be found.

It is proposed that the forthcoming removal of control over the home price and export quantities of coal shall be followed at the earliest possible moment by the complete restoration of the industry to its normal condition of freedom.

In accordance with the intention expressed in the Ministry of Transport Act, a Bill will be submitted to you for the reorganisation of the railways of Great Britain.

Bills will be laid before you dealing with the completion of land purchase in Ireland, and also for facilitating Church union in Scotland.

A Bill will also be presented dealing with the sale of alchoholic liquor in the light of the experience gained during the War.

My Ministers further trust that the work of the

Committee now examining the question of the Reform of the Second Chamber will be finished in time to permit of proposals being submitted to Parliament during the course of the present Session.

PROROGATION (10 November 1921)

My Lords and Members of the House of Commons:

The Session of Parliament which closes to-day has been marked by events of great importance to the welfare of the British Empire and to the peace of the world. It is not yet possible to say that peace is firmly established in Europe and it must be long before the world can recover from the strain and sacrifice of the War; but good progress has been made towards the solution of the most critical problems of home and foreign affairs.

I have welcomed with deep satisfaction the Prime Ministers of the Dominions and the Representatives of India, who have been in Conference with My Advisers here. They had questions of great moment to discuss in common and grave decisions to make. Their presence for that purpose has been invaluable, and I trust that it may be found possible to arrange regular meetings of a like character for the further exchange of views and the discussion of common interests.

Their deliberations on foreign policy dealt in particular with the problems of the Pacific and Far East and with the questions arising out of the Empire's obligations under the Treaty of Versailles and the other Treaties of Peace. I am happy to know that on all these issues My Governments here and oversea are in close accord.

The Conference gave serious attention to the defence of the Empire and to the maintenance of an adequate measure of sea-power. It was unanimously decided that the naval strength of the Empire should be equal to that of any other Power.

As a result of the proposals made by the Allied Powers to Germany last May and accepted by her, satisfactory progress has been made by the German Government in the execution of their financial and disarmament obligations under the Treaty of Versailles.

A serious rising of the Poles in Upper Silesia led to the British troops, which had been withdrawn in April, being sent back, and after difficult and anxious negotiations the insurrection was overcome, and the authority of the International Commission was re-established.

The insurrection unfortunately delayed the negotiations for a settlement of the frontier, and at a meeting of the Allied and Associated Powers in Paris in August last, it was decided to invite the League of Nations to examine the whole question and to make recommendations for a settlement.

Those recommendations have recently been received, and steps are being taken to give effect to them. There is reason to hope that they will be loyally carried out by the two parties principally concerned, and that a peaceful and honourable settlement will result.

Peace has been definitely established between the Allied Powers and Hungary. The Treaty signed at Trianon on the 4th June, 1920, having been ratified by the British Empire, France, Italy, Japan, Belgium, Czecho-Slovakia, Serbia, Rumania, Siam, and Hungary, the ratifications were deposited at the French Ministry for Foreign Affairs on the 26th July last.

The efforts, made by My Government at the Allied Conference in March and renewed in June, to establish peace in the Near East were in each case rendered fruitless by the renewed outbreak of hostilities between the Greek and Turkish forces in Anatolia. It is my earnest desire to see these hostilities followed by an early and just peace, and My Government are prepared, in conjunction with their Allies, to take the first opportunity of furthering this end.

I have followed with great satisfaction the steps taken by the President of the United States to promote the reduction of expenditure on armaments, an object which commands the fullest sympathy of My Government.

It was in this spirit that My Government gladly accepted the invitation extended by the United States Government to a Conference of Disarmament about to be held at Washington. It is My earnest hope that the labours of the Conference will be crowned with success.

Negotiations have for some time been in progress, but have not yet reached a conclusion, between My Government and a delegation nominated by His Highness the Sultan of Egypt with a view to determine the future relationship of that country with Great Britain.

Progress continues to be made in the reduction of expenditure in Iraq in accordance with the policy which has been explained in the House.

My son, the Prince of Wales, has embarked upon his Eastern voyage, and within a few days will land for the first time on Indian soil. I pray that his visit may still further strengthen the ties of affection which for so long have linked My house with the Princes and peoples of India. Upon the conclusion of his Indian tour he will proceed on a visit to the great and friendly Empire of Japan.

Members of the House of Commons:

I thank you for the provision for the public Service. Although trade and commerce have been undergoing a period of unexampled depression, I learn with satisfaction that it is nevertheless anticipated that, while the estimated surplus for redemption of debt will not be realised, the financial year will end without a deficit on the Budget.

Our debts, however, are great, our taxation heavy and burdensome to industry, and revenue cannot be maintained on the scale of the last three years. It is accordingly of vital importance to the financial stability of the country that expenditure should be still further restricted in every department of life, both public and private. The Government will continue to take advantage of every possible means to achieve this essential object in the field of public expenditure, and I confidently rely upon My people in their own practice to support the efforts of My Ministers.

My Lords and Members of the House of Commons:

The situation in Ireland still causes Me great anxiety. I earnestly exhort the leaders of all parties in Ireland, and all those in whose hands lies the power to influence the negotiations and discussions now proceeding, to exercise patience and moderation with the object of establishing friendship and loyal co-operation between My people of that country. It is My firm belief, as it is My earnest prayer, that with forbearance and goodwill, and with an honest resolve to tread the paths of oblivion and forgiveness, an enduring peace will finally be achieved.

The past summer has been notable for the occurrence of the most serious industrial conflict which has ever menaced the prosperity of the Realm. I take pride in the calm and serene spirit with which the trials of the coal stoppage were met by My people, and the freedom from strife and violence which characterised its course.

This dispute unhappily aggravated the adverse effect of the sudden world-wide trade depression, which has inflicted upon the industries of this country the most grievous experience in their history.

My Ministers have viewed with grave concern the continuance of the wide-spread unemployment which has attended the cessation of trade. Accordingly you have within the past few weeks given close and detailed consideration to this problem. Measures have received My assent designed, first, to encourage the revival of industry by facilitating the provision of capital for public undertakings and by assisting export trade, and, secondly, directly to provide employment on an extended scale by aiding local authorities and others to carry out various forms of beneficial works. Finally, in addition to the provision made by the Acts which you have already passed relating to Unemployment Insurance, a Measure has been framed to assist in mitigating the sufferings of those who remain unemployed, by the provision, out of moneys contributed by employers, employed and the State, of grants to wives and dependent children.

The peaceful settlement of many difficult disputes by mutual negotiation between employers and workpeople, together with some indications of a revival of trade, encourage My hope that the worst may be over and that the state of employment may show from now onwards a steady, if slow, improvement. But the position is still full of anxiety, and My Ministers will continue to devote to this problem their vigilant care.

It is not, however, so much to Acts of Parliament as to the proved good sense of employers and operatives, working together for the promotion of their common interests, that I look for the restoration of trade prosperity.

My assent has also been given to Measures for the reorganisation of the railways, and for the safeguarding of industry, and an Act for the Reform of the Licensing Laws has been passed with a universal and gratifying measure of agreement. But the legislation of the Session has been dominated by the difficult financial condition of the time. The imperative need for the avoidance of all fresh burdens and for the further curtailment of expenditure has required the modification of some Measures already passed and the postponement to happier times of the completion of other reforms.

FOURTH SESSION OF THE THIRTY-FIRST PARLIAMENT

1921

OPENING (14 December 1921)

My Lords and Members of the House of Commons:

I have summoned you to meet at this unusual time in order that the Articles of Agreement which have been signed by My Ministers and the Irish Delegation may be at once submitted for your approval.

No other business will be brought before you in the present Session.

It was with heartfelt joy that I learnt of the Agreement reached after negotiations protracted for many months and affecting the welfare not only of Ireland, but of the British and Irish races throughout the world.

It is my earnest hope that by the Articles of Agreement now submitted to you the strife of centuries may be ended, and that Ireland, as a free partner in the Commonwealth of Nations forming the British Empire, will secure the fulfilment of her national ideals.

PROROGATION (19 December 1921)

My Lords and Members of the House of Commons:

I have received with deep satisfaction the assurance of your approval of the Articles of the Irish Agreement and of your readiness to give effect to its provisions.

FIFTH SESSION OF THE THIRTY-FIRST PARLIAMENT

1922

OPENING (7 February 1922)

My Lords and Members of the House of Commons:

During the last three months the Washington Conference on the question of Disarmament and the Far East has continued its Sessions. A Treaty designed to maintain peace in the Pacific has been signed by the representatives of the British Empire, the United States, France and Japan, and awaits ratification. While this Treaty replaces the Anglo-Japanese Alliance, I am happy to feel that the long-standing concord between the two countries will remain as cordial as ever under the arrangements thus concluded. At the same time our relations with the United States of America enter upon a new and even closer phase of friendship.

Agreement has also been reached on the question of disarmament and a Treaty has been signed providing a large measure of relief from the burden of armaments. In all these respects great results have been attained; and the success of the Conference, for which the world will owe a deep debt of gratitude to the initiative of the President of the United States of America, will be of the happiest augury for the future of international relations.

The problem of securing the payment of reparations by Germany in the manner most conformable to the general interest engages the continuous consideration of My Ministers and of our Allies. The German Government, at the request of the Allies, have themselves submitted proposals, which are now under consideration.

Discussions were recently initiated and are now proceeding between My Goverment and the Governments of France and Belgium with a view to the conclusion of agreements for common action in the event of unprovoked attack by Germany.

The situation in the Near East continues to engage the anxious attention of My Government and it is My earnest hope that the forthcoming Allied discussions in Paris may result in an early solution, which will terminate the conflict in a manner honourable to all the parties concerned.

Members of the House of Commons:

The Estimates for the services in the coming year will be laid before you in due course. Every effort has been made to reduce public expenditure to the lowest possible limit, regard being had alike to the security and efficiency of the State, to public obligations and to the necessity of relieving our citizens to the utmost extent from the burdens which now rest heavily upon them. Retrenchment upon so

great a scale must necessarily involve hardship to individuals and postponement of public hopes. But in a time of great industrial depression such as that through which the world is at present passing it is a necessity of the situation that economy be practised by all and in every direction; and I look for your support in securing the economies which are essential.

My Lords and Members of the House of Commons:

The Articles of Agreement signed by My Ministers and the Irish Delegation, to which you have already signified your assent, have now been approved in Ireland, and the Provisional Government contemplated in that instrument is at the present moment engaged in taking over the administration of the country. The final establishment of the Irish Free State as a partner in the British Commonwealth is anxiously awaited throughout the world. You will, therefore, be invited at an early date to consider such measures as may be necessary, to give effect to the Agreement. A Bill of Indemnity will also be submitted to you.

The great and continued volume of unemployment among My people causes me the deepest concern, and will continue to receive the earnest attention of My Ministers. The only remedy for this distressing situation is to be found in the appeasement of international rivalries and suspicions, and in the improvement of the conditions under which trade is carried on all over the world. For these reasons I welcome the arrangements which are now being made for the meeting of an International Conference at Genoa at which, I trust, it will be possible to establish peace on a fair basis in Europe and to reach a settlement of the many important questions arising out of the pressing need for financial and economic reconstruction.

Proposals will be submitted to you for the Reform of the House of Lords and for the adjustment of differences between the two Houses.

Among the Measures which will be presented for your consideration the following Bills will be submitted: A Bill relating to the establishment of an International Trade Corporation; a Bill to enable the Government to give effect to the policy of co-operation in Empire settlement and Migration; a Bill to amend the Criminal Law Amendment Acts, 1885 to 1912; and a Bill relating to Allotments.

There will also be laid before you a Bill substituting yearly audit for half-yearly audit in the case of Rural District Councils and Boards of Guardians, and other Measures framed to give effect to the policy of retrenchment to which I have referred.

Proposals which were submitted to you last year will again be laid before you for the amendment of the law relating to real property and to the methods of land transfer.

Note: There was no Prorogation Speech. Parliament was Dissolved on October 26 during the Summer Recess.

FIRST SESSION OF THE THIRTY-SECOND PARLIAMENT

1922

OPENING (20 November 1922)

My Lords and Members of the House of Commons:
A Constitution for the Irish Free State having been passed by the House of the Parliament established under the Irish Free State (Agreement) Act of last Session sitting as a Constituent Assembly, and it being required by the terms of that Act that the Constitution should come into force by the sixth day of December next, I have summoned you to meet in order that the legislation necessary to give effect to that Constitution and to make the provisions consequential on the establishment of the Irish Free State may be at once submitted for your approval.

Members of the House of Commons:
Estimates for the public service will be laid before you.

My Lords and Members of the House of Commons:
The state of trade and employment continues to cause Me deep concern. The ameliorative measures prepared by My late Government are being examined afresh, and you will be asked to make provision for their continuance and extension and to guarantee a loan in accordance with the League of Nations scheme for the restoration of Austria.

Negotiations for the settlement of difficulties in the Near East are proceeding, and it is My hope that at the conference at Lausanne the efforts of My Ministers, acting in whole-hearted co-operation with the representatives of our Allies, may result in the re-establishment of peace and the restoration of security to the inhabitants of the regions which have recently been the scene of so much suffering.

PROROGATION (15 December 1922)

My Lords and Members of the House of Commons:
The discussion of problems affecting the peace of the Near East is proceeding at Lausanne, and I earnestly trust that a satisfactory solution will shortly be reached.

The execution of the Treaty of Peace with Germany has again been the subject of conversations between My Ministers and the Ministers of the Allied Powers. These conversations will be resumed in Paris at an early date.

The task of restoring conditions favourable to economic stability in Europe continues to give Me deep concern. The difficulties are great and complex, and can only be overcome by patient and sincere co-operation between the nations primarily affected.

Members of the House of Commons:
I thank you for the provision you have made for the public service.

My Lords and Members of the House of Commons:
I have given My Assent to Measures for the final enactment of the Constitution of the Irish Free State and for the consequent necessary provisions. It is My earnest prayer that the passing of these Measures may mark the inauguration of a period of prosperity and concord both for Ireland and for Great Britain.

An Act has been passed to continue and extend the measures already taken for improving trade, and My Ministers will continue to examine with great care all possible measures for dealing with Unemployment.

The condition of the agricultural industry, which is unfortunately passing through a period of serious depression, is receiving the careful consideration of My Ministers in the hope that means may be found to alleviate some of the difficulties confronting both farmers and labourers.

I have assented to a Bill to give effect to the Agreement entered into by My late Government with the representatives of the Government of My Dominion of Canada, for the amendment of the law with respect to the landing of imported animals in Great Britain.

THE SECOND SESSION OF THE THIRTY-SECOND PARLIAMENT

1923

OPENING (13 February 1923)

My Lords and Members of the House of Commons:

The Conference which was held in London early in December on the subject of the payment of Reparation by Germany was resumed in Paris, in January. My Government, in their desire to hasten a complete settlement of the Reparation question, offered to the Allied Governments far-reaching concessions on Allied debts to this country. I greatly regret that it proved impossible to reach a general agreement. The French and Belgian Governments have, therefore, proceeded to put into force the plan which they favoured, and the Italian Government have countenanced their action. My Government, while feeling unable either to concur or participate in this operation, are acting in such a way as not to add to the difficulties of their Allies.

During the past three months, the plenipotentiaries of My Government, in conjunction with those of the other Allied Powers, have been engaged at Lausanne in a sincere and patient effort to bring to a close the conditions of warfare which for over eight years have desolated the regions of the Near East.

I greatly regret that, in spite of the conciliatory spirit shown by the Allies, and of the immense concessions which they were prepared to make, the Treaty, when on the verge of signature, was declined by the Turkish Delegation. But I cherish the hope that, when a full report of the proceedings has reached the Turkish Government, the latter may still be disposed to accept the Treaty, and that the opportunity, so earnestly and laboriously prepared, of rebuilding the peace of the East and the stability of the future Turkish State, may not be sacrificed.

I welcome the prospective settlement of our War Debt to the United States of America, which reflects the determination of our people to meet their obligations.

Members of the House of Commons:

The Estimates for the public service in the coming year will be laid before you in due course.

The financial burdens of the country are heavy, and reductions in public expenditure remain essential to the well-being of the State.

My Lords and Members of the House of Commons:

The serious state of unemployment among My people causes Me the deepest concern, and must continuously engage the attention of My Ministers. The increase which has recently taken place in our

oversea trade gives ground for confidence in the future, and I earnestly trust that we may anticipate a continued improvement in both our external and our home trade. I look forward more particularly to a greater development of inter-Imperial trade in co-operation with the various Governments of My Empire. Meanwhile, full effect will be given to the special measures which have been initiated to afford relief to the situation.

The condition of agriculture continues to receive the careful consideration of My Ministers. With a view to the alleviation of some of the difficulties in the industry you will be invited to consider proposals for granting credit facilities to agriculturists.

The anomalies and inequalities of the present system of local taxation have long called for reform, and My Ministers are examining the whole question. It is hoped that it may be found pracitcable to deal with the subject on a comprehensive basis, and, in particular, to remove some of the burdens which press on the agricultural industry.

Among the measures which will be presented for your consideration will be Bills dealing with unemployment insurance benefit, housing, trade boards and industrial assurance.

The Departmental Committee appointed to consider the operation of the Increase of Rent and Mortgage Interest (Restrictions) Act has now made its final reports, and proposals will be made to you to carry into effect certain of the Committee's recommendations. You will also be asked to deal with difficulties arising out of the legal interpretation of the Act.

Measures will be submitted to you for simplifying legal procedure, and effecting economies, especially in the County Courts, and for the consolidation of various branches of the law, particularly that relating to the Supreme Court and to Real Property and Conveyancing.

PROROGATION (16 November 1923)

My Lords and Members of the House of Commons:

My Government have recently initiated negotiations aiming at the appointment, with the collaboration of the United States, of a Commission of Enquiry to determine Germany's capacity to pay Reparation. Unfortunately it has not been possible to secure the assent of the French Government to these proposals, which it had been hoped would lead to a solution of the Reparation problem. My Government regard with profound anxiety the continuance of the present economic conditions in Europe, which depend so largely on the settlement of this question.

A serious situation has developed in Germany which is engaging the close and earnest attention of My Government.

The arduous negotiations for peace with Turkey, begun in November, 1922, have, I am happy to say, been brought to a successful conclusion. A Bill to carry into effect certain provisions of the settlement reached at Lausanne on the 24th July last will be laid before Parliament as soon as possible.

It is My earnest hope that the conclusion of this Treaty may bring real peace to the Near East, and may herald an era of political and commercial prosperity for Turkey and for the countries which are renewing friendly relations with her.

Negotiations are proceeding with the United States Government for a settlement of the difficulties with regard to the carriage of liquor in transit, and illicit importation, into the United States.

I deplore the disaster which has recently befallen Japan. The heartfelt sympathy of My country is with the Japanese Government and people, our former allies and close friends, who are bearing this national tragedy with characterestic fortitude and heroism.

My Government have welcomed the opportunity afforded them during the last few weeks of meeting so many of My Ministers from the self-governing Dominions and the representatives of India.

The Conferences which have just terminated have been marked throughout by a spirit of great cordiality and good-will. Important questions affecting the foreign relations and the defence of My Empire were carefully examined, and particular attention was devoted to the promotion of trade and settlement within the Empire upon which the well-being of My people so largely depends at this time. I am convinced that meetings of this kind are of the highest value in promoting the spirit of mutual co-operation amongst My people at home and overseas.

Members of the House of Commons:

I thank you for the provision you have made for the public service.

My Lords and Members of the House of Commons:

The position of agriculture and the problem of unemployment throughout the country continue to cause Me deep anxiety. Despite all the efforts of My Government to stimulate trade and to alleviate distress, the circumstances of large numbers of our fellow-citizens still remain deplorable. My Ministers are convinced that unless measures for the safeguarding and development of the home market are adopted, no permanent improvement in their situation can be expected.

FIRST SESSION OF THE THIRTY-THIRD PARLIAMENT

1924

OPENING (15 January 1924)

My Lords and Members of the House of Commons:

My relations with Foreign Powers continue to be friendly. I am glad to be able to record definite progress in the solution of questions which have hitherto blocked the pathway of mutual understanding and have retarded the recovery of the world.

The Reparation Commission has set up two Committees, on which Experts from the United States of America will co-operate with others from Great Britain, France, Italy and Belgium in examining the very serious financial questions involved in the position of Germany.

The future status of the Tangier zone of Morocco, which has been a longstanding source of trouble, has been the subject of an Agreement between the delegates of the Powers principally concerned, which provides for the creation of an international *regime* and for the promotion of communications and trade.

A Bill will be introduced to give effect to the Lausanne Treaty with Turkey. As soon as it has been passed, the Treaty will be ratified, and a new era of peaceful relations with Turkey will open.

My Ministers, in common with the Dominion representatives, have been anxious to remove the difficulty with regard to the illicit importation of liquor into the United States, and have made proposals for an agreement which is on the eve of conclusion, and which should further strengthen the happy relations prevailing between the two countries and peoples.

It will continue to be My object to support by every means in My power the steady growth in influence of the League of Nations.

The recent series of murders on the North-West Frontier of India by criminals who have sought refuge in Afghan territory or are Afghan subjects, has caused Me much concern. My Government have made vigorous representations to the Government of His Majesty the Amir, and I earnestly trust that these persons will be punished, and more satisfactory relations on the frontier be established, at a very early date.

The recent Imperial Conferences marked a very definite progress in Imperial co-operation. More particularly was it found possible, without departure from the existing fiscal system in this country, to meet the wishes of the Dominions by a substantial extension of the principle of Imperial Preference established by the Conference of 1917 and in force since 1919. Proposals to give effect to the conclusions of both Conferences will be submitted to you.

I welcome the opportunity that will be afforded by the British Empire Exhibition to increase the knowledge of the varied resources of My Empire and to stimulate inter-Imperial trade.

Members of the House of Commons:

Estimates for the public services will be laid before you.

My Lords and Members of the House of Commons:

While I am glad to note that the schemes for providing employment now in operation have had an appreciable effect during the last year in reducing the numbers of those actually unemployed, the number still unable to find work causes Me the gravest concern. My Ministers recently laid before the country proposals which, in their judgment, would have contributed materially to a solution of this problem by affording to industry a greater measure of security in the home market and an improved outlet for its products in My Dominions overseas and in foreign countries; but these proposals were not accepted by the country.

In these circumstances your assent will be invited to an extension and amendment of the Trade Facilities and Export Credit Schemes, to the proposal of the Imperial Economic Conference for expediting and assisting the execution of certain public enterprises throughout the Empire by the grant of financial aid from public funds, and to an extension of the contributions towards the cost of Public Utility Works, whether undertaken by local authorities or promoted by statutory and private corporations.

You will also be asked to assist in providing work in the shipbuilding industry by the immediate construction of cruisers and auxiliary craft in anticipation of the Naval Programme.

Steps will be taken to develop the existing system of Juvenile Unemployment Centres and to provide increased facilities for general and technical education.

The condition of agriculture remains a source of serious anxiety. My Ministers propose to summon a conference representative of all those interested in agriculture, and of the various political parties, with the object of arriving at an agreed policy, by which the acreage of arable land may be maintained, and regular employment at an adequate wage secured for the agricultural worker.

Bills will be introduced to improve the position of pre-War pensioners, and to deal with the discouragement of thrift involved in the present means limitation to the grant of Old Age Pensions.

You will be asked to develop the probationary system of dealing with offenders. Bills will be introduced to amend and consolidate the Factory and Workshop Acts, to legitimize children born out of wedlock whose parents have subsequently married, and to amend the law relating to separation and maintenance orders.

Under the Housing Act of last Session My Ministers have approved the erection of a large number of houses, both by local authorities and by private enterprise. The local authorities are being approached with a view to increased activity under those sections of the Act which enable the working population to become the owners of their homes.

Measures will be laid before you to complete Land Purchase in Northern Ireland, and to guarantee the principal and interest of bonds issued by the Government of the Irish Free State under the Land Act recently passed in that Dominion.

The obligation to alleviate hardship caused by the former disturbances in Ireland is one which is recognised by My Government and will continue to engage their active attention.

Proposals will be submitted to you for the expansion of the Royal Air Force in connection with Home Defence.

Preparations have also been made for measures dealing with the property and endowments of the Church of Scotland, the improvement of the road traffic of London, for the reform of the system of valuation and rating in England and Wales, and of rating in Scotland, for the improvement of the administration of civil and criminal justice, for making valid certain charges imposed during the War, and for the ascertainment of costs and profits in connection with the distribution of milk.

PROROGATION (9 October 1924)

My Lords and Members of the House of Commons:
My relations with Foreign Powers continue to be of a friendly nature.

The acceptance of the Dawes Report by the Powers concerned was confirmed by the Conference held in London in July and August, when practical measures required in order to allow of the recommendations being put into force were unanimously approved. This happy result is due to the broadminded spirit of co-operation with which the very difficult problems involved were approached by the Powers concerned. I believe that this settlement will contribute largely to the restoration of international commerce, on which the material prosperity of this country so largely depends.

Following the close understanding reached between the British and French Delegations at Geneva, the fifth Assembly of the League of Nations by formulating proposals for dealing with the problem of general arbitration and security has made an important advance on the road to the reduction of armaments. The issue of its discussion has been embodied in a protocol which will be laid before Parliament as soon as possible, and which it is hoped will lead to the first practical measures for lightening the heavy burdens under which the nations are suffering.

My Government have renewed diplomatic relations with the Union of Socialist Soviet Republics and have concluded with the Government of the Union the two Treaties which have been laid before you. These Treaties have for their object the re-establishment of political and commercial ties between Great Britain and Russia as a necessary element in the general pacification and economic reconstruction of Europe.

Under the terms of the Treaty the question of the frontier between Turkey and Iraq has been referred to the Council of the League of Nations, who have decided to appoint a special Commission to report to them on the matter. Pending a final settlement both parties have undertaken to maintain the *status quo* on the frontier.

I regret that, as explained in a Paper recently laid before you, the informal discussions with the Prime Minister of Egypt did not lead to negotiations which might have resulted in the conclusion of a satisfactory agreement. In the absence of such agreement the position of my Country in relation to Egypt will continue to be governed by the policy adopted when the Protectorate was withdrawn.

Steps have been taken by My Ministers in conjunction with the Governments of My Dominions for the formation of a committee to devise means for the more efficient marketing in this country of various articles of food.

Members of the House of Commons:
I thank you for the provision you have made for the public service.

My Lords and Members of the House of Commons:
Though there are, I am glad to say, signs of distinct improvement in some of the principal industries and in certain branches of trade and commerce, severe depression continues. My Ministers have been actively engaged in the development of a constructive policy with a view to stimulating industry and encouraging trade as the only means of dealing fundamentally with the unemployment from which a large proportion of Our fellow-citizens are still suffering. Meanwhile, the measures taken by My Ministers for the provision of increased and continuous unemployment benefit have not only lightened the

burden upon the ratepayers in the most necessitous
areas, but have also alleviated the sufferings of the
innocent victims of industrial depression.

The measures taken by My Ministers, with the
support of Parliament, to enable Local Authorities
and the building industry to engage in a fifteen
years' uninterrupted building programme will, I hope,
afford an effective remedy for the serious overcrowding which continues to be a source of grevious
harm to the character and physique of many
hundreds of thousands of My people.

Steps have also been taken by My Government
to assist agriculture by loans to Farmers' Co-operative
Societies and by increasing grants-in-aid of
agricultural education and research. An Act has also
been passed to regulate the wages of agricultural
labourers in England and Wales.

The taking of a new Census of Production,
together with various other inquiries which have been
set on foot, will, I hope, afford valuable indications of
the directions in which the industrial and commercial
organisation of the country can be improved.

The advance of educational development has
been freed from the restrictions recently imposed
upon it and the lines for further progress have been
laid down towards a more universal system of
secondary education.

FIRST SESSION OF THE THIRTY-FOURTH PARLIAMENT

1924–1925

OPENING (9 December 1924)

My Lords and Members of the House of Commons:

My relations with foreign Powers continue to be friendly.

The campaign of hostility to British rights and interests in Egypt and the Sudan, inspired rather than discouraged by the Government of Zaghlul Pasha, culminated in the murder of Sir Lee Stack in the streets of Cairo and obliged My Government to demand redress.

Their demands, which the present Egyptian Government have accepted, are designed to secure respect for those interests which are of vital concern to My Empire and which My Government specifically reserved to their absolute discretion when My Protectorate over Egypt was withdrawn.

I follow with deep interest the important deliberations of the League of Nations. My Secretary of State for Foreign Affairs has proceeded to Rome to act as British representative at the meeting of its Council. He is taking the opportunity of this Journey to meet the Prime Ministers of France and Italy.

My Government have not yet had time to study, in consultation with the Governments of the Dominions, the Protocol for the pacific settlement of disputes drawn up at the last Assembly of the League of Nations with the attention which its character demands. They have already begun to examine this weighty question.

My Government are unable to recommend to your consideration the Treaties with the Government of the Union of Socialist Soviet Republics, signed on the 8th August. It is My desire that normal intercourse between the two countries shall not be interrupted. I trust that the attainment of this object will be made possible by the strict fulfilment of those conditions of friendly international intercourse which have been repeatedly placed before the Soviet Government, and accepted by them, particularly at the moment of the establishment of diplomatic relations. The Trade Agreement of the 16th March, 1921, does all that is at present possible to foster mutual trade.

I have concluded a Treaty of Commerce and Navigation with the President of the German Reich in order to put the commercial relations of the two countries on a stable footing. You will be invited to give legislative effect to its provisions.

A Bill will be laid before you for giving approval to the Treaty with Italy signed in July for the cession of a portion of the province of Jubaland, in the Kenya Colony and Protectorate.

The visit of My eldest son, the Prince of Wales, to South Africa, which was unavoidably postponed this year, has now been arranged to take place in the spring of next year. In the course of his journey he will also visit My possessions in West Africa and St. Helena. I have no doubt that the happy results which attended his previous visits to other parts of My Dominions will be repeated on this occasion.

I have received an invitation from the President and Government of the Argentine Republic for the Prince of Wales to visit the Argentine next year. I have gladly accepted this invitation on behalf of My son.

It is the firm conviction of My Government that in the closest co-operation with the Governments of My Dominions and of India in all matters of mutual concern lies the key both to industrial progress and to the increasing unity and strength of the Empire, and this will be a guiding principle of their administration.

The policy of encouraging Empire settlement and mutual trade between the various parts of My Empire is one which My advisers deem to be of the greatest importance, and to which they will steadfastly adhere. Proposals based upon the recommendations of the Imperial Economic Conference of last year will be submitted for granting further preferences on goods imported into this country from the Empire.

My Government propose, in accordance with the resolution of the last Imperial Conference, to proceed with plans already made for enlarging the Naval Base at Singapore.

Members of the House of Commons:

Estimates for the public services will be laid before you in due course. Every effort will be made to reduce public expenditure to the lowest possible limit consistent with the security and efficiency of the State. The present heavy burdens of the taxpayer are a hindrance to the revival of enterprise and employment. Economy in every sphere is imperative if we are to regain our industrial and commercial prosperity.

My Lords and Members of the House of Commons:

While I am glad to note the signs of improvement in the state of trade and industry, the present extent of unemployment continues to cause Me grave concern and will receive the constant attention of My Ministers. More stable economic and political conditions throughout the world, and the greater development of facilities for inter-Imperial commerce, will, I hope, promote the growth both of our internal and our overseas trade. A Bill is under consideration, and will be submitted to you at an early date, for safeguarding employment in efficient industries where, after inquiry, the need for such exceptional action is established.

The various schemes which have already been initiated for the relief of unemployment, including those relating to juvenile unemployment, will be examined with great care, and you will be asked to make provision for the continuance and extension of all such measures as are likely to alleviate the present distresses.

But no less important for the prosperity of My country than the action of Parliament is that there shall be among all parties concerned in the industrial life of the nation increased goodwill, frankness and mutual confidence, without which full advantage cannot be taken of any improvement in other conditions.

My Ministers are deeply impressed by the continued shortage of housing accommodation. They are convinced that the encouragement of the private builder and the occupying owner is an essential element in the successful treatment of the problem, and substantial progress has been made in this direction. My Ministers will devote their attention to overcoming the rising cost of houses and the shortage in the available supplies of skilled labour. With this object they will endeavour to supplement the building resources of the country by encouraging new methods of construction calculated to promote the rapid production of houses of approved design and moderate cost, and, at the same time, to assist in the reduction of unemployment.

The housing problem is not merely one of over-crowding, but also of the existence of large numbers of houses which fall below modern standards of propriety and sanitation. Something is already being done under existing legislation to clear the worst areas and to remedy sanitary and structural defects in those which remain. As new building increases it will be possible largely to develop this process, and My Government will take every opportunity of pressing it forward with vigour.

My Ministers are engaged upon inquiries into the possibility of combining with existing systems of insurance, provisions for improved old age pensions and pensions for widowed mothers.

They will also endeavour, in co-operation with the Local Education Authorities, to promote the steady and continuous development of the public system of education.

A Conference of representatives of landowners, farmers and workers has already been invited to consider whether an agreement can be arrived at by these different interests which might provide the stable basis of a national agricultural policy. Meanwhile,

measures will be laid before you to give effect to the proposals of the late Government for the encourage-ment of the sugar beet industry; to provide where practicable for the marking of imported foodstuffs and for dealing with the readjustment and redemption of Tithe Rent-charge.

Steps will be taken to carry out the principal recommendations of the Committee on the use of preservatives and colouring matter in food and for the ascertainment of costs and profits in the distribution of milk.

In view of the prevalence of high food prices and their adverse effect upon the cost of living, I have appointed a Commission to investigate the extent and causes of the differences between the prices received by producers of foodstuffs and those paid by consumers.

Measures will be presented for the consolidation of the Law of Property and of the enactments relating to the procedure of the Supreme Court, for the reform of the system of rating and valuation in England and Wales and of rating in Scotland, for the prolongation of the Rent Restrictions Act and of the Agricultural Rates Act, 1923. You will be asked to facilitate the completion of Land Purchase in Northern Ireland and to guarantee the principal and interest of bonds issued by the Government of the Irish Free State under the Land Act recently passed in that Dominion.

Bills will be introduced dealing with legitimation by subsequent marriage, separation and maintenance orders, guardianship of children and the improvement of the probationary system.

Preparations are being made for legislation dealing with the Property and Endowments of the Church of Scotland and with the foundation of a National Library for Scotland.

Bills will also be laid before you to give effect to three International Conventions dealing with wages in the case of shipwreck and with medical examination and stoke-hold employment of young seamen, to validate certain charges imposed during the War, and to amend and consolidate the Factory and Workshop Acts and the law with regard to the use of road vehicles.

My Government are hopeful that, with the support of the community at large, they may be able, on the lines here indicated and to be developed as time proceeds, to expedite the solution, in a spirit of unity, of many of the problems that are weighing heavily on the national life, and in this way to remove some of the obstacles that have not ceased, since the termination of the War, to retard the industrial and economic recovery of My people.

PROROGATION (22 December 1925)

My Lords and Members of the House of Commons:

The grevious loss which I and My family have sustained by the death of My beloved Mother is first in My thoughts. It has been a solace to Me in My grief to have received from all conditions and classes, from all parts of My dominions and from all foreign countries, the touching assurances of their deep sympathy in My sorrow and the expression of their affectionate regard for One who was enthroned in the love of My people.

I was happy to welcome home My Son, the Prince of Wales, on his recent return from his visit to South Africa, West Africa, and South America. I have been deeply touched by the account which he has given Me of the warm welcome everywhere accorded him, and I am proud to think that his visit has served to deepen the affection which unites My people and to strengthen the bonds which link this country with the peoples of South America.

My relations with Foreign Powers continue to be friendly.

It was a source of great satisfaction to Me to welcome in London the distinguished Plenipotentiaries of Germany, Belgium, France, Italy, Poland and Czechoslovakia, who, on the 1st December, signed the diplomatic instruments initialled at Locarno on the 16th October.

It is My belief and My earnest hope that these instruments, by giving security to the peoples immediately concerned, will prove to be not only the foundation of a true peace between them but the beginning of a friendly co-operation which cannot fail to benefit the whole world.

I rejoice at the part which My Government was able to play in the negotiations leading up to this happy event.

I have given My assent to a Bill for the Confirmation of an Agreement reached between My Ministers and the Governments of the Irish Free State and Northern Ireland, to amend and supplement the Articles of Agreement of the 6th December, 1921. It is my heartfelt prayer that this measure may advance co-operation and strengthen goodwill in Ireland.

The British Empire Exhibition at Wembley has now come to a close, and I feel that I should take this opportunity of expressing My gratitude to all those throughout My Empire who have co-operated in this great enterprise; I am sure that the increased knowledge which it has brought of the resources and activities of My people will have lasting and beneficial results.

Further preferences on goods imported into this country from other parts of the Empire have been accorded by legislation, and other measures for the development of Empire Trade are receiving the close consideration of My Government.

An Act has been passed to give effect to certain provisions contained in the Treaty of Commerce and Navigation with Germany, and ratifications of that Treaty have since been exchanged.

Members of the House of Commons:

I thank you for the provision you have made for the public service.

My Lords and Members of the House of Commons:

Progressive depression in the coal trade led, at the end of July, to a grave economic crisis, which threatened to result in a disastrous industrial conflict. The danger was averted by the decision to afford temporary financial assistance to the industry. This has made it possible to conduct, under My Commission, a full and impartial inquiry into the economic position of the industry. I am following the course of the inquiry with anxious interest, and I am hopeful that the task of My Commissioners will be lightened by ungrudging and singlehearted effort on the part of all concerned to find a solution for the problems of this great and vital industry.

By the passing of the Widows', Orphans' and Old Age Contributory Pensions Act a further important stage has been reached in the process whereby the resources of the State are made available for the encouragement of thrift and self-reliance. Provision has thus been made, through insurance, against those risks which have been a source of anxiety and apprehension to so many of My people.

An Act has been passed to simplify the law of rating, to provide for greater uniformity in valuation, and to improve the local administration of these services in England and Wales.

Acts have been passed for consolidating the laws relating to workmen's compensation in cases of accident, and to real property, and conveyancing, and also for consolidating the Judicature Acts and for simplifying and amending the procedure in criminal cases.

During the past year there has been a great increase in the number of houses built in England and Wales, and I hope that this improvement, so important to the health and well-being of My people, may continue. The housing position still gives cause for concern in Scotland, where special measures have, however, been taken by My Ministers.

Encouragement has been given to the establishment of the sugar beet industry in this country by an Act providing for a Government subsidy during a period of 10 years.

An Act has also been passed to amend the law relating to tithe rentcharge and the payment of rates thereon.

In pursuance of the policy announced at the opening of the Session, measures have been enacted for safeguarding by means of Customs duties certain industries which have been proved after inquiry to be suffering from unemployment due to exceptional foreign competiton of an unfair nature.

My assent has also been given to an Act establishing a permanent system of superannuation for teachers, to the Church of Scotland (Property and Endowments) Act, and to a measure providing for the institution of a Scottish National Library.

SECOND SESSION OF THE THIRTY-FOURTH PARLIAMENT

1926

OPENING (2 February 1926)

My Lords and Members of the House of Commons:

My relations with foreign Powers continue to be friendly. Since Parliament rose My Ambassador at Constantinople has proceeded to Angora with a view to arrive at a definite settlement of questions in connection with the Turco-Iraq frontier. My Government cordially reciprocate the desire of the Turkish Government for the promotion of the friendliest relations between Turkey and Great Britain.

A Treaty between Myself and His Majesty the King of Iraq, carrying out the stipulation laid down in the decision of the Council of the League of Nations, has been signed by our respective representatives and has been approved by the Parliament of Iraq. It will be submitted to you without delay.

One of My Ministers will proceed to Geneva as British representative of the Preparatory Committee on Disarmament which is to work out the bases of a general conference on the reduction of armaments. In the opinion of My Government, a substantial step forward in that direction should now be possible as a result of the system of security created by the Treaty of Locarno and subsidiary agreements.

My Government have recently received in London the Finance Minister of Italy, accompanied by a distinguished Delegation, and have concluded an agreement which provides for the funding of the Italian War Debt to this country on fair and honourable conditions. I rejoice that a friendly settlement has been reached of this difficult question.

Invitations are being issued to the Governments of Belgium, France, Germany and Italy to attend a Conference in London to consider the possibility of securing an effective international agreement for regulating hours of labour.

Members of the House of Commons:

The Estimates for the Public Services will be laid before you in due course. My Ministers have given earnest consideration to the increasing need for national economy. Proposals for effecting reductions of public expenditure are now being formulated and you will be asked to pass Measures required to give effect to them without delay.

Proposals will be laid before you for authorising My Government to guarantee loans for the development of the British dependencies in East Africa and of mandated territories.

My Lords and Members of the House of Commons:

The improvement in trade and industry at the end of 1924, which it was then thought would result in an appreciable decrease in the volume of unemployment, was unfortunately checked early last year by the widespread depression which occurred in coal mining.

Since the autumn of last year signs of a revival of industry have again begun to appear, but the growth of confidence on which revival depends is being arrested by the fear of industrial strife.

The result of the Inquiry into the economic condition of the Coal Industry, which is now being conducted by My Commission, will shortly be laid before you. I am well aware of the difficulties that are inherent in the whole situation. But the interests of the nation are paramount, and I appeal to all parties to face the future in a spirit of conciliation and fellowship and to avoid action which would again postpone the return of good trade and prosperity for which we have so long hoped.

With the object of securing greater economy and efficiency in the generation and transmission of electrical energy in the future, My Government have devised a scheme of reorganisation. A Bill to give effect to these proposals has been prepared and will shortly be introduced.

The condition of agriculture has received the earnest consideration of My Ministers. The question of the provision of better credit facilities for the industry is receiving special attention and discussions are proceeding with a view to the formulation of definite proposals on the subject. A Bill will be presented to enable County Councils to continue and extend the provision of small holdings and cottage holdings, both for owner occupiers and for tenants.

A measure will be laid before you to provide in suitable cases for marking imported agricultural produce and manufactured goods, so that they may be distinguished from the products of this country, and Empire goods distinguished from those of foreign origin.

While I learn with satisfaction of the progress made in the building of new houses in the urban areas of England and Wales, the conditions under which many of My people are compelled to live, both in country districts and in the congested areas of numerous towns, still occasion Me deep concern. My Ministers are now examining certain proposals for the improvement of these conditions, and if time permits they will submit to you measures designed to hasten the removal of the worst defects both in town and country.

My Ministers hope that it may be possible to carry further the process of consolidating the main statutes regulating the local government of the country.

I propose to appoint an additional Secretary of State to replace the Secretary for Scotland, and you will be asked to pass the necessary legislation providing for the transfer of functions.

Bills will be laid before you, if time and opportunity permit, dealing with the following matters:– National Health Insurance; Unemployment Insurance; The rating of railways; The control of road vehicles; The finance of Poor Law in London and the position and powers of Boards of Guardians; Rating, and the valuation of machinery, in Scotland.

PROROGATION (15 December 1926)

My Lords and Members of the House of Commons:

I have had great pleasure in acceding to the wishes of My Ministers in the Commonwealth of Australia that My Son and Daughter-in-Law should visit Australia for the inauguration of the new Federal Capital at Canberra. They will extend their visit to New Zealand at the invitation of My Ministers in that Dominion, and in the course of their journeys will also be able to see several of the Colonies. The occasion of thus personally renewing the ties of affection which unite My Family with the peoples of the different parts of the Empire will, I know, be as welcome to the Duke and Duchess of York to-day as it was to the Queen and Myself more than twenty-five years ago.

I have rejoiced at the opportunity given by the recent meeting of the Imperial Conference to welcome in London so many of My Ministers from the Dominions, and the Representatives of the Empire of India. The report of the proceedings of the Conference, which has recently been presented to you, bears eloquent testimony to the spirit of good will and mutual understanding which marked its deliberations. I am confident that its work will prove of lasting value to all parts of My Empire.

The situation in China is being watched by My Government with the closest attention. Our Country is animated by strong sympathy for that vast majority of the Chinese people whose aspirations are for settled conditions, for a new era of prosperity and for friendly relations with the foreign Powers.

Members of the House of Commons:

I thank you for the provision you have made for the public service.

My Lords and Members of the House of Commons:

During the greater part of the present year the Nation has lived in the shadow of the most protracted and ruinous industrial conflict in its history. When last addressing you I expressed the earnest hope that the Report of the Commissioners upon the economic condition of the coal industry would, with the willing co-operation of all concerned, pave the way to a peaceful solution of this great social and economic problem. This hope was not fulfilled. It remains to us now to unite in effacing all bitter memories of the past, and to set our eyes steadfastly upon the future, inspired by a common impulse towards genuine fellowship and sustained endeavour, upon which alone the prosperity and happiness of My People can be firmly based.

The improvement in housing accommodation continues. A larger number of new houses have been completed than in any previous year. In order to make available to rural workers further and better accommodation at rents adapted to their means Parliament has provided from public moneys grants for the reconstruction of existing houses and buildings in rural areas.

By the passing of the Electricity (Supply) Bill an important and overdue step has been taken towards extending the provision of electrical energy throughout Great Britain.

I have given assent to a measure to provide in suitable cases for marking imported agricultural produce and manufactured goods with an indication of origin. This measure will enable the purchasing community to give a preference to goods and produce of this country and of other parts of the Empire.

A Bill has also been passed for preventing short weight and measure in the retail sale of foodstuffs.

Bills have also been passed to unify and simplify the rating system of Scotland and to extend the right of appeal in criminal cases in Scotland.

A number of Bills relating to the agricultural industry have received My assent, including a measure to extend facilities for small and cottage holdings.

THIRD SESSION OF THE THIRTY-FOURTH PARLIAMENT

1927

OPENING (8 February 1927)

My Lords and Members of the House of Commons:

My relations with foreign Powers continue to be friendly. The League of Nations has been strengthened and a further step taken towards the restoration of normal international relations in Europe by the entry of Germany into the League and her appointment to a permanent seat on the Council of the League. In continuance of this policy, it was found possible at the end of last month to terminate the system of Allied military control in Germany as set up by the Treaty of Versailles and to hand over to the League all questions affecting the military clauses of the Treaty.

The continuance of civil war in China and the anti-foreign and particularly the anti-British agitation by which it has been accompanied have caused Me grave anxiety. In consequence of what happened at Hankow and in other places, My Government have felt it necessary to despatch to the Far East a sufficient force to protect the lives of My British and Indian subjects against mob violence and armed attack. But I earnestly desire a peaceful settlement of the difficulties which have arisen, and My Government have caused proposals to be made to the Chinese authorities which should convince public opinion in China and throughout the world that it is the desire of the British people to remove all real grievances, to renew Our treaties on an equitable basis, and to place Our future relations with the Chinese people on a footing of friendship and goodwill.

My Government will maintain Our traditional policy of non-interference in the internal affairs of China.

I rejoice that a fair and friendly settlement has been reached regarding the funding of the War Debt due to this country by Portugal.

Members of the House of Commons:

The Estimates for the Public Services will be laid before you in due course.

My Lords and Members of the House of Commons:

There are, I am happy to note, encouraging signs of improvement in the state of trade and industry. I earnestly pray that those engaged in the various industries of the country will use their utmost endeavours to ensure that the improvement in the volume of employment among My people, which may now be reasonably anticipated, will not be arrested by industrial strife.

Proposals will be laid before you at an early date to enable effect to be given to the change in the style and titles of the Sovereign to which, on the recommendation of the Imperial Conference, I have given My approval. At the same time you will be invited to make consequential alterations in the title of Parliament.

Recent events have made evident the importance of defining and amending the law with reference to industrial disputes. Proposals for this purpose will be laid before you.

Proposals will also be made for an amendment of the law relating to leasehold premises so as to secure to an outgoing tenant compensation for the loss of his goodwill and unexhausted improvements.

Bills in connection with Agriculture will be laid before you.

You will be invited to pass a Measure dealing with Insurance against Unemployment.

A Bill to encourage the production and exhibition of British films will be presented to you.

Proposals for the amendment of the Companies Acts will be introduced to your notice.

Proposals will also be submitted to you for the reorganisation of certain of the Departments of Scotland.

Other important Measures, as the time of the Session permits, will be introduced to your notice.

PROROGATION (22 December 1927)

My Lords and Members of the House of Commons:

I have followed with constant interest the journeys of My Sons, the Prince of Wales and Prince George, to Canada, and also of My Son and Daughter-in-Law, the Duke and Duchess of York, to New Zealand, Australia and other parts of My Dominions. I rejoice in their return, and I have learned from them with deep satisfaction of the loyal and enthusiastic welcome which they invariably experienced throughout their journeys.

It gave Me particular pleasure in the course of the summer to receive in My capital the President of the French Republic accompanied by the French Minister for Foreign Affairs. The visit gave fresh evidence of the cordial relations so happily established between My Government and the Government of the Republic and afforded My people a welcome opportunity of demonstrating their affection for France in the persons of these two eminent statesmen.

The visit of the King of Egypt was a source of gratification to Me and afforded an opportunity for a full exchange of views between the Egyptian Prime Minister and My Foreign Secretary. The frank and friendly nature of these conversations was in itself of good augury for the future and it is My hope that their outcome may prove of lasting benefit to both countries.

I have watched with profound sympathy and satisfaction the steady growth in influence of the League of Nations and the increasing part which it plays in composing international differences and preserving peace. The recent meeting of the Council at Geneva marked a further stage in this progress. My Government will continue to base its policy on loyal co-operation with the League.

A Conference with representatives of the United States of America and Japan was held at Geneva, at which the delegates of My Government put forward proposals for the future limitation of armaments, which if accepted would have led to substantial reductions in naval strengths and costs.

I regret that though much community of view was revealed, it was not possible to reach a general agreement. But in spite of this temporary failure, My Government have no intention of embarking upon an increase of their naval building programme, which is based upon a considered view of the defensive needs of My wide-spread Empire.

A Conference, attended by Governors or other senior officials representing twenty-six Colonies, Protectorates and Mandated Territories, assembled in May to exchange views on proposals of common interest to the Colonial Empire. This year has also been marked by important Inter-Imperial Conferences in London dealing with education and agricultural research. I am confident of the great value of such meetings, not only in the results achieved and the recommendations made, but also in bringing together, in a spirit of comradeship and mutual assistance, those who are engaged in similar work in widely separated parts of My Dominions.

My Government having decided that the time is ripe for the initiation of the Inquiry into the working of the system of government in India for which the law provides, I have, with the concurrence of both your Houses, issued a Commission to seven of your number who will shortly embark upon their momentous task. I earnestly trust that their labours may be crowned with success, and that from their counsels may emerge a system of government which shall give contentment to the peoples of India and strengthen the bonds that unite My Empire.

A new treaty between Myself and His Majesty the King of Iraq, to replace the existing treaties between us, has been signed by Our respective representatives. The text of this treaty has been laid before you.

During the past year Agreements have been concluded with the Greek and Serb-Croat-Slovene Governments providing for the settlement of their respective war debts to this country. The terms of the Agreements have been presented to Parliament, and, as in previous cases, they give effect to the policy adopted by My Government to limit the claims on our Allies to such amounts as, together with our Reparation Receipts, will cover the obligations My Government has itself to meet in respect of War Debts. I note with satisfaction that funding Agreements have now been signed in respect of all the Allied War Debts to this country, except that of Russia.

Members of the House of Commons:
I thank you for the provision you have made for the public service.

My Lords and Members of the House of Commons:
My Ministers continue to watch closely the state of employment which, though showing welcome signs of improvement in some parts of the country, still gives cause for anxiety in others. To facilitate the transfer of labour from industries with restricted opportunities for employment and in particular the coal-mining industry, a Board is to be appointed to recommend the executive action to be taken by the Departments concerned. My Ministers look with confidence for co-operation from all who can assist in this work both at home and overseas.

A Bill has been passed placing the system of insurance against unemployment upon an improved permanent basis.

Striking progress has been made during the past year in providing housing accommodation for the people and the number of new houses completed in England and Wales since the Armistice now exceeds one million.

During the past year a greater number of new houses have been completed in Scotland that in any previous year. Substantial progress is also being made with the clearance of insanitary areas and the rehousing of displaced tenants.

A Bill has been passed to declare and amend the law with regard to Trade Disputes and Trade Unions.

I have given My assent to the Landlord and Tenant Bill, the provisions of which will secure to certain classes of tenants compensation for the loss of goodwill attaching to their premises and for unexhausted improvements, and will effect other desirable alterations in the law.

A Bill has been passed which it is hoped will materially assist the development of the British Cinematograph Film Industry.

A Bill has also been passed providing for the reorganisation of certain legal services and the amendment in certain respects of the law relating to Sheriff Court business in Scotland.

FOURTH SESSION OF THE THIRTY-FOURTH PARLIAMENT

1928

OPENING (7 February 1928)

My Lords and Members of the House of Commons:

My relations with foreign Powers continue to be friendly. It is the constant effort of My Government, in co-operation with the League of Nations, to secure the settlement of international differences and to promote the cause of peace.

I have invited the King of Afghanistan to visit Me in March and I look forward to welcoming His Majesty to My capital. It will be a particular pleasure to Me to receive His Majesty on his first visit to Europe.

The position in China has so far improved as to permit large reductions in the naval and military forces sent to the Far East for the protection of My British and Indian subjects resident in the Concessions, but the situation caused by internal disturbances and civil wars and the consequent insecurity of life and property, both Chinese and foreign, still give cause for anxiety. In spite of these discouraging circumstances, My Government adhere to the declaration of policy published by them a year ago, as the basis on which they are prepared to meet Chinese aspirations when the Chinese can assure satisfactory protection for British lives and property.

On the 29th December last the United States Government communicated to My Ambassador at Washington, for consideration and as a basis for negotiation, the draft of a new Treaty of Arbitration between Myself and the President of the United States of America, to take the place of the Treaty of Arbitration concluded at Washington on the 4th April, 1908. The terms of the new draft are being carefully and sympathetically studied by My Government in Great Britain and will be considered in communication with My Governments in the Dominions.

Members of the House of Commons:

The Estimates for the Public Services will be laid before you in due course.

My Lords and Members of the House of Commons:

Although the condition of affairs in some of the principal industries continues to give cause for serious anxiety, I am glad to observe that in the general state of trade and industry there are many encouraging signs of progressive improvement in both our home and external trade which justify the hope that with co-operation and good-will steady progress will be made in the coming year.

The burdens imposed upon industry and agriculture by the present incidence of local rates have attracted the anxious attention of My Ministers. They are now engaged upon inquiries into the possibility of affording some relief from these burdens to the producing community and into the changes in local government which would thereby be involved.

Proposals will be brought before you for amending the law relating to the Parliamentary and local government franchise.

Measures will be presented to you for giving effect to certain recommendations of My Commission on National Health Insurance, and for increasing the credit facilities of persons engaged in agriculture.

Among other Bills which you will be invited to pass are Measures dealing with the laws relating to the Supreme Court of Judicature and to Arbitration, with the amendment of the Companies Acts, with the valuation for rating purposes of property in London, and with the law relating to the Metropolitan Common Poor Fund.

You will also be asked to consider proposals for the reorganisation of certain of the Departments in Scotland.

Bills dealing with other Measures of importance will be introduced and proceeded with as time and opportunity allow.

PROROGATION (3 August 1928)

My Lords and Members of the House of Commons:

The visit of Their Majesties the King and Queen of Afghanistan in March last was an auspicious event in the history of Our two countries. To Me it will always be a pleasant memory, and I have received with much gratification messages from King Amanulla expressing His warm appreciation of the welcome accorded to Their Majesties. It is a matter of national congratulation that the visit has confirmed and strengthened the good relations existing between Afghanistan and the British Empire.

My Government have been happy to accept the proposed treaty for the renunciation of war in the form in which it was finally proposed to them by the Government of the United States. The proposed treaty has similarly been accepted by My Governments in the Dominions and by the Government of India. It is My confident expectation that, when completed it will constitute a new and important guarantee of the world's peace.

Negotiations between My Government and the French, Italian and Spanish Governments for the revision of the Tangier Statute have just reached a successful conclusion. Under the terms of the instrument embodying the results of these negotiations, which I have caused to be laid before you, Italy becomes a contracting party to the Statute and Spain receives additional guarantees for the security of her zone.

A treaty between Myself and His Imperial Majesty the Shah of Persia, regulating the commercial relations between Our countries, and providing for the abrogation of existing treaty provisions which limit the right of Persia to settle her customs tariff autonomously, has been signed by Our respective representatives. They have also recorded agreements on other important questions in subsidiary notes. The texts of these documents will be laid before you in due course.

In harmony with the Resolution of the Imperial Conference of 1926, recommending the further development of the present system of consultation between My Governments, arrangements have been completed for the appointment by My Government in Great Britain of a representative in Canada, with the title of High Commissioner. He will proceed to Ottawa in September.

The Imperial Wireless and Cables Conference has submitted a unanimous Report on the improvement of telegraphic communications between the several parts of My Empire. To the principles underlying the Report the Governments concerned are favourably disposed. I hope that with wholehearted co-operation the telegraph systems which unite its various parts will be organised to the lasting benefit of My Empire.

The Order in Council under the British Guiana Act, 1928, enabling Me to create a new Constitution for that Colony, has been passed.

The Commission appointed to examine the Constitution of Ceylon has now presented its Report, and its recommendations will receive the careful consideration of My Ministers.

The Commissioners appointed to inquire into agriculture and rural economy in British India have submitted a unanimous Report, containing many recommendations for the promotion of the welfare of the rural population. I am confident that these recommendations will receive sympathetic and fruitful consideration from the competent authorities in India.

Members of the House of Commons:

I thank you for the provision you have made for the public service.

My Lords and Members of the House of Commons:

The condition of our basic industries and the high level of unemployment continue to cause Me anxiety. My Ministers have prepared a scheme for relieving agriculture and other productive industries from the onerous burden of rates. The relief will affect not only the direct burden of rates but also the indirect burden thrown specially upon the basic industries by the present system of rating railways, docks and canals. This policy involves as a necessary consequence the enactment of long-desired reforms in local government and in the financial relations between the State and local authorities. My Ministers are hopeful that in respect of selected industrial and agricultural traffic the relief may come into force at the end of the present year. I trust that these comprehensive proposals will not only increase employment generally, but will also bring special relief to the areas which are most in need of it.

I have given My assent to a Measure assimilating the Local Government and Parliamentary Franchise of men and women. This will confer equal electoral rights on the two sexes.

A Bill has been passed, based generally on the recommendations of My Commission on National Health Insurance, whereby the existing system will be materially simplified and improved.

Steady progress has been made during the year in the provision of housing for the people, and the price of house construction has continued generally to fall.

I have given My assent to a Measure for assisting the credit of persons engaged in agriculture in England and Wales, and My Government have prepared a scheme for effecting the same object in Scotland.

A Bill has been passed to provide for the grading and marking of agricultural produce.

It is a source of special satisfaction to Me that it has been found possible, subject to suitable safeguards, to secure permanently the present rates of disability pension for the Great War against any reduction owing to a fall in the cost of living. This will remove an element of uncertainty which disturbs the minds of those who are, unhappily, still suffering from the effects of their War Service.

The rapid growth of road traffic has created new problems which demand investigation. I have appointed a Commission which will, I hope, result in measures for the wise development of all available means of transport.

Bills have also been passed to reorganise certain Scottish Departments, and for setting up a Commission to deal with educational endowments in Scotland.

FIFTH SESSION OF THE THIRTY-FOURTH PARLIAMENT

1928–1929

OPENING (6 November 1928)

My Lords and Members of the House of Commons:

My relations with foreign Powers continue to be friendly.

My Government have been happy to accept the Treaty for the Renuniciation of War in the form proposed by the Government of the United States. To My great satisfaction this Treaty was signed in Paris on the 27th August by Plenipotentiaries on behalf of all My Governments, and on behalf of the United States, France, Germany, Italy, Japan, Belgium, Poland and Czecho-Slovakia.

In pursuance of their fixed policy My Government have continued to accord their full support to the League of Nations. They are co-operating in all its current activities, and in particular they have sought fully to discharge their obligations under Article 8 of the Covenant by reducing the armed forces of this country to the lowest point consistent with national safety and by assisting the League to formulate plans for a general reduction of armaments.

Agreement has been reached with the Governments of Belgium, France, Germany, Italy and Japan that negotiations should be opened in regard to the possibility of a complete and definite settlement of the problem of reparations; and it has also been recognised that negotiations should take place relative to the German Government's request for the evacuation of the Rhineland at present occupied by British, French and Belgian troops.

The Coronation of the Emperor of Japan is shortly to take place, and I take this opportunity in the name of Myself and My people, of wishing His Imperial Majesty a long and glorious reign. The historic friendship which for so many years has united Japan and My country has always been a potent factor in the maintenance of peace in the Far East.

I welcome the efforts which China is making to establish a central government for the whole of that great country and to cope with those forces of disorder which have distracted it for many years past. I regard the progress of these endeavours as being of the highest importance, not only for the safety and prosperity of My subjects resident in China, but also for the peace of the world.

Members of the House of Commons:

The Estimates for the Services in the coming year will be laid before you in due course. They are being prepared with strict attention to the continuing need for economy in public expenditure. In anticipation of the general scheme for relieving agriculture and productive industry from the burden of rates, you will be asked to make provision enabling railway companies to make lower charges on important traffics of concern to agriculture, and to the coal, iron and steel industries.

My Lords and Members of the House of Commons:

The situation in the mining areas continues to engage the earnest attention of My Ministers, who are taking energetic steps to promote the success of the scheme of industrial transference and migration. The abnormal expenditure out of the Unemployment Fund entailed by the displacement of labour from the mines will render necessary an increase of borrowing powers, and a Bill dealing with this question will be laid before you.

Measures will be presented to you for giving effect in this country and in Scotland to the comprehensive scheme which has been prepared by My Ministers for the reform of the rating system on a more equitable basis, for the reorganisation of local government and for the readjustment of the financial relations between the state and the Local Authorities.

I trust that the relief from the burden of rates afforded under the scheme may benefit agriculture and lead to a greater measure of employment in industry generally, and in particular in those basic trades whose condition still causes concern. The proposed changes in local government and in the relations between the Exchequer and Local Authorities are measures of far-reaching importance. My Ministers anticipate that they will promote efficiency and economy in local government, will enable better provision to be made for the health of the people, and will direct assistance particularly to those areas whose needs are most pressing.

Proposals for extending the Export Credits Guarantee Scheme for a further period will be laid before you.

You will be invited to pass a Bill authorising the appointment of two additional members of the Judicial Committee of the Privy Council and of one additional Lord of Appeal in Ordinary.

Among other Measures a Bill for assisting persons engaged in agriculture in Scotland to obtain credits required for the pursuit of their industry will be introduced.

PROROGATION (10 May 1929)

My Lords and Members of the House of Commons:

My relations with Foreign Powers continue to be friendly.

The negotiations for My participation in the multilateral Treaty for the Renuniciation of War in the form proposed by the Government of the United States were successfully concluded on the 2nd March last when My ratifications of this instrument in respect of all parts of My Empire were deposited in Washington.

I have entrusted My Son, the Duke of Gloucester, with the Mission of conferring the Insignia of the Order of the Garter upon the Emperor of Japan as a token of My high regard for His Imperial Majesty, and as a pledge of the friendship which unites Our two countries in their determination to co-operate for the peaceful settlement of international questions, both in the Far East amd in the world at large.

I hope that events in China will continue to show improvement and gradual progress towards more stable conditions. I am glad that it has been possible for full recognition to be accorded to the National Government established at Nanking and for My Government to conclude with them a Treaty recognising the principle of complete tariff autonomy.

Owing to the uncertain situation in Afghanistan and the absence of a settled Government, My Representative was withdrawn from Kabul at the end of February. It is My earnest hope that internal peace may soon be restored and a Government established acceptable to the people generally with which My Government will be able to resume the friendly intercourse of the past.

My Government have continued to press for the reduction of armaments in consultation with other Governments at Geneva. New hope of an early settlement of the question of further naval disarmament has recently been given by the speech of the United States delegate there, of which My Government were not slow to express their appreciation.

My Government have announced their intention of taking the necessary action to enable Me to accept, subject to reciprocity, the Protocol prohibiting chemical and bacteriological methods of warfare. All My Governments in My Dominions have announced a similar intention.

The seven members of your two Houses, to whom, eighteen months ago, I issued a Commission to enquire into the working of the existing system of government in India, have now completed the first part of their task. They have visited India twice to acquire information and collect evidence for the purpose of their enquiry. They have enjoyed the co-operation of Committees of Provincial Legislatures,

as well as that of a Committee of members of the Central Legislature who, at the invitation of My Government, will be associated with them also in the final stages of their enquiry. There lies before them, to complete their arduous task, the duty of framing a Report which, when drawn, will be presented to the Parliament at that time assembled. I pray that success may crown their labours.

In pursuance of the recommendations of the Imperial Conference of 1924, arrangements have been made for the meeting in London in October next of an Expert Committee on the Operation of Dominion Legislation, consisting of representatives of My Governments, and for the holding of a Sub-Conference on Merchant Shipping Legislation.

Members of the House of Commons:

I thank you for the provision you have made for the public service.

My Lords and Members of the House of Commons:

The number of persons unemployed in certain industries during the past year has continued to cause anxiety, but a substantial improvement has taken place and there are good grounds for the belief that we are moving towards a higher level of employment in all parts of the country. The re-organisation of industry, and its development in new directions, are steadily proceeding and, with continued co-operation and goodwill between employers and workers, will lay the foundation for a lasting improvement. It is clear, however, that owing to the altered needs of industry a redistribution of workers must take place on a large scale and it has been the policy of My Ministers to aid and guide this movement by schemes of training and transference.

I have given My assent to the measures embodying the comprehensive scheme which has been before you for relieving agriculture and other productive industries from the burden of rates, for the reorganisation of local government and for the readjustment of the financial relations between the State and the local authorities. The measure of relief in respect of railway freights which it has been possible to give in regard to selected industrial and agricultural traffics in anticipation of the general scheme has proved of value. It is a hopeful augury of the greater and more widespread benefits that should accrue, particularly to the basic trades whose conditions are least satisfactory, when the full scheme of relief takes effect.

I have given My assent to a Measure providing that in the case of agriculture this relief from rates shall come into force immediately.

My Ministers are confident that the reforms in local government, which include recommendations made by My commission on Local Government, and the reorganisation of the financial relations between the State and the local authorities will promote

efficiency and economy in local administration, will
enable better provision to be made for the health
and welfare of the people, and will in particular
direct special relief to those areas whose needs are
most pressing.

Steady progress continues to be made in the
provision of houses, and the reductions in costs which
are being secured should materially facilitate the
erection of houses for the less well-paid members of
the community.

My Ministers have initiated an inquiry into the
radium requirements of the country in the light of
the knowledge and experience gained as to the
importance of radium in the treatment of cancer,
and in accordance with the recommendation made
to them they have agreed to contribute to a fund
for the acquisition of a stock of radium. It is My
earnest hope that this action may prove a
substantial step forward in the campaign against one
of the most distressing maladies known to mankind.

I have given My assent to a Bill effecting a
consolidation of the law as to companies.

A Bill has also been passed which, it is hoped,
will assist the further development of the gas
industry.

Measures have been passed for the reform of
Local Government in Scotland and for granting
substantial relief from the burden of rates to
agricultural, industrial and freight-transport lands
and heritages.

Provision has also been made to increase the
available facilities for the supply of credit to the
agricultural industry in Scotland.

The Scottish Departments of Health,
Agriculture, Prisons and other Departments have
been reorganised in accordance with the terms of the
Reorganisation of Offices (Scotland) Act of last
Session.

FIRST SESSION OF THE THIRTY-FIFTH PARLIAMENT

1929–1930

OPENING (2 July 1929)

My Lords and Members of the House of Commons:

While I regret that it is not possible to address you in person, I thank Almighty God that I can look forward with confidence to that complete restoration of health, for which the prayers of My people throughout the Empire, with a sympathy and affection which call forth My deepest gratitude, were offered during the months of My long and serious illness.

My relations with foreign Powers continue to be friendly.

The independent financial experts appointed to draw up proposals for a complete and definitive settlement of the German reparation problem have presented a unanimous report which is at present being considered by My Government in preparation for a Conference of representatives of the Governments concerned. A settlement of this problem will enable the occupying Powers to proceed with the evacuation of the Rhineland.

Conversations have commenced with the Ambassador of the United States of America on the subject of naval disarmament, in consequence of which it is the earnest hope of My Government to ensure, in co-operation with My Governments in the Dominions, the Government of India and the Governments of foreign Powers, an early reduction of armaments throughout the world.

My Government consider that the time has come to submit to judicial settlement international disputes in which the parties are in conflict as to their respective rights. For this purpose they are now consulting with My Governments in the Dominions and the Government of India regarding the signing of the Optional Clause embodied in the statute of the Permanent Court of International Justice. My Government are examining the conditions under which diplomatic relations with the Government of the Union of Soviet Socialist Republics may be resumed and are in communication with My Governments in the Dominions and the Government of India on the subject.

Members of the House of Commons:

Estimates for the public service will be laid before you.

My Lords and Members of the House of Commons:

It will be the foremost endeavour of My Ministers to deal effectively with the continuing evil of unemployment.

Schemes are being prepared for the improvement of the means of transport, for the stimulation of the depressed export trades, for the economic development of My Overseas Dependencies, for the improvement of the condition of agriculture, for the encouragement of the fishing industry, and for the improvement of the facilities for the marketing of farm and fishery outputs. In co-operation with My Governments in the Dominions measures are being considered with the object of providing greater opportunities for overseas migration.

My Government have under consideration the question of the reorganisation of the coal industry including hours and other factors and of the ownership of the minerals. Proposals to this end will be submitted in due course.

Inquiries will be undertaken immediately into the condition of the iron and steel and the cotton industries in order to discover means for co-operating with them to improve their position in the markets of the world.

Bills will be laid before you for amending and consolidating the existing factory legislation, and for giving effect to the obligations entered into in Washington in 1919.

My Ministers propose to introduce legislation to promote an extensive policy of slum clearance and to make further provision for housing in urban and rural areas.

My Ministers have decided that the time has come to investigate the whole field of legislation relating to the sale and supply of intoxicating liquor and on their recommendation I propose to appoint at an early date Commissioners for this purpose.

My Ministers are engaged on a general survey of the various National Insurance and Pensions schemes. Meanwhile a Bill is being prepared to amend the Widows', Orphans' and Old Age Contributory Pensions Act, 1925, so as to modify the conditions applicable to certain pensions, and to make some increase in the classes of persons entitled to them.

A measure will be introduced to remedy the situation created by the Trade Disputes and Trades Unions Act, 1927.

At the recent General Election an extended franchise placed in the hands of the whole of My people of adult years the grave responsibility for guarding the well-being of this nation as a constitutional democracy, and My Government propose to institute an examination of the experiences of the election so that the working of the law relating to parliamentary elections may be brought into conformity with the new conditions.

PROROGATION (1 August 1930)

My Lords and Members of the House of Commons:

My relations with foreign Powers continue to be friendly.

It has given Me great pleasure to welcome in My capital Their Imperial Highnesses Prince and Princess Takamatsu, and to learn from His Imperial Highness of the gratification which the Emperor of Japan derived from the visit of My son, the Duke of Gloucester, to Japan last year to convey to His Imperial Majesty the insignia of the Order of the Garter.

At the Conference held at The Hague last January Agreements were concluded for the definite settlement of the reparation liabilities of Germany, Austria, Hungary and Bulgaria. These Agreements, together with that subsequently concluded at Paris, solved a number of difficult and delicate problems which have impeded the political as well as the financial progress of Europe; and their conclusion enabled the evacuation of the Rhineland by the Armies of Occupation to be completed on the 30th June last. The Hague Conference thus marks a decisive stage in the financial reconstruction and political tranquillisation of Europe and its success has given Me profound satisfaction.

In January it afforded Me great pleasure to open at Westminster an international conference for the limitation and reduction of naval armaments. After three months of deliberation, a Treaty embodying many important points of agreement in regard to the principles of naval limitation and achieving effective economies in the sphere of naval armaments was signed by representatives of the United States of America, France, Italy and Japan and of My Governments in the United Kingdom, the Dominions and India. In addition the Treaty embodies an agreement between My Governments and those of the United States of America and Japan fixing for a period a total tonnage limit for certain categories of warships. In this agreement the representatives of France and Italy were unable at the time of the signature of the Treaty to participate. The Conference was accordingly adjourned so as to give further time for negotiations, and these will, I trust, result in a full agreement at no very distant date.

The Optional Clause of the Statute of the Permanent Court of International Justice was signed at Geneva in September last in respect of the United Kingdom of Great Britain and Northern Ireland. My self-governing Dominions and India, and the several instruments of ratification are now completed or nearing completion.

In October last the Prime Minister visited Washington for the purpose of an informal discussion with the President of the United States upon various questions bearing on the peace of the world and an international agreement regarding reduction and limitation of naval armaments. Subsequently the Prime Minister visited Ottawa. The very cordial manner in which he was received caused Me the liveliest satisfaction.

A mission under the Chairmanship of Viscount D'Abernon was appointed in 1929 to consider Anglo-Argentine and Anglo-Brazilian relations, industrial, commercial and financial, with a view to their development to the mutual advantage of the countries respectively concerned.

The failure of the recent negotiations for an Anglo-Egyptian settlement occasioned Me sincere disappointment, but I hope that a successful conclusion may soon be reached.

Diplomatic relations with the Union of Soviet Socialist Republics were resumed in December last, and placed on a normal basis by the appointment of Ambassadors.

I am happy to say that the restoration of more settled conditions in Afghanistan has enabled Me to accredit a Minister to His Majesty King Nadir Shah, and to receive a representative of His Majesty in My capital.

A new Treaty of Alliance between Myself and His Majesty the King of Iraq to regulate the future relations between Our two countries, has been signed by Our respective representatives. The text of this Treaty has been laid before you.

I am glad that arrangements have been made for a meeting of the Imperial Conference in London at the end of September. I welcome the opportunities afforded by such meetings between the representatives of My several Governments for the promotion of mutual understanding and of co-operation in all matters of common concern. The Expert Conference on the Operation of Dominion Legislation which met in London last year presented a Report which will come before the Imperial Conference for consideration.

In accordance with an Address to Me from the Senate and Commons of Canada, the British North America Act, 1930, has been passed for the purpose of confirming and validating certain agreements entered into between My Government in Canada and the Governments of the Provinces of Manitoba, British Columbia, Alberta and Saskatchewan.

A Conference attended by Governors and other senior officials from the Colonies, Protectorates and Mandated Territories assembled in June to discuss matters of common interest to the various territories of the Colonial Empire.

During the Session the Commission appointed by Me in pursuance of the provisions of the Government of India Act have completed their arduous duty and have submitted to Me their Report, which has been presented to both your Houses. My Government will shortly be approaching the task of framing and submitting for your consideration proposals for the future government of India..For guidance in this matter, it is their intention to summon into conference in London representatives of the wide variety of interests in India. I earnestly pray that a spirit of mutual trust and friendship may unite all races and creeds in India, and the representatives of both countries, in their discharge of the responsibilities which the Conference will impose upon them; and I am confident that the single purpose of promoting the welfare of My Indian people will be the inspiration of every member of the Conference.

Members of the House of Commons:

I thank you for the provision you have made for the public service.

My Lords and Members of the House of Commons:

The high level to which unemployment has risen during the past year and the world-wide depression in trade is causing Me very grave anxiety. Measures have been passed with the object of promoting works of economic development in this country and in My Overseas Dependencies. It is encouraging to find that schemes have been designed to provide useful employment in works of public utility of a total value of over £100,000,000. This has been made possible by a substantial contribution granted by My Government.

I have given My assent to a further Measure to facilitate more speedy execution of works of this character by local authorities and other bodies.

Reports have been received on the inquiries undertaken into the condition of the iron and steel and cotton industries in order to discover means of improving their position in the markets of the world, and discussion of the recommendations made is actively proceeding between all the interests concerned.

A Bill has been passed which amends the Unemployment Insurance Scheme in several important respects, and other legislative measures have been necessary to provide for the heavy expenditure on unemployment benefit occasioned by the great volume of unemployment.

I have given My assent to a Measure for ameliorating the conditions of miners by reducing their hours of labour and for effecting an improvement in the organisation of the mining industry.

A Measure, based generally on the recommendations of My Commission on Land Drainage, has been passed to enable essential comprehensive drainage works to be undertaken for the prevention of flooding and the consequent benefit of agriculture, and the increase of employment in rural areas.

Acts have also been passed to make further provision with respect to the drainage of agricultural land in Scotland and to provide additional moneys for improving medical service in the Highlands and Islands.

Steps are being taken to appoint an Agricultural Research Council, and with this purpose in view a Committee of the Privy Council has been appointed.

I have given My assent to Measures to facilitate the clearance and prevention of slums and the provision of better housing accommodation, both in urban and rural areas in Great Britain.

It is My earnest hope that these Measures will improve the unsatisfactory conditions under which so many of My people dwell.

I have given My assent to a Bill which modifies the conditions applicable to certain pensions under the Widows', Orphans' and Old Age Contributory Pensions Act, 1925, and brings some new classes of persons within the benefits of the Act; to a Measure designed to improve and extend the facilities for the treatment of mental illness, and also to a Bill amending and consolidating the law relating to the regulation and control of motor vehicles.

SECOND SESSION OF THE THIRTY-FIFTH PARLIAMENT

1930–1931

OPENING (28 October 1930)

My Lords and Members of the House of Commons:

It has given Me much pleasure to receive My Ministers from the Dominions and the Representatives of India who are attending the Imperial Conference. I watch with deep interest the progress of their labours, the satisfactory result of which I shall confidently await.

I hope soon to welcome the Representatives of the Princes and Peoples of India who are about to join with members of all Parties in both Houses of Parliament to consider the future constitutional position of India.

My intention is to inaugurate this Conference, and I earnestly trust that in the conclusion of its proceedings may be found agreed and wise solutions of those important questions upon which it will be called to deliberate.

My relations with Foreign Powers continue to be friendly.

I was very glad to entrust My Son, the Duke of Gloucester, with the duty of representing Me at the coronation of the Emperor of Ethiopia.

My Government took an active part in the proceedings of the Assembly of the League of Nations in September last. General agreement was reached upon the Treaty of Financial Assistance to States Victims of Aggression which was recently signed at Geneva. The application of this Treaty is conditional upon the coming into force of a General Disarmament Convention, which I trust will shortly be concluded.

Members of the House of Commons:

Estimates for the Public Service will be laid before you.

My Lords and Members of the House of Commons:

I follow with grave concern and sympathy the continuance of heavy unemployment among so many of My People.

Economic depression unfortunately continues to dominate the markets of the world and the accompanying restriction of international trade is felt with particular severity in those industries which are especially dependent on export.

My Government will persist in its efforts to develop and extend home, Imperial and foreign trade and to help in measures which will lead to greater efficiency in industry.

Proposals will be laid before you for the promotion of increased settlement and employment on the land, and of large-scale farming operations, and for the acquisition and improvement of agricultural land in need of re-conditioning; and for the organisation of producers for marketing purposes.

I propose immediately to set up a Commission to inquire into the whole question of Unemployment Insurance and in particular into the allegations of abuse of its provisions. The Commission will be asked to present interim Reports on the most pressing questions and, if required, legislation based upon them will be introduced. In the meantime a measure to make further financial provision for the Unemployment Fund will be laid before you.

My Ministers propose to introduce legislation to secure for the community its share in the site value of land.

Measures will be submitted to you for raising the Age of Compulsory School Attendance, for amending the law relating to Trade Disputes and Trade Unions, and for the setting up of a Consumers' Council.

My Ministers propose to introduce legislation for the modification and extension of the Law relating to town planning and to the preservation of rural amenities; and for the amendment and consolidation of the Factory Acts.

A Measure of Electoral Reform will be submitted to you.

Bills will also be laid before you to enable the ratification of the Washington Hours Convention and of the International Convention for the Safety of Life at Sea and for the establishment of a new statutory authority to deal with passenger traffic in London.

PROROGATION (7 October 1931)

My Lords and Members of the House of Commons:

My relations with Foreign Powers continue to be friendly.

I have been following with interest and sympathy the resumed deliberations of the Round Table Conference. I trust that joint endeavour may produce an agreement on a plan which will commend itself to the judgment of wise statesmanship.

Members of the House of Commons:

I thank you for the provision you have made for the public service.

My Lords and Members of the House of Commons:

In the last few weeks My people have been called upon to face a financial and economic crisis which continues to give cause for anxiety. The measures taken by My Ministers, with the support of Parliament, to meet this emergency, involve sacrifices from every member of the community. I am confident that as on former occasions in the history of the Country, every citizen will co-operate to the utmost of his power in restoring prosperity to the Nation.

I have given My assent to Measures necessary to balance the National Budget.

An Act has been passed to amend the law relating to the Gold Standard.

My assent has also been given to a Measure to ensure the public against exploitation in regard to the supply or price of certain articles of general consumption.

FIRST SESSION OF THE THIRTY-SIXTH PARLIAMENT

1931–1932

OPENING (10 November 1931)

My Lords and Members of the House of Commons:
My relations with foreign Powers continue to be friendly.

My Government intend to pursue the policy of promoting peace and goodwill and to continue their active interest in the work of the League of Nations. Particularly, they are giving close attention to the preparations for the approaching Disarmament Conference, the successful result of which would, I am convinced, produce great and universal benefit.

The serious financial and economic situation of the world deeply concerns My Government. They will do their utmost in co-operation with other Governments, and in the spirit of mutual helpfulness, to find ways for restoring the volume of international trade.

The Indian Round Table Conference continues its work, and a Conference with Representatives of Burma will very shortly assemble. It is My earnest prayer that the deliberations of both these Conferences may be crowned with success.

In conformity with the undertaking given to the Representatives of My Dominions in 1930, a Measure will be laid before you to give statutory effect to certain of the Declarations and Resolutions of the Imperial Conferences of 1926 and 1930. This Measure is designed to make clear the powers of Dominion Parliaments and to promote the spirit of free co-operation amongst Members of the British Commonwealth of Nations.

My Government have received from the Government of My Dominion of Canada a proposal that the Economic Conference, which was adjourned in 1930, should be convened at Ottawa as soon as possible. This invitation has been welcomed by My Ministers and will be considered in the most sympathetic spirit and with an earnest desire to come to some mutually advantageous arrangement with the Governments of My Dominions.

Members of the House of Commons:
The Estimates for the public services will be laid before you in due course.

My Lords and Members of the House of Commons:
The Nation, at the General Election, endorsed those measures for securing economy and balancing the National Budget which constituted the first essential steps in the solution of the financial and economic problems with which the country has been confronted.

The Nation was also invited by My Ministers to empower them to pursue a policy designed fully to re-establish confidence in our financial stability and to give them authority to frame plans for ensuring a favourable balance of trade.

They further sought from the Nation unfettered discretion to consider every proposal likely to be of assistance in these matters.

My Ministers have now received a clear and emphatic mandate to that effect.

The important problems involved are already under detailed examination by My Government. Decisions will be taken and applied with the least possible delay, and in due course any legislation that may be required will be submitted to Parliament.

PROROGATION (17 November 1932)

My Lords and Members of the House of Commons:
The admission of the Kingdom of Iraq to membership of the League of Nations as a fully independent sovereign State marks the successful issue of the policy which My Government and their predecessors have consistently pursued during the last 12 years.

At the Lausanne Conference held in the summer the Governments concerned collaborated with success in devising the conditions of a lasting settlement of the question of German reparations as an essential preliminary to the economic recovery of the world.

I am deeply gratified at the successful conclusion of the Economic Conference held at Ottawa between representatives of the Governments of the different parts of My Empire, and I trust that it will add strength to the ties between My Peoples and stimulate Imperial trade. I have given My assent to the Measure necessary to give effect in the United Kingdom to the recommendations of the Conference.

I regret that certain questions which have arisen between the United Kingdom and the Irish Free State have not yet, despite the efforts made, been found capable of adjustment.

In accordance with the Resolutions approved by both your Houses, My Ministers have been investigating the many difficult questions involved in the revision of the Indian Constitution, and they have removed a serious barrier to progress by issuing a Declaration on the subject of communal representation.

Members of the House of Commons:

I thank you for the provision you have made for the public service.

My Lords and Members of the House of Commons:

The measures taken to meet the crisis of last autumn and the readiness of the community to make all necessary sacrifices have succeeded in re-establishing a balance between income and expenditure in our national finances.

Within the last few months operations on a scale never hitherto attempted have been carried through with complete success for the purpose of reducing the charge to the public for the service of the National Debt.

The adverse balance of trade which occasioned so much anxiety last year has been checked by the passing of the Import Duties Act and a substantial addition to the Revenue has been obtained by the same means, while a reasonable protection has been afforded to British industry on the recommendations of an impartial advisory committee.

Since the passing of this Act approaches have been made to My Government, by the Governments of a number of foreign countries, with a view to the negotiation of trade agreements. My Ministers welcome these approaches and conversations have already begun which will, I trust, lead to mutually satisfactory arrangements.

The condition of the agricultural industry has received the anxious consideration of My Ministers. The serious position in the live-stock industry has demanded emergency measures and a scheme for the voluntary regulation of imports of meat into this Country is now being brought into operation with the co-operation of the Governments and commercial interests in the Dominions and Foreign countries concerned. I am gratified to learn that this co-operation has been so readily forthcoming.

I have given My assent to a Measure for the assistance of growers of wheat in this Country, and provision has been made for the protection and encouragement of the fruit growing and market gardening industries.

An Act of great constitutional significance, namely, the Statute of Westminster, 1931, which makes clear the powers of Dominion Parliaments, has been passed. This Act gives effect to certain resolutions passed by the Imperial Conferences of 1926 and 1930 setting out the relationship of the United Kingdom and the Dominions.

I have given My assent to a Bill laying down the rules to be observed with regard to certain matters in the assessment of transitional payments to the unemployed, and enabling the same rules to be applied to outdoor relief.

A Measure has been passed consolidating and amending the law of town planning, whereby the responsible authorities will in future be enabled, subject to due consideration of all interests concerned, to study and deal with problems of development in relation to areas, whether built up or not.

A number of other Measures of public utility have been added to the Statute Book.

On the advice of My Ministers, I have appointed a Commission to inquire into the existing law and the practice thereunder relating to lotteries, betting, gambling and cognate matters, and to report what changes, if any, are desirable and practicable.

SECOND SESSION OF THE THIRTY-SIXTH PARLIAMENT

1932–1933

OPENING (22 November 1932)

My Lords and Members of the House of Commons:

My relations with foreign Powers continue to be friendly.

In accordance with the conclusions reached by the Conference at Lausanne, a World Economic Conference is to be convened by the League of Nations and will be held in London as soon as possible next year. It is My earnest hope that the Conference will be able to reach agreement on the measures required to deal with the causes which have brought about the present economic and financial difficulties of the world.

The Conference for the Reduction and Limitation of Armaments now sitting at Geneva embodies the hope and the effort of mankind to reach the greatest measure of general disarmament that can be attained. My Government will continue, in full co-operation with all the other members of the Conference, to work for an international convention which will be a foundation for a lasting peace.

My Ministers and other Members of both your Houses are meeting in conference representatives of the Indian States and of British India. They hope thereafter to place before you proposals for further constitutional development in India. The decisions to be taken will be of great moment to the whole of My Empire, and I shall watch your deliberations with deep interest.

Members of the House of Commons:

The Estimates for the Public Service will be laid before you in due course.

My Lords and Members of the House of Commons:

Although the various conversion schemes which have been successfully carried through offer the prospect of large reductions in the service of the National Debt, it is still necessary to exercise careful supervision over public expenditure, both national and local.

The measures already taken to assist British industry in the home market and to improve our markets overseas have created a feeling of greater confidence. My Government will continue to do everything in their power to stimulate the recovery of trade.

Agriculture has long been depressed by the general fall in the wholesale prices of its products. My Ministers recognise that though the measures recently taken in regard to meat and other products have been of real assistance to producers, further plans are necessary to enable agriculture as a whole to take its proper place in the economy of the nation. While the restoration of prosperity to agriculture cannot be expected until wholesale prices have risen to a more normal level. My Government believe that the various steps which they have taken, combined with action upon the investigations concluded, or still proceeding, will enable the industry to put itself in a position to take full advantage of a return to more favourable conditions.

Large numbers of My people are still unable to find employment and the persistence of this situation causes Me the greatest anxiety. Unemployment as we have known it for some years is undoubtedly the gravest of our social problems. In particular I am distressed that many young men and women have never in their lives had an opportunity of regular employment.

In the view of My Ministers any provision for unemployed persons should not only afford material assistance but should also be designed to maintain their morale and their fitness to resume work when opportunities can be found. My Government intend to bring forward Measures dealing comprehensively with Unemployment Insurance and with the treatment of those unable to obtain work, and the considerations I have mentioned will be borne in mind in framing their proposals.

Bills relating to Scotland will be introduced to amend the procedure governing private legislation, to facilitate the administration of civil justice, and for other purposes.

Measures dealing with Rent Restriction, London Passenger Transport, and other matters of importance will be introduced and proceeded with as time and opportunity offer.

PROROGATION (17 November 1933)

My Lords and Members of the House of Commons:

I rejoice to observe the steady improvement in trade and employment among My people.

Trade Agreements, which will, I trust, be found mutually advantageous, have been concluded with a number of foreign countries. Negotiations with other countries for the conclusion of similar Agreements will shortly be begun.

I have been gratified to learn that the question of Flag Discrimination in Portuguese ports, which has for some years been a subject of discussion, has now been satisfactorily settled by an Agreement between My Government and that of the Portuguese Republic.

I had pleasure in welcoming to London in June last year the delegates to the session of the World Monetary and Economic Conference. My Prime Minister acted as President of the Conference at the request of the Council of the League of Nations.

Considerable progress was made with certain questions but owing to unexpected developments in the international monetary and financial situation the Conference was, to My regret, unable to reach conclusions on certain important matters before its adjournment on the 27th July. It is, however, satisfactory that a joint declaration as to their views on some of the principal subjects raised at the Conference was drawn up by Delegations of the British Commonwealth and published. The Conference has left in being suitable organisations charged with the task of fixing the date of reassembly and of making the preliminary arrangements necessary for the purpose.

My Government have throughout taken an active part at the Disarmament Conference, and the British Draft, which was presented on the 16th March, was adopted in June last as the basis of the proposed Convention. I earnestly trust that the difficulties which have since arisen may be surmounted. The withdrawal of Germany a month ago from the deliberations at Geneva has necessarily dislocated the programme, but the work for international disarmament by agreement between nations must be vigorously pursued.

Members of the House of Commons:
I thank you for the provision you have made for the public service.

My Lords and Members of the House of Commons:
The continued willingness of My People to bear heavy sacrifices has made it possible for this country, almost alone among the great countries of the world, to maintain a satisfactory balance between its national income and expenditure.

Confidence has been restored by the pursuit of a sound financial policy, accompanied by the establishment of a reasonable measure of protection for the industry of the United Kingdom. The steps taken to promote the re-organisation of various sections of agriculture and the sea-fishing industry have not yet had time to show their full results, but I am pleased to note that there are already definite signs of improvement.

The numbers of the unemployed, though still unhappily far too large, have fallen substantially and continuously in recent months, despite the usual seasonal trend in the opposite direction.

Bills have received My assent providing for the amendment and continuation of the Rent and Mortgage Interest (Restrictions) Acts, for the re-organisation of London passenger transport, for the licensing and regulation of goods motor vehicles, for the consolidation of the law relating to children and young persons and for the amendment of the law relating to the national status of married women.

A number of other Measures of public utility have been passed into law.

THIRD SESSION OF THE THIRTY-SIXTH PARLIAMENT

1933–1934

OPENING (21 November 1933)

My Lords and Members of the House of Commons:

My relations with foreign Powers continue to be friendly.

The central purpose of My Government in international affairs is to promote and to sustain, by every means in their power, peace in the world. With this object in view, My Government will continue to co-operate with other Governments in endeavouring to reach a satisfactory solution of the complicated questions of disarmament in order to achieve a settlement acceptable to all and to attain fruitful results from the prolonged labours of the Disarmament Conference. My Government remain determined to uphold the work of international co-operation by collective action through the machinery of the League of Nations and in all other ways calculated to further good relations between all States and peoples.

During the past Session a Joint Committee of both your Houses considered, in conference with delegates from India, proposals for Indian constitutional reform. You will be invited to re-constitute the Committee, and My Ministers hope that the Committee may find it possible to complete their arduous task in time to enable definite proposals, in legislative form, to be laid before you during the coming Session. I am deeply conscious of the burden of responsibility which lies upon all those whose duty it is to guide or to take decisions as to the form of the future government of My Indian Empire, and I pray that wisdom may inform their judgment.

The Report of the Royal Commission on Newfoundland is about to be laid before you, and any legislation which may be found necessary in connection with their recommendations will be submitted to you.

Members of the House of Commons:

The Estimates for the public services will be laid before you in due course.

My Lords and Members of the House of Commons:

The past year has been marked by a steady growth of confidence in the future prospects of British trade and industry. In the opinion of My Government it is of the first importance that this confidence should be maintained and increased, since it lies at the root of any lasting improvement in the condition of the country.

By careful attention to sound principles both in the control of expenditure and in measures calculated to encourage enterprise My Ministers will endeavour to promote the return of the nation, step by step, to conditions which will permit the easing of its present burdens.

My Ministers will continue their efforts to create favourable conditions for the export trade, especially by the negotiation of trade agreements. In this way it is hoped that opportunities will be afforded for the development of the cotton, coal and other exporting trades.

You will be invited to give immediate consideration to a comprehensive Measure which will put the Unemployment Insurance scheme on a sound and permanent footing and will establish a new system for the assistance and welfare of the unemployed outside insurance.

My Ministers intend, in conjunction with the Local Authorities, to press forward with the improvement of housing conditions by the clearance or re-conditioning of houses unfit for human habitation, and their replacement, when demolished, by dwellings which accord with modern standards and can be let at reasonable rents.

Measures dealing with the law relating to betting and gambling, the continuation of a beet sugar subsidy for another year, the reconditioning of working-class houses and regulating the hours of employment of young persons and other conditions in the distributive trades will be submitted to you.

Bills relating to Scotland will be introduced to accelerate the provision of small holdings, to deal with illegal trawling, to amend the Poor Law, and for other purposes.

Other Measures of importance will be laid before you and proceeded with as time and opportunity offer.

PROROGATION (16 November 1934)

My Lords and Members of the House of Commons:

The murder of the former Austrian Chancellor in July, and the assassination of the King of Yugoslavia and of M. Barthou in October, profoundly shocked the world and evoked the deep sympathy of Myself and all my People. These tragedies undoubtedly caused a serious setback to movements then on foot for European appeasement, and I have therefore noted with satisfaction the untiring efforts which My Government have made in many directions to counsel moderation and promote more friendly relations between nations.

In continuation of the conversations which took place last summer, representatives of My Government are at present engaged in preliminary discussions with representatives of the Governments of the United States and Japan in preparation for the Naval Conference, which is due to take place next year. It is My earnest hope that their efforts may be attended with success, in order that the world may be spared the evil of unrestricted competition in naval armaments so effectively averted in recent years by the international engagements freely entered into by the parties concerned.

Two of My sons have been able to make visits during the present year to My Dominions overseas. The welcome which the Duke of Kent received during his recent visit to South Africa and that given to the Duke of Gloucester first in Ceylon and then in Australia have been a source of great pleasure to the Queen and Myself.

An Act has been passed making fresh provision for the administration of Newfoundland in accordance with the recommendations of the Royal Commission on Newfoundland. A Commission of Government has been set up and will, I trust, succeed in restoring prosperity to the Island.

The Joint Committee of both your Houses, after patiently and assiduously examining the problem of the future government of India, have concluded their task, and their recommendations will shortly be before you. Seldom, if ever, has an enquiry covered a wider or a more important field, and I do not doubt that your Committee have discharged their duty in a manner worthy of the task entrusted to them:

Members of the House of Commons:

I thank you for the provision you have made for the public service.

My Lords and Members of the House of Commons:

Notwithstanding the continuance of difficult conditions affecting international trade, the purchasing and saving power of My people has been strengthened and the national finances have so far improved as to justify a substantial alleviation of the burdens which were accepted three years ago.

The continued improvement in trade and employment among My People gives Me great satisfaction. I am especially pleased at the welcome expansion in the export trade of this country, which has been materially assisted by the trade agreements which have been concluded with a number of foreign States, and by the development of trade within the Empire on the basis of mutual preference.

I regret that unhappily some areas have not shared in this improvement and their special conditions are receiving the sympathetic attention of My Ministers.

I have given My assent to a Bill providing for the amendment of the unemployment insurance scheme and for the establishment of a system of unemployment assistance on a national basis.

Bills have received My assent providing for the amendment of the law relating to betting and gambling, for the prevention of incitement to disaffection, and for regulating the hours of employment of young persons in the distributive trades.

Measures have also been passed for meeting the situation arising from the long continued drought, and for assisting the livestock and dairy sections of the agricultural industry.

Bills relating to Scotland have received My assent providing for the acceleration of the provisions of small holdings, for the suppression of illegal trawling, and for the amendment of the Poor Law.

A number of other Measures of public utility have been passed into law.

FOURTH SESSION OF THE THIRTY-SIXTH PARLIAMENT

1934–1935

OPENING (20 November 1934)

My Lords and Members of the House of Commons:

My relations with foreign Powers continue to be friendly.

The maintenance of world peace does not cease to give My Government the most anxious concern. They will continue to make the support and extension of the authority of the League of Nations a cardinal point of their policy. They earnestly trust that the general work of the Disarmament Conference may be actively resumed in a political atmosphere more favourable to the attainment of definite results. In the meantime, strenuous efforts will be made to secure international agreement on such matters as are capable of separate treatment.

The Report of the Joint Committee of both your Houses on Indian Constitutional Reform is about to be placed in your hands, and it will be the duty of My Ministers to lay before you their legislative proposals for the future government of India. I pray that both your Houses, upon whom now rests the responsibility of deciding these issues, may approach the task which lies before them with the single aim of furthering the well-being of My Empire.

Members of the House of Commons:

The Estimates for the public services will be laid before you in due course.

My Lords and Members of the House of Commons:

Although factors adverse to the full resumption of international trade still exist, it is My earnest hope that the coming year will be marked by a continuance of the spirit of confidence and enterprise which has enabled this country to take the lead in world recovery.

The condition of the shipping industry is receiving the anxious consideration of My Ministers. The serious position of tramp shipping calls for early treatment, and you will be invited to consider a measure for providing temporary assistance to this section of the industry.

My Ministers, in conjunction with the local authorities, are pressing forward with the task of clearing the slums in regard to which the national conscience has been so deeply stirred. So great a measure of progress is being attained that My Ministers are able to contemplate the next step in the process of improving the housing conditions of the people. A Bill will accordingly be submitted to you for preventing overcrowding and making provision for the rehousing of those found to be living in overcrowded conditions.

A similar Bill applying to Scotland will also be introduced.

A Measure will be submitted to you to assist certain areas in which prolonged unemployment has created problems of an exceptional character. A Bill will also be laid before you to amend the law relating to the supply of electricity.

My Ministers have for some time past had under consideration the further development and acceleration of Imperial air communications, and Measures to this end will be brought forward in due course.

The condition of Agriculture and the reorganisation of the herring industry are closely engaging the attention of My Ministers.

Measures will be introduced, if time permits, for the control of building development along the main thoroughfares, for providing better housing of the Metropolitan Police, and other subjects.

PROROGATION (25 October 1935)

My Lords and Members of the House of Commons:

To both the Queen and to Myself this—My Silver Jubilee year—will ever remain one of Our happiest memories. The wonderful tributes of affection which We have received from every part of My Empire will be treasured in Our hearts so long as We live.

I was happy to welcome in London My Prime Ministers from My Dominions overseas, and the representative of India, who came to take part in the celebrations of My Silver Jubilee.

My relations with foreign Powers continue to be friendly.

The critical situation which has unhappily arisen between Italy and Abyssinia has aroused My gravest concern. From the moment that a dispute occurred between the two countries as the result of a frontier incident in December of last year My Government have exerted themselves to the utmost, both individually and in co-operation with other States members of the League of Nations, to promote a peaceful settlement. To My regret these persistent endeavours did not avail to prevent a resort to force, and My Government have loyally supported the efforts of the League of Nations with a view to the restoration of peace and the achievement of an equitable settlement in the spirit of the Covenant.

I have given My assent to a Bill to make

provision for the future government of India and Burma, which must stand in the records of both your Houses as one of the weightiest and most complex measures with which Parliament has ever dealt. I trust that when the further steps required to bring the Act into operation have been taken its provisions will not only bring contentment and well-being to the people of India and Burma, but draw closer the bonds of amity between them and the rest of My Empire.

Members of the House of Commons:

I thank you for the provision you have made for the public service.

My Lords and Members of the House of Commons:

The more confident spirit of industry, the continued growth in the national revenue, and the prudent and successful management of our financial affairs have permitted a further considerable advance towards prosperity. I rejoice that it has been possible for My Government, notwithstanding new and pressing claims from many directions, to remove the greater part of the extra burdens imposed four years ago and, in particular, to grant substantial relief to the small taxpayer.

I am gratified to observe a further steady increase in employment among My people during the past year. Despite many adverse conditions in the international trade position, the overseas trade of this country continues to expand, especially with the other Parts of the Empire and with the foreign countries with which trade agreements have been concluded.

The effects on the increase in employment cannot but be felt, to a greater or less degree, in all localities, but in some areas the problem of unemployment continues to present special difficulties. Among other measures an Act passed at the beginning of the Session provided for the appointment of Commissioners for the Special Areas in England and Wales and in Scotland, respectively, who are devoting their attention to improving the condition of those areas under the powers conferred upon them. Interim Reports made by these Commissioners were laid before Parliament in July. Further progress has since been made, and My Ministers are continuing to give close and anxious attention to the problems of these areas in all their bearings.

Regulations relating to unemployment assistance were approved by Parliament in December. Unexpected difficulties were met in the apllication of these Regulations and an Act passed in February contained temporary provisions for dealing with the situation thus arising.

While My Government have not ceased, and will not cease, their continuing efforts to promote the limitation and reduction by international agreement of all forms of armament, it has been found impossible to postpone further the expansion of the Royal Air Force to a strength which will enable it to fulfil its vital duties in National and Imperial Defence; and the programme necessary to give effect to this has now been undertaken.

Far-reaching proposals have been announced for the improvement and acceleration of Imperial air communications and plans for their further development are under active consideration.

Important postal, telegraph and telephone concessions have been introduced during the year.

Highway authorities have been asked to submit their programmes of road improvements on a quinquennial instead of an annual basis. The response augurs well for the scientific planning of our roads to meet modern requirements.

I have given My assent to a Bill providing for the control of ribbon development along the frontages of roads and for the prevention of interference with traffic.

My assent has also been given to a Bill which provides, for the first time, for a full survey of overcrowding and equips local authorities with new powers for dealing with the twin evils of slums and overcrowding, while at the same time remedying certain anomalies in the law which pressed unfairly on owners of house property.

During the year progress both in the clearance and replacement of slums and in the provision of additional houses has been on an unprecedented scale.

Provision has been made for safe-guarding insured persons against the loss of their pension rights and certain of their health insurance rights by reason of unemployment.

Measures have been enacted providing for further assistance to the agricultural industry, for the reorganisation of the herring industry, for a temporary subsidy to assist tramp shipping and for the grant of loans to shipowners to facilitate the replacing of obsolete with modern cargo vessels.

Acts have been passed amending the law relating to the legal position of married women, and to the right to recover damages against joint tortfeasors, to make provision for an increase in the number of Judges attached to the King's Bench Division, and to make improvements in the procedure of the Probate, Divorce and Admiralty Division.

I have given My assent to a Bill providing that persons who have failed to pay fines or other money payments, in pursuance of the order of a Court of Summary Jurisdiction, shall not be committed to prison without a further adjudication by the Court on their circumstances.

Among Bills relating to Scotland which have received My assent are measures providing for the better housing of the people, and for the continuation and amendment of legislation relating to the Education Endowments Commissioners.

FIRST SESSION OF THE THIRTY-SEVENTH PARLIAMENT

1935–1936

OPENING (3 December 1935)

My Lords and Members of the House of Commons:

I deeply regret that I am not addressing you in person to-day.

My relations with foreign Powers continue to be friendly.

My Government's foreign policy will as heretofore be based on a firm support of the League of Nations. They will remain prepared to fulfil, in co-operation with other members of the League, the obligations of the Covenant. In particular, they are determined to use at all times the full weight of their influence for the preservation of peace.

In pursuance of these obligations My Government have felt compelled to adopt, in co-operation with some fifty other States Members of the League, certain measures of an economic and financial nature in regard to Italy. At the same time they will continue to exert their influence in favour of a peace acceptable to the three parties in the dispute, namely, Italy, Ethiopia, and the League of Nations.

My Government have issued invitations to the Governments of the other countries which were parties to the Washington and London Naval Treaties to attend a Conference in London this month with a view to the conclusion of a new international treaty for the limitation of naval armaments. I have learned with satisfaction that all the invitations to this Conference have been accepted, and I trust that its labours will be crowned with success.

Members of the House of Commons:

The Estimates for the Public Service will be laid before you.

The fulfilment of our international obligations under the Covenant, no less than the adequate safeguarding of My Empire, makes it urgently necessary that the deficiencies in My Defence Forces should be made good. My Ministers will in due course lay before you their proposals, which will be limited to the minimum required for these two purposes.

My Lords and Members of the House of Commons:

The policy of My Ministers, while continuing to foster the general recovery of trade, industry, and agriculture, will pay special regard to those areas in which the burden of unemployment is greatest and to the development of any measures likely to be advantageous to them.

The problem of securing improved conditions in the coal-mining industry is receiving the anxious consideration of My Ministers. Active steps are being taken to co-ordinate the selling arrangements of the industry and the necessary orders under Part 1 of the Coal Mines Act, 1930, will be laid before you.

In pursuance of the policy of re-organisation, a Measure will be introduced to provide for the unification of coal royalties under national control.

In the opinion of My Government the time has come when the existing provisions for the safety of workers in mines should be reviewed in the light of modern scientific knowledge. I shall, as soon as possible, appoint Commissioners to inquire fully into this important matter.

Proposals for making improved arrangements for assistance to the unemployed and for the insurance of agricultural workers against unemployment will be laid before you.

A Bill will be introduced to authorise the guarantee by the State of a loan to be raised for the purpose of enabling the Railway Companies to carry out special developments which will add to transport facilities and to the convenience of travellers.

A Measure will be submitted to you for promoting the further development of our civil air communications, both in this country and throughout the Empire; and for dealing with other matters relating to air navigation.

It is the intention of My Ministers to proceed at an early date with the proposals laid before the last Parliament for dealing with the problem of surplus productive capacity in the spinning section of the cotton industry.

My Government are convinced of the need for an early and substantial development of the educational services of the country. A Bill will be introduced to amend the law in England and Wales relating both to the age of compulsory school attendance and to assistance from public funds towards expenditure on Voluntary School buildings. Action will also be taken, in co-operation with Local Authorities and others, to increase the effectiveness of the other educational services. In particular, the improvement of the school medical arrangements, the extension of physical education, and the development of Technical Schools, will receive the attention of My Government.

My Ministers will continue to promote actively the development of the social services, and to take vigorous measures to improve the health and physique of the nation. They will press forward the work of slum clearance in order to ensure that the programmes submitted by local authorities are carried out within the period contemplated, and they will encourage the active administration of the Housing Acts of 1935 which enable local authorities to make a direct attack upon the evils of overcrowding.

Careful consideration has been given by My Government to the organisation of the maternity services with a view to providing better care for women in child-birth, and a Bill will be introduced for the provision by local authorities in co-operation with voluntary associations of an organised service of salaried midwives.

My Ministers will continue to give close consideration to the further improvement of conditions in Scotland and among Measures to that end a Bill will be introduced providing for the raising of the school age.

Other Measures of importance will be laid before you and proceeded with as time and opportunity offer.

PROROGATION (30 October 1936)

My Lords and Members of the House of Commons:
I am addressing you for the first time as your Sovereign. I desire before all to express once more My deep appreciation of the sympathy which has been extended to Me and to My dear Mother in every part of My dominions. I have been profoundly touched by the universal expression of the affection and respect with which My beloved Father was regarded. I am well assured that the memory of King George's life of devotion and unremitting service will long live in the hearts of His people.

My relations with foreign Powers continue to be friendly.

On the 26th August a Treaty of Alliance with the King of Egypt was signed in London by delegates representing My Government and the Egyptian Government. It is My earnest hope that this Treaty when ratified will be the beginning of a new era in which the friendly co-operation that has marked the relations between My country and Egypt in the past will be confirmed and strengthened.

A Conference was held at Montreux in the summer for the revision of the Straits Convention of Lausanne. The successful outcome of this Conference, to which I am pleased to think that My Government contributed, has set a happy example for the future.

The Assembly of the League of Nations have recently opened an inquiry into the working of the Covenant, and My Government, which remain firmly attached to the principles of the Covenant of the League, have made known their views upon the manner in which its application might be improved.

My Ministers have been engaged in negotiations for a meeting between the Five Powers signatory to the Treaty of Locarno on the basis of the agreement reached by My Government and the Governments of France and Belgium in London on the 23rd July. The negotiations are continuing.

I have viewed with concern and anxiety the events in Spain during the last three months. My Government have spared no pains to promote and encourage humanitarian efforts to mitigate the suffering of the people of Spain. My Navy has acted in accordance with its high traditions in relieving the distress caused by these disturbances. It has been the consistent policy of My Government to attempt to localise this unhappy struggle, and with this end in view they seconded the initiative of the French Government for a non-intervention agreement and have energetically co-operated in its negotiation and application.

My Ministers were glad to be able, in conjunction with the Government of the United States of America, to lend their co-operation to the scheme for the re-adjustment of the value of the French currency. I trust that the measures taken recently by the French and several other Governments will pave the way for a further improvement in international trade.

Members of the House of Commons:
I thank you for the provision you have made for the public service.

I thank you for the arrangements you have made for the maintenance of the honour and dignity of the Crown.

My Lords and Members of the House of Commons:
The measures essential for improving and strengthening all three of My defence forces, which were laid before you this year, have been steadily pursued.

I rejoice at the further marked increase in trade and employment during the year. I note, with much gratification, that unemployment generally is still diminishing and that employment has reached the highest level ever recorded. Schemes for the amelioration of the conditions in those districts where the problem of unemployment still presents special difficulties have continued to engage the close attention of My Ministers and of the Commissioners appointed for those areas.

Steps have been taken to reduce the rate of contributions under the general unemployment insurance scheme.

Regulations relating to unemployment assistance and measures for bringing to an end the period of standstill which has existed since February, 1935, received your approval in July, and will come into effect in November.

The development of the national health services has received the close attention of My Ministers. Good progress has been made in the clearance and replace-ment of slums, the surveys of overcrowding required

under the Housing Acts, 1935, have been completed
by local authorities, and the work of providing new
accommodation under those Acts has been begun. The
high rate of house production in general has been well
maintained.

Acts have been passed for the improvement of the
maternity services by the provision of an organised
service of salaried midwives, and for the consolidation
and amendment of the law relating to public health.

I have given My assent to a Bill to amend the
law in England and Wales relating to compulsory
school attendance and to assistance from public
funds towards expenditure on voluntary school
buildings; and also to a Bill providing for the raising
of the school-leaving age in Scotland and for certain
improvements in the educational system, in particular
as regards children suffering from physical and mental
defects.

Action has been taken, in co-operation with
Local Authorities, to improve and extend the
provision of physical education in the schools.

Measures have been enacted providing for a
solution of the problem of tithe rentcharge upon a
permanent footing, and for the maintenance of the
beet sugar industry as part of the general agricultural
policy of this country. Assistance to the cattle and
dairying sections of the agricultural industry has been
continued.

An Act has been passed for insuring agricultural
workers against unemployment, which will enable
such workers, if unemployed during the coming
winter, to receive benefit.

I have given My assent to Bills to facilitate the
elimination of surplus productive capacity in the
spinning section of the cotton industry, and to
continue for a further year the temporary subsidy
granted to tramp shipping in 1935. Steps have been
taken to enable the selling arrangements of the coal
industry to be co-ordinated.

A number of other measures of public utility
have been added to the Statute Book.

SECOND SESSION OF THE THIRTY-SEVENTH PARLIAMENT

1936–1937

OPENING (3 November 1936)

My Lords and Members of the House of Commons:

My relations with foreign Powers continue to be friendly.

The policy of My Government continues to be based upon membership of the League of Nations. They desire to see the League strengthened for its work in the pacific settlement of international disputes, and they have already made known at Geneva their proposals for the improved working and wider authority of the League. My Government will co-operate with other Governments in the work of the Committee of the League which has been set up to examine these and other proposals.

My Government will continue to do all in their power to further the appeasement of Europe. With this object in view they will persist in their efforts to bring about a meeting between the Five Powers signatory to the Treaty of Locarno.

I trust that, as a result of the negotiations at present in progress, the Treaty for the limitation of naval armaments, which was signed in London on March 25th by representatives of the United States of America, France, the United Kingdom, Canada, the Commonwealth of Australia, New Zealand and India, will form the basis of an international agreement to which all naval Powers will eventually become parties.

My Government have followed with concern the political situation in the Far East, where peace and tranquillity are so essential to the important interests of My people in that part of the world. It is My hope that the negotiations now in progress between China and Japan may result in a satisfactory solution.

My Ministers, while maintaining their determination to support the international agreement for non-intervention in Spain, will continue to take every opportunity to mitigate human suffering and loss of life in that unhappy country.

I trust that before the end of the present year the Treaty of Alliance with Egypt will have been ratified by Myself and the King of Egypt, and that it will prove to be the means of loyal co-operation between our two Governments and peoples whose destinies are inseparably bound together by common aims and interests.

A meeting of the Imperial Conference is to be held in London next May, and I am confident that the opportunity thus afforded for discussions between representatives of My several Governments will once more prove its value in promoting a closer understanding between all My peoples. I am glad to think that this meeting will coincide in time with the occasion of My Coronation.

It is My hope, when the solemnity of My Coronation has been celebrated, to revisit My Indian Dominions and there to make known in the same manner as My revered Father to the Princes and Peoples of India My succession to the Imperial Crown.

You will be asked to approve the drafts of various instruments which are required to implement your decision that the provisions of the Government of India Act affecting the Provinces and of the Government of Burma Act shall come into operation in April next. I have every confidence that the great responsibilities which will devolve upon the representatives of the people of India and of Burma will be faithfully and effectively discharged.

I deeply regret the serious disturbances which have taken place in Palestine during the last six months, and which made it necessary to despatch additional troops. I welcome the recent improvement in the situation and the Royal Commission, which I have appointed, will leave England this week to undertake their inquiry. I sincerely trust that their examination of the very difficult problems which will come before them will lead to a just and permanent settlement.

Members of the House of Commons:

The Estimates for the Public Services will be laid before you.

The work of strengthening My defence forces is being pressed on with the utmost energy and is now making rapid progress. My Government are satisfied that the measures they are taking are essential to the defence of My Empire and to the ability of this country to discharge its international obligations. My Ministers will nevertheless lose no opportunity of promoting general international appeasement and the limitation of expenditure on armaments which would naturally follow upon such an improvement of relations.

My Lords and Members of the House of Commons:

I am gratified to note that the general trade and industrial outlook continues to be favourable, and that there is good ground for expecting that there will be further improvement. My Ministers will continue to foster industrial activity at home and, in the belief that the attainment of general prosperity here depends on further expansion of our overseas trade, to maintain their efforts to promote the freer exchange of goods throughout the world.

You will be invited to extend the period of operation of the Special Areas (Development and Improvement) Act, 1934.

The position of the shipping industry is receiving the careful consideration of My Ministers, with a view to deciding what measures are required to secure the maintenance of a mercantile marine adequate for the needs of the country.

You will be invited to consider proposals for the furtherance of re-organisation in the coal industry, and for the unification of coal royalties under national control.

My Ministers have come to the conclusion that the existing law requires amendment in order to deal more effectively with persons or organisations who provoke or cause disturbances of the public peace. A Bill for strengthening the law without interfering with legitimate freedom of speech or assembly will be submitted to you.

The present law regulating the conditions of work in factories is based upon the Act of 1901, and though it has from time to time been modified in certain particulars, further amendment and consolidation are long overdue. My Ministers intend to invite Parliament to undertake and carry through this important task in the course of the present Session.

My Ministers will continue to promote by an active and constructive policy the development of home agriculture and fisheries. The position of the livestock industry has been engaging their close attention and legislation will be introduced to promote increased efficiency in that industry and to provide for assistance to the producers of fat cattle.

A Bill will be introduced with a view to transferring from the county councils to the Minister of Transport the principal roads which constitute the national system of through traffic routes in Great Britain.

I am impressed with the need for more comprehensive efforts to improve the physical condition of the nation, especially among the younger members of the community, and My Ministers will in due course submit to you proposals designed to carry out this purpose.

Encouragement will continue to be given to the development of the existing public health services. Vigorous action for the provision of housing accommodation to replace slum dwellings and abate overcrowding will be maintained.

Legislation will be introduced to provide medical care for young persons who have left school and entered employment, and to extend to persons with limited income voluntary insurance for the purpose of pensions.

Measures will also be submitted to you to reduce the age limit for the award of pensions to blind persons and to make further provision for the superannuation of local government officers.

A Bill will also be laid before you to remove certain anomalies in the present standing of Ministers by adjustments and alterations in their salaries, and for other purposes.

Close attention will continue to be given to the improvement of conditions in Scotland. My Ministers are examining the Report of the Committee on Scottish Health Services and among measures relating to health a Bill for the development of Scottish maternity services will be introduced. Legislation affecting agriculture in Scotland will also be submitted to you.

Among other Bills you will be invited to pass are measures to make better provisions for preventing abuses of the law relating to clubs, to regulate unit trusts, to improve the efficiency of the organisation of the fire brigade services of the country, and to amend the scheme of railway freight rebates.

Other measures of importance will be laid before you and proceeded with as time and opportunity offer.

PROROGATION (22 October 1937)

My Lords and Members of the House of Commons:

It was with deep satisfaction that the Queen and I on the solemn occasion of Our Coronation received the proofs of the loyalty and affection of My peoples and of their devotion to the Crown. The significance of this Ceremony was emphasised by the presence of Prime Ministers of My Dominions, and representatives of My Empire of India and every part of My Empire overseas.

The deliberations of the Imperial Conference which followed immediately after the Coronation, afforded ample evidence of the value of such meetings for the discussion of matters of common concern, and I earnestly trust that their result may be to enhance the security as well as the prosperity and happiness of My peoples in all parts of the British Commonwealth of Nations.

My relations with foreign Powers continue to be friendly.

The Treaty of Alliance with Egypt has been duly ratified by Myself and the King of Egypt. In the spring of this year an international Conference was held at Montreux for the abolition of the capitulations in Egypt. Thanks to the practical and conciliatory spirit in which the complex issues involved were faced by the delegations of the participating Governments, the Conference was brought to a successful issue.

Throughout the course of the past year My Ministers have followed with concern and anxiety the tragic events in Spain, and have persisted in their endeavours to prevent the spread of the conflict beyond that country's borders. I am happy to note the successful outcome of the Conference at Nyon.

I have seen with the greatest concern the development of hostilities between Japan and China. The sufferings which have been inflicted upon the innocent noncombatants by attacks from the air and sea have caused Me particular distress. I trust that the Conference of Powers, which is shortly to be called together, may contribute to bring this deplorable conflict to an end.

In the field of naval limitation I am happy to state that the London Naval Treaty signed in London on the 25th March, 1936, has now been ratified by all the signatories. Further, with a view to extending the scope of that Treaty, bilateral naval agreements have recently been concluded between My Government and the Governments of Germany and of the Union of Soviet Socialist Republics.

The provisions of the Government of India Act, giving responsible government to the Provinces of India, and of the Government of Burma Act have come into operation during the year, and I am watching with deep interest developments in both countries. I hope that in no distant time there may be realised the full project of a Federation of India.

Members of the House of Commons:

I thank you for the provision you have made for the Public Service.

I thank you for the provision you have made for the honour and dignity of the Crown.

My Lords and Members of the House of Commons:

I note with much satisfaction the continued strengthening and improvement of all three of My defence forces, as a result of the measures laid before you last year. The heavy burden of this necessary rearmament is to some extent lightened by the continued growth of trade, employment, saving and purchasing power among My people.

The provision of facilities for recreation and healthy outdoor activity, more especially for the younger members of the community, has always been a matter of special interest to Me. It was therefore with particular pleasure that I gave My assent last summer to the Physical Training and Recreation Act. It is My hope that the fullest possible use will be made of this contribution to the physical well-being, and through it the happiness, of the nation.

The national health services have been further developed and improved. The rate of progress in the clearance and replacement of slums, has been satisfactorily maintained, the abatement of over-crowding is proceeding, and house building has continued at a high rate.

The Act relating to the Special Areas has been continued for a further period and additional powers have been conferred with the object of further promoting the establishment of new industrial undertakings in those areas and in other areas of heavy unemployment.

I have given My assent to a Bill in which the law regulating the conditions of work in factories has been codified and brought up to date, and greatly improved provision has been made for securing the safety and health of factory workers.

My assent has also been given to Bills extending voluntary insurance for pensions to persons with limited income, making further provision for the superannuation of local government officers, and providing for the distribution of Exchequer grants with increased regard to the needs of local authorities.

Bills have been passed into law to assist the livestock industry and to promote its efficiency; to increase the productivity of agriculture by measures to encourage the application of lime and basic slag to the soil; to promote land drainage; to provide further assurance for the cultivation of cereals and to combat animal diseases. Assistance to the milk industry has been continued for an additional period.

I have given My assent to a Measure extending, with certain amendments, the operation of the Empire Settlement Act, 1922, for a further period of fifteen years.

Acts have been passed to authorise the raising of defence loans, to increase the amount which may be issued to the Exchange Equalisation Account, to continue the temporary subsidy granted to tramp shipping and to consolidate and amend the law relating to export guarantees.

The Bills relating to Scotland which have received My assent have included, in addition to Bills dealing with Exchequer grants to local authorities and the superannuation of local government employees, Measures for the development and improvement of maternity services, for the regulation of the wages of agricultural workers, and for the better custody of public records.

A number of other Measures of public utility have been passed into law.

THIRD SESSION OF THE THIRTY-SEVENTH PARLIAMENT

1937–1938

OPENING (26 October 1937)

My Lords and Members of the House of Commons:

My relations with foreign Powers continue to be friendly.

I have invited the King of the Belgians to visit Me in November and a similar invitation has been extended to the King of Roumania for the spring of next year. I shall welcome the visits of Their Majesties to My capital and trust that they will conduce towards the consolidation of the friendly relations existing between our nations.

My Ministers have followed with growing concern the continuance of the conflict in Spain. It is their aim to do everything which lies in their power to assist towards the restoration of peace among the Spanish people. They believe that a strict application of the international policy of non-intervention in Spain will materially contribute to this end.

The position in the Far East will continue to engage the earnest attention of My Government, who will persist in their policy of attempting, in co-operation with other Governments, whether members of the League of Nations or not, to mitigate the suffering caused by the conflict and to bring it to a conclusion.

I am looking forward with interest and pleasure to the time when it will be possible for Me to visit My Indian Empire.

Members of the House of Commons:

The Estimates for the Public Services will be laid before you.

My Lords and Members of the House of Commons:

With the full co-operation of My people the work of expanding and equipping My defence forces is now making rapid progress.

My Ministers are anxious that energetic steps shall be taken to complete the measures for the protection of the civilian population against air raids. A Bill to put the necessary arrangements on a statutory basis will be brought forward for your consideration.

I rejoice to know that the outlook for trade and industry remains favourable, and that there is every indication that the progress made in the last year will be maintained. My Government will continue to take all possible measures to encourage industrial activity at home, and to develop our overseas trade.

A Bill will be submitted to you to provide for the unification of coal royalties under national control and for the furtherance of re-organisation in the coal-mining industry.

A Measure for improving the distribution of electricity will be laid before you.

My Government have announced their intention to assist the production and to increase the consumption of milk, and to facilitate the improvement of milk distribution. A Bill to this end and further proposals for the welfare of agriculture will be submitted to you.

You will be invited to pass legislation to provide for the reorganisation of the white fish industry, and for other matters related to sea fisheries.

A comprehensive publicity campaign is being undertaken to ensure the fullest use of the public health services and to encourage their expansion. The policy of improving housing conditions will be energetically pursued.

My Government will further develop their social policy by introducing legislation to enable meals to be supplied to boys and girls attending junior instruction centres; to provide medical care for young persons who have left school and entered employment; to reduce the age limit for the award of pensions to blind persons; to enable further information to be obtained for the study of the population problem; to amend the financial provision for slum clearance and the abatement of overcrowding; and to make further provision for the improvement of agricultural housing.

A Measure will be laid before you to amend the penal law and to enable improved arrangements to be made for dealing with offenders, including juveniles and those who commit repeated offences.

Proposals will be laid before you for providing such additional judicial strength for the Probate, Divorce and Admiralty Division as will enable the High Court to discharge the additional duties laid upon it by the Matrimonial Causes Act of last Session; for carrying out some of the recommendations of the Royal Commission on the Despatch of Business at Common Law; and for giving effect to certain recommendations of the Law Revision Committee on the subject of the limitation of actions.

Among other Measures which you will be invited to pass will be Bills to amend the present scheme for securing the renting and exhibition of a certain proportion of British films; to prevent frauds in share dealings; to make better provisions for preventing abuses of the law relating to clubs; to improve the efficiency of the organisation of the fire brigade services of the country; and to regulate wages and conditions of employment in the transport of goods by road.

Scottish affairs will continue to receive the close attention of My Ministers. Legislation on the subject of rural housing in Scotland and on other matters of Scottish interest will be submitted to you.

Other Measures of importance will be laid before you and proceeded with as time and opportunity offer.

PROROGATION (4 November 1938)

My Lords and Members of the House of Commons:

My relations with foreign Powers continue to be friendly.

In response to an invitation from the President of the French Republic, the Queen and I paid a visit in July last to Paris. We were profoundly moved by the evident sincerity and spontaneity of the welcome extended to us by the French Government and people. Nothing could more clearly have demonstrated the strength of the bonds which so happily unite our two countries.

I have followed with deep anxiety the developments of the grave crisis through which Europe has just passed. Throughout the whole period My Government in close accord with the French Government, made every endeavour both in Prague and in Berlin to ensure a lasting and peaceful settlement of the problem of the German minority in Czechoslovakia. Their efforts were ably assisted by a mission of investigation and mediation in Czechoslovakia, headed by Viscount Runciman.

In view of the increasing gravity of the crisis the Prime Minister on the 14th September decided to fly to Berchtesgaden in order to establish personal contact with the German Chancellor. This initiative was followed on the 22nd September by a further visit by the Prime Minister to Godesberg. At this stage the prospect of a peaceful settlement seemed almost to have vanished, but at the last moment the Prime Minister made a proposal to the German Chancellor for a Four-Power Conference. Signor Mussolini gave valuable support to the suggestion and on the 29th September the German Chancellor, the French President of the Council, the Head of the Italian Government and the Prime Minister met at Munich and came to an agreement. The settlement thus arrived at was accepted, with a dignity that has earned general admiration, by the Government and people of Czechoslovakia.

The cause of peace was powerfully aided by the timely action of the President of the United States of America. The desire of all peoples not to be drawn into war with one another is manifest and significant, and everywhere men and women share with Me, I am convinced, a feeling of deep thankfulness that the imminent peril was thus averted. I pray that, with the passing of this peril, a new era may have opened for Europe.

During this period of anxiety it became necessary to put into force certain measures, including the mobilisation of the Navy, the calling out of a considerable portion of the personnel of the auxiliary Forces and the initiation of certain precautions against air raids. All these arrangements were carried out with admirable promptitude. In every department of national life men and women alike came forward to serve their country. I was proud to observe the calmness and determination displayed by all My people and I thank them for their spirit of service.

In the spring of this year My Government concluded an Agreement with the Italian Government regulating a number of questions of mutual concern. My Ministers have now decided to bring that Agreement into full operation as soon as possible. They are confident that this decision will still further strengthen the good relations already existing between Italy and this country.

My Ministers have continued to participate in the work and deliberations of the League of Nations. They have taken the lead at the recent meeting of the Assembly in providing for the explicit recognition of the independent existence of the Covenant of the League, apart from the Treaties of Peace, and in securing a comprehensive and practical review of the obligations devolving on Members thereunder. It gave Me great pleasure to meet representatives of the Governing Body of the International Labour Organisation, which on the invitation of My Government, held their October meeting in London.

The civil war in Spain has continued to engage the earnest attention of My Ministers. They have maintained their efforts to make the international policy of non-intervention more effective and they have noted with satisfaction the recent decision of the Spanish Government to repatriate all its foreign combatants and the decision of the Administration at Burgos to dispense with a proportion of those on the other side.

I regret that the hostilities between China and Japan still continue with great loss of life to both combatants and with considerable damage to the rights and interests of third parties. I earnestly hope that this conflict will be brought to an early termination.

The cordial co-operation in matters of common interest between My Government and the Government of Egypt has been amply confirmed during the recent anxious months. Certain provisions of the Anglo-Egyptian Treaty of Alliance, the cost of which, owing to the increasing complexity of Military and Air Force requirements, was found likely greatly to exceed the original estimates, have been revised in a Protocol, the text of which has been laid before you. It is My confident hope that this revision will strengthen the sincere friendship between My Government and the Royal Egyptian Government and will expedite the important work of construction of barrack and other accommodation for My Forces.

It was with great satisfaction that I gave My assent to a Bill confirming certain Agreements with Eire. I welcome these Agreements, and I hope that they will promote closer co-operation and good feeling between the two countries.

I have been deeply distressed by the continuance and recent intensification of violence and lawlessness in Palestine, which have necessitated the despatch in the past few weeks of strong military reinforcements. The Technical Commission have now completed their labours, and their Report is being carefully studied by My Ministers.

The conditions prevailing in the West Indies have given Me concern, and I have appointed a Commission to visit certain of the Colonies in that area and to make recommendations with regard to the social and economic position in them.

Members of the House of Commons:

The continued strengthening of our defence has required additional taxation, which has been accepted as necessary by the country.

I thank you for the provision you have made for the Public Service.

My Lords and Members of the House of Commons:

Defence requirements have engaged the unremitting attention of My Ministers, and are being reviewed in the light of recent experience.

I have given My assent to a Measure requiring local authorities to prepare schemes of air-raid precautions for their areas. Such schemes are an essential part of the defence organisation of the country.

The development of the national health service has continued and steps have been taken with success to make those services more widely known and to encourage their use.

Active progress both in house building and in the clearance of the slums has been maintained and the abatement of overcrowding is proceeding. Acts have been passed amending the financial provision in England and Wales for slum clearance and for the abatement of overcrowding and making further provision for the improvement of agricultural housing.

My assent has also been given to Bills providing medical care for young persons who have left school and entered employment, reducing the age limit for the award of pensions to blind persons, enabling further information to be obtained for the study of the population problem and continuing, with modifications, for a further period the statutes relating to rent restrictions.

Acts have been passed amending the Unemployment Insurance Acts; regulating wages and conditions in their road haulage industry; enabling certain wage-fixing authorities to require the grant of holidays with pay; regulating the hours of employment of persons under the age of eighteen in certain previously unregulated occupations; and enabling officers in the Merchant Navy to assign part of their wages for the purpose of paying pensions contributions.

Measures have been enacted providing for the better organisation and development of the bacon and pig producing industries and for certain important matters relating to sea fisheries, including the re-organisation of the white fish industry, and the improvement of conditions in the herring fishing industry. An Act has also been passed continuing assistance to the dairy industry.

The administration of justice in the Supreme Court has had My careful consideration, and the numbers of the judges in the Probate Division of the High Court and the Court of Appeal have been increased. Greater facilities having been given for the appointment of legally qualified persons as chairmen of the Courts of Quarter Sessions, provision has been made for enlarging the jurisdiction of those Courts where the chairman is legally qualified.

Acts have been passed providing for the setting up of a Coal Commission to unify coal royalties under national control and to further the re-organisation of the coal mining industry; requiring local authorities throughout Great Britain to provide fire brigade services and containing various provisions for improving the fire brigade organisation of the country; and continuing the assistance afforded to the British film industry by previous legislation.

Progress in the improvement of housing conditions and of public health in Scotland has been maintained, and among the Bills relating to Scotland to which My assent has been given has been a Measure to facilitate the better housing of the agricultural population.

A number of other Measures of public utility have been added to the Statute Book.

FOURTH SESSION OF THE THIRTY-SEVENTH PARLIAMENT

1938–1939

OPENING (8 November 1938)

My Lords and Members of the House of Commons:

My relations with foreign Powers continue to be friendly, and My Government will do all in their power to promote the development of good understanding in the spirit of the joint Anglo-German declaration made at Munich on the 30th September last.

The agreement negotiated last April between My Government and the Italian Government will now shortly be brought into force. I believe that this action will confirm the traditional good relations, so happily and so long subsisting between our two countries, and thus further the cause of European peace.

I have invited the King of Roumania to visit Me this month and I look forward with pleasure to his stay in My capital.

I have also invited the President of the French Republic to visit Me in the spring of next year and I feel assured that this visit will cause great satisfaction to all My people.

The Queen and I are anticipating with the keenest pleasure the visit which We are hoping to pay to My Dominion of Canada next summer.

I have been happy to accept an invitation extended to The Queen and Myself by the President to visit the United States of America before the conclusion of My Canadian tour. I warmly welcome this practical expression of the good feeling that prevails between our countries.

My Ministers deeply regret the continuance of the hostilities in Spain. While adhering to the policy of non-intervention, they will lend their assistance in any way possible towards the restoration of peace in that country.

My Government will be ready at any time, if desired by the parties to the dispute in the Far East, to aid in reaching a settlement which will ensure lasting peace in that region. Meanwhile, My Ministers will do all in their power to safeguard British interests in the areas affected.

My Ministers will shortly lay before you the Report of the Palestine Commission and will make a statement of future policy.

Members of the House of Commons:

My Ministers have already arranged for an advance of £10 millions to be placed at the disposal of the Czechoslovak Government to meet urgent requirements, and legislation will be laid before you dealing with financial assistance to that Government.

The Estimates for the Public Services will be laid before you.

My Lords and Members of the House of Commons:

Although the equipment and expansion of My Defence Forces are now making rapid progress, the emergency through which we have passed has shown that certain deficiencies in our military and civil defence preparations remain to be remedied. My Ministers have reviewed these matters in the light of the experience gained, and will in due course take steps to accelerate and supplement the measures already in hand.

The problems of civil defence, including that of the effective utilisation of the resources of the nation for national voluntary service, will in future receive the undivided attention of a Minister, the Lord Privy Seal.

The active furtherance of peace in Europe, which is the constant aim of My Government, will, I trust, lead to a wider spirit of confidence and supply a fresh impulse for expansion in trade, industry and employment. My Ministers will persist in their efforts to establish favourable conditions for the development of oversea markets.

My Government will press forward with better housing, both urban and rural, and will proceed with the development of the educational services. They will vigorously continue the campaign for the improvement of the public health, and in particular will submit to you proposals for the earlier and more effective treatment of cancer.

The policy of My Government will continue to be directed to improving conditions in the Special Areas.

A Bill will be laid before you to amend the penal law dealing, in particular, with young offenders and those who commit repeated offences.

My Ministers recognise the important place which home agriculture must occupy in the national economy and defence. They will continue to promote by an active and constructive policy the economic development of the industry and the improvement of the conditions of those engaged in it. Measures will be laid before you to assist the production, improve the quality and increase the consumption of milk, to assist the poultry industry, and to effect certain amendments in the Wheat Act, 1932, including further reviews of the standard price of wheat.

The difficulties of the cotton industry are engaging the attention of My Ministers and proposals, which would require legislation, are before them. Among the Measures which you will be invited to pass will be Bills to prevent fraud in relation to investments; to amend the law relating to the carrying on of the business of insurance; to amend the Unemployment

Insurance Acts; and to raise the amount of the Miners' Welfare Levy, in order to provide additional funds for the building of pithead baths.

A Bill will be submitted to you for the purpose of re-organising Scottish administration, and centralising the Government Departments in Edinburgh. Further action will be taken to deal with slums and overcrowding in Scotland, and a Measure relating to the financial provision for this purpose will be submitted to you. You will also be invited to consider other Scottish Measures, including a Bill for the amendment of the marriage law.

Other legislative proposals will be laid before you and proceeded with as time and opportunity offer.

PROROGATION (23 November 1939)

My Lords and Members of the House of Commons:
The shadow of war has once more fallen over Europe.

Despite the efforts of My Government to preserve peace, Germany, in violation of her solemn undertakings, wantonly invaded Poland. This new instance of German aggression and bad faith was a challenge which we could not have declined without dishonour to ourselves and without peril to the cause of freedom and the progress of mankind.

We seek no material gain. Liberty and free institutions are our birthright which we, like our forefathers, are resolved to preserve.

Members of the House of Commons:
I thank you for your ready acceptance of the heavy financial burdens rendered necessary as a contribution towards meeting the severe expense of war. So prompt and ungrudging a response has deeply impressed the world and demonstrates the unflinching determination of My people to make every sacrifice necessary for victory.

My Lords and Members of the House of Commons:
The issue is clear. With united will My peoples here and overseas have dedicated themselves to the struggle. The spontaneous decision of My Dominions to participate in the conflict and the invaluable help which they are giving, and are about to give, to the common cause have been of the greatest encouragement to Me. With the aid of our faithful French and Polish allies we cannot doubt that our cause will prevail.

FIFTH SESSION OF THE THIRTY-SEVENTH PARLIAMENT

1939–1940

OPENING (28 November 1939)

My Lords and Members of the House of Commons:

The prosecution of the war commands the energies of all My subjects. My Dominions overseas are participating wholeheartedly and with an effectiveness which is most gratifying to Me.

Throughout the world My Navies, together with the Merchant Navy and Fishing Fleets, are keeping free and open the highways of the sea. At home, in France and in all stations overseas, My Armies and Air Forces are fulfilling their tasks. I am well assured that they will be equal to any efforts and sacrifices to which they may be called.

Members of the House of Commons:

You will be asked to make further financial provision for the conduct of the war.

My Lords and Members of the House of Commons:

Grave responsibilities rest upon you at this time. You will, I am convinced, express the resolution of the Nation.

The measures which will be submitted to you are such as seem necessary to My Advisers for the welfare of My people and the attainment of the purpose upon which all our efforts are set.

PROROGATION (20 November 1940)

My Lords and Members of the House of Commons:

For over a year My Forces by sea, land and air have been defending the cause of freedom. My people everywhere, enduring with fortitude in their homes and work places, and at sea, the brutal attacks of the enemy, have nobly sustained the common effort.

By calculated treachery and violence Germany has brought under her yoke many free nations devoted to the arts of peace. I have been happy to receive here the Governments of countries thus overrun. I rejoice that their armed forces, together with brave men of other nations, are now fighting side by side with My own.

In the early summer France, overtaken by military disaster, felt compelled to sue for terms of armistice. Taking advantage of French misfortunes Italy seized the opportunity to range herself with the aggressor and has now launched a wanton attack on Greece. I welcome in the struggle against tyranny a new comrade to whom My Empire will bring all possible aid. By her courageous resistance Greece is proving herself worthy of her glorious past.

My Forces in the Mediterranean are prepared to give a good account of themselves in all emergencies, and My country enjoys, in that region, the benefit of valued Treaties of alliance with Egypt and Turkey.

It was with gratification that I learnt of the decision of the Government of the United States to transfer fifty destroyers to My Navy, and I trust that the grant to that Government of defence facilities in certain territories on the Atlantic seaboard may equally serve to defend the heritage of free men.

Members of the House of Commons:

I thank you for the provision you have made towards the increasingly heavy costs of war. The readiness of My people to accept these burdens confirms Me in My belief that they will think no financial sacrifice too great to ensure the triumph of our cause.

My Lords and Members of the House of Commons:

I am glad that despite the heavy preoccupations of the war My Government have found it possible to promote various measures for improving social conditions in this country.

The frustration of German plans for the invasion of Britain, the attacks upon the sources of German military power, the firm defence of Egypt and the Sudan and the successful attack upon the Italian Navy give proof of our strength, and justify our confidence in final victory.

The present war is not only a struggle between nations. It springs from the clash of fundamental ideals. We shall not falter or lay aside our arms until the high purposes, to which we have pledged our faith, are achieved.

SIXTH SESSION OF THE THIRTY-SEVENTH PARLIAMENT

1940–1941

OPENING (21 November 1940)

My Lords and Members of the House of Commons:

My peoples and My Allies are united in their resolve to continue the fight against the aggressor nations until freedom is made secure. Then only can the nations, released from oppression and violence, again work together on a basis of ordered liberty and social justice.

I am confident that victory is assured, not only by the prowess of the Armed Forces of My Empire and of those of My Allies, but also by the devotion of the Civil Defence Forces and the tenacity and industry of My peoples. These are now enduring, where they live and labour, the perils as well as the hardships of war.

The staunchness of the men of the Merchant and Fishing Fleets has added lustre to the ancient traditions of the sea.

The resistance of My people has won the admiration of other friendly Powers. The relations of My Government with that of the United States of America could not be more cordial, and I learn, with the utmost satisfaction, of the ever-increasing volume of munitions of war which is arriving from that country. It is good to know in these fateful times how widely shared are the ideals of ordered freedom, of justice and security.

Members of the House of Commons:

You will be asked to make further financial provision for the conduct of the war.

My Lords and Members of the House of Commons:

Measures will be submitted to you for compensating those whose home or business property has, at any time since the outbreak of hostitlities, been destroyed or damaged by enemy attack, and for extending insurance against the risk of such damage to all forms of moveable property which are not at present protected.

Further proposals for legislation will also be made to improve the conditions of those who may now or in the future require assistance from public funds.

Apart from these and such other measures as may be required for the effective prosecution of the war, My Government will take every possible step to sustain the health and well-being of My people in their ordeal.

PROROGATION (11 November 1941)

My Lords and Members of the House of Commons:

My Peoples have entered upon the third year of war with heightened vigour and resolution. I have seen the courage and fortitude with which they have endured savage attacks from the air, and I have watched with admiration the selfless devotion of the Civil Defence Forces.

During the past year My Forces, by sea, land and air, have continued, with the powerful support of the Armed Forces of My Allies, to defend the cause of freedom throughout the world. The enemy has added to the number of countries temporarily over-run, but the epic struggle of Greece and Yugoslavia, worthy of their glorious history, has inspired the civilised world.

I heartily welcome as an Ally the great Union of Soviet Socialist Republics. On the 12th July My Government and the Government of the Soviet Union agreed to aid each other in the war against Germany and to conclude no separate armistice or treaty of peace. The heroic resistance of the armies of the Soviet Union has won My deepest admiration. A Conference on aid to Russia between representatives of My Government and of the Governments of the United States of America and the Union of Soviet Socialist Republics has been held in Moscow with eminently satisfactory results, and, in co-operation with the United States of America, My Empire is affording the Soviet Union all possible assistance against the common foe.

The life-time of this Parliament has been memorable for the strengthening of the already close ties between My Governments and Peoples and the Government and People of the United States of America. A striking illustration of this growing intimacy was afforded by the meeting at sea between The President of the United States and the Prime Minister of My Government in the United Kingdom. On the seas and the oceans, commanded by our two Navies in closest fraternity, a Charter was agreed upon and published to the world, which will stand as a beacon in history radiating resolution, justice and unselfish purpose.

My Navy has continued to attack the enemy wherever it has been able to find him. Aided by its Auxiliaries and the Fishing Fleet, it has maintained unceasing vigil and has kept open the seaways on which My gallant Merchant Navy, and the Merchant Fleets of My Allies, have brought an increasing flow of food-stuffs and munitions.

The position of My Forces in the Middle East has been greatly strengthened. The brilliant campaigns

in East Africa, where the enemy, despite great
numerical superiority, was evicted from the mountain
fastness of Eritrea and Ethiopia and either destroyed
or captured, prove the skill of My Commanders and
the endurance of My Forces from many parts of the
Empire. These operations, which augur well for the
future, were rendered possible by the annihilation last
winter of the hostile army which sought to invade
Egypt from Cyrenacica.

My Air Force has carried the war into the
enemy's territory and has attacked with growing
power his industries, communications, naval bases and
shipping. By the boldness of its assaults, it has
compelled the enemy to keep large air formations in
the West.

Developments in the Far East have engaged the
close and constant attention of My Government, and
it has been necessary to increase the Forces which
defend My territories in those regions.

It has been a source of great gratification to Me
that My Prime Ministers of Canada, the Commonwealth of Australia, and New Zealand have found it
possible to visit this country and confer with My
Ministers in the United Kingdom. Valuable discussions
have been held in Egypt with My Prime Minister of
the Union of South Africa. These personal exchanges
are of the utmost value to My Ministers in the
prosecution of the war.

Members of the House of Commons:

I thank you for the increased provision you
have made towards the cost of the war. The
unprecedented measures you have taken have been
whole-heartedly supported by My People, who have
willingly borne the heavy additional taxation imposed
upon them and have also freely responded to the call
for loans.

My Lords and Members of the House of Commons:

The War Damage Act for damage to property
caused by enemy action has afforded immediate relief
to many of My People, and the compensation which
it provides has further strengthened the war economy
of the country.

Under Providence, and thanks to the unexampled
efforts of the seafaring and farming communities, the
food supplies of My People are assured.

SEVENTH SESSION OF THE THIRTY-SEVENTH PARLIAMENT

1941–1942

OPENING (12 November 1941)

My Lords and Members of the House of Commons:

The developments of the past year have strengthened the resolution of My Peoples and of My Allies to prosecute this war against aggression until final victory. Meanwhile, My Government, in consultation with the Allied Governments, and with the goodwill of the Government of the United States of America, are considering the urgent problems which will face them when the nations now enduring the tyranny of the oppressor have regained their freedom.

I well know that My People will continue to respond wholeheartedly to the great demands made upon them to furnish My Forces with the instruments of victory, and that they are determined to meet, to the utmost of their power, the needs of the Soviet Union in its heroic conflict.

The United States are furnishing My Peoples and My Allies with war supplies of all kinds on a scale unexampled in history.

My relations with Turkey, with whom I have a valued treaty of alliance, remain firmly based on trust and friendship.

I welcome the restoration to his Throne of His Majesty the Emperor of Ethiopia. Thus, the first country which fell a victim to aggression has been the first to be liberated and re-established.

My loyal subjects in Malta continue to face air attack with a fortitude that commands My deepest admiration.

Members of the House of Commons:

You will be asked to make further financial provision for the conduct of the war.

My Lords and Members of the House of Commons:

The fulfilment of the task to which we are committed will call for the unsparing effort of every one of us. I am confident that My People will answer this call with the courage and devotion which our forefathers never failed to show when our country was in danger.

My Government will continue to take all practical steps to sustain the health and well-being of My People under the stress of war.

PROROGATION (10 November 1942)

My Lords and Members of the House of Commons:

During the past year the forces fighting for honour and freedom throughout the world have gained a most notable accession of strength. Japan's treacherous and unprovoked assault has spread the conflict of war throughout the Eastern Hemisphere; and has brought fresh danger to My peoples in Asia and in the Pacific. But this extension of the war has brought to our side, as comrades in arms, the United States of America, who had already long sustained the Allied Cause by their sympathy and material aid, and has also brought Me into a close alliance with the Republic of China, which has so long and so gallantly resisted the aggression of Japan.

I welcome too as Allies in the great battle for freedom those other American Republics which have joined the United Nations, and I am gratified that yet others have severed their diplomatic relations with the enemy Powers.

I share to the full the admiration of My people for the glorious feats of arms of the Soviet forces. In the defence of Stalingrad, which has been a hard blow struck at our enemies, a new chapter of heroism has been written in the annals of war. My Government and My people are determined to do their utmost to assist our Russian Allies, both by the supply of materials of war and by offensive action against the common foe.

On New Year's Day 1942 My Government signed a Joint Declaration endorsing the principles embodied in the Atlantic Charter and pledged themselves to devote, in common with their Allies, their full resources to the defeat of the Axis Powers. To-day a great company of nations are united in their determination to win victory; and their support gives to Me and to My people fresh encouragement in the struggle in which we have been engaged for more than three years.

The relations between My peoples and those of the United States of America are becoming ever closer. Since this Parliament was opened, My Prime Minister in the United Kingdom has twice crossed the Atlantic to visit Washington and Ottawa, and the generous welcome extended to him both in Canada and by the President and the people of the United States of America, has afforded Me and My people the greatest pleasure. The work of the Combined Staff and the Combined Boards established in Washington and London has already gone far to perfect the mutual assistance between the two countries and to make more effective the organisation of our common offensive against the enemy.

We have enjoyed with profound satisfaction the privilege of welcoming Mrs. Roosevelt among us. I welcome, too, the presence in this country in such large numbers of the soldiers, sailors and airmen of our American Allies, a happy augury of the great offensive strength which they are building up in their own country.

On the 26th May I concluded with the Presidium of the Supreme Council of the Union of Soviet Socialist Republics a new Treaty of Alliance in the war against Hitlerite Germany and her associates in Europe. This Treaty also provides for post-war collaboration with the Soviet Union and for mutual assistance against aggression.

The welcome visit of the Soviet People's Commissar for Foreign Affairs to this country and to the United States of America, following on the visit of My Foreign Secretary to Moscow, together with the visit of My Prime Minister of the United Kingdom accompanied by a special envoy of President Roosevelt to Mr. Stalin in August last, provided an opportunity for far-reaching discussions on the general conduct of the war by the three Allies.

My Government in the United Kingdom have offered to the Chinese Government a Treaty for the relinquishment of extra-territorial jurisdiction in China. The close collaboration of the Government of the United States of America in this matter will be a source of special satisfaction to My people. The offer of this Treaty is an earnest of the close and equal collaboration which I am confident will regulate My relations with My valued Chinese Ally in the future. I am glad that in these difficult times for the Chinese people you have been able to send a delegation of your members to Chungking to assure them of the goodwill and determined support which My peoples will always give them.

It has been a great pleasure to me to welcome to this country My Prime Minister of the Union of South Africa. His participation at this time in the discussions and decisions of My Government here will prove of great value. Many other of My Ministers and counsellors have also come to this country during the year from My Dominions and from India for the purpose of conferring with My Government here. The cordial friendship existing between all My Governments has been a great factor in forwarding the war effort of all My people.

My Government in the United Kingdom have declared to the Princes and peoples of India their desire to see India assume full freedom and independence within the British Commonwealth of Nations on the basis of a Constitution framed by Indians themselves immediately after the termination of hostilities. In the meantime, representative Indian political leaders were invited to co-operate fully in the government of their country and in the prosecution of the war. I regret profoundly that hitherto they have not been willing to accept this offer. I sincerely hope that wiser counsels may prevail, and that a speedy and successful solution to these difficulties may be brought about through a wider measure of agreement amongst the Indian peoples themselves.

All My peoples have met with courage and endurance the increasing calls upon their services both for the armed forces and for the great production industries. Particularly remarkable during the last year has been the response of the great numbers of women who have entered the Services and civil employment and who in both spheres have shown a high degree of skill and devotion in their work.

The extension of the war to the Far East created fresh and grave problems of profound concern to My peoples in Australia and New Zealand, as well as to the whole of my Indian Empire. At the outset heavy reverses were sustained by the Allies. I have watched with increasing confidence the steady growth of the Allied strength and the resumption of the offensive by United States and Australian forces.

I have followed with a sympathy and admiration which I know is shared by my peoples throughout the Commonwealth the magnificent fortitude shown by the Island of Malta in resisting the strongest attacks which the enemy could bring to bear upon it. I was happy to award the George Cross to this gallant Island which, by its long continued bravery and resistance, has played so noble a part in the battles of the Middle East.

My Navy has been compelled by the extension of the war and the growth of the U-boat and air menace to shipping to extend its protection over an ever-widening area of the oceans. Aided by its auxiliaries and by the fishing fleet, it has succeeded, thanks to the bravery and endurance of My officers and men, in what might well have seemed an impossible task. My gallant merchant seamen and the merchant seamen of the United Nations have shown steadfast courage and determination in maintaining a flow of supplies through all the perils of sea and air to our Soviet Allies, to our forces in the Mediterranean and to other theatres of war, while at the same time maintaining the essential supplies of food and raw materials to this country.

The Eighth Army in the Middle East, with the devoted support of units of the Royal Air Force and the Royal Navy, has dealt a crushing blow at the Axis forces in the Western Desert. This famous victory, in which forces of the Dominions, of India and of the Allies have all played a notable part, is now driving the enemy from Egypt. In conjunction with these operations, powerful United States and British forces, under United States command, supported by units of the Royal Navy and Royal Air Force, have landed in French North Africa in order to forestall an enemy occupation of these territories and to preserve them for France.

Throughout the year the training and preparation of My Army has gone forward. Those officers and men who are compelled to remain in this country are playing an important role both in our defence and in the preparation for attack. Upon them and upon their high morale we shall depend for our victory in the future.

My Indian Army is growing in strength month by month, and has displayed its historic valour upon many fields of battle. We are proud that more than a million men have already voluntarily engaged in our Indian land, sea and air forces; and we place our full confidence in their courage and fortitude in the days of struggle that lie before them.

My Air Force has added fresh achievements to its already famous record. It dominates the air over this Island and over the North of France. In every encounter it has proved its ascendancy over our enemies. In close co-operation with My Navy and My Army it has taken an increasing part in our campaigns, both by sea and by land in all theatres of war. Over Malta and Egypt it has inflicted heavy defeats on the air forces of the enemy; and it has carried the offensive with ever-increasing weight and strength into Germany and Italy, devastating their factories and disrupting their transport.

The strength of My Armed Forces in the Dominions is continually increasing, and they have shown by sea, land and air the courage and resolution in the face of the common enemy.

In their encounters with the enemy, My Navy, Army and Air Force have fought side by side with the Allied Forces; both those of the United States, now gathering its strength month by month, and those of My other Allies, undaunted by the overrunning of their homelands.

In those countries now occupied by the enemy Powers and subjected to every form of oppression, starvation and savagery, the ever-growing tide of resistance brings courage and inspiration to all who are determined to see freedom established in the world. It is the firm and unchangeable purpose of My peoples and of our Allies, not only to defend the cause of freedom wherever it may be attacked, but to carry the war into enemy territory so that we may liberate as speedily as lies in our power those countries and peoples now under a hateful domination.

You have carried on your task through times of difficulty and of stress as Members of a free Parliament and, by your unswerving determination to maintain those free institutions which have been built up in this our country, you have given an example to all the world of the value and strength of our Democracy.

Members of the House of Commons:

I thank you for the provision that you have made towards the cost of the war. The enormous expenditure which is necessary to carry the war to a successful conclusion continues to be met by the efforts of My people both by way of taxation and by their readiness to put their savings at the disposal of the State.

My Lords and Members of the House of Commons:

Once again, thanks to the great efforts of the whole agricultural community and of our seamen, the food supplies essential for My people have been assured.

My assent has been given to an Act making possible an increased degree of mobilisation of the man and woman power of the country. Almost the entire man and woman power of our country is now mobilised, and we must rely upon the constant and continuous drive for efficiency and economy in manpower and material to increase the production of arms and supplies which are essential if My Armed Forces are to be victorious over the enemy.

EIGHTH SESSION OF THE THIRTY-SEVENTH PARLIAMENT

1942–1943

OPENING (11 November 1942)

My Lords and Members of the House of Commons:

In this fourth year of war My Peoples look forward with unshakable courage. They are determined to fight on to complete victory, with no thought of parley. Whatever the future may hold, I know that they will respond wholeheartedly to every new demand made upon them.

I look with gratitude and pride upon the great and ever-growing war effort of My loyal Subjects throughout the Empire. Their comradeship and unity in war will be an inspiration and source of power in the years to come.

In the last few days Providence has blessed our arms and those of our American Allies. The brilliant victory in the Western Desert, and the great operation forestalling the attack of our enemies upon the French territories in Northern Africa, are notable steps towards final victory.

My Forces by sea, land and air continue to meet with courage and devotion the calls which the extension of the war has made upon their resources. Aided by the powerful support of the Armed Forces of My Allies and sustained by the growing output of our munition factories, they are now bringing an increasing weight of attack against the enemy.

The declaration of the United Nations endorsing the principles of the Atlantic Charter provides a foundation on which international society can be rebuilt after the war. As a first step My Government have entered into consultation with the Governments of the United Nations in preparation for the urgent needs which will arise when the victims of oppression regain their freedom. When the time comes, these tasks will, I am confident, be faced with the same spirit of comradeship and resolution as has been shown in the war.

My Government desire to do their utmost to raise the standards and to improve the conditions of My Peoples in the Colonies, who are playing their full part in the united war effort.

Members of the House of Commons:

You will be asked to make further financial provision for the conduct of the war and for the other necessary services.

My Lords and Members of the House of Commons:

My Government's first concern must be to seek and secure the means of achieving complete and speedy victory; and they will put before you such proposals for emergency legislation as may be necessary for the effective prosecution of the war or for meeting conditions arising out of the war. You will be asked to pass legislation with respect to war damage suffered by public utility undertakings.

A start has, however, been made in working out the measures which will be necessary when peace comes. My Government have already received and are examining Reports upon compensation and betterment in respect of public control of the use of land and upon land utilisation in rural areas. Renewed consideration will be given to the position of Old Age and Widowed Pensioners and further measures will be laid before you.

Conversations are taking place between My Ministers and others concerned with the provision and conduct of education in England and Wales with a view to reaching an understanding upon the improvements necessary. My Ministers hope that these discussions will result in such a wide measure of agreement being reached that further progress can be made with plans for the better education of My people. The system of education in Scotland is also under review.

My Ministers will continue to take all measures open to them to promote the health and well-being of My people in war-time by securing the better care of young children, by the prevention of disease, by the treatment of the sick and by the alleviation wherever possible of the housing difficulties consequent upon the war.

Our enemies yet remain powerful and we can look forward to no easy task. All our fortitude and all our determination will be needed to win through to victory. But I know that nothing will shake your purpose or cause your steps to falter on the way.

PROROGATION (23 November 1943)

My Lords and Members of the House of Commons:

During the past year My peoples and those of My Allies have been brought, by God's providence, to a turning point in their unceasing fight for freedom. The mounting strength of the United Nations has enabled them to wrest the initiative from the enemy and to take the offensive in all parts of the world.

Our common purpose has been furthered by an ever closer co-operation between the United Nations —above all between My Governments and those of our Allies in the United States and the Soviet Union.

My Prime Minister has three times met in conference the President of the United States. The Foreign Secretary has recently returned from concerting with M. Molotov and Mr. Cordell Hull plans for the joint conduct of the war and for a united approach to the problems of the transition from war to peace. It is a matter for gratification that the Chinese Government associated themselves with one of the more important instruments resulting from that Conference. The results of this most fruitful meeting in Moscow have brought new hope to all who look to a speedy victory over our enemies and a just and enduring peace. I rejoice in the warmth of the reception accorded to My Ministers in Washington and Moscow and in the historic city of Quebec in My Dominion of Canada.

In the various theatres of war throughout the world My Navy, Army and Air Force have fought in close and continuous fellowship with their comrades from My Dominions and India and My Colonial Empire, and with the forces of the United States and My other Allies. Their united efforts have produced solid and striking achievements in every theatre of war.

The dangerous attack of the U-boats has been largely broken by our Navies and Air Forces, whose continued success rejoices all our hearts. Their task will be notably eased by the facilities granted by My oldest Ally, Portugal, in her Atlantic islands. Over Germany itself our Air Forces are striking increasingly heavy blows at the heart of the enemy, in the face of the most desperate opposition. Throughout Europe a mounting tide of resistance is rising against the oppressor.

In the Mediterranean resounding victories have been won. The enemy has been driven from the soil of Africa; Sicily, Sardinia and Corsica have been liberated; the Italian fleet is in our hands; one-third of Italy has been occupied; and My troops and those of the United States confront the foe on the mainland of Europe. The Italian people's repudiation of their false leader and their readiness to strike against their German oppressors have shaken the guilty confederacy of our enemies to its foundation.

It was a special pleasure to Me to visit My Navies, Armies and Air Forces in the midst of these memorable operations and Myself to witness their courage and ardour.

I continue with My people to watch with admiration the increasing successes of the armies of our heroic Russian Allies, and rejoice with them in the liberation of great regions from the ravages of our common foe.

In the Far East the advance of the enemy has been halted and the offensive of the United Nations has begun. I trust that this may soon bring some relief to our Chinese Allies, whose long struggle against the Japanese invader has inspired our deepest sympathy. In South-East Asia a new Command has been created and new Commanders appointed. In the Western Pacific freedom has already been restored to some of the islands which were overrun by the enemy. I look forward to the day when we shall, with God's help, restore to all My peoples the blessings of peace and progress.

These successful operations in all theatres of war have been sustained and supplied by the untiring efforts of the men and women working in the industries and services essential to the prosecution of the war—in the great manufacturing industries, in agriculture, in the mines, and in transport by land and by sea. For the third successive year we have been blessed with a bounteous harvest.

The splendid courage and determination of My merchant seamen and those of the United Nations, and of the men of the fishing fleets, with the untiring aid of the minesweepers, have continued to assure the flow of supplies essential to the prosecution of the war and to the life of My peoples.

I have also watched with pride the fortitude and endurance shown by those whose duties, though no less necessary, are less directly concerned with the activites of war—the women at home, so many of whom combine their domestic duties with other work, and the men and women working in the industries supplying the essential civil needs of My people.

The perseverance and industry of My people in the United Kingdom has been emulated by My peoples in My Dominions and Colonial territories and in India. I trust that the special hardships which the war has lately brought to many among My Indian subjects will be relieved; and that the steps My Government have already taken will assist the Governments in India in relieving the grave shortage of food in certain areas of India.

The unity of My peoples with those of My Allies has continued to hearten our friends and confound our enemies. Once again we have had the advantage of the wise counsel of My Prime Minister of the Union of South Africa; and several of My Ministers from other Dominions have also been able to visit us, with beneficial results. The Secretary of State for Dominion Affairs has visited My Dominion of Canada and Newfoundland; and the Secretary of State for the Colonies has recently returned from a visit to My territories in East and West Africa. We have been happy to welcome here many distinguished members of the United States Administration.

Matters of great import for the future of the United Nations and of freedom-loving peoples everywhere have been considered at international discussions; and My Ministers here have welcomed the opportunity of exploratory conversations on the future of civil air transport with representatives from My Commonwealth and Empire.

The Treaty for the abolition of extra-territorial rights has been successfully concluded with My Chinese Ally. In the summer we had the pleasure of welcoming Dr. T.V. Soong, the Chinese Minister for

Foreign Affairs, on a brief visit, which unhappily was overshadowed by the death of the Chinese President, Dr. Lin Sen.

My Government have welcomed the establishment of the French Committee of National Liberation at Algiers, and have recognised it as the body qualified to ensure the conduct of the French effort in the war within the framework of inter-Allied co-operation. We look forward to the liberation of France and her restoration to the ranks of the Great Powers.

Members of the House of Commons:

I thank you for the provision that you have made towards the cost of the war. The ready support given by My people to the measures you have adopted has ensured that the very heavy expenditure required by the war has been met with due regard to the social and economic interests of My country.

My Lords and Members of the House of Commons:

It is a matter of especial satisfaction to the Queen and Myself that Parliament has complied with My request that the Regency Act should be so amended as to enable Our beloved daughter Princess Elizabeth, when she attains the age of eighteen, to serve as one of the Counsellors of State should occasion arise for their appointment.

I have given My Assent to a number of measures which have been brought before you during the course of the year. These have included Acts providing for the reorganisation of My Foreign Service, for strengthening public control over the planning of town and country, and for the development of hydro-electric power in Scotland. Legislation has been passed to introduce a new system of taxation of wages and salaries, which will be of substantial convenience to all employees, particularly those whose earnings are liable to fluctuation. An Act has been passed to facilitate electoral registration under war conditions. Provision has been made for the development of the catering trades and for regulating the conditions of employment in those trades, for improving the administration of pensions, and for further temporary increases in the rates of workmen's compensation.

Steps have also been taken to establish machinery for dealing with questions of wages and conditions in the coal-mining industry.

My Government have taken the necessary action to ratify the International Labour Conventions concerning the Regulation of Written Contracts of Employment of Indigenous Workers and Penal Sanctions for Breaches of Contracts of Employment by Indigenous Workers.

NINTH SESSION OF THE THIRTY-SEVENTH PARLIAMENT

1943–1944

OPENING (24 November 1943)

My Lords and Members of the House of Commons:

In the fourth year of war the Forces of the United Nations assumed the offensive in all theatres of war. The enemy has been cast out of Africa; freedom has been brought to Sicily, Sardinia and Corsica; and in Italy My Forces and those of My American Ally are now engaging the enemy on the mainland of Europe. On his eastern front the enemy has given ground before the massive and unrelenting advance of the Russian Armies, whose magnificent achievements we have watched with ever-deepening admiration. The captive peoples of Europe are everywhere preparing to throw off the yoke of the oppressor; and we shall continue to afford them such help and encouragement as lies in our power. On the frontier of India and in the Pacific, Japanese aggression has been halted, and the Forces of the United Nations are now moving to the offensive. At sea My Navies and those of our Allies continue to maintain their mastery over the enemy, and important successes have been won in the struggle against the enemy's U-boats. The Air Forces of the United Nations have maintained their ascendancy in all theatres of war, and have increased the weight of their blows at the enemy's heart.

The mounting scale of our offensive is the fruit of the devoted and untiring efforts of My peoples throughout the Commonwealth and Empire; and in the coming year we shall, with God's help, be able to bring to bear upon the enemy a still greater weight of attack. With the growing help of our great American Ally, and together with the other United Nations, we shall go forward with confidence in our cause until we have delivered the peoples of the world from the fear of the aggressor.

My Government, taking counsel with My Allies and building upon the foundations laid at the recent Conference in Moscow, will devote continuous attention to the study of plans for the future settlement of Europe.

Members of the House of Commons:

You will be asked to make further financial provision for the conduct of the war and for the other necessary services.

My Lords and Members of the House of Commons:

My Government will continue to concentrate their powers and energies upon the prosecution of the war; and, until final victory is won, that will be their primary task. You will be invited to pass such further legislation as may be necessary to provide for the needs of the war and to meet abnormal conditions arising from the war.

At the same time My Ministers are resolved that, so far as the future can be foreseen, they shall be ready to meet the different tasks that await them when victory has been won. They have undertaken a special review of the problems which are likely to arise as hostilities in Europe come to an end and of the adjustments which will have to be made when we turn to prosecute with fresh vigour the war against Japan; and in the months to come My Ministers will complete their provisional plans for the period of transition through which we must pass before the troubled times of war give place to settled conditions of peace. It will be the primary aim of My Government to ensure that in this period food, homes and employment are provided for My people, that good progress is made with the rebuilding of our damaged cities, and that in industry, mining, and agriculture a smooth transition is made from war to peace. For some of these purposes fresh powers will be needed; and, as the preparations proceed, proposals for the necessary legislation will be laid before you. You will, in the immediate future, be asked to make provision for the training and employment of disabled persons, and to amend the law regarding the reinstatement in their civil employment of persons discharged from the Armed Forces.

In certain fields it is already possible to look beyond the transitional period and to frame proposals for social reforms designed to confer lasting benefits on My people.

A measure embodying My Government's proposals for the reconstruction of the national system of education in England and Wales will be laid before you. An Advisory Council is now preparing reports which are expected to form the basis for educational developments in Scotland.

My Ministers will present to you their views and proposals regarding an enlarged and unified system of social insurance, a comprehensive health service and a new scheme of workmen's compensation; and they will decide, in the light of your discussions, what specific proposals for legislation on these matters can be brought forward at this stage.

You will be invited to pass legislation conferring special powers for the re-development of areas which, by reason of enemy action, over-crowding or otherwise, need to be re-planned as a whole.

My Government will lay before you the results of their examination of the Reports which have been made recommending the assumption of further powers to control and direct the use of the land of Great Britain.

It is the desire of My Government that full consideration should be given to various proposals which have been put forward for changes in the existing franchise law, and you will be invited to give your early attention to this question.

My Ministers will maintain and develop the measures for promoting the health and well-being of My people which, by God's providence, have been so successful during the past four years of war.

PROROGATION (28 November 1944)

My Lords and Members of the House of Commons:

The past year has seen the intensification of the efforts of My peoples and of those of My Allies to free the world from German and Japanese oppression and we are now reaping the reward of the long years of endurance and preparation that have gone before.

The victories achieved are the fruits of the close friendship which knits together My Governments and those of My Allies—a friendship fostered by the meetings between Allied leaders which have played such a notable part in the furtherance of our common purpose.

Within the Commonwealth and Empire the ties that unite My peoples were further strengthened by the meetings in London at which the Prime Ministers of My Dominions, the Prime Minister of Southern Rhodesia and representatives of My Empire of India conferred with the Prime Minister of the United Kingdom. The declaration which they issued at the conclusion of their meetings expressed the common resolve of My peoples to devote their whole energies towards victory in the struggle in which we are engaged.

In the wider sphere, the meeting at Teheran, where for the first time the leaders of the United States and of the Soviet Union met in joint conference with My Prime Minister, settled the co-ordinated strategy which has unfolded itself in the past year. In Cairo My Prime Minister and the President of the United States were able to confer with the leader of the Chinese people. And this autumn My Prime Minister has undertaken further arduous journeys, to Quebec to concert with the President of the United States plans for the conduct of the war in the Far East, and to Moscow to co-ordinate with Marshal Stalin plans for achieving the final downfall of Hitlerite Germany and to review with him the problems of Europe. More recently he has paid, at the invitation of the President of the French Provisional Government, a visit to Paris, which has demonstrated afresh the cordial friendship which unites the French and British peoples. In all these visits he has been assisted by the presence of My Foreign Secretary.

In the theatres of war throughout the world, the Forces of all My peoples have continued to fight in close comradeship with the gallant Forces of the United States and My other Allies.

My Forces from the United Kingdom and from Canada, with their comrades from the United States, successfully launched the long-prepared assault on the shores of Western Europe, established a foothold in the face of determined opposition, and, after destroying the German armies which opposed them have advanced through France and Belgium to the gates of Germany.

Never before in our history has a single enterprise so completely absorbed the energies of the whole nation. Military success has been rendered possible only by the devotion with which the Home Guard, the Civil Defence Services and the Active Air Defences of Great Britain have fulfilled their task of guarding this island base on which the whole undertaking in Western Europe depends.

In the Mediterranean, maintaining the advance which began at El Alamein, the Forces of the United Nations have by hard and determined fighting driven the enemy from Rome and reached the Northern plains of Italy.

In Burma, My Fourteenth Army, including African Colonial Forces and aided by the Forces of the United States and China, has turned the attempted Japanese invasion of India into a disastrous retreat. In this campaign My Indian Forces have contributed brilliantly to the defence of their country.

In all these victories My Air Forces, fighting in the closest association with the Allied Air Forces, have played a conspicuous part. They have everywhere engaged the enemy with confidence and courage and their sustained and gallant attacks in Western Europe, in co-operation with the Air Forces of the United States, opened the way for the successful invasion of the Continent.

My Navies have been heavily and continuously engaged throughout the world. In conjunction with My Air Forces they have gained great successes against those enemy submarines and surface craft which have dared to show themselves. They secured the safe passage of the vast invasion convoys for the assault on the shores of Western Europe and they continue to maintain the flow of supplies to My Armies as well as to ensure the safe and timely arrival of the food and material on which the life and work of the nation depends. This would not have been accomplished without the spendid bravery of our merchant seamen and those of the United Nations and Denmark.

It has given Me particular pleasure to have been able to visit units of all My Forces both in Western Europe and in the Mediterranean.

Resounding victories have continued to reward

·the skill and valour of My Russian Allies, whose advances have carried them into Eastern Germany and brought to an end the German domination of South-Eastern Europe.

In the Pacific theatre of war the Forces of the United States, valiantly supported by Australian and New Zealand Forces, have rapidly advanced across vast spaces of the ocean and have broken into the outer defences of Japan.

The victories achieved and the successful invasion of the Continent have been made possible by the tireless effort and inventive genius of all those who have planned, produced and transported the manifold types of equipment and munitions of war for My Forces and who have maintained the services essential to the prosecution of the war. Our farmers and agricultural workers and the courageous men of the fishing fleets have toiled without respite to provide food for My people, and, in the Forces, in trade amd industry, in voluntary service and in the home, women have continued to make their invaluable contribution towards victory.

The civil population and the Police, Fire and Civil Defence Services have again shown those qualities of courage and fortitude which earned the admiration of the world in 1940 and 1941. The sympathies of the Queen and Myself extend to all those who have suffered as a result of the enemy's attacks, and We are thankful that the advance of the Allied Forces on the Continent has put an end to the shelling of the south-east coast and reduced the enemy's capacity to launch attacks by flying-bombs and long-range rockets.

I rejoice at the freeing of the territory of France, Belgium, Luxembourg, Greece and Yugoslavia, and our sympathy goes out to the Dutch people in their present ordeal. It is My earnest hope that before long deliverance will have come to the whole of occupied Europe.

In every occupied country the enemy has been increasingly harassed by the resistance of the oppressed peoples and I have watched with warm admiration the great part which the French Forces of the Interior have played in ridding their country of the invader.

My Government have welcomed the establishment in France of a Provisional Government, which will govern the country in accordance with the laws of the Republic until general elections can be held. My Government have also been glad to join with the Government of the United States of America and the Government of the Soviet Union in inviting the Provisional Government of France to appoint a representative to join as a full and permanent member in the important work of the European Advisory Commission in London.

It is our earnest desire to promote peaceful co-operation among the nations of the world, and to this end important conversations have been held with officials of the United States, the Soviet Union and the Republic of China which have resulted in the submission to each of the four Governments concerned of agreed suggestions for the formation of an international organisation designed to maintain peace and security.

My Government were represented at the twenty-sixth session of the International Labour Conference, at the second council meeting of the United Nations Relief and Rehabilitation Administration and at the United Nations Monetary and Financial Conference.

My Government have concluded an agreement with the Governments of other maritime United Nations, ensuring through a United Maritime Authority that their combined shipping resources shall continue to be available for the prosecution of the war in Europe and the Far East and for all the purposes of the United Nations.

The need for an enlightened international settlement under which civil air transport will flourish as an aid to prosperity and peace continues to engage the attentions of My Ministers. Further discussions have been held with representatives from other parts of My Commonwealth and Empire, and the Minister for Civil Aviation has headed a delegation to an international conference convened by the United States of America.

Members of the House of Commons:

I thank you for the provision which you have made towards the cost of the war. The heavy financial sacrifices which My people have continued to make during the fifth year of the war have been an essential and outstanding factor in our war effort.

My Lords and Members of the House of Commons:

Although the successful prosecution of the war has been first in the thoughts of My Government and people, progress has been made with plans for the resettlement of the men and women who during the war have been employed in the various forms of national service, and for the reconversion of industry from war production to the production of goods for the needs of My people and for export.

I have given My Assent to a number of Measures which have been brought before you during the course of the year.

A comprehensive Act has been passed to reform the law relating to education in England and Wales in all its aspects, and to secure its progressive development at all stages. This Measure will open new opportunities to the individual, and will secure to the future service of the community the fullest advantage from the resources inherent in the national character and capacity.

Measures have been passed to provide for the rehabilitation and re-entry into employment of disabled persons and for the reinstatement in the civil employment of men and women in the Services;

to facilitate the building of houses; to improve water
supply and sewerage in rural areas; to assist the herring
industry, and to provide for the redevelopment of
war damaged and obsolescent areas and regulate the
price of acquisition of land for public purposes.

Legislation has also been passed to establish a
Ministry of National Insurance; to increase the rates
of unemployment insurance benefit, and so set up
permanent machinery for the redistribution of
Parliamentary constituencies and provide for an
immediate redistribution of abnormally large
constituencies.

My Government have outlined the policy which
they propose to follow with a view to the maintenance
of a high and stable level of employment after the
war. They have also published for examination and
discussion proposals for a national health service, for
a comprehensive system of national insurance and a
new scheme of industrial injury insurance, and for a
national water policy.

TENTH SESSION OF THE THIRTY-SEVENTH PARLIAMENT

1944–1945

OPENING (29 November 1944)

My Lords and Members of the House of Commons:

The United Nations look back on a year of resounding achievement. They now look forward with greater confidence than ever to those final victories which will give to the peoples of the world the just peace which is our chief desire. In Western Europe My Forces from the United Kingdom and Canada and their comrades from the United States, with the valuable aid of the Armed Forces of My European Allies and of the peoples who have risen to meet them, have routed the enemy in a series of decisive battles and are now pressing him on the borders of his own country. In Italy the Forces of the United Nations have advanced to the northern plains and in Greece and Yugoslavia the Germans are being driven from the countries which they have oppressed for three bitter years. In the East the massive achievements of My Russian Ally have deprived the Germans of vast stretches of territory which they hoped would feed their armies and provide an impassable barrier to prevent the soil of Germany from becoming a battle-ground. Both in the East and in the West, Germany is invaded. The plight in which her armies now find themselves is a measure of the success which by God's grace has crowned our arms.

In the war against Japan, the enemy has been thrown back from India and My American Ally continues to reduce the shrinking area still under Japanese control in the Pacific. We intend to reinforce as rapidly and powerfully as possible the United Kingdom Forces who are now sharing with their comrades from all parts of the British Commonwealth and Empire and from the United States, China, the Netherlands and France the burden of the struggle against Japan.

My Navies everywhere have maintained their mastery over the enemy and have achieved great successes, in which My Air Forces have fully shared, in driving his surface and submarine forces from the seas. My Air Forces, in concert with the Air Forces of the United States, have delivered increasingly heavy blows against Germany and have maintained their support of military and naval operations in all theatres.

The success of My Armed Forces would not have been achieved but for the devoted labours of those throughout the Commonwealth and Empire who have striven ceaselessly to arm and equip them. It is over five years now since My peoples first took up the struggle to free the world from aggression and the contribution of the civil population is beyond all praise.

The United Nations await with sober confidence the unrolling of future events. Joined in an unbreakable alliance and fortified by constant collaboration between the Governments concerned and by frequent personal meetings between their leaders, they look forward to that day on which the aggressor is finally defeated and the whole world can turn to the rebuilding of prosperity and the maintenance of an unassailable peace.

Members of the House of Commons:

You will be asked to make further financial provision for the conduct of the war and for the other necessary services.

My Lords and Members of the House of Commons:

Victory remains our supreme aim and to this end you will be invited to pass such further legislation as may be required for the effective prosecution of the war.

Once, however, the war in Europe is over, the transition from war to peace will begin; and My Ministers are actively preparing plans to ensure that, without in any way prejudicing the active prosecution of the war against Japan, an increasing part of our resources is made available for civilian production. They will try to create conditions favourable to the expansion of our export trade and the re-equipment of our industry and to maintain a high level of food production at home. They are considering the methods by which the policy for the maintenance of a high level of employment can be implemented, especially with regard to the distribution of industry in the Development Areas. Progress will be made in fulfilling the urgent tasks of providing additional housing accommodation and of increasing supplies of civilian goods. My Ministers will continue their policy of ensuring a fair distribution of the necessaries of life so long as there is any scarcity.

My Government intend that, as opportunity serves, progress should be made with legislation arising out of the proposals already made public for a comprehensive health service, an enlarged and unified scheme of national insurance, a new scheme of industrial injury insurance and a system of family allowances. They will also invite you to approve measures embodying proposals for a national water policy which have already been presented to you.

A Bill will be laid before you dealing with electoral reform based on the recommendations of Mr. Speaker's Conference, and a Bill providing for the resumption of local elections at the appropriate time. You will be invited to pass measures relating to the provision of finance for the capital expenditure which local authorities will incur after the end of hostilities in Europe and proposals for the adjustment of local government areas in England and Wales will also be laid before you.

You will be asked to approve legislation designed to extend export credit facilities and to conserve, subject to appropriate safeguards, the use or value of assets created at the public expense on requisitioned and other land.

Measures will also be laid before you making further provision for the regulation of wages and conditions of employment and for the development of the public educational system in Scotland.

There will be presented to you legislation making further provision for assistance towards the development of the Colonial Empire both by prolonging the period covered by the Colonial Development and Welfare Act of 1940 and by substantially increasing the provision of funds authorised to be made under that Act.

PROROGATION (15 June 1945)

My Lords and Members of the House of Commons:

The present Parliamentary session, which I am now bringing to a close, has seen the final overthrow and unconditional surrender of our enemies in Europe. Their leaders, almost without exception, are either dead by their own hand or held in Allied custody. At last, after more than five years of mortal strife, Europe is liberated from the foul tyranny that threatened to enslave it. This deliverance is due not only to the resolution with which My people in these islands have carried on the struggle, but also to the stalwart aid so freely given by the peoples and governments of My Commonwealth and Empire overseas, to the splendid Armies, Fleets and Air Forces of the United States and the vast supplies which they have afforded, and to the heroic deeds of the Forces of much-suffering Russia. I must also express My deep admiration for the exertions of all those other Allies who fought by our side on sea, land and in the air and of the resistance of their peoples, now happily restored to their former independence. So persistent, so wide-spread and so united a co-operation of States to rescue European freedom from a hideous menace has never before been seen in the history of the world. I, with all My peoples, take pride in the thought that it was we who stood alone to face the foe in the darkest days, and who now share in the common triumph.

It has given the Queen and Myself particular pleasure to have been able to visit My loyal subjects in the Channel Islands; and I rejoice that they, who suffered so long under the German invader, are once more free.

I have already had an opportunity in replying to your loyal Addresses of Congratulation, to pay tribute to all that has been done by My peoples, whether in the Armed Forces or in any of the other forms of national endeavour. It is a wonderful record of constancy, faith and courage in every part of our national life and a striking manifestation of the historic character and quality of the British people.

My thoughts have been constantly with the peoples of the Commonwealth and Empire whose lands still suffer from the tyrannous Japanese occupation and with all others who have experienced the same calamity. The resounding victory gained in Burma and the swift advances made in the Pacific by the powerful Forces of the United States, who, together with Forces from these islands and from Australia, New Zealand and other parts of My Dominions, are closing in on Japan, have brought nearer their liberation. Though heavy labours and tribulations may still lie ahead, the downfall of our enemy in Europe enables us to bend all our energies to the task, which we shall share with our Allies, of crushing the aggressor in the Far East.

The grievous sacrifices which My peoples and My gallant Allies have had to bear in these long years of war will not have been in vain if they lead to the establishment of a new world order based upon justice and respect for human rights, and equipped to crush any future attempt to disturb the peace of the world. At San Francisco My Ministers have striven to further the framing of an international organisation by which future generations may be spared from the horrors of war.

My Government have authorised the Governor-General of India to invite the participation of Indian political leaders in the Government of British India. I earnestly hope that this invitation will be accepted, so that the immediate tasks of the waging of the war against Japan and the post-war development of India may be undertaken with the full co-operation of all sections of Indian public opinion.

I have assented with great satisfaction to the Colonial Development and Welfare (Amendment) Act, which both substantially increases the amount of money to be made available to assist colonial development and prolongs the period of assistance. The resources so provided will be of the greatest help to Colonial Governments in those plans which they are now preparing to improve the conditions and standards of living of the people in their territories.

Members of the House of Commons:

I thank you for the provision which you have made towards the heavy cost of conducting the war and the cost of the public services.

My Lords and Members of the House of Commons:

Plans have been completed for the orderly release of men and women from the Armed Forces under a scheme which ensures fair treatment to serving men and women, and there has been a recent relaxation of the control over the employment of labour. Much progress has also been made with the arrangements for training men and women released from the Forces or from industrial war work and for compensating and resettling those who are disabled as a result of their service.

Steps have been taken, in close co-operation with the Governments of the United States, Canada and other Dominions to overcome the grave shortages in world supplies of many essential foods. These shortages make yet more necessary the vigorous and sustained efforts of the agricultural community and the men of the fishing fleets in providing food for My people.

The destruction of our homes by the enemy and the urgent need to concentrate our man-power for nearly six years on tasks directly connected with the prosecution of the war have led to a widespread shortage of houses. Energetic measures have already been taken to restore houses damaged by enemy attack and to prepare housing sites, and the maximum effort is being devoted to the production and erection of new houses. To this end arrangements have been made to augment the number of those available for house building both by special releases of building workers from other industries and from the Armed Forces and by the training of new recruits for the building industry.

I have given My assent to a number of measures which have been brought before you during the course of the year.

Legislation has been passed to provide for a scheme of family allowances, in which the families of serving men will be included. A measure has been passed to assist employers and workpeople in securing the wider observance of jointly agreed terms and conditions of employment and in maintaining reasonable standards of remuneration. A much needed reform has been effected in the law concerning contributory negligence. Henceforward a claimant who proves that his injury is due to another's fault will not fail to secure some compensation merely because a certain degree of fault is attributable to him. Among the Bills relating to Scotland which have received My assent is a measure to amend the law relating to education and to introduce reforms which will promote the progressive development of the educational system.

Provision has been made for the resumption of local elections, and reforms have been made in the law relating to the representation of the people. Effect has been given to the Report of the Boundary Commission for England regarding the division of abnormally large constituencies.

Measures have been passed to finance capital expenditure incurred by local authorities; to assist the improvement and equipment of modern industry by the reform of the income tax law; to extend export credit facilities; to maintain the use or value of assets created at the public expense on requisitioned or other land, and to provide for the maintenance of employment by a better distribution of industry.

Legislation has been passed to transfer to the Agricultural Ministers responsibility for forestry, with a view to promoting schemes of intensive afforestation; for continuing the functions of the Minister of Fuel and Power; and for the appointment of a Minister of Civil Aviation.

I have also given My assent to measures for the adjustment of local government areas in England and Wales; for the conservation of water resources and the better organisation of water supplies, and for the re-development of war damaged and obsolescent areas and the regulation of the price at which land can be acquired for public purposes in Scotland.

FIRST SESSION OF THE THIRTY-EIGHTH PARLIAMENT

1945–1946

OPENING (15 August 1945)

My Lords and Members of the House of Commons:

The surrender of Japan has brought to an end six years of warfare which have caused untold loss and misery to the world. In this hour of deliverance, it is fitting that we should give humble and solemn thanks to God by whose grace we have been brought to final victory. My Armed Forces from every part of My Commonwealth and Empire have fought with steady courage and endurance. To them as well as to all others who have borne their share in bringing about this great victory and to all our Allies our gratitude is due. We remember especially at this time those who have laid down their lives in the fight for freedom.

It is the firm purpose of My Government to work in the closest co-operation with the Governments of My Dominions and in concert with all peace-loving peoples to attain a world of freedom, peace and social justice so that the sacrifices of the war shall not have been in vain. To this end they are determined to promote throughout the world conditions under which all countries may face with confidence the urgent tasks of reconstruction, and to carry out in this country those policies which have received the approval of My people.

At Berlin My Ministers, in conference with the President of the United States and Premier Stalin, have laid the foundations on which the peoples of Europe, after the long nightmare of war, may restore their shattered lands. I welcome the establishment of the Council of Foreign Ministers which will shortly hold its first meeting in London and will continue the work begun at Berlin in preparation for a final peace settlement.

My Ministers will submit to you the Charter of the United Nations which has now been signed without reservation by the representatives of all the fifty States who took part in the Conference at San Francisco and which expresses the determination of the United Nations to maintain peace in accordance with justice and respect for human rights and to promote the welfare of all peoples by international co-operation. The devastating new weapon which science has now placed in the hands of humanity should bring home to all the lesson that the nations of the world must abolish recourse to war or perish by mutual destruction.

It has given Me special pleasure to meet the President of the United States on his brief visit to My Country after the Conference at Berlin. I have also been glad to express the gratitude of this country to the Supreme Commander of the Allied Expeditionary Force for his inspiring leadership in the campaign for the liberation of Europe..

My Forces in Europe continue to discharge the duties entailed in the occupation of enemy countries and the repatriation of the many thousands of persons who were deported from their homes by the enemy. My Navy, aided by the Navies of My Allies, is clearing the seas of mines so that merchant ships and fishing fleets may once more sail in safety.

In the Far East My Ministers will make it their most immediate concern to ensure that all prisoners in Japanese hands are cared for and returned to their homes with all speed. The bringing of relief to those who have suffered under Japanese tyranny and the disarmament and control of the enemy will continue to impose heavy demands on My Forces.

Members of the House of Commons:

You will be asked to make further financial provision, not, happily, for the continuance of the war, but for expenditure on reconstruction and other essential services.

My Lords and Members of the House of Commons:

My Government will continue the orderly release of men and women from the Armed Forces on the basis of the plans announced in the autumn of last year and will take every step to secure that these plans are carried out with the greatest speed consistent with our military commitments and fair treatment to serving men and women. The arrangements already in operation for the resettlement in civil life of men and women released from the Forces and from war work, including those who have been disabled during their service, will be continued and, where necessary, expanded.

The continuing shortages in the supply of many necessaries, especially houses, food, clothing and fuel, will call for the same spirit of tolerance and understanding which the nation has displayed during the six years of war.

It will be the aim of My Ministers to see that the national resources in labour and material are employed with the fullest efficiency in the interests of all and that the standard of living is progressively improved. In the pursuit of this aim the special problems of Scotland and Wales will have the attention of My Ministers.

My Government will take up with energy the tasks of reconverting industry from the purposes of war to those of peace, of expanding our export trade and of securing by suitable control or by an extension of public ownership that our industries and services shall make their maximum contribution to the national well-being. The orderly solution of these difficult problems will require from all My people efforts comparable in intensity and public spirit to those which have brought us victory in war.

In order to promote employment and national development machinery will be set up to provide for the effective planning of investment and a measure will be laid before you to bring the Bank of England under public ownership. A Bill will also be laid before you to nationalise the coal-mining industry as part of a concerted plan for the co-ordination of the fuel and power industries.

Legislation will be submitted to you to ensure that during the period of transition from war to peace there are available such powers as are necessary to secure the right use of our commercial and industrial resources and the distribution at fair prices of essential supplies and services.

An urgent and vital task of My Ministers will be to increase by all practicable means the number of homes available both in town and country. Accordingly they will organise the resources of the building and manufacturing industries in the most effective way to meet the housing and other essential building requirements of the nation. They will also lay before you proposals to deal with the problems of compensation and betterment in relation to town and country planning, to improve the procedure for the aquisition of land for public purposes, and otherwise to promote the best use of land in the national interest.

You will be asked to approve measures to provide a comprehensive scheme of insurance against industrial injuries, to extend and improve the existing scheme of social insurance and to establish a national health service. Legislation will be introduced to repeal the Trade Disputes and Trade Unions Act.

My Ministers will develop to the fullest possible extent the home production of good food. To this end they will continue, with suitable adaptations, those war-time policies under which food production has been organised and the efficiency of agriculture improved, and will take all necessary steps to promote a healthy fishing industry. The ravages of war have made world food supplies insufficient to meet demands, but My Ministers will do all in their power to provide and distribute food to My peoples at prices which they can afford to pay; and they will keep in being and extend the new food services for the workers and for mothers and children which have been established during the war.

A measure will be laid before you for the reorganisation of air transport.

It will be the aim of My Ministers to bring into practical effect at the earliest possible date the educational reforms which have already been approved.

My Government will continue to work in close consultation with the other Members of My Commonwealth on all matters of mutual concern.

In accordance with the promises already made to My Indian peoples, My Government will do their utmost to promote in conjunction with the leaders of Indian opinion the early realisation of full self-government in India.

They will also press on with the development of My Colonial Empire and the welfare of its peoples.

PROROGATION (6 November 1946)

My Lords and Members of the House of Commons:
When I opened this Session, the first of a new Parliament, there was in all our hearts a deep thankfulness to Almighty God for our deliverance from the war and an urgent desire to do everything in our power to repair the ravages which it had caused, both at home and abroad. A notable beginning has been made with this task.

My Government have taken a leading part in formulating treaties of peace with Italy, Roumania, Bulgaria, Hungary and Finland. The conference of My Allies convened in Paris to consider the draft treaties and to submit recommendations on them to the Council of Foreign Ministers has concluded its labours. I have welcomed the thorough discussion which has given an opportunity for a full expression of views by My Dominion Governments and My many gallant Allies and has enabled the general belief to be expressed that the treaties should be based not on vengence but on justice. I hope that these peace treaties will soon be signed and will substantially contribute to the rehabilitation of a devastated continent.

It gave Me great pleasure to welcome to this country the delegates to the inaugural session of the General Assembly of the United Nations. My Government have given every possible help and support to the United Nations Organisation, its Economic and Social Council and Security Council, and the many international bodies which are to be associated with it. Representatives of the United Kingdom have shared fully in the work of the International Labour Organisation.

My Government have accepted membership of the International Monetary Fund and the International Bank for Reconstruction and Development, and it is My hope that these institutions will help to bring greater security and a better standard of life to the peoples of the world. It is a source of gratification to Me that the

Chancellor of the Exchequer has been selected as Chairman for the coming year of the Board of Governors of the Fund and of the Bank.

Financial agreements have been concluded with the Government of the United States and with My Government in Canada, under which substantial credits have been extended to My Government to assist them in overcoming the difficulties of transition from war and in moving towards a freer and more stable system of international trade. Important economic agreements have also been made with various countries.

In defeated Germany and also in Austria My Forces of occupation and civil authorities, co-operating with those of My Allies, have continued to carry out with great devotion and diligence the tasks of restoring ordered government, repatriating displaced persons, preventing famine and disease, and finally eliminating Nazism. I welcome the progress which has been made towards the restoration of the freedom and independence of Austria and the close co-operation which is being established with My United States Allies as a step towards the treatment of Germany as an economic whole; and I trust that it may be possible to lighten the heavy financial burden which the present state of Germany imposes on the people of the United Kingdom.

The trial of major German war criminals at Nuremberg has been carried through with dignity and impartiality, and in full accordance with the best judicial traditions. The proceedings were a signal example of inter-Allied co-operation and the principles laid down by the Court, which represent an important development in international law, will, I earnestly hope, prove a lasting deterrent against aggression.

One of the first concerns of My Government on the surrender of Japan was the repatriation of all My subjects who had been held captive by the Japanese. We give thanks to Almighty God for their safe return after their many sufferings.

In Japan British Commonwealth Forces are making their contribution towards the work which is being undertaken under the direction of the Supreme Commander of the Allied Powers for the restoration of a peaceful and productive way of life in that country.

In other parts of the world My Forces are playing their part in helping a return to the conditions of peace; and many members of them have been engaged, both overseas and at home, on the difficult and dangerous task of mine clearance.

It gave Me special pleasure to welcome the Prime Ministers and other Ministers of the self-governing members of the British Commonwealth to this country in April and May for discussions with My Ministers in the United Kingdom on many important matters. These discussions contributed greatly to the elucidation of many problems and to a mutual understanding of the issues involved. Discussions have also taken place in London with representatives of other parts of the Commonwealth on other matters of common concern, including scientific collaboration and commercial policy.

My Government have given their most earnest attention to the affairs of India, where changes of unparalled importance are taking place. The visit of three of My Ministers to India earlier this year has resulted in the election of a Constituent Assembly to frame a constitution for India on the basis of the statement made by My Government on the 16th May last. Provision has also been made for associating the Indian States with this work.

Pending the completion of the work of the Constituent Assembly, an Interim Government has been formed which is representative of all important elements in British India. I pray that India will prosper under their guidance and will achieve through the deliberations of the Constituent Assembly that freedom which it has long been the policy of My Ministers and Parliament to promote.

In Burma the Governor has reconstituted his Executive Council on a broader basis and with a wider authority which will enable the principal political parties to make their contribution to the economic and political reconstruction of their country.

In Newfoundland a National Convention has been elected to make recommendations with a view to a subsequent referendum as to the future form of the Government of the Island, and it is My earnest hope that they will be successful in achieving their object.

I have made an Order in Council providing for a new constitution in Ceylon under which responsibility for the internal affairs of the island will pass to a Parliament of Ceylon. I congratulate My people in Ceylon on this achievement and extend to them My best wishes for the future.

During the past Session the territories of North Borneo and Sarawak have come under My sovereignty. I have been glad to extend a warm welcome to their inhabitants and to assure them that it will be the constant care of My Government to promote their welfare.

Members of the House of Commons:

I thank you for the provision which you have made for expenditure on reconstruction and other public services.

My Lords and Members of the House of Commons:

Despite the heavy responsibilities of My Armed Forces, no fewer than four million men and women have been released from them since June, 1945. During the same period the transfer of two and a half million workers from war to peace-time production has been smoothly effected without giving rise to any large measure of unemployment in the in the country as a whole. Good progress has also been made with the rehabilitation of disabled persons and their resettlement in employment.

The Merchant Navy is rapidly returning to its normal peace-time tasks and My Government have taken part in an International Labour Conference designed to secure improvements in the conditions of employment of merchant seamen.

Controls imposed during the war over labour, materials and other resources have been relaxed, wherever the removal of restrictions could be carried out without damage to the national interest; and arrangements have been made for regular consultation with a National Joint Advisory Council, representing organisations of employers and workers.

At home there has been an increasing flow of consumer goods and a substantial advance has been made towards that great increase in exports which is necessary to secure and pay for the imports of raw materials and other commodities which we need from abroad. The Exhibition of Industrial Design which I opened in September is an impressive sign of the achievements of our manufacturers and designers.

In the face of a continuing and most serious world shortage of food My Ministers have been concerned to maintain the essential supplies of My peoples and also, so far as lies in their power, to help in preventing the spread of famine overseas. In accordance with the policy of ensuring that the necessaries of life are fairly distributed, My Government have been obliged to continue, and even to extend, the rationing of the main foodstuffs.

Farmers and agricultural workers have made great efforts to maintain a high level of food production in the United Kingdom. They have had to contend with exceptionally adverse weather conditions during the harvest months and My sympathy goes out to them in the difficulties which they have had to face.

The repair of war damage to schools and colleges and the return of teachers from war service have helped towards the rebuilding of our educational service. Improved arrangements for granting assistance to students at Universities will make it easier for young men and women to continue their education. Milk has been made available free for all attending school; and facilities for children to have meals at school are still increasing rapidly. The provision of milk and vitamin supplements for mothers and young children has also been continued with good results.

The financial credit of My Government has been fully maintained. In the course of the Session rates of interest for both short-term and long-term borrowing have been substantially reduced. This policy has lightened the burden of the national debt and has assisted the financing of capital expenditure on reconstruction incurred by My Government and by local authorities.

I have given My assent to a large number oi important measures during the Session.

A measure has been passed to nationalise the coal-mining industry. Thereby it has become possible to set in hand the reorganisation of this great industry which is one of the foundations of our country's strength and prosperity.

I have also given My assent to legislation to nationalise the Bank of England, to regulate the borrowing and the raising of money and the issue of securities, to enable guarantees to be given for loans for industrial reconstruction or development, and to substitute cupro-nickel for silver in the coinage.

Provision has been made for a national health service in England and Wales; for the creation of a national scheme of insurance against industrial injuries in place of the present system of workmen's compensation, and for the expansion and improvement of the existing schemes of social insurance. A system of family allowances and the higher rates of old age pension under the new social insurance scheme have been brought into operation.

I have given My assent to legislation to finance the production of houses by My Government and to subsidise house building by local authorities. I have also assented to a measure to control the rents of furnished houses.

Legislation has been passed to improve the procedure for the acquisition of land for public purposes and to provide for the creation of new towns to help in securing a properly balanced distribution of the the population.

Acts have been passed to improve the efficiency of the police services, to increase the productive capacity of hill farming areas and to assist fishermen in obtaining boats and gear for the white fishing industry.

I have assented to legislation to secure the development of air transport services under public control, to bring overseas telegraph and wireless services under public ownership, and to facilitate the provision of nationally owned airports.

A measure has been passed to promote and control the development of atomic energy.

My Government have welcomed the proposal of the Pilgrims Society to erect in the gardens of Grosvenor Square a memorial to that great and far-sighted statesmen, the late President Roosevelt, and by a measure to which I have given My assent they have undertaken the duty of maintaining the statue and the gardens.

SECOND SESSION OF THE THIRTY-EIGHTH PARLIAMENT

1946–1947

OPENING (12 November 1946)

My Lords and Members of the House of Commons:

During the Session that lies before you My Government will seek by all means in their power to promote the well-being of My people and to enable the nation, by its example and leadership, to play a worthy part in the advance of all nations of the world towards greater freedom and prosperity.

My Ministers will shortly meet representatives of the United States, Russia and France to discuss the future of Germany. It will be their aim to establish in Germany conditions which will foster true democracy, will guarantee the world against further attempts at world domination, and will remove the financial burden which the occupation has laid on My people.

I trust that at an early date a treaty will be concluded with Austria which will enable all forces of occupation to be withdrawn from that country.

The control of Japan and the measures taken to bring about a stable and just settlement in the Far East will remain the concern of My Ministers.

The General Assembly of the United Nations has resumed in New York the session begun in London last January. It will be the policy of My Government to share fully both in these discussions and in the meetings of those other international bodies which have been created to foster mutual help and understanding among the nations of the world.

I earnestly hope that the preparatory work for an International Conference on Trade and Employment which is now proceeding in London will lay the foundations for an increase in international trade over a wide area and for the maintenance of a high and stable level of employment in all the countries of the world. My Government will use every endeavour to bring these and wider international discussions to a successful conclusion.

My Ministers will continue to develop the existing intimate understanding and close working relations between this country and the self-governing members of the British Commonwealth.

My Government will forward by every means at their disposal the policy with regard to the goverance of India laid down in the statements made by them and by the Mission of My Ministers which recently visited India.

Steps are being taken to hold elections in Burma early next year, as the necessary preliminary to further constitutional progress.

In the territories for which My Government are responsible they will seek actively to promote the welfare of My peoples, to develop the economic life of the territories and to give My peoples all practical guidance in their march to self-government.

The Queen and I are looking forward with the greatest pleasure to the visit which We propose to pay to South Africa next year.

Members of the House of Commons:

Estimates for the public services will be laid before you in due course.

My Lords and Members of the House of Commons:

My Government will press on with the conversion of the national economy from war to peace and will endeavour to ensure that the resources of the nation are effectively employed for the common good.

It will be an urgent task of My Ministers to encourage an increase in the productivity of industry and so to secure the greatly increased flow of both consumer and capital goods needed for the raising of the standard of living of My people and the expansion of the export trade. In particular, My Ministers will, in fostering the growth of industry, continue to pay special attention to the needs of the development areas.

My Ministers recognise the urgent need for securing an adequate flow of volunteers for the Regular Forces, and their efforts to stimulate recruitment will be intensified. The reconstitution of the Territorial and Reserve Forces will be begun at an early date and My Government will bring forward a measure providing for the continuation of national service from the date when the present transitional scheme comes to an end.

My Ministers will do all in their power to increase the supply and variety of food and to see that it is efficiently and equitably distributed. They will also prosecute with the utmost vigour the task of providing suitable homes for My people, and will seek to ensure that those most in need of it have first claim on new accommodation. They recognise that the housewives of the nation have had to bear a specially heavy burden owing to the shortages of houses, of food-stuffs and of other consumer goods. It will be their constant endeavour to alleviate the hardships and inconveniences caused by this legacy from the years of war.

All necessary action is being taken to enable the school-leaving age to be raised in April of next year.

A measure will be laid before you to bring inland transport services under national ownership and control; and you will be asked to approve proposals to deal with compensation and betterment in relation to town and country planning and otherwise to improve the machinery of planning.

A Bill will also be submitted to you to bring into national ownership the electricity supply industry as a further part of a concerted plan for the co-ordination of the fuel and power industries.

Valuable reports have already been received from working parties appointed to make recommendations for the better organisation of a number of important industries, and you will be asked to approve legislation to enable effect to be given to their recommendations.

A measure dealing with exchange control will be placed before you, and you will be asked to approve legislation to provide for the amendment of the Companies Act and for the establishment of a commission to purchase, import and distribute raw cotton.

Proposals will be laid before you to give effect to the plans prepared by My Ministers for the efficient development of agriculture in this country, based on the system of guaranteed prices and assured markets for the principal farm products, and to give permanent effect to the transfer of wage-fixing powers from the local agricultural wages committees to the central Wages Boards.

Legislation will be submitted to you to provide for the establishment of a comprehensive health service in Scotland, and to consolidate, with amendments, the local government law of Scotland.

You will be asked to approve a Bill to provide for the establishment of a Ministry of Defence.

Measures will be laid before you providing for the arrangements consequent upon the termination of the National Fire Service and for empowering local authorities to operate civic restaurants.

A Bill will be introduced to give effect to the Convention on International Civil Aviation, signed at Chicago on the 7th December, 1944.

Other measures will be laid before you if time permits.

PROROGATION (20 October 1947)

My Lords and Members of the House of Commons:
During the Session which is now concluding substantial progress has been made in the work of reconstruction, but the economic difficulties resulting from the war, both at home and abroad, have presented My Ministers with serious problems and have required continuing efforts and sacrifices by My people. To enable My Ministers to deal rapidly and effectively with these problems, a measure has been enacted extending the purposes for which emergency powers can be used, and a new organisation for

economic planning has been established. In order to secure a redistribution of labour to assist those industries which are essential to economic recovery, My Government have reintroduced a measure of control over the engagement of labour, supported by some limited use of the power of direction of workers.

My Ministers have given unremitting attention to the serious deficit in the overseas balance of payments and to the continuing need to stimulate exports and limit imports. In order to protect our reserves of gold and foreign exchange, it has been necessary temporarily to suspend the convertibility of sterling. My Government have been fully aware that our own difficulties cannot be overcome except in conjunction with other Governments. They have, therefore, warmly welcomed the initiative of the United States in seeking to promote joint action by the Governments of the European nations to increase production and extend international trade, and they have given this initiative their strongest backing.

My Government have contined to give full support to the United Nations in the task of promoting international understanding and co-operation. They have played a leading part in establishing the Trusteeship Council and have continued to share fully in the deliberations of the Economic and Social Council, the International Labour Organisation, the Food and Agriculture Organisation and other specialised agencies. They have also put forward proposals for defining and safeguarding the fundamental liberties which it is the right of all peoples to enjoy.

A Treaty of Alliance has been concluded with the Government of the French Republic.

My Ministers have persisted in their efforts to establish true democracy in Germany, and they have approved the establishment of popularly elected regional Governments in the British Zone and encouraged a gradual transfer of powers to the German people.

Treaties of Peace with Italy, Roumania, Bulgaria, Hungary and Finland have been signed and brought into force, and My Government have consequently resumed diplomatic relations with those countries. The technical state of war between the United Kingdom and Austria has been terminated and diplomatic relations have been resumed between the two countries.

The Queen and I were deeply moved by the warmth of the welcome which We received throughout Our visit to South Africa, and will always treasure the happiest memories of Our journey.

It is with very great pleasure that I have given My consent to the engagement of My beloved daughter, Princess Elizabeth, to Lieutenant Philip Mountbatten, R.N.

Ministers from the United Kingdom have attended a Conference of Ministers and other representatives of My several Governments held in

Canberra at the invitation of My Government in the Commonwealth of Australia. This Conference resulted in a valuable exchange of views of problems likely to arise in the drawing up of a Peace Treaty with Japan.

In July I assented to the Indian Independence Act under which on 15th August two new Dominions, India and Pakistan, came into being. Thus was brought to fruition the declared policy of Parliament that the peoples of British India should achieve complete autonomy within the British Commonwealth. I trust that the most cordial relations will rule between India and Pakistan and the other members of the British Commonwealth.

The relationship which had so long subsisted between the Crown and the Ruling Princes of India has inevitably also changed. I acknowledge with gratitude the loyalty and devotion of the Indian Rulers to Myself and to My Royal predecessors and I hope that in association with India or Pakistan their ties with the Commonwealth will endure.

I remember gratefully the services of all those men and women who have served the Crown in India and all those who have given their best in the service of the peoples of India; particularly I am mindful of the faithful and gallant services of the men of My Indian Forces in time of war.

I am grieved at the grave disorders now occurring in India and Pakistan. My sympathy goes out to the Governments and peoples of both Dominions in their present troubles and especially to the refugees seeking new homes.

It gives Me much pleasure to record that self-government in internal affairs has been restored to Malta, that gallant island whose signal contribution to the common cause in the late war has been a source of ·pride to us all.

Delegates chosen by the legislatures of My possessions in the Caribbean have discussed the question of the closer association of those territories. I am confident that this conference will contribute to the progress and well-being of My peoples in this valued section of the British community of nations.

My Government have referred the question of the future status of Palestine to the United Nations, whose recommendations are now awaited as the result of the present discussions in the Assembly. Meanwhile they have made it clear that, in the absence of a settlement, they must plan for an early withdrawal of British Forces and of the British Administration from Palestine.

At the invitation of My Government in the United Kingdom, a conference of representatives of British Commonwealth Governments in the sterling area has been held in London to discuss questions of common interest arising out of the general financial situation.

My Government have taken an active part in the discussions preparatory to an International Conference on Trade and Employment. I hope that these efforts will assist the expansion of international trade and will create world conditions favouring its further expansion and the maintenance of a high and stable level of employment in all countries.

Members of the House of Commons:

I thank you for the provision which you have made for the public services.

My Lords and Members of the House of Commons:

I have assented to legislation setting up a Ministry of Defence charged with ensuring the formulation and general application of a unified policy relating to the Armed Forces and their requirements.

In many parts of the world My Forces continue to make their contribution to the maintenance of order and the restoration of peaceful conditions; their devotion to duty and the forbearance displayed in many difficult and trying circumstances are deserving of the highest praise.

Despite the responsibilities of My Forces overseas and the many tasks at home arising from the aftermath of war, the progress of demobilisation has brought the total number of men and women released from them since June, 1945, to about four and three-quarter millions. The resettlement in civil life of those released has been continued with success.

The National Service Acts have been amended to provide for the continuation of national service for a further period of five years from 31st December, 1948.

The exceptionally severe winter weather, followed by unprecedented floods, inflicted grievous damage on agriculture. In order to mitigate the losses sustained, My Government contributed to the Lord Mayor's National Flood Distress Fund and to the Agricultural Disaster Fund, and a measure was passed to provide special assistance to farmers cropping abnormally flooded land and rebuilding depleted flocks.

My Ministers are acutely aware of the distress caused by the housing shortage. They have continued to regard the provision of houses as a matter of the utmost urgency and have made substantial progress with their programme.

Steps have been taken to provide the additional teachers and the accommodation required as a result of the raising of the school-leaving age, and facilities for enabling promising students to obtain university and advanced education have been increased. The Universities are responding readily to the demand for an expansion of their activities and they have been aided by largely increased grants from the Exchequer.

My Ministers have devoted continuous attention to the development of industry in Scotland and Wales in order to provide increased opportunities for employment. New industrial projects have been started, substanial progress has been made in the diversification of industry, and a large programme of afforestation is proceeding. Scottish hydro-electric schemes have been advanced and an Advisory Panel for the Highlands has been set up. Special attention has been given to improving the Government machinery for the consideration of Welsh problems.

Measures have been passed for the better organisation of inland transport services under public ownership and control, for the co-ordination of the electricity supply industry under public ownership, and for continuing the centralised buying of cotton.

I have given My assent to legislation making fresh provision both in England and Wales and in Scotland for planning and controlling the development and use of land.

Bills have been passed into law to promote the stability and long-term development of agriculture in England and Wales, to extend the powers of the central agricultural wages boards, and to enable land to be dedicated permanently to forestry purposes.

I have assented to legislation providing for exchange control, for a far-reaching measure of company law reform, for the establishment of development councils with a view to increasing efficiency and output in industry, and for the collection of statistics showing the use made of the nation's resources and the changing structure of its economy.

A measure has been passed to amend the law relating to civil proceedings by and against the Crown.

My assent has also been given to legislation providing for the arrangements consequent on the termination of the National Fire Service.

Provision has been made for a National Health Service in Scotland and legislation has been passed consolidating the law relating to the constitution and general administration of local authorities in Scotland.

THIRD SESSION OF THE THIRTY-EIGHTH PARLIAMENT

1947–1948

OPENING (21 October 1947)

My Lords and Members of the House of Commons:

In the Session which opens today the nation is faced with grave economic difficulties affecting almost the entire world. Upon their successful solution depends the well-being of My people. My Government are determined to use every means in their power to overcome these difficulties.

I am confident that in these times of hardship My people will demonstrate once again to the world their qualities of resolution and energy. With sustained effort this nation will continue to play its full part in leading the world back to prosperity and freedom.

The first aim of My Ministers will be to redress the adverse balance of payments, particularly by expanding exports. This will demand increased production and the sale abroad of a larger share of output. The task to be performed by each industry has been set out and, in conjunction with all those engaged in industry, My Government will do their best to provide the means to carry out these tasks.

My Ministers will give all possible help to those who work on the land in order to increase still more the home production of food. Legislation will be introduced to provide for the improvement and development of Scottish agriculture so that Scotland may play its full part in the campaign for higher production.

With a view to increasing exports and saving imports which can be replaced by home products, steps will be taken to ensure that man-power is used to the best national advantage, and, in particular, to expand the numbers employed in the coal-mining, agricultural and textile industries. The working of the reimposed labour controls will be watched closely and My Government will take measures to bring into essential work those who are making no contribution to the national well-being. They will also encourage in every way the close joint consultation in industry which is necessary if the greatest volume of production is to be secured.

My Government will continue to devote their earnest attention to securing from overseas the essential foodstuffs and raw materials for My people. They will do all in their power to find new sources of supply and they will seek to enter into further long-term agreements with overseas countries. A measure will be laid before you designed to promote the expansion of production of all kinds within the Empire.

My Government will continue to participate in the work of European reconstruction put in hand in the recent conference in Paris and will do their utmost to forward the projects formulated at that meeting for the benefit of Europe and of the world as a whole.

The present obstacles to co-operation and understanding between the peoples of the world have strengthened the determination of My Government to support the United Nations and to seek by that means to promote the mutual trust and tolerance on which peaceful progress depends.

It is My earnest hope that the forthcoming conference of Foreign Ministers will result in a measure of agreement leading towards a democratic and self-supporting Germany which will not threaten world security, and to the satisfactory settlement of the international status of Austria.

I trust that a Treaty of Peace with Japan, which will contribute to the welfare of all countries in the Far East, may be concluded at an early date.

A measure will be laid before you to enable the future governance of Burma to be in accordance with the free decision of the elected representatives of its people.

I hope that the discussions now in progress will enable legislation to be laid before you to confer on Ceylon fully responsible status within the British Commonwealth.

Members of the House of Commons:

Estimates for the public services will be laid before you in due course, and you will be asked to approve supplementary financial measures at an early stage of the session.

My Lords and Members of the House of Commons:

My Ministers will accelerate the release of men and women from the Armed Forces to the maximum extent consistent with the adequate fulfilment of the tasks falling to the Forces:

They will press on with the reorganisation of the Forces on their peace-time basis and the task of obtaining the necessary voluntary recruits to build up the Regular Forces and the Auxiliary Services.

Legislation will be introduced to amend the Parliament Act, 1911.

A Bill will be laid before you to reform the administration of criminal justice in England and Wales.

You will be asked to approve legislation to abolish the poor law and to provide a comprehensive system of assistance for all in need. This will complete the all-embracing scheme of social security, the main lines of which have been laid down in measures already enacted.

A Bill will be laid before you to bring the gas industry under public ownership in completion of the plan for the co-ordination of the fuel and power industries.

A measure will be laid before you to extend the scope of public care of children deprived of a normal home life and to secure improved standards of care for such children.

Legislation will be introduced to provide a new and more equitable basis for the distribution of general Exchequer grants to local authorities. Provision will also be made for centralising the machinery of valuation for rating purposes and amending the law as to the valuation of small dwellinghouses in England and Wales.

You will be asked to approve a measure to reform the franchise and electoral procedure and to give appropriate effect to recommendations of the Commissioners appointed to consider the distribution of Parliamentary seats.

A Bill will be laid before you to enable a common national status to be maintained throughout the Commonwealth and to amend the existing law governing the national status of married women.

You will be asked to approve a measure for the establishment of river boards to take over from existing authorities certain responsibilities for land drainage, fisheries, and the prevention of pollution.

You will also be invited to pass a Bill to amend the present scheme for securing the exhibition of a fair proportion of British films.

A measure will be laid before you to reform the law relating to actions for personal injuries.

It is hoped that various measures consolidating important branches of the law will be introduced during the Session; and other measures will be laid before you if time permits.

PROROGATION (13 September 1948)

My Lords and Members of the House of Commons:

During the Session which is now ending economic difficulties have gravely delayed the recovery of all the countries of the eastern hemisphere. Through the sustained energies of My people in achieving a great and continuing expansion of exports and their resolute acceptance of a prolonged period of inevitable difficulty, progress has been made in redressing the adverse balance of payments. But world circumstances—including a persistent rise in the price of many commodities essential to our economy—have proved unfavourable, and further effort and sacrifice will be needed if the problem is to be surmounted. A great contribution towards lessening our dependence

on imports has been made by our agricultural industry, all sections of which have responded to the call for increased production. In the face of world shortages My Ministers have vigorously sought both to establish new sources of supply of foodstuffs and to safeguard the future by entering into long-term agreements with overseas countries.

The way before us is still hard, and it is only with courage and endurance, and by intensifying our present efforts, that we can, under God, overcome our difficulties and attain to that degree of prosperity and well-being for which we all hope.

In these anxious times we have all been encouraged by the far-sighted and generous action of the United States of America in extending financial assistance to the United Kingdom and other European countries. It is the policy of My Government to work with the Government of the United States and with other European Governments to bring about the fullest possible measure of European recovery by the wise use both of our own resources and of the aid afforded us. To this end they have entered into the Convention for European Economic Co-operation, and have signed the Economic Co-operation Agreement with the United States.

Close links have been forged with our neighbours in Western Europe. A Treaty of Economic, Social and Cultural Collaboration and Collective Self-Defence has been signed with the Governments of Belgium, France, Luxembourg and the Netherlands; permanent machinery for the co-ordination of defence with those countries has been established; and satisfactory progress is being made with the other matters dealt with in the Treaty. It is My prayer that out of these hopeful beginnings there will develop an increasing degree of union between all the countries of Western Europe; and that ultimately, in furtherance of the aims of the United Nations, they may, with their common heritage of culture and freedom, constitute an area of peace, prosperity and ordered progress, in association with the peoples of My Commonwealth overseas and with the United States of America.

My Government, together with the United States and French Governments and in co-operation with the heads of the Governments of the Western German States, have taken political, economic and financial measures to enable Western Germany to play her part in the community of European nations. My Government are still doing their utmost to reach agreement with the Soviet Union on fundamental problems affecting Germany as a whole.

My beloved daughter, Princess Elizabeth, together with the Duke of Edinburgh, paid an official visit to the French Republic in May. The affectionate reception which they were accorded formed a heartening demonstration of our good relations with our nearest Continental neighbour.

I have been happy to welcome to the United

Kingdom the Prime Minister of Australia. My Ministers in the United Kingdom greatly valued this opportunity of personal discussions with him. These have already led to economic arrangements of advantage to both countries, and I have learned with pleasure of the gift which My Government in Australia have made to My Government in the United Kingdom.

I am gratified that arrangements have been made for a general meeting of My Prime Ministers to be held in London in October.

A comprehensive trade agreement between the United Kingdom and Eire has recently been signed. This agreement will, I am confident, prove to be of benefit to both countries, and will further contribute to the growth of friendly relations between them.

My Government in the United Kingdom have concluded mutually satisfactory agreements on financial matters with My Governments in India and Pakistan.

During the past year, Ceylon has become a fully self-governing Member of the Commonwealth. I wish her people all happiness and prosperity and I trust that her relations with the other nations of the Commonwealth will be close and cordial.

My Government have continued to press ahead with the economic development of the Colonial territories, in order to provide a firm foundation for the social and political advancement of My Colonial peoples and to increase the world supply of essential foodstuffs and raw materials.

I have given assent to Constitutional Instruments designed to facilitate the operation of essential common services in the East African territories.

The new Federation of Malaya has been inaugurated and the new Legislative Council of the Colony of Singapore has met. My Ministers are determined to restore law and order in these territories and to suppress the outbreaks of violence which have so unhappily disturbed the peace of the Federation; and to that end the police forces have been greatly strengthened and military reinforcements have been sent to Malaya.

I note with satisfaction the measures taken by the Governor-General of the Sudan to set up in that territory an Executive Council and an elected Legislative Assembly as a first step towards self-government, and I regret that the Egyptian Government have so far felt unable to join in assisting this advance.

In accordance with plans announced some months earlier My Government relinquished the Mandate for Palestine on 15th May. At the same time the Assembly of the United Nations adopted a resolution setting up a United Nations Mediator for Palestine, thus putting into effect a suggestion made by the United Kingdom representative. I deeply regret the loss of life caused by hostilities which broke out between the Arabs and Jews in Palestine. These

hostilities have been brought to an end by the energetic action of the Mediator based on truce resolutions adopted by the Security Council. The last British forces have now been withdrawn from Palestine.

Our gratitude is due to the services rendered for so many years by the British civil administration in Palestine, by members of the Palestine Police Force and by the British Armed Forces who have served there. Amid conditions of great difficulty and danger they have discharged their tasks with an impartiality, forbearance and skill deserving of the highest praise.

I have given My assent to the Burma Independence Act, by which Burma became an independent State on 4th January, 1948. The Treaty previously concluded between My Government and the Provisional Government of Burma was ratified on the same date. I wish well to the Government and people of Burma.

My Government have become parties to the Protocol of Provisional Application of the General Agreement on Tariffs and Trade. They have also taken part in Conferences at Geneva and Havana to draw up the draft Charter of the International Trade Organisation and have signed the Final Act of the Havana Conference.

Members of the House of Commons:

I thank you for the provision which you have made for the public services and for My beloved daughter, Princess Elizabeth, and her husband.

My Lords and Members of the House of Commons:

My Forces have continued honourably to discharge the tasks assigned to them throughout the world.

I have assented to legislation under which women may be enlisted and commissioned in the Army and the Royal Air Force, and this, with the continuance of the Women's Services of the Royal Navy in their existing form, will enable women to maintain their high tradition of service with My Forces.

My Ministers are anxious to ensure the fullest possible growth of good industrial relations, on which efficiency in industry and the necessary increase in production so largely depend. To this end they have encouraged the extension of joint consultation between management and workers at all levels.

Acts have been passed to abolish the Poor Law and establish arrangements for assistance to all in need, and to make improved provision for children deprived of a normal home life. Thus has been discharged the great task, which it has fallen to this Parliament to undertake, of giving legislative effect to a comprehensive scheme of social security. That scheme, which has now been brought into operation, will promote the health and well-being of My people, provide a substantial resource in any periods of unavoidable unemployment, and relieve those anxieties which in the past so often attended sickness, disability or old age.

Steps have been taken to improve the facilities for the consideration of Scottish affairs by the establishment of a Scottish Economic Conference and by providing for the greater use of the Standing Committee of the House of Commons on Scottish Bills.

I have assented to legislation amending the financial relations between the Exchequer and local authorities, centralising the machinery of valuation for rating purposes, and amending the law as to the valuation of small dwelling houses in England and Wales.

In furtherance of the plan for the co-ordination of the fuel and power industries a measure has been passed to bring the gas industry under public ownership.

I have given My assent to measures to reform the administration of criminal justice in England and Wales, and to assimilate and reform the Parliamentary and local government franchise and electoral procedure and revise the distribution of Parliamentary seats. A measure has also been passed to enable a common national status to be maintained throughout the Commonwealth and to amend the law governing the national status of married women.

Legislation has been enacted to promote, in fulfilment of My Government's agricultural policy for the United Kingdom, the stability and long-term development of agriculture in Scotland; to establish River Boards in England and Wales; to enlarge the facilities for veterinary training and improve the status of the profession; and to provide assistance to the white fish and herring industries.

I have assented to Bills to encourage the exhibition of British cinematograph films, to provide for the payment of grants for the modernisation of cotton-spinning mills and to set up a body to develop and exploit inventions in the national interest.

An enactment has been passed enabling enquiry by an independent Commission to be made into restrictive business arrangements and monopolies, and authorising corrective measures where these are found necessary.

Substantial progress has been made with the work of consolidating and revising the Statute Law and I have given My assent to several Bills introduced for this purpose.

FOURTH SESSION OF THE THIRTY-EIGHTH PARLIAMENT

1948

OPENING (14 September 1948)

My Lords and Members of the House of Commons:

I have summoned you to meet at this time in order that you may give further consideration to the Bill to amend the Parliament Act, 1911, on which there was disagreement between the two Houses last Session.

It is not proposed to bring any other business before you in the present Session.

PROROGATION (25 October 1948)

My Lords and Members of the House of Commons:

The Session now ending has been marked by the meeting of My Prime Ministers and other Ministers representing Commonwealth countries. I have been happy to welcome to this country those who have come from overseas to attend the meeting and I am sure that great good must come of this personal exchange of views between the Leaders of My Governments.

I am also gratified that the Commonwealth Parliamentary Conference has brought together in the United Kingdom many other distinguished citizens from Commonwealth countries.

Representatives of My peoples in Africa have conferred in London with My Ministers. Their meetings will, I am confident, promote closer understanding, co-operative endeavour and mutual benefit.

My Government have continued to take an active part in the work of the Organisation for European Economic Co-operation, which has recently agreed upon recommendations about the division of the first year's aid from the United States. My Government, together with the other members of the Organisation, have also signed a convention to facilitate trade and payments among the countries concerned.

My Government have taken certain measures to strengthen My Armed Forces. They have also, in association with the other Governments signatory to the Treaty.of Brussels, set up the nucleus of a command organisation for the defence forces of the Five Powers, and made arrangments to deal with problems of production and equipment.

The two Houses have again failed to agree on the Bill to amend the Parliament Act, 1911.

My Ministers have drawn counsel and support from your valuable debates on the international situation on defence and on economic affairs.

FIFTH SESSION OF THE THIRTY-EIGHTH PARLIAMENT

1948–1949

OPENING (26 October 1948)

My Lords and Members of the House of Commons:

The Session beginning today opens in a troubled world still suffering from the ravages of war. To spend all our energies on repairing these ravages has been our constant desire, but we have been hindered by distrust and dissension between the nations. Yet, with mutual confidence and goodwill, the problems now facing us would not defy solution, and the peoples of the would would be able to live in peace and enjoy the fruits of their labours. Meanwhile, as the recent meeting in London of Prime Ministers and their representatives has shown, the peoples of My Commonwealth offer an example of voluntary and useful co-operation.

My Government will continue to work closely and harmoniously, within the framework of the Treaty of Brussels, with the other Governments which are party to it; to give full support to the United Nations; and to strive to fulfil the aims of world peace and well-being set forth in the Charter.

In the Western Zones of Germany, economic revival has begun. Currency reform has brought stability and renewed faith in the value of money. The Germans themselves are working hard to design a democratic constitution for Western Germany.

In Berlin, however, a difficult situation has arisen as a result of the action of the Soviet Government in cutting surface communications between the city and Western Germany. My Government hold the view that this action constitutes a threat to peace and therefore referred the matter to the Security Council of the United Nations. The resolution of the Security Council has been vetoed by the Soviet representative, and the situation thus created is under consideration by My Government in consultation with the two other Governments concerned. Meanwhile, Berlin is being supplied by air; and aircraft from the United Kingdom, some of them flown by crews from other Commonwealth countries, are combining with those of the United States to keep Berlin linked with Western Europe.

The Queen and I look forward with pleasure to visiting Australia and New Zealand next year. We shall welcome the opportunity of meeting again My peoples of those countries, whose generous support both in war and peace has never failed Us.

Legislation will be laid before you to give effect to whatever decisions may result from the negotiations for admitting Newfoundland to the Canadian Confederation.

My Ministers will continue to devote themselves to the problem of the balance of payments. Fortified by the generous aid of the United States, and working together with the other members of the Commonwealth and of the Organisation for European Economic Co-operation, we shall hope to progress further towards paying our way abroad and restoring the prosperity of our country and the world. It is only by our continued exertions and self-restraint that we shall win through. Inventive thought matched to hard work is necessary to enable workers and management, in common effort and counsel, to make the fullest use of our available resources. By increasing the individual contribution of skill and labour we must build up our production still further.

My Ministers are taking steps to ensure that My Armed Forces shall be efficient and well equipped, and that the best use shall be made of men called up under the National Service Act. Recruiting for the Regular Forces will be stimulated, and the Reserve and Auxiliary Forces will also be built up. A Bill to amend the Territorial and Reserve Forces Act will be laid before you.

You will be asked to consider a measure for the future organisation of Civil Defence.

Members of the House of Commons:

The Estimates for the public services will be laid before you in due course.

My Lords and Members of the House of Commons:

You will be asked to consider further the Bill to amend the Parliament Act, 1911, on which during the last two Sessions your Houses have disagreed.

A measure will be laid before you to bring under public ownership those companies extensively engaged in the production of iron ore, or of pig iron or steel, or in the shaping of steel by a rolling process.

Legislation will be introduced to establish national parks in England and Wales; to improve the law relating to footpaths and access to the countryside; and to ensure the better conservation of wild life.

You will be asked to consider proposals for making legal aid and advice more readily available to persons of small or moderate means.

Legislation will be introduced to improve the organisation of Magistrates' Courts in England and Wales and to amend the law relating to Justices of the Peace.

A Bill will be laid before you to provide for the payment of jurors and for the abolition, with limited exceptions of special jurors.

Measures will be laid before you to extend the powers of local authorities in regard to new housing, and to promote the improvement of existing dwellings by local authorities and by private owners. You will also be asked to pass a measure to provide for reviewing the rents of shared rooms, and of houses and flats let for the first time since the war.

Legislation will be introduced to change the constitution of the General Nursing Council and to provide for the better training of nurses.

A Bill will be laid before you to amend and consolidate the law of patents and designs.

Legislation will be introduced to protect the coast from erosion by the sea.

Bills will be laid before you to modify the constitution and powers of producers' marketing boards; to encourage the development of the white fish industry, and to provide for safer milk.

You will be invited to pass a measure to enable My Government to ratify an international convention on safety of life at sea.

You will be invited to consider Bills to improve water supplies in Scotland, and to amend the Scottish criminal law.

Other measures will be laid before you if time permits; and it is hoped to make further progress with the task of consolidating and revising the Statute Law.

PROROGATION (16 December 1949)

My Lords and Members of the House of Commons:

The long Session which is now ending has been marked by a continuance of the economic difficulties with which we have been confronted since the end of the war. Fortunately there is work for all, and through the sustained efforts of My People a notable increase in production has been achieved. I pray that, under the guidance of Almighty God, we shall overcome the difficulties that still beset us and reach the goal of a stable and prosperous economy.

During last winter our overseas account as a whole was brought into balance. Trade with North America still presented special problems, but the size of the gap between receipts and payments in respect of that area was being progressively reduced as the drive to increase direct and indirect dollar earnings gathered momentum. Thanks to generous assistance from the Governments and Peoples of the United States and Canada, together with the continued efforts of My People, there was every reason to believe that the gap would be closed.

In the early part of 1949 a fall in demand for goods from the United Kingdom, and from the other countries linked with sterling, seriously affected our earnings of dollars and the resulting difficulties were much intensified by a widespread belief that there would be an alteration in the value of the pound

sterling in terms of the United States dollar. My Ministers took prompt action to reduce imports and to initiate discussions on some of the wider aspects of the problem. In July, a meeting of Commonwealth Finance Ministers was held in London to exchange views on the urgent economic problems confronting us. In September, My Ministers in the United Kingdom and Canada met representatives of the United States Government in Washington and discussed with them the trade and financial relations between the sterling and dollar areas. Complete understanding was achieved in these talks. There was recognition that the freer development of world trade required the sustained effort, not only of these three countries, but of all other countries which desired to promote a free exchange of goods throughout the world.

Before the Washington discussions began My Ministers had reached the conclusion that a radical adjustment would be necessary in the rate of exchange between sterling and the dollar, and an alteration in the rate was announced on 18th September. In order to make the devaluation of sterling an effective aid in foreign trade, My Ministers decided upon substantial reductions in Government expenditure and capital investment, thus maintaining their policy of disinflation as well as encouraging an increase in exports, especially to the dollar and other hard-currency areas.

An outstanding event during the Session was the conclusion of the North Atlantic Treaty, a defensive alliance of twelve Powers, each of whom has agreed, in harmony with the Charter of the United Nations, to give mutual assistance in case of armed attack. I am convinced that this Treaty will be a powerful aid to the preservation of peace and the defence of freedom.

My Government, in association with the other Governments signatory to the Brussels Treaty, have strengthened and developed the various organisations set up under that Treaty and My Navy and Air Force have taken part in joint Western Union exercises.

Persuaded of the need for closer unity between European Nations, My Government also decided to join with other European Powers in the establishment of a Council of Europe. Members of both Houses of Parliament attended the first meeting of the Consultative Assembly at Strasbourg in August as representatives from the United Kingdom. I shall watch with close interest the progress of this venture in international co-operation.

My Government have continued to play their full part in the work of the Organisation for European Economic Co-operation and have taken the lead, both in proposals and in action, to free a substantial part of international trade from import controls.

My Government will continue to give whole-hearted support to the purposes and principles of the United Nations.

In Germany considerable progress has been achieved by My Government in close collaboration with the Governments of the United States and France. The German Federal Government has been established after free elections and a wide measure of responsibility has now been transferred to the German authorities. I welcome particularly the Petersberg Agreement recently concluded between the Allied High Commission and the Federal Chancellor. After Berlin had been sustained for eleven months by the Allied airlift, adequate transport services were restored and the city has established closer relations with the Federal Republic. My Government, together with the United States and French Governments have continued, unhappily without success so far, their efforts to reach an agreement with the Soviet Union on fundamental problems affecting Germany.

My Forces continue to bear throughout the world heavy responsibilities in maintaining order and preserving the peace. In Hong Kong, Malaya and elsewhere they are discharging their duties with their accustomed efficiency and devotion.

The Queen and I greatly regret that it was not possible for us to visit Australia and New Zealand , this year, as we had hoped: and I look forward to the time when I shall have an opportunity of meeting again My Peoples in those parts of the Commonwealth.

A special conference of the Prime Ministers and other Ministers of the self-governing members of the British Commonwealth was held in London in April and I am happy to record the historic agreement then reached whereby India, whilst assuming the status of a sovereign independent Republic, will continue in full membership of the Commonwealth, with the good will of all its members. In consequence I have assented to an Act which will preserve to India and her citizens the privileges of Commonwealth status under the laws of the United Kingdom and Colonies.

On 31st.March, Newfoundland became a province of Canada. My good wishes attend this union of the two countries which I pray may bring them lasting prosperity and well-being.

I have learned with pleasure of the further generous gift which My Government in the United Kingdom have received from my Government in Australia.

The steady progress of My Colonial Peoples towards self-government within the Commonwealth has recently been demonstrated by the important proposals for constitutional advance in the Gold Coast. I warmly welcomed the success of the Colonial Month and Exhibition which I inaugurated in London last June.

Members of the House of Commons:
I thank you for the provision which you have made for the public services.

My Lords and Members of the House of Commons:
I have given My Assent to a measure to amend the Parliament Act, 1911, which reduces the period during which the House of Lords may delay legislative proposals in cases of disagreement between the two Chambers. I regret that it was not possible to secure agreement between both Houses on the provisions of this measure.

Legislation has been enacted extending the housing functions of local authorities; providing financial assistance towards the improvement of housing accommodation by local authorities and by private persons; and providing for the control of rents of houses and flats let for the first time since the war and for the abolition of premiums.

I have given My Assent to a Bill to establish in due course an Iron and Steel Corporation to which will subsequently be transferred the securities of certain companies extensively engaged in the iron and steel industry.

There has been a further notable advance in the output of British agriculture, to which all those engaged in the industry have contributed. In this and other ways redoubled efforts are being made to lessen our dependence on food from areas to which we export less than we import.

The general economic situation has required continued adherence to the policy of restraint in regard to personal incomes and limitation of dividends. The co-operation of employers and workers in giving effect to this policy deserves high praise.

An Act has been passed to give My Government the necessary powers to implement the provisions of the International Convention for the Safety of Life at Sea.

Important changes have been made in the laws relating to patents for inventions and to registered industrial designs.

Legislation has been passed for the better protection of the coast against erosion.

I have given My Assent to an Act enabling National Parks to be established in England and Wales and nature reserves to be provided in Great Britain for the better protection of wild life.

Preparations for the Festival of Britain, 1951, are now taking shape with the cordial support of local authorities and voluntary organisations in all parts of the United Kingdom.

I have given My Assent to legislation to improve water supplies in Scotland; to protect the tenants of shops; and to amend the criminal law in Scotland and the law relating to education in that country.

A measure has been passed to make further provision for the organisation of civil defence.

The arrangements for dealing with Welsh affairs have been strengthened by the establishment of the Council for Wales and Monmouthshire.

An Act has been passed to improve the

administrative and financial arrangements for magistrates' courts in England and Wales and to amend the law relating to justices of the peace. Provision has also been made for the payment of jurors and for the virtual abolition of special juries.

I have assented to measures for schemes of legal aid and advice in England and Wales and in Scotland.

Steady progress is being made in the consolidation of statute law. The law relating to agricultural holdings and agricultural wages in Scotland, civil aviation, elections, marriage, patents, registered designs and taxation of vehicles has been consolidated in this Session.

FIRST SESSION OF THE THIRTY-NINTH PARLIAMENT

1950

OPENING (6 March 1950)

My Lords and Members of the House of Commons:

I am proud to recognise that My people, by a sustained endeavour, have increased industrial and agricultural production and thereby helped our country forward to greater prosperity. In this task they have been greatly assisted by the help and co-operation of the Governments and peoples of other parts of the Commonwealth.

The world shortage of dollars, in which this country has shared, has again been eased by generous help from the United States of America and Canada. Renewed efforts will, however, be required to secure a balance in the country's overseas trade and, in particular, to increase earnings in North America.

My Government will maintain their whole-hearted support of the Organisation for European Economic Co-operation, through which it is hoped to work out a new European payments scheme.

I look forward with great pleasure to the visit of the President of the French Republic and Madame Auriol.

My Government in the United Kingdom warmly welcomed the opportunity provided by the recent meeting of Commonwealth Ministers in Colombo for a valuable exchange of views on foreign affairs. In accordance with the recommendations of the meeting, My Ministers look forward to co-operating with other Commonwealth Governments in matters of common interest in South and South-East Asia.

My Government welcome the inauguration on the 27th December last of the Republic of the United States of Indonesia as an independent sovereign state, with whom diplomatic relations have been established.

On the 6th January My Government accorded recognition to the Central People's Government of the People's Republic of China.

On the 7th February My Government granted recognition to the States of Viet Nam, Laos and Cambodia, as associate states within the French Union.

My Government will continue to give full support to the United Nations, for it is only through an effective system of security that world peace can be assured. In particular, they will use their utmost endeavours, through the United Nations, to assist in finding a durable solution of the tremendous problem of atomic energy so that international agreement for adequate control and supervision of the production of atomic energy may be secured.

My Government will do their utmost to ensure the success of the Council of Europe.

The formation of a Federal German Government has made possible a progressive transfer of responsibilities from the Western Allies to the Germans. As a result My Government have been able to make substantial reductions in the cost of their administration in Germany.

My Ministers will maintain the closest relations with the other Powers signatory to the North Atlantic and Brussels Treaties, and will play their due part, in collaboration with the other Powers, in strengthening common means of defence. My Government will continue to take all necessary steps to ensure that My Armed Forces are ready to meet their responsibilities in all parts of the world. The new organisation of Civil Defence will be developed.

My Government are actively promoting the economic and social development of the Colonial territories, and the Colonial Development Corporation is proving a useful instrument to this end.

Members of the House of Commons:

The Estimates for the public services will be laid before you in due course.

You will be asked to approve orders making certain changes in the Customs Tariff arising from the agreements which My Government concluded last summer at the meeting at Annency, at which the Governments of the Commonwealth were represented.

My Lords and Members of the House of Commons:

The economic difficulties of this country have emphasised the need for renewed effort to expand the production of food from our own soil, and My Government will continue to take all practical steps to encourage our agricultural population to increase output by every efficient means and to make better use of marginal land. The improvement of water supplies, particularly in rural areas, will continue to occupy the attention of My Ministers and preparatory steps will be taken with a view to the introduction of legislation as soon as circumstances permit.

In view of the restricted time available and the heavy volume of financial business to be transacted, My Government propose only a limited programme of legislation for the present Session. Nevertheless, should other measures prove in their view to be immediately necessary for the maintenance of full employment and the national well-being, My Ministers will not hesitate to submit them to Parliament, even though they may seem likely to prove contentious.

Bills will be laid before you to amend the law relating to allotments in England and Wales and in Scotland.

A Bill will be laid before you to amend the Medical Acts so as to raise the standard of medical education and to modify the constitution and disciplinary procedure of the General Medical Council. Legislation will also be introduced to vary the constitution of the Central Midwives Boards and to make other alterations in the law relating to midwives.

A measure will be laid before you to provide a uniform code for regulating the breaking-up of streets by public utility undertakings; also a measure to empower highway authorities to place and maintain cattle grids in highways.

You will be invited to pass a Bill to regulate and improve the living conditions of the crews of fishing trawlers.

You will be asked to approve legislation giving further encouragement to the transfer of industrial undertakings to the development areas.

On receipt of a.further report from the committee which is examining the law relating to leasehold, My Ministers will consider what legislation can be introduced to amend the law in respect of residential and business premises.

Other measures will be laid before you if time permits; and it is hoped to make further progress with the consolidation and revision of the Statute Law.

PROROGATION (26 October 1950)

My Lords and Members of the House of Commons:

The increase in production, which is vital to the economic progress of the country, is most encouraging. At the same time, there has been continued restraint in claims for increases in personal income of all kinds. The efforts which My People have made, not without sacrifices, have enabled us to maintain a healthy internal economy and to achieve a great improvement in the balance of overseas trade, notably with North America. Generous help from the United States of America and Canada has also continued to strengthen the general economic life of the country.

My Government have fully supported the United Nations' measures to combat the unprovoked aggression launched upon the Republic of Korea on 25th June, and My Forces are contributing by land, sea and in the air to the action now being taken in Korea by members of the United Nations in pursuance of the recommendations of the Security Council.

My Government, together with other friendly Powers, have also presented to the United Nations proposals for an ultimate settlement of a unified, independent and democratic Korea. These proposals have been approved by an overwhelming majority of member states gathered together in the General Assembly.

My Government have continued to play a prominent part in the economic and social activities of the United Nations, conscious of the great contribution which higher standards of living can make to the maintenance of peace and order in all parts of the world.

My Government, in association with other Governments signatory to the North Atlantic Treaty, have contributed to the strengthening of the Treaty Organisation by the appointment of a permanent body of Deputies to the Foreign Ministers. Together with these Governments they are initiating an urgent programme of production to ensure the adequate defence of the North Atlantic area. They acknowledge the powerful support which the United States of America are giving to the efforts of the North Atlantic Treaty Organisation to maintain greater security in this region.

My Government have taken two important steps towards peace and stability in the Middle East. In April they granted *de jure* recognition to the Government of Israel together with the simultaneous recognition of the union with the Hashemite Kingdom of Jordan of that part of Palestine which is under Jordan control. In May My Government, with the Governments of France and the United States of America, jointly issued the tripartite statement concerning the stability of the Middle East.

In August this year the Consultative Assembly of the Council of Europe began its second session. I shall continue to follow with interest this new and important development in international co-operation.

Together with the Governments of France and the United States, My Government have continued to work for the closer association of the German Federal Republic with the Western community of nations. I welcome both the accession of the Federal Republic as an associate member of the Council of Europe and the conclusions regarding Germany which the Foreign Ministers of the three Governments reached at their conference last month in New York.

In the economic field, My Government continue to collaborate to the full in the work of the Organisation for European Economic Co-operation.

I welcome the establishment of the European Payments Union which will enable the Organisation to facilitate trade and payments among its members.

It is gratifying that the countries participating in the international discussions on tariffs and trade have elected to hold their meetings in this country.

My Ministers in the United Kingdom welcomed the invitation of My Ministers in Australia to attend a meeting in Sydney in May to discuss with other Commonwealth Governments plans for the economic development of South and South-East Asia; My Government were hosts to further meetings in London in September at which countries in South-East Asia outside the Commonwealth were represented.

Discussions have also been held in London

between My Ministers in the United Kingdom and Ministers from Commonwealth countries overseas, which have afforded a valuable opportunity for an exchange of views on general trade and economic questions.

The visit of the President of the French Republic and Madame Auriol in March was an occasion of great pleasure to The Queen and myself and further strengthened the bonds of friendship between our two Peoples.

My Forces continue to assist the peoples of Malaya and the Civil Administration in their task of restoring law and order.

Important steps have been taken to bring about a rapid improvement in the size and efficiency of My Forces, whose rates of pay have been substantially increased. I have given My Assent to a measure extending to two years the period of whole-time National Service.

My Government in Canada have undertaken to train pilots and navigators of the Royal Air Force in Royal Canadian Air Force establishments. This measure of co-operation, which will materially help to advance training has been warmly welcomed by My Government in the United Kingdom.

Members of the House of Commons:

I thank you for the provision which you have made for the public services.

My Lords and Members of the House of Commons:

I have received your Addresses praying for the continuance for a further period of one year of certain emergency powers and will give effect to your wishes.

Over a large part of the country unusually bad weather has robbed farmers and the nation of the full fruits of what had promised to be a bountiful harvest, and they and their workers are to be commended for their unfailing courage and skill in fighting this adversity.

Legislation has been passed to help the provision and use of allotments throughout Great Britain.

Provision has been made for temporary assistance to the white fish industry pending the introduction of permanent legislation.

A comprehensive development plan for the Highlands and Islands of Scotland has been laid before you.

A Committee has been appointed to enquire into the financial and economic relationships between Scotland and the rest of the United Kingdom.

The Council for Wales and Monmouthshire have continued to do useful work and have recently submitted a valuable report.

The Medical Acts have been amended so as to ensure that, from a day to be appointed, medical practitioners shall have had experience in hospitals or other approved institutions before they are finally registered, and so as to improve the constitution and procedure of the General Medical Council.

I have assented to legislation which, by enabling wife maintenance, guardianship of infants and adoption orders to be made and enforced throughout the United Kingdom, will relieve much hardship and give a remedy to many women who have hitherto been barred from the exercise of their just claims.

My Ministers have continued to develop the organisation of the Civil Defence Services.

My Ministers have taken steps to impress upon all industries the need to help men to return to civil employment after service in the Regular Forces and I am gratified at the measure of response so far received.

Legislation has been passed giving further encouragement to transfers of industrial undertakings to the Development Areas.

Measures have been passed to provide a uniform code for regulating the breaking-up of streets by public utility undertakings and to empower highway authorities to place and maintain cattle-grids in highways.

I have assented to a Bill to provide relief from the hardship suffered by some owners and occupiers of small dwelling-houses which are damaged by coal-mining subsidence.

An Act has been passed for further promoting the revision of the Statute Law and the publication of Revised Editions of Statutes; progress has also been made in the consolidation of Statute Law.

SECOND SESSION OF THE THIRTY-NINTH PARLIAMENT

1950–1951

OPENING (31 October 1950)

My Lords and Members of the House of Commons:

Five years ago, in the hour of our deliverance from war, I declared it to be the firm purpose of My Government to work, in concert with the Governments of all other peace-loving nations, for the attainment of enduring world peace. Yet despite the untiring efforts to this end of all My Peoples, helped by My Allies across the seas, the world is once more troubled with the menace of war. The avoidance of war remains the supreme desire of My Ministers, and under this new peril they will seek by all means in their power to ensure the success of the measures for rearmament which they have taken. In the Session which lies before you the necessary increases in production for defence will call for further efforts and sacrifices, but I am confident that with the unfailing support of all My loyal subjects the nation will be enabled to play its full part in the defence of freedom and the preservation of peace.

In Korea forces, for the first time under the flag of the United Nations, are overcoming the invaders. The success of this historic action in which My Forces are playing their part marks a decisive moment in world affairs, and is arousing fresh hopes of achieving a united, free and democratic Korea. It has already given proof of the ability of the United Nations to meet a threat to world peace.

My Government also support strongly the efforts of the Specialised Agencies of the United Nations which are directed to improving the standard of living in impoverished or backward countries.

My Ministers in the United Kingdom will maintain the closest relations with the other Governments of the Commonwealth in order to safeguard freedom and peace. They will also continue to work with the Governments signatory to the North Atlantic and Brussels Treaties to strengthen the North Atlantic Treaty Organisation, to improve the defence of the North Atlantic area and thus to achieve security against attack.

In consultation with other Commonwealth Governments, My Ministers will give further study to plans for promoting the economic development of South and South-East Asia.

The development of the Colonial Territories and the welfare of their peoples will continue to receive the attention of My Government, and they will introduce legislation to supplement the sums made available for these purposes by the Colonial Development and Welfare Act, 1945.

I look forward with great pleasure to the forthcoming visit of the Queen of the Netherlands and the Prince of the Netherlands.

Members of the House of Commons:

The Estimates for the Public Services will be laid before you in due course.

My Lords and Members of the House of Commons:

I am glad to know that preparations are going forward throughout the United Kingdom for the Festival of Britain, 1951, which will demonstrate to the world the greatness of British achievement in the arts and sciences and in their application to industry and agriculture. The Queen and I look forward with high expectation to the opening of the Festival next May.

Although the rearmament programme will make heavy demands upon the nation, My Government will continue to give high priority to housing and will maintain the essentials of their social policy. They will do their utmost to ensure as far as possible the stability of costs and prices and to continue the export drive.

In order to defend full employment, to ensure that the resources of the community are used to best advantage and to avoid inflation, legislation will be introduced to make available to My Ministers on a permanent basis but subject to appropriate Parliamentary safeguards, powers to regulate production, distribution and consumption and to control prices.

My Ministers propose the further development of the Civil Defence Services both as a responsibility of local authorities and, after due consultation with managements and workers, within large industrial units.

A Bill will be laid before you to provide for the hearing of appeals against convictions by courts-martial.

You will be asked to approve a measure to confer rights of reinstatement in civilian employment on reservists recalled to My Forces and on National Service men who, before the coming into force of the National Service Act, 1950, voluntarily undertook an additional six months' wholetime service.

Legislation will be laid before you to provide for the restoration of land devastated by ironstone extraction.

The disturbed international situation emphasises the need to intensify the efforts which My Ministers have been making to expand the production of food at home. A Bill will be laid before you still further to encourage the rearing of livestock in upland areas.

A measure will be laid before you to place on a permanent basis the legislation relating to the beet sugar·industry and to transfer to public ownership the shares in the British Sugar Corporation which are not held by the Exchequer.

My Government will introduce legislation providing for the establishment of an authority with powers to reorganise and develop the white fish industry, and of a Scottish Committee of that authority.

A Bill will also be laid before you proposing more effective means of dealing with the poaching of salmon and trout in Scotland.

A Bill will be laid before you to amend the Restoration of Pre-War Trade Practices Act, 1942.

My Ministers have under consideration the reform of the law relating to leaseholds and meanwhile measures will be introduced to provide for the continuation for a short period of ground leases relating to residential premises, so as to prevent some of the hardships which would otherwise arise on the termination of tenancies. Provision will also be made for facilitating the renewal of certain business tenancies.

A measure will be laid before you to provide River Boards with more effective powers to deal with the pollution of rivers and streams.

Other measures will be laid before you if time permits; and it is hoped to make further progress with the consolidation of the Statute Law.

PROROGATION (4 October 1951)

My Lords and Members of the House of Commons:

My Ministers have continued to give the fullest support to the United Nations in the maintenance of international peace and security.

It is My earnest hope that the efforts which are being made to restore peace in Korea will be successful. Under the United Nations My Forces have continued to take a prominent part in the arduous campaign in that country. The land forces from the various Commonwealth countries have been grouped together to form the First (Commonwealth) Division. The heroic action of the First Battalion, the Gloucester Regiment, maintained the highest traditions of My fighting services and has been justly acclaimed throughout the world.

My Ministers deeply regret that, although they made earnest efforts to find a basis for discussion, success did not attend the recent negotiations for a meeting of the Foreign Ministers of the Soviet Union, France, the United States and the United Kingdom.

My Government, in association with the other Governments signatory to the North Atlantic Treaty, have accepted the necessity for making greatly increased provision for defence, and the consequent strengthening of My Forces is already becoming apparent. I pray that, with God's help, the defence programme will succeed in its purpose of averting war

and laying the foundations of a lasting peace throughout the world.

My Government have watched with sympathy and interest the progress made in building up, within the wider framework of the North Atlantic partnership, a European community in which Germany will play her part. My Government desire to establish a close association with this community at all stages of its development.

I welcome the appointment of General of the Army Eisenhower as Supreme Allied Commander, Europe. Units of My Forces have been placed under his command.

In order to increase the readiness of our defences, members of My Reserve and Auxiliary Forces have been recalled for periods of training of between fifteen days and three months, and for periods of service amounting in some cases to eighteen months.

My Ministers have tried to achieve by negotiation a solution of the unfortunate dispute which has arisen in connection with the oil industry in Iran, but these efforts, despite the help rendered by the President of the United States and his special representative, have so far been unsuccessful.

My Government, jointly with the Government of the United States, sponsored the Treaty of Peace with Japan which was signed by forty-eight nations at San Francisco on the 8th September. The Treaty was the result of a prolonged series of international consultations in which My Government in the United Kingdom and My Governments in other Commonwealth countries had played a leading part.

In Malaya further progress has been made in associating all communities with the administration of government and in furthering their welfare and prosperity. With the assistance of the peoples of Malaya and the civil administration, My troops have, with increasing success, continued their efforts to restore law and order and to bring communist banditry to an end.

The Prime Ministers of all the self-governing countries of the Commonwealth, or their representatives, met in London in January last to review the international situation and to consider what further positive action Commonwealth Governments could take to secure and preserve world peace. Since then, Ministers from the United Kingdom, Australia, New Zealand, South Africa and Southern Rhodesia have met in London to consider defence problems in regions of common concern, including the Middle East, and South African Ministers have met representatives of other interested Governments in Nairobi to consider defence facilities in Africa.

The increase in production, which has been among the outstanding achievements of this country since the war, has continued in the face of many difficulties. For this success great credit is due to workpeople and management throughout the whole range of industry, agriculture and commerce. Despite the obstacles caused by shortages of materials and the high prices of many imports, full employment has been maintained, our exports have continued at a high level and the rearmament programme has been further advanced.

During the past session My Ministers were able to announce that, in agreement with the United States Government, it had been decided to suspend further allotments of Marshall Aid which had been so generously given to us by the people of the United States.

In order to restrain the rise in living costs provoked by high import prices, measures have been taken, by the operation of price control, and otherwise, to limit the rise in the prices of goods and services.

I regret that, largely because of higher import prices, the balance of payments, which was remarkably favourable last year, has become less favourable in recent months.

I warmly welcomed the State visits of Her Majesty the Queen of the Netherlands and His Royal Highness Prince Bernhard of the Netherlands, Their Majesties the King and Queen of Denmark and His Majesty the King of Norway.

It gave Me great pleasure to open in May last the Festival of Britain, in which the whole nation has displayed its talents and traditions in the arts and sciences. Despite the clouds which hang over the world, the celebrations throughout the land have given a powerful stimulus to the arts of peace and have provided opportunity for well-earned recreation of spirit. I am pleased that so many visitors from overseas have attended the Festival, which has thus contributed to international friendship and under-standing.

My Ministers continue to attach importance to international co-operation and mutual aid in economic and social matters through the United Nations and other bodies. They welcomed delegates from Commonwealth and foreign countries to the tariff negotiations which were held last winter in Torquay, and have participated with other Commonwealth Governments in the plans for the economic develop-ment of South and South-East Asia. My Government continue to collaborate fully in the work of the Organisation for European Economic Co-operation.

My Ministers were glad to be able to exchange views at a meeting in London with My Ministers in other Commonwealth Governments concerned with the production of raw materials and the supply of manufactured goods, and to have the assistance of representatives from a number of Colonial territories in these deliberations.

My deep sympathy went out to My people in Jamaica when many parts of the island were devastated by a hurricane on the 17th August. My Ministers in the United Kingdom announced an immediate grant for relief.

Members of the House of Commons:
I thank you for the provision which you have made for the public services.

My Lords and Members of the House of Commons:
Thanks to the determination of farmers and agricultural workers throughout a trying season, the programme for the expansion of the production of food at home has been carried on with unabated vigour.

An Act has been passed to extend the help given to farmers rearing livestock in upland areas.

My assent has also been given to a measure providing for the restoration to agriculture and other useful purposes of land broken up by the open-cast working of ironstone.

Legislation has been passed to establish a White Fish Authority with powers to reorganise, develop and regulate the white fish industry; and a new scheme has been approved conferring wider powers on the Herring Industry Board.

New provisions have been enacted for ensuring the purity of the rivers and other inland or coastal waters. An Act has also been passed to increase the contributions which may be made from the Exchequer towards the cost of schemes for rural water supply and sewerage.

My Government were gratified by the response which they received to their appeal for extra output from the coal mines. Higher levels of industrial production have, however, greatly increased the demand for fuel and power; and My Ministers have taken, and will continue to take, all practicable steps to encourage the recruiting of more miners, and to increase the supply of fuel, electricity and other forms of power and ensure their more efficient use.

Both sides of industry have recognised the need to remove obstacles to increased production and, with the full agreement of employers and work-people, provision has been made to postpone the restoration of pre-war trade practices in industry.

The war-time measures for the prevention and settlement of trade disputes have been withdrawn and replaced by provisions more appropriate to peace-time conditions.

Legislation which will be of great benefit to a large number of My People has been passed to augment retirement pensions and the provision for widowed mothers and for children under the National Insurance Acts. National Assistance scales have been increased and improvements made in certain supplementary allowances paid to war pensioners.

Increases have been granted in the retired pay and pensions of My Regular Forces.

An Act has been passed to safeguard the civil interests of My Reserve and Auxiliary Forces.

Provision has been made for the setting up of a Court-Martial Appeal Court to hear appeals against convictions by courts-martial.

My Ministers have continued to develop the organisation of the Civil Defence Services and have been in consultation with representatives of industry and commerce about civil defence in industrial and commercial undertakings.

I gave My assent to legislation to make temporary provision for the protection of the occupiers of certain classes of leasehold property in Great Britain.

An Act was passed which extends the powers and duties of the Forestry Commissioners to establish and maintain adequate reserves of growing trees.

A measure has been passed to provide more effective means of dealing with the poaching of salmon and trout in Scotland.

Further sums were made available for the development of the Colonial territories and the welfare of My peoples there.

Progress has been made in the consolidation of the Statute Law.

FIRST SESSION OF THE FORTIETH PARLIAMENT

1951–1952

OPENING (6 November 1951)

My Lords and Members of the House of Commons:

It is a matter of sincere regret to Me that I cannot address you in person on this Opening of a New Parliament. I have been sustained and strengthened through My illness by the prayers and the sympathy of all My peoples.

It has given Me great satisfaction that The Princess Elizabeth, accompanied by her husband, has been able to undertake her projected journey to Canada and the United States of America, and I have been deeply moved by the warmth of the reception accorded both to her and to the Duke of Edinburgh.

The Queen and I are deeply touched by the sympathy and understanding shown by My peoples in Australia, New Zealand and Ceylon on learning that We had, for the second time, been prevented by My illness from carrying out Our plan to visit them. Happily My elder daughter and her husband will make this journey in Our stead; and they ardently look forward to their visit to these and other Commonwealth countries through which they will pass in the course of their journey.

My Ministers will ever be anxious to maintain the intimate and precious ties of friendship and understanding which exist between all the peoples of the Commonwealth and Empire.

My Government will make it their first duty to ensure our national safety and, in concert with the other members of the Commonwealth, the United States of America and our European partners, will share in a supreme effort to build a more tranquil and prosperous world. They will take the necessary measures to strengthen our defences both in trained men and in equipment, to re-establish the Home Guard and to develop Civil Defence.

My Government will faithfully support the United Nations as the World instrument for peace and security. They will continue to play their part in Korea with the aim of restoring peace and well-being.

My Ministers will try to repair the injuries our rights and interests have suffered in Persia.

My Government regard the abrogation by the Egyptian Government of the Anglo-Egyptian Treaty of Alliance of 1936 and the Sudan Condominium Agreements of 1899 as illegal and without validity. They are resolved, in conjunction with the Governments of the United States, France and Turkey, to press forward with their proposals for joint defence arrangements in the Middle East. In the meantime they will maintain their position in the Canal Zone under the terms of the 1936 Treaty and will safeguard the international highway. Nothing can be allowed to interfere with the rights of the Sudanese to decide for themselves the future status of their country.

The text of the Japanese Peace Treaty signed at San Francisco on the 8th of September will be presented to you before ratification. Legislation will be introduced to give effect to certain provisions of the Treaty.

My Government will introduce legislation to regulate the position of Commonwealth and foreign armed forces who are stationed in this country.

Members of the House of Commons:

The estimates for the public services will be laid before you.

My Lords and Members of the House of Commons:

First steps will be taken to fulfil the plans of My Ministers for the management of Scottish affairs.

I have approved new arrangements to bring added strength to the counsels of My Government upon the special problems and interests of Wales.

My Government view with grave concern the economic situation of the United Kingdom about which a full disclosure must be made to the nation. The recent deterioration in the balance of payments causes increasing anxiety and must be urgently remedied in order to restore the fullest confidence in the purchasing power of the pound, so that we may continue to be able to obtain from overseas the supplies necessary to maintain employment and an increasingly high level of production. The measures to this end must include drastic action to reduce the growing inflation in our economy which threatens the maintenance of our defence programme and which, if unchecked, must cause a continuing rise in the cost of living. My Government regard this problem as overshadowing all other domestic matters. They are giving it urgent examination and will announce their conclusions and make proposals to Parliament in the immediate future. They will make a searching inquiry into Government expenditure with a view to reducing it wherever possible. While pressing on with domestic remedies they will also invite the other Governments of the Commonwealth to confer together on action which should be taken in concert to remedy the adverse balance of payments.

My Government will seek to promote flexibility in those industries which have been brought under public management and to stimulate free enterprise by giving it a fuller share in our economic activity. They will be mindful of the great demands on our productive capacity, and will consider all methods for creating that spirit of partnership between management and workers on which industrial harmony and a higher level of productivity must depend.

My Government view with concern the serious shortage of labour, particularly of skilled labour, which has handicapped production in a number of essential industries. They will review, in consultation with representatives of those concerned, the possibilities of making available more labour for those industries and of ensuring the best use of the existing labour force.

A Bill will be placed before you to annul the Iron and Steel Act with a view to the reorganisation of the industry under free enterprise but with an adequate measure of public supervision.

Proposals will be made to facilitate the extension of private road haulage activities.

A measure will be laid before you for strengthening and widening the activities of the Monopolies Commission.

You will be asked to authorise for a period the continuation in force of certain emergency enactments and defence regulations which are due to expire next month. My Ministers will, however, review the whole subject with the aim of reducing the number of these controls and regulations and, wherever possible, embodying those which must be kept in legislation requiring annual renewal by Parliament.

My Government will do their utmost to stimulate the building of new houses for My people, using to the fullest extent both public and private enterprise. Their housing policy will have regard to the desire of many people to own their homes and to the special needs of the elderly.

In their policy towards the social services My Government will pursue the aim of ensuring efficiency and providing value for money spent.

My Ministers will vigorously encourage production of food by the basic industries of agriculture, horticulture and fisheries.

Further progress will be made with the consolidation of the statute law.

Other measures will be laid before you in due course.

PROROGATION (30 October 1952)

My Lords and Members of the House of Commons:
My thoughts turn first to My beloved Father whose death was so deeply mourned throughout the Commonwealth and beyond. The countless expressions of devotion to Him have moved Me deeply and encourage Me in My resolute determination to prove worthy of a sacred trust.

My Ministers have continued to give the fullest support to the United Nations Organisation in its efforts to promote international co-operation and to maintain peace.

My Forces are playing their full part in collective resistance to aggression in Korea and have enhanced their high reputation for efficiency and for readiness to carry out whatever task is demanded of them by land, at sea or in the air. I mourn the loss of gallant lives which has brought sorrow to many homes. My Government in the United Kingdom and in the other countries of the Commonwealth have worked ceaselessly to achieve an armistice agreement in conformity with the principles for which the United Nations stand.

In Malaya My Forces and the civil administration are carrying out a difficult task with patience and determination. In spite of great loss and suffering all communities are playing an ever more active part in the defence of their freedom.

My Government, in close association with our Allies, have shared in the steady development of the North Atlantic Treaty Organisation. They have welcomed the notable contribution made to the strengthening of the Organisation and of its member countries by the people of the United States of America who are bearing so large a share of the heavy cost of mutual defence. I have watched with hope and confidence the measures which these countries, now happily joined by Turkey and Greece, have taken to secure themselves against the threat of armed aggression. The continued strengthening of My Forces has contributed to the growing power of the free world to deter aggression and so to preserve peace.

My Government have worked for the promotion of unity and prosperity in Europe and are taking a leading part in the work of the Organisation for European Economic Co-operation. They have also appointed a permanent delegation to the High Authority of the European Coal and Steel Community.

A treaty of mutual assistance has been concluded between the United Kingdom and the members of the European Defence Community and My Government have joined with the Governments of the United States of America and France in reaffirming their guarantee to Berlin. It is their confident hope that these and other related measures will contribute powerfully to the stability of Western Europe and of the democratic world.

My Ministers have supported the inclusion of the German Federal Republic in the European community and by ratifying the Bonn conventions have formed a new relationship between the United Kingdom and Germany. I regret, however, that prolonged exchanges between My Government and the Soviet Government have not yet ended in agreement upon the unification of Germany in conditions of freedom and that the efforts of My Government to conclude an Austrian State Treaty have not yet been successful.

The Japanese Peace Treaty has been ratified and legislation has been passed to give effect to certain of its provisions.

My Government, with the help of other Commonwealth Governments and of the Sterling Area as a whole, have taken effective steps to redress the balance of payments and to maintain the strength of sterling as an international currency.

Members of the House of Commons:

I thank you for the provisions which you have made for the public services.

I thank you for the provision you have made for the honour and dignity of the Crown.

My Lords and Members of the House of Commons:

My Ministers have continued to develop the organisation of civil defence both as a responsibility of local authorities and in industry and commerce.

An Act has been passed to establish the Home Guard.

My Ministers have taken fiscal measures to aid the textile industries and have brought forward a number of Government contracts to help these industries over their immediate difficulties.

My Government have called special attention to the need to increase the numbers of skilled workers and have set up a Committee to advise on the provision of opportunities for the employment of older men and women. An Act has been passed for the better organisation of miners' welfare.

All engaged in agriculture have rallied to My Government's call for increased food production. Measures have been passed to provide grants to increase the acreage under the plough and to pay subsidies on calves and fertilisers.

The welfare of the fishing industry has engaged the attention of My Ministers. The white fish subsidy and other measures of assistance have been continued.

My Ministers have vigorously carried out the expansion of the housing programme and the production of building materials necessary to sustain it. Housing Bills have been passed together with measures to encourage town development in County districts and to make financial provision for the building of New Towns.

Additional Ministers have been appointed to ensure ever closer attention to Scottish affairs. A Royal Commission on Scottish Affairs has begun its deliberations.

Ministers have also been appointed with special responsibilities for Wales.

Other legislation of benefit to My people has been passed. Family allowances, National Insurance payments and certain State pensions have been increased, and the National Assistance scales have been raised.

Consolidation of the laws relating to Customs and Excise and to Income Tax has been accomplished.

SECOND SESSION OF THE FORTIETH PARLIAMENT

1952–1953

OPENING (4 November 1952)

My Lords and Members of the House of Commons:

On this first occasion when I speak to you in person as your Queen I gratefully acknowledge the sympathy which has been extended to Me and My Family from every part of the Commonwealth. By His selfless devotion to His duties as your Sovereign My Father set an example which it will be My constant endeavour to follow. I am well assured that My peoples everywhere will accord Me that same loyalty and understanding which ever supported Him in the service of His peoples.

I look forward with deep pleasure to fulfilling at the end of next year My long cherished hopes of visiting, in company with My dear Husband, My peoples in Australia, New Zealand and Ceylon.

I earnestly pray that in Korea an early armistice will be arranged. Until this is accomplished the continued participation of My Forces in this conflict will be clear proof of My Government's whole-hearted attachment to the ideals of the United Nations.

My Ministers are determined to make ever closer that co-operation with the other Members of the Commonwealth and with the Colonial Empire which must be the keystone of our policy. To this end they have invited Commonwealth Prime Ministers to meet together this month to confer on vital problems of finance, commerce and economic policy.

My Government will continue to take their full share in the work of the North Atlantic Treaty Organisation as the bulwark of Western defence and the embodiment of the common aspirations of the Atlantic Community. Within that Community and in every other way they will seek to maintain the closest and most friendly relations with the Government and people of the United States of America.

It will be My Government's aim to strengthen the unity of Europe. They will work in close association with our neighbours in Western Europe and give all possible support to their efforts to forge closer links with one another.

My Ministers will continue to work for the conclusion of an Austrian State Treaty and for a fair and equitable settlement of the problem of German unity.

Active measures will be taken to strengthen the long-standing ties of friendship and of mutual trade between the United Kingdom and the countries of Latin America.

Further consideration will be given to the draft scheme for federation in Central Africa. For this purpose My Government have invited the three Central African Governments to a further conference in London in January.

My Ministers will continue the rearmament of My Forces and the development of the Civil Defence organisation, with due regard to the need for maintaining economic strength and stability.

Members of the House of Commons:

The estimates for public services will be laid before you in due course.

My Lords and Members of the House of Commons:

My Government will proceed resolutely with the task of placing the national economy on a sound foundation. They will not hesitate to take any further steps necessary to hold and improve the more favourable position now reached in our overseas payments.

My Ministers will encourage all engaged in agriculture, mining and industry to co-operate in increasing productive efficiency and thus to produce at lower cost the goods needed at home and by the export trades.

In the interests of the employment and the standard of living of My people, My Government will persevere with measures to curb inflation and to reduce the heavy load of Government expenditure.

A steadily increasing number of houses will be built under My Government's programme.

Bills will be laid before you for the reorganisation of the Iron and Steel Industry and to provide for changes in the Transport Industry.

Further measures will be promoted relating to the Town and Country Planning Acts of 1947, to Local Government superannuation and to the date for depositing new rating valuation lists.

The question of the supply of electricity in Scotland is being attentively examined with a view to legislation.

A Bill will be introduced to make certain changes within the framework of the Education Acts in the law affecting voluntary schools.

My Government will continue to give every encouragement to the fishing industry. A Bill will be laid before you to provide financial help for the building of fishing vessels.

Proposals will be made to you for improving the maternity benefits of the National Insurance Scheme and also for the further amendment of the National Insurance (Industrial Injuries) Act.

My Ministers will propose an extension of the existing temporary Acts on leasehold property in

England and Wales and in Scotland and will seek an opportunity of making known their policy on this subject.

Other measures will be laid before you in due course.

PROROGATION (29 October 1953)

My Lords and Members of the House of Commons:

I acknowledge with deep gratitude the expressions of loyalty and devotion which marked My Coronation and the prayers of My Peoples which sustained Me on that solemn occasion. The presence of so many leading representatives of the Commonwealth and Empire and of other countries was an added source of support and happiness to Me and My dear Husband.

My Government have continued their whole-hearted support of the United Nations.

In Korea My Forces played a notable part in the successful resistance to aggression. My Government have continued to work with others in seeking a peaceful settlement of the Korean problem and I received with deep thankfulness the news of the armistice which brought the fighting to an end.

In Malaya My Forces, together with the local security forces, have been increasingly successful in their campaign. I have watched with sympathy and admiration the gallant efforts of My loyal subjects of all races in Kenya to restore peace and order in that country.

My Ministers regret that it has become necessary to suspend the Constitution of British Guiana.

My Government have continued in the North Atlantic Treaty Organisation to develop the combined strength of the West.

My Government have given full support and encouragement to the promotion of European unity and prosperity. They have offered to enter into close political and military relations with the European Defence Community and have continued to take a leading part in the work of the Organisation for European Economic Co-operation.

My Government and the Governments of France and the United States have renewed their invitation to the Soviet Government to a meeting to discuss the problems of Germany and Austria.

My Government have been discussing with the Egyptian Government means of settling the differences between the two countries while safe-guarding the security of the Middle East and the Suez Canal.

My Government have signed with the United Kingdom of Libya a Treaty of Friendship and Alliance which provides for mutual defence and recognises the common interest of the two countries in the maintenance of international peace and security.

Prime Ministers of the Commonwealth met in London last November and again immediately after My Coronation. At their first Conference they agreed on a course of action to strengthen the economies of Commonwealth countries, to bring about by international agreement more rapid progress towards freer trade and currencies and to maintain the improvement in the balance of payments of the sterling area. At their second Conference the Prime Ministers reviewed the international situation and considered what contribution Commonwealth Governments could make towards composing the differences which divide the world.

An Act was passed conferring on Me powers, which I have exercised, to provide for a Federation of Rhodesia and Nyasaland. I earnestly hope that a harmonious and prosperous future lies before the new Federation.

The peoples of My Colonial territories and protectorates are moving towards a larger share in the management of·their own affairs within the Commonwealth. My Ministers have held discussions with representatives of the peoples of Nigeria on the future of their Constitution. A further step has been taken towards Federation in the West Indies. My Government are considering proposals for the future constitutional advance of the Gold Coast.

The development and rearmament of My Forces have continued during the year.

I grieved at the loss of life and destruction from the recent severe earthquake in Cyprus and rejoiced that My Forces were able to bring rapid aid to the victims of a like calamity in Greece.

Members of the House of Commons:

I thank you for the provision which you have made for the Public Services.

My Lords and Members of the House of Commons:

I was greatly distressed by the wide-spread damage and suffering caused by the storm and floods on the East Coast of England and in Scotland. My Government took energetic steps to ensure the speedy restoration of essential services and have undertaken to meet the full cost of restoring the damaged sea defences. This work is now largely complete and in certain areas excellent progress has been made with major improvements. Emergency legislation was passed to facilitate this work in England and to give financial assistance for the restoration of flooded land. Financial assistance was also provided to facilitate the disposal of wind-blown timber in Scotland.

Legislation has provided for the continuance of grants for new fishing vessels and of assistance to the fishing industries.

All concerned with the land have worked resolutely in response to My Government's call to increase food production. Cereals and feeding-stuffs have been released from control and a new method of guaranteeing the return which the farmer receives has been introduced for 1954.

Building and the production of building materials have alike increased and My Ministers have continued to expand their building programme.

Measures have been passed to make further financial provision for the building of new towns and to provide for the revaluation of dwelling houses for rating purposes, to abolish development charges, and to improve the superannuation benefits available to local government officers.

I have given My assent to a measure to establish an Iron and Steel Board for the supervision of the iron and steel industry and to provide for the return of iron and steel under-takings to private ownership.

An Act has been passed which amends the powers, duties and composition of the British Transport Commission and provides for the return to free enterprise of the long distance carriage of goods by road, for the reorganisation of the railways and for greater freedom for the Commission in the charges they may make.

Legislation has been passed to improve the maternity benefits under National Insurance and the working of the Industrial Injuries Scheme.

An Act has been passed to amend the provisions of the Education Acts including those relating to voluntary schools.

A measure has been enacted providing for the reorganisation of the University of St. Andrews.

A measure has been passed to enable grants to be made towards the preservation of buildings of outstanding historic and architectural importance and to strengthen the legislative provisions for the protection of Ancient Monuments.

I have given My assent to measures to strengthen the Monopolies Commission and the law relating to merchandise marks.

With the object of promoting administrative efficiency and public economy My Government have merged the Ministry of Civil Aviation with the Ministry of Transport and the Ministry of Pensions with the Ministry of National Insurance.

THIRD SESSION OF THE FORTIETH PARLIAMENT

1953–1954

OPENING (3 November 1953)

My Lords and Members of the House of Commons:

I look forward eagerly to the visits which I am about to pay with My dear Husband to My peoples in overseas countries of the Commonwealth and Empire.

My Government will continue to regard the relaxation of international tension and the preservation of peace as prime objects of their policy. To this end they are persisting in their efforts to bring about an early meeting between the Soviet Union and the three Western Powers.

My Government will continue to take their full part in all efforts by the United Nations to promote international co-operation. The North Atlantic Alliance is fundamental to My Government's policy and they will do their utmost to keep it vital and strong.

My Government are resolved to work constantly in harmony with the Government of the United States of America. They will also continue to co-operate with their partners in Western Europe to promote European unity and economic well-being. They hope to see the early establishment of the European Defence Community and will afford it all possible support.

My Government will continue to work for a settlement of the problem of German unity, in conjunction with the Governments of France and the United States and in consultation with the German Federal Government. They will also maintain their efforts for the conclusion of an Austrian State Treaty.

Though the fighting has ceased in Korea My Forces have still a part to play there under the United Nations Command. My Government are co-operating in efforts to bring about a political conference on Korea.

My Government hope for a renewal of those friendly relations which have been traditional between this country and Persia and for an early resumption of normal diplomatic relations between the two countries.

My Government attach the utmost importance to continued consultation with their partners in the Commonwealth and will take part in the Conference of Commonwealth Finance Ministers which will be held in Australia in January.

My Ministers will continue to work for the progress and well-being of the peoples of My Colonial territories and protectorates. They will seek to ensure that measures of social and political advancement and of economic development are promoted in the interests of all races.

My Government will ensure that My Forces continue to make their full contribution to world peace and stability.

A measure will be introduced to strengthen and improve the effectiveness of My Reserve Forces and a proposal to continue the present National Service Scheme for a further period will also be presented to you.

Members of the House of Commons:

The Estimates for Public Services will be laid before you in due course.

My Lords and Members of the House of Commons:

It will be the constant aim of My Ministers to strengthen the national economy and thereby to safeguard the high standards of the social services and the stability of employment. To this end they will strive for a further improvement in the balance of overseas payments by encouraging the expansion of exports and of services earning income from abroad.

My Ministers will continue to encourage the building of houses and schools. They will also stimulate a vigorous resumption of slum clearance. Legislation will be introduced to facilitate the repair and improvement of existing houses both by local authorities and private owners.

Bills will be laid before you to amend the financial provisions of the Town and Country Planning Acts and the existing arrangements for payment of equalisation grant to local authorities in Scotland.

Legislation will be introduced to effect lease-hold reform in England and Wales and in Scotland.

My Ministers will continue to encourage the agricultural industry to increase food production and improve the quality and efficiency of home output. My Ministers are consulting farmers and the trades concerned about new methods of providing price guarantees and of marketing which will be required as rationing and allocation cease to be necessary.

My Government will also continue to pay close attention to the welfare of the fishing industry.

Proposals will be laid before you for the transfer of responsibility for atomic energy from the Ministry of Supply to a statutory corporation.

A measure will be introduced to bring the salaries of the judges of My Superior Courts of Law in the United Kingdom more into keeping with the dignity and responsibilities of their office.

Legislation will be proposed to revise, consolidate and extend the law on the safety, health and welfare of miners and quarrymen, to provide benefit for certain further cases of disablement from industrial diseases, to amend and consolidate the law relating to food and drugs and to restrict night working in the baking industry.

My Ministers are attentively examining the Road Traffic Acts with a view to introducing further legislation to improve road safety and promote the orderly use of the roads.

Bills will be introduced to amend the constitution of the National Gallery and the Tate Gallery, to provide for a new governing body for the National Museum of Antiquities in Scotland and to prolong the powers of the National Film Finance Corporation.

Among other measures which you will be invited to pass will be Bills to remove the restrictions at present imposed upon private persons wishing to trade in raw cotton and wind up the Raw Cotton Commission and to reorganise electricity supply in Scotland.

My Ministers will lay before you their proposals for carrying out their policy for television development.

My Ministers will give further consideration to the question of reform of the House of Lords.

PROROGATION (25 November 1954)

My Lords and Members of the House of Commons:

I shall always remember the visits which with My dear Husband I paid to My Peoples in overseas countries of the Commonwealth and Empire. I and My Husband were deeply moved by the warmth of the welcome and the demonstration of affection and loyalty we received from My Peoples everywhere.

I am greviously distressed at the sufferings caused by the recent hurricane in Ontario, and by the calamitous floods in India and Pakistan, and in the Kingdom of Nepal. In token of their sympathy My Government have sent aid to the afflicted.

My Government have maintained their firm support of the United Nations, and in the North Atlantic Treaty Organisation have helped to develop the combined strength of the West.

In concert with the Governments of France and the United States My Government have striven to reach agreement with the Soviet Government on the future of Germany and Austria.

My Government have sought for means of ending the occupation of Western Germany, of associating the German Federal Republic more closely with the West and of enabling Germany to contribute to the defence of the free world. It is a matter of profound satisfaction to Me that at the Conferences held recently in London and Paris agreement was reached on the methods of achieving these ends.

My Government took a leading part in the meeting of Foreign Ministers at Geneva where agreements were reached bringing to an end the fighting in Indo-China. They have been ancouraged by the readiness with which My Government in **Canada** and the Government of India have accepted membership of the Commissions to supervise the Geneva settlement.

My Government also took part in the Manila Conference in company with My Governments in Australia, New Zealand and Pakistan, and signed the South East Asia collective Defence Treaty negotiated there.

My Government have signed an Agreement with the Egyptian Government about the future of the Suez Canal Base. It is My sincere hope that this Agreement will mark the beginning of a new era of friendly co-operation with Egypt.

My Government welcome the settlement of the oil dispute with Persia and the resumption of the traditional relations between the two countries.

In concert with the Governments of the United States of America, Italy and Yugoslavia, My Government have concluded a Memorandum of Understanding providing for the future of the Free Territory of Trieste. My Forces and those of the United States have thus completed their task in that area.

My Government have supported the efforts of the United Nations to bring about peaceful relations between Israel and the Arab States, and to alleviate the lot of the Arab refugees from Palestine.

I was glad to receive a visit from Their Majesties the King and Queen of Sweden in a year which marked the three hundredth anniversary of the Treaty by which the interests of our two countries are so closely linked.

I have also been happy to welcome to My capital and country His Imperial Majesty, the Emperor of Ethiopia, and to have had this opportunity of strengthening the ties between our countries.

The Government of the Rhodesia and Nyasaland Federation has progressively assumed the powers awarded to it under its constitution. The Federal Assembly has been elected and opened its first session.

Important constitutional reforms have been introduced in the Gold Coast, Nigeria, the Gambia and Kenya.

In Malaya and Kenya My Forces, together with the local security forces, have vigorously pursued their campaign, which must be continued until complete success has been achieved.

Finance Ministers of the Commonwealth met in Sydney last January, and Ministers of the Member Governments of the Organisation for European Economic Co-operation in London last July, to consolidate the progress made in our advance towards freer trade and currencies and to agree upon future steps towards that end.

A measure has been passed to strengthen My Reserve Forces. The National Service Scheme has been extended for a further five years, and a Bill has been passed to enable civil defence training to be given to certain National Service Reservists.

Members of the House of Commons:

I thank you for the provision which you have made for the Public Services.

My Lords and Members of the House of Commons:

Farmers and farm workers have striven to maintain and increase their output and have shown great determination and resourcefulness in getting in the harvest.

My Ministers have ended food rationing and a large number of controls. With the restoration of private trade, guarantees of price and market for home food production have been continued in new forms, and certain import duties have been revised in the interest of the horticultural industry.

Acts have been passed to effect leasehold reform in England and Wales and in Scotland.

Measures have been enacted which make further provision for the clearance and replacement of slums; for the improvement of structurally sound houses or their conversion into more convenient dwellings; and for allowing sufficient increase in the rental income of older houses to enable them to be maintained in good repair.

The number of houses built, both for letting and owner-occupation, has continued to increase.

Legislation has been passed to amend the financial provisions of the Town and Country Planning Acts.

I have given My assent to Measures to provide benefit for certain further cases of disablement from industrial diseases, to improve and consolidate the law concerning the safety, health and welfare of mine and quarry workers, and to restrict night-working in the baking industry.

A Measure has been enacted to amend the law relating to Food and Drugs in England and Wales.

An Act has been passed providing for the dissolution of the Raw Cotton Commission.

Legislation has been passed establishing the Independent Television Authority to provide additional television broadcast programmes.

Measures have been enacted to increase the Exchequer Equalisation Grant payable to local authorities in Scotland and to authorise the Secretary of State to appoint a new Board with responsibility for the supply of electricity in southern Scotland.

I have given My assent to a Measure setting up the United Kingdom Atomic Energy Authority.

FOURTH SESSION OF THE FORTIETH PARLIAMENT

1954–1955

OPENING (30 November 1954)

My Lords and Members of the House of Commons:

In the Session which lies before you My Ministers will strive unremittingly to promote the well-being of My People and the peace of the world.

My Government are convinced that a strong and united Commonwealth can take a leading part in the councils of the nations. They look forward keenly to the meeting of Commonwealth Prime Ministers to be held in London early next year.

My Ministers will promote the development of the Colonial Empire, and for this purpose will prolong the Colonial Development and Welfare Acts and increase the funds available under them. They will also continue to give full support to the Columbo Plan.

My Government re-affirm their belief that the United Nations Organisation is essential to the furtherance of international concord, and will give it their wholehearted support. They will at the same time co-operate fully in the work of the North Atlantic Alliance, which they regard as vital to the preservation of peace.

My Government attach the highest importance to maintaining and strengthening close and friendly relations with the United States of America. It is upon this intimate association that world survival depends.

My Government will continue their efforts to promote security and prosperity in South East Asia and to uphold the Indo-China settlement concluded at Geneva.

My Government will persevere in their efforts to conclude an Austrian State Treaty.

In consultation with other Governments concerned, My Government will seek to give early effect to the agreements reached at the recent Conferences in London and Paris, whereby the occupation of Western Germany will end, the German Federal Republic and Italy will accede to the Brussels Treaty, and the German Federal Republic will join the North Atlantic Alliance. My Government trust that these policies, steadfastly pursued in co-operation with other Governments concerned, will so develop the unity and strength of the free nations that the essential basis will be established on which an understanding with the Soviet Union may be sought.

My Forces will continue to make their full contribution to world stability. Their strength on the mainland of Europe will be maintained in accordance with the public undertakings recently given by My Government; and at home a strategic reserve will be developed and measures taken to meet possible new forms of warfare.

Members of the House of Commons:

The Estimates for public services will be laid before you in due course.

My Lords and Members of the House of Commons:

My Ministers will continue to encourage the expansion of industry and the full employment of My People.

In company with other Governments of the Commonwealth, My Government are taking part in the present review of the General Agreement on Tariffs and Trade. In this and other ways My Government will seek to maintain the advance towards a freer system of trade and payments, and to extend the markets for our exports.

My Ministers will be vigilant in preserving the soundness of the public finances, the control of expenditure and the curb on inflation.

On these sure foundations of national prosperity My Ministers will find increasing scope for pursuing social policies directed to the happiness and well-being of all My People.

My Government are very sensible of the difficulties of many of My People who are old age or disablement pensioners. The first five-yearly review of the National Insurance Scheme enables My Ministers to revise its provisions in the light of all the information available about their effects on both this and future generations. They will introduce early legislation to authorise increases in retirement pensions and the other benefits provided for the victims of industrial accidents and diseases, for widows, the sick and the unemployed. There will be corresponding increases in pensions for those disabled in war and for war widows.

My Ministers will ensure the continuance of a high rate of house-building, for letting and for purchase, and are now able to resume an active campaign to clear the slums.

Legislation will be laid before you to deal with certain problems connected with requisitioned dwellings and other matters relating to housing.

My Ministers are greatly concerned at the grievous toll in death and injury that is taken by road accidents, at the inadequacy of our highway system for the ever-increasing volume of traffic, and at the damage done to our national economy by traffic congestion and delays. My Ministers have accordingly decided to embark upon an expanded programme of road construction and improvement, designed both to increase safety on the roads and to promote the freer flow of traffic. The Road Traffic Acts will also be amended to further these aims.

Legislation will be proposed to authorise an increase in the borrowing powers of the British Transport Commission.

To provide better education for children and young people, My Ministers will continue to encourage the building and improvement of schools and technical colleges. Special attention will be paid to the provision of secondary schools, village halls and playing fields in the rural areas. In consultation with the teachers and local authorities, My Ministers will prepare a new scheme for ensuring a sound financial basis for teachers' pensions.

My Government will stimulate the expansion of facilities for higher technological education, so that advances in scientific research may be matched by increased industrial efficiency and production.

My Ministers recognise that the transition from control to freedom has brought problems for all engaged in farming and kindred industries. They will not relax their efforts to promote the efficient production and marketing of food. These will enable stability for the industry to be combined with the flexibility of a free market so that the consumer may enjoy plentiful supplies, and the producer a fair return.

My Ministers will continue to foster the interests of the fishing industry, and will introduce a Bill to provide further assistance to the herring industry.

A Bill will be laid before you to enable My Government to carry out their obligations under the Commonwealth Sugar Agreement, whilst bringing to an end the present system of state trading in sugar.

In order to relieve pressure of business in My courts of law measures will be laid before you to increase the jurisdiction of the county courts in England and Wales and to set up new criminal courts at Liverpool and Manchester.

My Ministers will give close attention to the development of health services in factories.

Legislation will be proposed to enable My Government to accept the Convention adopted by the International Conference on Pollution of the Sea by Oil.

Legislation will be introduced to amend and consolidate the law relating to crofting and to provide for the appointment of a Crofters' Commission.

The Report of the Royal Commission on Scottish Affairs has received the close attention of My Ministers and steps are being taken to carry out its recommendations.

Other measures will be laid before you in due course.

PROROGATION (6 May 1955)

My Lords and Members of the House of Commons:
I followed with the closest interest the visits which My dear Sister paid recently to My Peoples in the Caribbean Islands. The warmth of the welcome She received there was a source of great happiness to Me.

Commonwealth Prime Ministers met in London in January. They reviewed the course of world affairs, and reaffirmed their Governments' resolve to do their utmost to ease international strain and to promote conditions in which real peace can grow and thrive. My Ministers were greatly heartened to learn how far their views upon the means of furthering these common purposes were shared by other Commonwealth Governments.

My Government have continued to give full support to the United Nations, and are striving in the Disarmament Sub-Committee to secure agreement on a comprehensive and properly supervised plan for world-wide disarmament in order to prevent the overwhelming disaster of nuclear warfare.

My Ministers attended meetings of the North Atlantic Council in December, when further plans for collective defence were approved.

The ratification of the Paris Agreements is a matter of great satisfaction to My Government. These Agreements will end the occupation of Western Germany and will associate the German Federal Republic with the countries of the West. They will also provide a basis on which My Government hope to enter into fruitful negotiations with the Soviet Union.

My Government welcome the improved prospect of the conclusion of the Austrian State Treaty.

My Government have signed an Agreement which will promote a more intimate association between the United Kingdom and the European Coal and Steel Community.

My Government have continued to support efforts to bring about peaceful relations between Israel and the Arab States.

My Government have acceded to the Pact of Mutual Co-operation between Turkey and Iraq and have concluded thereunder a Special Agreement with Iraq to replace the Anglo-Iraqi Treaty of Alliance of 1930. It is their belief that this Agreement will fortify friendly co-operation between the two countries, and thereby contribute to the security of the Middle East.

My Government have continued their efforts to uphold the Geneva Agreements on Indo-China and took part in the Bangkok Conference, at which arrangements were carried forward under the Manila Treaty further to safeguard the security of South East Asia. My Government have also continued to encourage economic development in this area through the Colombo Plan.

My Government have been greatly concerned at the dangers of the situation in the Formosa Strait. They have been in constant consultation with the various Governments concerned, in order to open the way for a peaceful settlement.

I have been happy to learn of the agreement reached in the West Indies on the Plan for a British Caribbean Federation, which has enabled My Government to proceed with the next stages towards its achievement.

Legislation has been passed to prolong the Colonial Development and Welfare Acts until 1960, and to provide an additional sum of £80 millions to be spent under these Acts during the next five years.

My Government have strengthened and reorganised My Forces, and have made clear their determination by all means in their power to deter aggression. To this end, My Ministers have felt it their duty to continue the development and production of nuclear weapons.

My Forces have discharged with devotion their many responsibilities throughout the world. Operations against the terrorists in Malaya and Kenya have been vigorously pursued.

Legislation has been passed to effect an extensive revision of the Army and Air Force Acts.

My Ministers have continued to strengthen the Civil Defence Services, and to review the many problems of home defence. They have taken steps to establish a Mobile Defence Corps as part of My Reserve Forces, and to train all members of My Forces in civil defence duties.

Members of the House of Commons:

I thank you for the provision which you have made for the Public Services.

My Lords and Members of the House of Commons:

My Government have continued the policy of freeing trade and payments, and to this end have played a leading part in securing improvements in the General Agreement on Tariffs and Trade and in promoting freer trade in Europe through the Organisation for European Economic Co-operation.

It is a source of great satisfaction to Me that My People's employment has been fully maintained. Fresh incentives have been given to production and to productive investment; and substantial programmes of road and rail development have been announced.

Farmers and farm workers have laboured tirelessly to remedy the situation resulting from an exceptionally severe season. My Ministers have fixed price guarantees and grants for home food production, which should assure stability and encourage an increase in output where this would assist our balance of payments.

War pensions and retirement pensions have been raised. Rates of benefit under the National Insurance and Industrial Injuries Schemes have been increased, and improvements made in the scales of National Assistance.

My Government have approved a scheme, on lines agreed by the National Whitley Council, for the gradual introduction of equal pay for women doing equal work with men in the non-industrial Civil Service.

The provision of houses, both for letting and owner-occupation, has been maintained at a high level. A measure has also been passed to facilitate the release of requisitioned houses, with safeguards for the present occupants.

Legislation has been enacted to authorise further capital expenditure on the development of new towns.

A measure has been passed to amend and consolidate the law relating to crofting, and provide for the appointment of a Crofters' Commission. Legislation has also been enacted to authorise additional grants for the herring industry; and to simplify the procedure for assisting the construction and improvement of fishery harbours.

Local Education Authorities in England and Wales are responding to My Ministers' request to put in hand a five-year programme for reorganising schools in rural areas. Special grants have been made for the expansion of facilities for technological education.

An Act has been passed to protect the youth of the country from the influence of certain harmful publications.

In furtherance of an International Convention legislation has been enacted to strengthen the law relating to the prevention of pollution of the sea by oil.

The recommendations of the Royal Commission on Scottish Affairs are now being carried out.

FIRST SESSION OF THE FORTY-FIRST PARLIAMENT

1955–1956

OPENING (9 June 1955)

My Lords and Members of the House of Commons:

The grave situation created by the interruption of the railway services has made it necessary to advance the date of the Opening of Parliament. I have proclaimed a state of emergency under the Emergency Powers Act, 1920, to enable My Ministers to take the steps needed to maintain supplies and services which are essential to the life of the community.

In their relations with foreign Powers My Government will resolutely go forward with the policies to which they are pledged. The United Nations the Atlantic Alliance and the new association of Western European Union will all receive their whole-hearted support. They will continue to work in close accord with the United States of America.

Fortified by the growing unity and strength of the free nations, My Government look forward, in a spirit of confidence and goodwill, to fruitful negotiations with the Government of the Soviet Union.

My Government welcome the progress which has recently been made in the United Nations' discussions on disarmament and will zealously maintain their efforts to reach agreement on a comprehensive disarmament plan designed to bring peace and security to all countries.

My Government have warmly welcomed the signature of the State Treaty for the re-establishment of an independent and democratic Austria. The text of this Treaty will be presented to you before ratification.

In consultation with the other Governments concerned, My Government will continue earnestly to seek a peaceful settlement of the situation in the Formosa Strait.

My Government will continue their efforts to uphold the Indo-China settlement concluded at Geneva and to promote the peace, security and prosperity of South East Asia through the regional organisations set up for that purpose.

My Government will maintain and strengthen consultation within the Commonwealth for the fulfilment of our common aims and purposes.

The economic development of the Common-wealth and Empire will be steadily encouraged, and My Government will continue to support the Colombo Plan.

My Government look forward to further progress in establishing the British Caribbean Federation.

My Forces will continue to play their full part in maintaining peace and stability in the world.

My Ministers are reviewing the problems of Home Defence and the measures required to meet new forms of warfare.

Members of the House of Commons:

Estimates for the public services will be laid before you in due course.

My Lords and Members of the House of Commons:

The full employment of My People will continue to be the first care of My Ministers. To this end they will actively seek the co-operation of employers and workers in ensuring that full employment and expanding output shall not be jeopardised. They are convinced that, with a steady expansion of production in industry, commerce and agriculture, an ever higher standard of living can be secured for the whole nation.

My Government will actively promote the development of nuclear energy for peaceful purposes.

Legislation, consistent with My Government's international obligations, will be introduced to permit the imposition of countervailing and anti-dumping duties on imported goods.

My Ministers will take such further action as may be required in the public interest to deal with abuses in the field of monopolies and restrictive practices.

It will be the aim of My Government to strengthen the balance of payments and to extend overseas markets for our goods and services. Together with the other Governments of the Commonwealth and of Europe, and with the Government of the United States of America, they will work for a further advance towards a free flow of international trade and payments.

My Ministers will not relax their efforts to secure the utmost economy in public expenditure, and by sound handling of financial affairs to check the dangers of inflation.

My Ministers recognise the need for maximum economic production from our land. They will continue, through guaranteed prices and assured markets, to ensure a fair return to producers, and will encourage the efficient marketing of food.

Legislation will be introduced to safeguard the health and provide for the safety and welfare of those employed in agriculture and forestry.

My Ministers will continue to promote the well-being of the fishing industry and to support the efforts of the White Fish Authority and the Herring Industry Board to improve the condition of the fishing fleets and enable them to operate on an efficient basis.

My Ministers will ensure that steady progress is made with the modernisation and re-equipment of the railways, so that they may give better service to the public and provide improved working conditions for railway workers.

My Government will press forward their far-reaching programme of road construction and improvement and their plans to ease the flow of traffic and reduce danger on the roads. A Measure will be laid before you to amend the Road Traffic Acts.

In the light of proposals recently agreed among the local authority associations My Government are examining the problems of local government in England and Wales with a view to introducing legislation on this subject.

While maintaining a high rate of house building, My Ministers will encourage action to secure the more rapid clearance of slums in both town and country and to relieve urban congestion. They will introduce such legislation as may be found necessary to further these objects.

In step with the continued expansion in the building and improvement of schools My Government will give close attention to the number and needs of the teaching profession. They have very much in mind the special requirements of rural areas. Secondary schools will be encouraged to provide a choice of courses; and facilities for technical education will be extended.

My Ministers will propose amendments to the scheme of superannuation for teachers following the discussions now proceeding with representatives of teachers and local authorities.

A Bill will be laid before you to extend the period during which family allowances are payable for children who remain at school.

Legislation will be introduced to amend the law of valuation and rating in Scotland in the light of the recommendations of a Departmental Committee; and an inquiry into the working of the arrangements for ascertaining Equalisation Grant in Scotland will be made in consultation with the associations of local authorities.

You will also be invited to pass a Measure to amend the law relating to valuation and rating in England and Wales.

Legislation will be proposed to reform the law of copyright on the basis of recommendation in the report of the Copyright Committee.

My Government will proceed with a Bill to enable them to carry out their obligations under the Commonwealth Sugar Agreement, and to bring to an end the present system of state trading in sugar.

My Ministers will bring forward legislation to reduce the pollution of the air by smoke and other causes.

Steps will be taken to extend legal aid to proceedings in county courts in England and Wales, and the jurisdiction of these courts will be increased. A Measure will also be introduced to set up new criminal courts at Liverpool and Manchester, and to amend the law relating to recorders and stipendiary magistrates.

An inquiry will be held to consider practice and procedure in relation to administrative tribunals and quasi-judicial inquiries, including those concerning land.

Further consideration will be given to the question of the composition of the House of Lords.

Other Measures will be laid before you in due course.

PROROGATION (5 November 1956)

My Lords and Members of the House of Commons:
I shall always retain the happiest recollections of the visit which I paid with My Dear Husband to the Federation of Nigeria and of the moving welcome accorded to us there. We also recall with pleasure our visits to the Kingdoms of Norway and Sweden and the gracious reception extended to us by the peoples of those countries. The warmth of the regard shown by My peoples of East Africa and Mauritius to My Dear Sister during her recent visit has been a source of great satisfaction to Me.

I have also been very happy to welcome to this country the President of our oldest ally, Portugal, and the King of Iraq, with whom we are so closely associated in the Bagdad Pact.

My Government have been gravely concerned at the outbreak of hostilities between Israel and Egypt. They resolved, in conjunction with the French Government, to make a quick and decisive intervention to protect the lives of our nationals and to safeguard the Suez Canal by separating the combatants and restoring peace. My Government have proposed that the United Nations should take over responsibility for policing the area, as a prelude to a satisfactory settlement in the Middle East. They earnestly trust that this purpose will be achieved.

My Government have maintained their efforts in the Disarmament Commission of the United Nations to achieve an international agreement on conventional and nuclear disarmament.

The Prime Ministers of the Commonwealth met in London at the end of June. Their discussions were prompted by a desire to further the common interests of their countries and to seek by all means to promote peace and security in the world. My Government have continued to support the purposes of the Colombo Plan and have increased their provision for technical assistance.

The situation in Cyprus has caused My Ministers profound concern. In the face of violence and provocation My Forces have shown exemplary steadiness and forbearance. My Government have taken a fresh initiative by appointing a Commissioner to make recommendations for a new and liberal Constitution for the Island.

I was deeply grieved at the loss of life and great devastation from a disastrous hurricane suffered by several of My West Indian territories. I am glad to know that with the aid of assistance from My Government in the United Kingdom, from others of My Governments, from foreign countries and public appeals they have since made good progress towards recovery.

A Round Table Conference was appointed to consider proposals for closer association of Malta with the United Kingdom. My Government accepted their report and discussions preparatory to the consequential legislation are now proceeding.

An Act was passed conferring powers on Me to provide for a British Caribbean Federation. It was agreed at a Conference with a delegation from the Federation of Malaya that a new Constitution providing for full self-government and independence within the Commonwealth should be introduced by August 1957, if possible. An Order in Council has been made providing for an elected majority in the Legislative Assembly of Sarawak.

The pay and conditions of service of members of the Services on regular engagements have been improved. Plans have been ·developed for using My Forces in support of the local civil defence services which have continued to play their part in home defence.

Members of the House of Commons:

I thank you for the provision which you have made for the public services.

My Lords and Members of the House of Commons:

It has been the constant concern of My Ministers to maintain full employment, to encourage savings by vigorous and imaginative incentives and to preserve the strength and stability of the economy.

In order to stimulate competitive enterprise an Act has been passed to provide for the registration of restrictive trading agreements and their judicial examination by a special court, and to prohibit the collective enforcement of resale price conditions.

The law dealing with copyright and related matters has been revised.

The price guarantees and grants determined by My Ministers have provided valuable support for the agricultural industry. Farmers and workers have faced with courage and determination the difficulties caused by the bad weather this year.

Further help has been provided for agriculture in the hill farming and livestock rearing areas.

Further financial assistance has been provided for the fishing industry.

An Act has been passed to safeguard the health, and to provide for the safety and welfare, of those employed in agriculture and forestry.

My Ministers have ended the Government purchase of imported bacon and have arranged for the import of sugar for home consumption to be returned to private trading. I have given My Assent to an Act to carry out the Government's obligations under the Commonwealth Sugar Agreement.

Measures have been enacted to introduce new arrangements for financing agricultural research and to amend the constitution of the Department of Scientific and Industrial Research.

My Government have announced a five-year plan for extending technical education. An Act has also been passed amending the schemes of superannuation for teachers.

The law relating to education in Scotland has been amended.

My Government have been much concerned with the problem of traffic on the roads and legislation has been passed to improve its regulation and to promote road safety.

New criminal courts have been set up in Liverpool and Manchester and legislation has been enacted to make further reforms in the administration of justice. The system of legal aid has been extended to proceedings in the county courts in England and Wales and the jurisdiction of these courts has been increased.

The law relating to rating and valuation in England and Wales has been amended. Legislation has also been passed to amend the law of valuation and rating in Scotland and to provide a new basis for the payment of equalisation grant to Scottish local authorities for an interim period.

Legislation has been enacted to abate the evils of air pollution.

The structure of the housing subsidies in England and Wales has been modified so as to encourage the building of houses to replace slums and to relieve the congestion of our cities. The compensation payable to certain owner-occupiers and businesses affected by slum clearance has been improved.

An Act has been passed to provide for the establishment of a General Dental Council.

Family allowances have been extended, improvements have been made in the war pensions and national insurance benefits of widows with children, the earnings rules for insurance pensioners have been relaxed, and provision has been made for those receiving workmen's compensation who are totally disabled. The national assistance scales have been raised. The pensions of retired members of the public services have been increased.

SECOND SESSION OF THE FORTY-FIRST PARLIAMENT

1956–1957

OPENING (6 November 1956)

My Lords and Members of the House of Commons:

I look forward with great pleasure to the visits which I shall pay with My Dear Husband to Portugal, France and Denmark. I am following with the closest interest the journey which My Husband is now making through many lands of the Commonwealth.

My Government will continue their efforts to achieve, by all possible means, a prompt and just settlement of the many problems arising from the grave situation in the Middle East. To this end they will welcome the broadest measure of co-operation with the Commonwealth, with our Allies in the Atlantic Alliance and in Europe, and with those international agencies of which the United Kingdom is a member.

Fortified by the unique advances in Parliamentary democracy and economic prosperity which the joint effort of the Commonwealth has already achieved, My Ministers will be concerned to further the progress and constitutional development of the territories for whose well-being they are responsible.

A Bill will be introduced early in this Session to grant independence to the Gold Coast under the name of Ghana, and it is the intention of My Ministers that independence should take effect on 6th March, 1957. The Gold Coast Legislative Assembly have expressed the desire that Ghana should be an independent State within the Commonwealth.

Orders in Council will be laid before you to provide for the constitution of the new British Caribbean Federation and for the inclusion of a number of elected members in the Legislature of British Guiana.

My Ministers, while continuing to take the measures which are unhappily necessary to deal with terrorist activity in Cyprus, will spare no effort to find a solution to the problems of the Island, through a new and liberal Constitution which will safeguard the rights of all communities and the essential interests of this country and our Allies.

My Government will pursue their policy of adjusting the structure of My Forces and the organisation of home defence to changes in the world situation in the light of scientific and technical advances.

It is My Government's intention to put forward during the present Session proposals for reforming the composition of the House of Lords.

Members of the House of Commons:

Estimates for the public services will be laid before you in due course.

My Lords and Members of the House of Commons:

My Ministers will continue to seek the collaboration of employers and workers in combining full employment, rising production and stable prices. They are convinced that the wisdom and experience of My People will be a powerful aid to them in this task.

It will be the aim of My Government to fortify the balance of payments and to extend oversea markets for our goods and services. My Ministers, while fostering the traditional and established Commonwealth preferential system, attach great importance to increasing and strengthening economic co-operation in Europe. To this end they are examining possible methods for creating in Europe an area within which restrictions on the free exchange of goods, other than foodstuffs, would be progressively removed.

Legislation, consistent with My Government's international obligations, will be introduced to allow countervailing and anti-dumping duties to be imposed on imported goods.

A measure will be laid before you to replace the existing emergency powers in respect of hire-purchase and hiring agreements and to regulate borrowing by hire-purchase finance companies.

Steps will be taken to continue the lending powers of the National Film Finance Corporation and to substitute a statutory levy on exhibitors for the present voluntary levy.

My Ministers will continue to make it their aim to promote conditions which will enable the agricultural industry to maintain its progress in increasing efficiency and to achieve the maximum economic production from our land.

A Bill will be introduced to continue financial assistance to, and to make further provision for modernising, certain sections of the fishing fleet.

A measure will be laid before you to give effect to proposals arising from the recent comprehensive review of the financial and economic position and prospects of the British Transport Commission.

My Ministers will proceed with a Bill to reorganise the electricity supply industry in England and Wales.

A measure will be introduced to provide a remedy for damage caused by subsidence resulting from coal mining.

My Government have been reviewing the finance of local government including the incidence of the rate burden between different classes of property.

Their conclusions will, in due course, be announced to Parliament.

Legislation will be laid before you to amend the laws dealing with rent control.

Legislation will be introduced to revise Scottish housing subsidies and to facilitate the relief of congested local authority areas in Scotland.

My Ministers will bring forward proposals to amend the law of homicide and to limit the scope of capital punishment.

My Ministers are resolved to maintain progress in improving social and working conditions, and you will be invited to approve a Bill to amend the law about the closing hours of shops and related matters.

Legislation will be proposed to enable increases in the pay and allowances of members of the police, fire and probation services to be given retrospective effect.

My Government will press on with their plans for expanding facilities for technical education. They will also continue to give a high place in the building programme to new schools.

Other measures will be laid before you in due course.

PROROGATION (1 November 1957)

My Lords and Members of the House of Commons:

A few days ago I returned to London with My Dear Husband on the conclusion of a short stay in Canada and a visit to the United States. It was a great joy to Me to have this opportunity to see again My People in Canada, to open the Canadian Parliament and to renew My personal experience of that great and developing Commonwealth country. I was also very happy to pay, at President Eisenhower's invitation, a second visit to the United States, and to meet members of the United States Government, Congress and the Supreme Court. Everywhere I received a most warm and friendly welcome. My visit has further convinced Me that the ties which bind our peoples are strong and enduring.

I shall always retain the happiest recollections of the visits which I paid with My Dear Husband to Portugal, France and Denmark, and the moving reception extended to us by the peoples of those countries.

My Dear Husband and I were deeply grieved at the death of King Haakon the Seventh of Norway, who held a special place in the hearts of My People. Our sympathy goes out to the members of His family and to the whole Norwegian people.

I recall with pleasure the reception accorded to Me and My Husband by the Secretary-General and by the General Assembly of the United Nations in the course of My visit to New York this month. My Government have continued to co-operate in the work of the Disarmament Commission of the United Nations and have joined in putting forward practical proposals for an international agreement on conventional and nuclear disarmament.

My Government have contributed to the continuing progress being made within the North Atlantic Treaty Organisation and Western European Union in strengthening the defence of the Atlantic Community and in broadening the scope of European co-operation. They have also continued to give their whole-hearted support to the South-East Asia Treaty Organisation and the Bagdad Pact. They welcome the decision of the United States Government to participate in the Military Committee of the Bagdad Pact, and have been much encouraged by the Joint Resolution of the United States Congress, designed to promote peace and stability in the Middle East.

After the cessation of hostilities between Israel and Egypt and the establishment of a United Nations force, United Kingdom Forces were withdrawn from the Suez Canal area. My Government have thereafter continued their efforts to bring about a just settlement of the dangerous situation in the Middle East.

In view of the long-standing ties of friendship between Muscat and Oman and the United Kingdom, My Government took prompt action in response to a request from the Sultan for armed assistance in quelling a rebellion in his dominions. There were no losses in action among the small number of United Kingdom troops engaged.

It gave Me great pleasure to meet the Prime Ministers and other representatives of Commonwealth countries in London at the end of June. Their meeting, at which they reviewed all the major international issues of the day which were of common concern to their countries, revealed a broad similarity of approach and purpose. They affirmed that in the interest of world peace and security they would continue to work for the wider adoption of the principle and practice of co-operation between nations, which is the foundation of their own association.

During the year Acts were passed as a result of which Ghana and the Federation of Malaya achieved independence within the Commonwealth. All Commonwealth Prime Ministers agreed to recognise them as follow members of the Commonwealth. I wish the peoples of Ghana and Malaya all happiness and prosperity; and I welcome their admission to the United Nations. I was much gratified at the cordial reception extended to My Dear Aunt, Her Royal Highness the Duchess of Kent, who represented Me at the celebrations in Ghana in March, and to My Dear Uncle, His Royal Highness the Duke of Gloucester, who represented Me in the Federation of Malaya in August.

My Government have entered into an Agreement

with the Government of the Federation of Malaya whereby United Kingdom Forces may be stationed in Malaya to assist that country in her external defence and for the fulfilment of Commonwealth and international obligations. United Kingdom Forces, together with Forces from other Commonwealth countries, are also continuing to support the Army of the Federation of Malaya in the campaign against the terrorists.

The Nigeria Constitutional Conference which was held in London in May and June, has led to the establishment, under the chairmanship of the Governor-General, of an All-Nigerian Council of Ministers with a Federal Prime Minister, and to the grant of Regional self-government in the Eastern and Western Regions. An Order in Council has been made providing for the establishment of the Federation of the British West Indies.

My Ministers have announced plans for reorganising My Armed Forces at home and overseas. Compensation terms and resettlement plans for those officers and men whose service will be prematurely terminated have been published. A new Naval Discipline Act has been passed.

My Government have approved a re-organisation and expansion of the information services overseas.

Members of the House of Commons:

I thank you for the provision which you have made for the public services.

My Lords and Members of the House of Commons:

My Government welcomed the opportunity, provided by the recent meeting of Commonwealth Finance Ministers in Canada, to exchange views with other members of the Commonwealth on problems of common economic concern.

Provision has been made for more effective long-term assurances to agriculture and for assistance towards the modernisation of farms in the United Kingdom. New provision has also been made for the development of the pig industry in Great Britain.

Legislation has been passed providing further assistance for the white fish and herring industries and for the modernisation of the fishing fleet.

An Act has been passed to amend the law of homicide and to limit the scope of capital punishment.

I have given My Assent to legislation to enable effect to be given to the four international conventions which provide for protection for the victims of war.

Legislation has been enacted amending the Rent Restrictions Acts and providing for a minimum period of notice for the termination of residential lettings. A measure has been passed to revise Scottish housing subsidies and to facilitate the movement of population from overcrowded areas in Scotland.

The law relating to rating and valuation in England and Wales has been amended.

An Act has been passed providing for the payment by all insured persons of a special weekly National Health Service contribution.

Provision has been made for reorganising the electricity supply industry in England and Wales.

A measure has been enacted permitting the imposition of countervailing and anti-dumping duties on goods imported into the United Kingdom.

An Act has been passed to impose a levy on exhibitors of cinematograph films, and to continue certain other provisions, to assist British film production.

I have assented to an Act to extend the right of redress for damage caused by subsidence resulting from coal mining.

Improvements have been made in the provisions for elderly and seriously disabled war pensioners.

THIRD SESSION OF THE FORTY-FIRST PARLIAMENT

1957–1958

OPENING (5 November 1957)

My Lords and Members of the House of Commons:

I look forward with much pleasure to the visit which His Excellency the President of the Italian Republic and Signora Gronchi will pay to this country next May.

I and My Dear Husband have been most profoundly moved by our recent stay in Canada and our visit to the United States of America. The warmth of the welcome which greeted us wherever we went was spontaneous evidence of the bond of common sympathy which unites the peoples of the Commonwealth and the English-speaking world. It will be the constant endeavour of My Government to foster this unity of sentiment and purpose among the free peoples, that they may be confirmed in their resolve to defend the right and to sustain those values on which our civilisation is founded. My Government have recently held discussions in Washington with the United States Government, the results of which, they confidently believe, will greatly further the achievement of this aim.

My Government will seek to strengthen the United Nations in the task of maintaining justice and peace throughout the world. They will pursue their endeavours to achieve an agreement on disarmament, mindful that, at this momentous time, the advance of science into the unknown should be inspired by the hopes, and not retarded by the fears, of mankind.

In accordance with their belief in responsible self-government by free peoples My Ministers will continue to promote the economic and constitutional development of the territories overseas which are in their care. They will introduce legislation to give effect to certain recommendations of the Conference held in April 1957 about the future Constitution of Singapore. They will endeavour, in agreement with the Government of Malta, to further the plans for the closer association of Malta with the United Kingdom. They will continue to seek a just and enduring solution of the problems of Cyprus, in conformity both with the interests of the local communities and with those of this country and our Allies.

Members of the House of Commons:

Estimates for the public services will be laid before you in due course.

My Lords and Members of the House of Commons:

My Ministers are resolved to take all steps necessary to maintain the value of our money, to preserve the economic basis of full employment by restraining inflation, to strengthen our balance of payments and to fortify our reserves, upon which depends the strength of sterling and hence the strength of the sterling area as a whole. My Government believe that these are purposes which should command the support of all sections of the nation.

My Government welcome the recommendation, made by the recent meeting of Commonwealth Finance Ministers in Canada, that a Commonwealth Trade and Economic Conference should be held in 1958. They consider that this would provide a valuable opportunity to reinforce still further the economic ties between the members of the Commonwealth. My Government also welcome the recent declaration by the Council of the Organisation for European Economic Co-operation of their determination to promote the establishment of a European Free Trade Area. It is the firm purpose of My Ministers to seek to bring these negotiations to a successful conclusion, and so to strengthen the resources of the free world.

A Bill will be introduced to revise and codify existing legislation relating to import duties.

My Ministers will continue to give support to agriculture and fishing. Legislation will be introduced to amend certain provisions of the Agriculture and Agricultural Holdings Acts and to improve agricultural drainage in Scotland. My Government have completed a comprehensive review of the emergency powers relating to land. They will propose the repeal of certain of these powers and their replacement, so far as necessary, by statutory provisions.

A measure will be laid before you to establish a Conservancy Authority for Milford Haven to regulate the increased maritime traffic which should result from the projected development of this important harbour.

My Ministers will seek to promote the progressive development of the institutions of government in this country, to enlarge the opportunities for public service and to foster the sense of shared responsibility for the efficient discharge of the manifold functions of government.

Thus legislation will be laid before you to establish machinery for the reorganisation of local government in England and Wales. This measure will also make adjustments in the rating system and in the system of Exchequer grants to local authorities. Separate legislation will be introduced for these two purposes in Scotland.

You will also be invited to approve a measure to permit the creation of life Peerages for men and women, carrying the right to sit and vote in the House of Lords.

My Government have considered with care the report of the Committee on Administrative Tribunals and Enquiries and will introduce legislation to give effect to certain of the recommendations of that Committee.

My Ministers will continue to promote the social welfare of My people. A Bill will be introduced to improve the arrangements for the industrial rehabilitation, training and resettlement of disabled persons. War pensions will be increased; legislation will be introduced to authorise increases in retirement and other benefits, and in contributions, under the National Insurance and Industrial Injuries schemes: and My Government will continue to study the wider problems of provision for old age. They will also introduce legislation amending the law relating to the adoption of children and providing for the supervision of those who take children into their care for payment. They will continue to pay particular attention to penal reform and the treatment of offenders, and they will develop improvements in the prison system in the light of an imaginative programme of research.

Other measures will be laid before you in due course.

My Lords and Members of the House of Commons:

Three weeks ago I opened the Parliament of Canada. Today, I open Parliament at Westminster, where our forefathers, many centuries ago, laid the first foundations of those institutions of Parliamentary democracy which peoples throughout the world have adopted as the guardian of their rights, their liberties and their hopes. From the New World I have brought a message of firm fellowship and the assurance of a common faith.

PROROGATION (23 October 1958)

My Lords and Members of the House of Commons:

My Dear Husband and I derived great pleasure from our visit to the Netherlands in March.

I was pleased to welcome to this country the President of Italy and Signora Gronchi, and the President of the Federal Republic of Germany.

I rejoice that the relations between this country and the United States of America are growing continually closer. My Government welcome the agreement concluded with the Government of the United States for co-operation on the development of modern weapons for purposes of collective defence.

My Government have continued to support the work of the United Nations Organisation. They have maintained their efforts to bring about further progress towards disarmament.

My Government have continued to play their full part in the North Atlantic Alliance and the other regional pacts to which they belong.

In response to an appeal by the Jordanian Government certain of My Forces were despatched to Amman to preserve the territorial integrity and political independence of the country. A few days earlier, United States Forces had landed in the Lebanon in response to a similar appeal from the Lebanese President and My Government had fully supported this action. My Government made it clear to the United Nations that British Forces would be withdrawn from Jordan either at the request of the legitimate Government or when satisfactory arrangements to preserve Jordanian independence had been made under United Nations auspices. As a result of action taken in the United Nations to improve relations between all the Arab States, My Government have agreed with the Jordanian Government that My Forces should be withdrawn and this withdrawal is now taking place.

My Government took part in the Conference at Geneva on the Law of the Sea and have signed the resulting Conventions on the régime of the high seas, the territorial sea, the continental shelf and fishery conservation. They have continued their efforts to negotiate a settlement with Iceland about fishery limits and have offered to submit the issue to the International Court of Justice. Meanwhile they are affording protection to British vessels engaged in fishing in the high seas around Iceland.

The enthusiastic welcome which My Dear Mother received during her recent visit to Australia and New Zealand has been a great joy to Me. The Federation of the West Indies was established in January of this year and in April My Dear Sister represented Me at the inauguration in Trinidad of the Federal Legislature. She subsequently visited Guiana and British Honduras. More recently she has visited Canada. I was happy to hear from her of the warmth and loyalty with which she was greeted everywhere.

My Government welcomed the opportunity for constructive partnership offered by the recent Commonwealth Trade and Economic Conference at Montreal. This meeting emphasised the important role which the countries of the Commonwealth are playing in measures directed towards the expansion of the world economy and the improvement of living standards.

The cordial reception given to My Prime Minister during his tour of India, Pakistan, Ceylon, Singapore, New Zealand and Australia afforded Me great satisfaction. The many discussions which he had with statesmen in these countries served to strengthen still further the ties of friendship within the Commonwealth.

My Government have persevered in their efforts to overcome the obstacles to a settlement in Cyprus;

and My Forces are discharging their unhappy task in the Island with courage and integrity in the face of great difficulties.

During the year an Act was passed enabling provision to be made for the grant of a new constitution to Singapore and for the extension of Commonwealth citizenship to all its citizens.

An Order in Council has been made providing for an all-African Executive Council in Sierra Leone under the presidency of the Governor.

Members of the House of Commons:

I thank you for the provision which you have made for the public services.

My Lords and Members of the House of Commons:

The constant endeavour of My Ministers to strengthen the economy has improved our balance of payments and fortified our reserves, while maintaining a high and stable level of employment for My People and securing greater stability in the value of their money. Additional legislation has been enacted with a view to increasing employment in particular areas.

Measures have been taken to remove controls over the supply and retail prices of coal and over iron and steel scrap prices; to revise and codify the law relating to import duties; and to establish a Conservancy Board at Milford Haven.

My Government have continued to support home agriculture in accordance with the long-term assurances given to the industry, and have provided further assistance for the fishing industry. Legislation has been passed to repeal the disciplinary powers of the State over owners and occupiers of agricultural land and to modify the law relating to security of tenure and the arbitration of rents on tenanted farms. An Act has been passed to facilitate the drainage of agricultural land in Scotland. Fresh provision has been made with respect to the licensing and regulation of slaughterhouses in England and Wales.

Acts have been passed to bring to an end certain emergency powers, notably those dealing with land used for defence purposes and opencast coal production, and to replace them, so far as necessary, with more limited permanent powers.

In accordance with the resolve of My Ministers to improve the institutions of government, machinery has been established by statute for re-organising local government in England and Wales.

Changes have also been made in the rating system and in the system of Exchequer grants to local authorities throughout Great Britain.

A measure has been passed to permit the creation of life Peerages for men and women, carrying the right to sit and vote in the House of Lords. Improvements have also been made in the law relating to the redistribution of seats in the House of Commons.

Measures have been taken to give effect to the majority of the recommendations of the Committee on Administrative Tribunals and Enquiries.

The social welfare of My People has continued to be the special care of My Government. War pensions have been raised; retirement pensions and other benefits under the National Insurance and Industrial Injuries Schemes have been increased; and improvements have been made in the scales of National Assistance. An Act has also been passed to improve the arrangements for the industrial rehabilitation, training and resettlement of disabled persons.

Legislation has been enacted to alleviate possible hardship to tenants of certain dwelling-houses released from control.

The Maintenance Orders Act will achieve a useful measure of social reform in England and Wales by facilitating the enforcement of maintenance orders while at the same time reducing the number of men committed to prison in default of payment.

Important reforms affecting the welfare of children are being effected by an Act amending the law of adoption and making fresh provision for the supervision of those who take children into their care for payment.

FOURTH SESSION OF THE FORTY-FIRST PARLIAMENT

1958–1959

OPENING (28 October 1958)

My Lords and Members of the House of Commons:

I look forward eagerly to the tour of Canada which I shall carry out next summer with My Dear Husband. The peoples of Canada and the United Kingdom have long shared a common destiny. It is our hope that the friendship and understanding between them will be strengthened still further by our visit.

We also look forward with much pleasure to our stay in Ghana in the autumn of next year. This will be My first opportunity of meeting My People in this new Member Country of the Commonwealth and I particularly welcome it. I hope that it will also be possible for Me to visit Sierra Leone and Gambia.

In the spirit which inspired the recent Trade and Economic Conference at Montreal. My Government will seek to promote the closest co-operation within the Commonwealth. It is their firm belief that the Commonwealth has a unique contribution to make to the progress of human society. They will also continue to foster the prosperity of the oversea territories which are in their charge. New legislation to maintain the provision of financial assistance for Colonial develop ment and welfare will be laid before you.

My Government will neglect no opportunity to promote the advance of the Colonial territories and the increasing association of their peoples with the management of their own affairs. They are taking energetic steps to protect the employment of the people of Malta and hope that the forthcoming constitutional discussions with the Maltese political parties will set the pattern of a stable and thriving future. They are deeply concerned at the situation in Cyprus and the tragic loss of life involved. They will persevere in their efforts to secure a settlement ensuring tranquillity and progress in the Island.

I shall be very happy to welcome the Shah of Iran on his visit to this country next May.

My Government will seek to play a full and constructive part in preserving peace and justice and promoting improved standards of life throughout the world. To this end they will actively support the United Nations, and the North Atlantic Alliance and other regional Pacts of which they are members. They will co-operate with the United Nations and the countries of the Middle East in any measures likely to relieve international tension in that troubled area and to take account of the needs and aspirations of its peoples.

Negotiations on the possibility of securing a controlled suspension of the testing of nuclear weapons are due to begin in Geneva on 31st October between My Government and the Governments of the United States of America and the Soviet Union. It is the earnest hope of My Government that these discussions, in which they, together with the Government of the United States, have taken the initiative, may prove fruitful. My Government will also continue to seek an agreement on disarmament in the hope that thereby the fear of war may be lifted from the minds of our own and succeeding generations.

Members of the House of Commons:

Estimates for the public services will be laid before you in due course.

My Lords and Members of the House of Commons:

My Ministers are resolved to ensure the strength of sterling at home and abroad and a high and stable level of employment. In co-operation with the Commonwealth, they will seek to expand our oversea trade both in Europe, by the creation of a Free Trade Area, and throughout the world.

A healthy and thriving agriculture will remain among the principal objectives of My Government. Legislation will be introduced to enable special assistance to be given to small farmers and to provide for further support for the Agricultural Mortgage Corporation.

A Bill will be laid before you for the protection and control of deer in Scotland.

My Ministers will continue to help the fishing industry. They are supporting in the United Nations a proposal that a second World Conference on the Law of the Sea should be convened soon. It is their hope that this may lead to a lasting settlement of the problems of the territorial sea and fishing limits, which are of grave concern to British fishermen.

It will be the special care of My Government to introduce measures to promote the social well-being of My People. Proposals will be laid before you for placing the National Insurance Scheme on a sound financial basis and enabling a larger section of My People to build up pension rights related to their earnings. Effect will be given to many of the recommendations of the Royal Commission on mental illness; and the provisions of a new Bill will replace the existing law on mental health in England and Wales. My Ministers will introduce legislation to amend and strengthen the Factories Acts. A Bill will also be brought in to repeal the Catering Wages Act and to convert the four Catering Wages Boards which are functioning at present into Wages Councils.

My Government will continue to encourage the extension of facilities for higher education in the universities and technical colleges. In addition they will announce new plans for developing the nation's schools intended, in particular, to improve the scope and quality of secondary education.

My Government view with gravity the increase in crime. In the light of the most up-to-date knowledge and research they will seek to improve the penal system and to make methods of dealing with offenders more effective.

My Ministers will continue their efforts to secure a just balance between the expanding demands of the modern State and the freedom and status of the individual. They will introduce Bills to improve the basis of compensation for compulsory acquisition of land: to give further encouragement to home ownership: and to provide for the future management of the New Towns in England and Wales. Legislation will also be proposed to establish a modern code for the general regulation of building in Scotland.

Believing that the traditional rights and liberties of My Subjects should be safeguarded by permanent statute, My Ministers will seek specific statutory sanction for the continuance, for a temporary period and in a restricted form, of certain economic controls deriving from war-time emergency powers and will allow the remainder to lapse.

Other measures will be laid before you in due course.

My Lords and Members of the House of Commons:

  Today, for the first time, this ceremony is being watched not only by those who are present in this Chamber, but by many millions of My Subjects. Peoples in other lands will also be able to witness this renewal of the life of Parliament. Outwardly they will see the pageantry and the symbols of authority and state; but in their hearts they will surely respond to the spirit of hope and purpose which inspires our Parliamentary tradition.

PROROGATION (18 September 1959)

My Lords and Members of the House of Commons:

  The six weeks' tour of My Realm of Canada which My Dear Husband and I undertook this summer was a great happiness to us. It gave us the opportunity to extend our knowledge of that mighty and developing country and to meet personally so many of My Canadian people. It was with special pleasure that, with the President of the United States of America, I opened the St. Lawrence Seaway, a practical illustration both of the co-operation of these two great neighbours and of the increasing industrial strength of the Canadian nation. We were able to make a brief visit to Chicago, where we were deeply impressed by our reception.

I was very glad to welcome President Eisenhower when he came here recently for discussions with My Prime Minister. The outstanding welcome extended to the President by My People was a clear testimony to the deep and abiding friendship between our two countries.

I was pleased to welcome to this country the Shah of Iran. His Imperial Majesty's visit, and also the Commerical Treaty and the Cultural Convention recently concluded with Iran, symbolise the ties of alliance and friendship between our two countries.

In March My Prime Minister and Secretary of State for Foreign Affairs paid an official visit to the Soviet Union which has helped to strengthen peaceful relations with that country. Following that visit a five-year Trade Agreement with the Soviet Union was signed.

My Government have taken part in the Conference on the Discontinuance of Nuclear Weapons Tests, and progress has been made in drafting an international agreement. My Government have also recently agreed with other Governments, including the Soviet Union, to set up a new body to facilitate further negotiations on general disarmament.

My Government have maintained their support of the work of the United Nations and its agencies.

My Government have continued to play their full part in the North Atlantic Alliance and the other regional pacts to which they belong.

During the year, members of My Family have visited many countries outside the Commonwealth. The warmth and generosity with which they were everywhere received have been a source of lasting pleasure to Me.

My heart was warmed also by the great friendliness with which My Dear Husband was greeted when he visited India and Pakistan to attend the Conference of the Indian Science Congress and the Pakistan Association for the Advancement of Science, and by the loyal welcome given him in those of My Territories he visited on his way home.

Other members of My Family have made visits to Nigeria, on the introduction of self-government for the Northern Region, and to others of My Territories and Peoples under My Protection in East and West Africa. The loyalty and friendship which met them everywhere has brought Me much happiness.

The Commonwealth Education Conference which met in Oxford in July reached agreement on important measures of Commonwealth co-operation in education, including mutual assistance in the supply and training of teachers and in technical education. As part of a Commonwealth scheme, My Government have offered to provide 500 scholarships.

I was glad to make My Palace of Marlborough

House available for Commonwealth meetings and for other Commonwealth purposes.

I was happy that, in co-operation with the Governments of Greece and Turkey and the representatives of the Cypriot communities, My Government were able at the London Conference in February to achieve an agreed foundation for the final settlement of the problem of Cyprus. Energetic action has subsequently been taken both in Cyprus and London towards the establishment of the new Republic.

An Order in Council has provided for internal self-government for Jamaica within the Federation of the West Indies. The Constitution of Northern Rhodesia has been advanced. The State of Singapore was inaugurated in June this year.

My Government regretted the need for a state of emergency to be declared in Nyasaland. More recently, provision has been made there for increased African participation in the Legislative Council and for the addition of two African members to the Executive Council.

An Act has been passed which provides a further £95 millions for Colonial Development and Welfare Schemes in the period up to 1964 and which enables My Government to make loans to Overseas Governments of up to £100 millions towards their development programmes.

An Overseas Research Council has been established, to further scientific development in Commonwealth and other countries overseas.

My Government have taken the first steps towards developing a British space research programme.

My Armed Forces have continued to play their part in the preservation of peace throughout the world.

Members of the House of Commons:

I thank you for the provision which you have made for the public services.

My Lords and Members of the House of Commons:

The economic affairs of the country have continued to improve. Production and employment have increased; the balance of payments has been favourable; and prices have remained stable. An Act has been passed providing for substantial assistance from public funds towards the reorganisation and re-equipment of the cotton industry.

Legislation has been enacted to remove remaining wartime emergency legislation and other dependent Defence Regulations, and specific statutory provision has been made for such few limited economic controls as are still required.

My Government have maintained their support for home agriculture. An Act has been passed to enable special assistance to be given to small farmers.

My Government have put into effect plans for further advances in education. An Act has been passed to give more help to denominational schools in England and Wales so that they may play their part in these developments.

The law on mental health in England and Wales has been reformed and fresh provisions made for the treatment and care of mental patients.

My Government have published a White Paper describing their immediate and long-term plans for meeting the challenge of the increase in crime.

I have given My Assent to legislation to improve the basis of compensation for compulsory acquisition of land; to provide for the future management of the New Towns in England and Wales; and to give further encouragement to house-purchase and the modernisation of dwellings.

Legislation has been passed to strengthen the Factories Acts.

My Government have made a number of advances in the field of pensions. Increased provision has been made for elderly war widows. In National Insurance, increases have been made in the pensions earned by those postponing retirement and the earnings rule has been further relaxed. Legislation has been passed which will place national insurance on a sound financial basis and will introduce a scheme of contributions and supplementary pensions related to earnings for employed people who cannot be covered by an appropriate occupational scheme. Action has also been taken to improve the standard of living of those receiving national assistance.

An Act has been passed to increase the pensions of those who have retired from the public services and the pensions of former members of My Armed Forces have also been increased.

For Scotland, legislation has been enacted to establish a modern code for the general regulation of building, and to further the conservation and control of red deer and prevent the illegal and inhumane taking and killing of any deer. A White Paper has been published reviewing the progress made in the development of the Highlands and Islands and setting out a programme of further development of the basic industries and services which contribute to the economic life of the area.

FIRST SESSION OF THE FORTY-SECOND PARLIAMENT

1959–1960

OPENING (27 October 1959)

My Lords and Members of the House of Commons:

I am glad that My dear Husband is to pay a short visit to Ghana next month and I hope that the visit which we had planned to make together may take place in 1961.

The warm and friendly welcome accorded to My Cousin, the Princess Alexandra, by the Government and people of Australia has given me great joy; and and I have learned with pleasure of the generous courtesy with which His Majesty the King of Thailand and His Majesty the King of Cambodia have received her in their countries.

I look forward with pleasure to the visit which the President of the French Republic and Mme. de Gaulle are to pay to this country next year.

My Government will work in the closest collaboration with the Governments of the Commonwealth in all matters which contribute to peace. They will seek to develop the material resources on which the standard of living of the peoples of the Commonwealth must depend and will at the same time foster the spiritual values which form our common heritage.

The Commonwealth Education Conference which met last July made a number of recommendations designed to spread the benefits of education more widely within the Commonwealth. The consequential legislation will be laid before you.

I confidently expect that a formal request will be received from the Nigerian Legislature for the grant of independence within the Commonwealth to the Federation of Nigeria in 1960. My Government intend to proceed with the appointment of an Advisory Commission in preparation for the review of the constitution of the Federation of Rhodesia and Nyasaland which is to take place next year. My Government welcome the prospect of the establishment of the Republic of Cyprus, in accordance with the Agreements concluded at the London Conference.

My Government will continue to work for the improvement of relations between East and West and will use all their efforts to this end.

My Government look forward to taking part in the work of the new Commission of ten nations which is to consider plans for comprehensive disarmament. They will maintain their efforts to achieve agreement at the Geneva Conference on the discontinuance of nuclear weapons tests. They will persist in their support of the United Nations and will seek to increase its influence. They will play their full part in maintaining the North Atlantic Alliance and other regional pacts to which they belong. My Armed Forces will continue to make their contribution to the preservation of peace throughout the world.

The improvement of conditions of life in the less developed countries of the world will remain an urgent concern of My Government. They will promote economic co-operation between the nations and support plans for financial and technical assistance. They have entered into negotiations for setting up a free trade association of seven countries in Europe, and intend that this should assist in the establishment of wider European trading arrangements which will be in the best interests of the Commonwealth and of the world as a whole.

Members of the House of Commons:

Estimates for the public services will be laid before you in due course.

My Lords and Members of the House of Commons:

My Ministers will strive to maintain full employment, together with steady prices, a favourable balance of payments and a continuing improvement in standards of living based on increasing production and a rising rate of investment.

In recognition of the place of science and technology in the modern world a Cabinet Minister has been entrusted with the task of co-ordinating and promoting development in research and other scientific activity.

My Ministers will give urgent attention to the problems of those areas in which there is need to provide further opportunities for employment, and a Bill will be introduced to replace the Distribution of Industry Acts.

In order to develop a sound system of communications throughout the country, My Government will press forward with their policy of building new highways and improving existing roads. They will encourage further modernisation of the railways and will devote special attention to the future of the aircraft industry. A Bill will be laid before you for improving the arrangements for licensing air services and airline operators and to ensure the maintenance of high standards of safety.

My Government will initiate an enquiry into the working of the Companies Act and will introduce a Bill to strengthen the present law relating to building societies. They will put before you legislation to permit the payment of wages through a bank to any employee who so requests.

The well-being of all those whose living depends on the land will remain one of the first cares of My Government. The system of guaranteed prices and the long-term assurances in the Agriculture Act of 1957 will be continued. Legislation will be introduced to provide grants for horticultural growers and My Government will encourage the more economic marketing of produce. In particular, proposals will be put before you for reorganising and improving Covent Garden Market.

Proposals will be put before you also to continue the subsidies and grants given to the fishing industry and to make further provision for co-operation in international measures of conservation. At the Second World Conference on the Law of the Sea, to be held next spring, My Ministers will work for a just and reasonable settlement of the unresolved problems of the breadth of the territorial sea and of fishery limits.

My Government will give close attention to the social welfare of My people, including the needs of the war-disabled and their dependants and of old people. The earnings rules for pensioners and widowed mothers will be further relaxed. New house building will be maintained at a high level and the slum clearance campaign will continue. Measures will be introduced to modernise the law in Scotland relating to mental health and to succession. A Bill will also be laid before you providing for the registration of certain professions auxiliary to medicine.

The needs of the young in the society of today demand special attention. My Government will press forward with their plans to improve school buildings and to enlarge opportunities in the schools, technical colleges and universities. More teachers will be trained, and this will help to reduce the size of classes. With the aid of more trained youth-leaders, with an improved Youth Service and by other means young people will be enabled to put their leisure to better use.

A Bill will be introduced to amend and modernise the law on betting and gaming. A measure will be prepared to bring up to date the various statutes relating to Charitable Trusts. Legislation will be laid before you to make legal aid and advice more widely available.

Further advances will be made in penal reform. A Bill will be introduced to provide more effective means of dealing with young offenders and to extend compulsory after-care to prisoners who, by supervision or discharge, may be prevented from reverting to crime.

Other measures will be laid before you in due course.

PROROGATION (27 October 1960)

My Lords and Members of the House of Commons:

I am deeply grateful for the many expressions of good will which came to me on the birth of My second Son, Prince Andrew. This year has also brought me the great happiness of My Sister's marriage.

In the course of the year the friendships existing between My People in this country and peoples overseas have been reinforced by a number of visits.

In April I had the special pleasure of welcoming to London the President of the French Republic and Madame de Gaulle. I have been happy to greet here their Majesties the King and Queen of Thailand and, ten days ago, the King and Queen of Nepal.

I was glad that the President of Peru was able to meet members of My Family when he came here in February and that I was myself able to receive the President of the Argentine Republic.

I was moved by the warmth and sincerity of the reception accorded to My Husband when he visited New York in June to open the British Exhibition.

My Mother has visited the Federation of Rhodesia and Nyasaland to open the great Kariba Dam. Both she and I were deeply affected by the enthusiastic welcome which she received throughout her journeys in the Federation.

The visits of members of My Family to the Caribbean were a vivid reminder to all My Peoples in that area of their links with the Crown and with My People in the United Kingdom.

My Government have supported the work of the United Nations and its agencies and are taking their full share in the work of the General Assembly. My Government have continued to play their full part in the North Atlantic Alliance and other regional pacts.

They have continued to take part in the Geneva Conference on the Discontinuance of Nuclear Weapons Tests, in which progress has been made towards agreement on the prohibition of tests under effective international control. They played a notable role in the Ten-Nation Committee on Disarmament at Geneva and supported the resolution of the United Nations recommending the earliest possible resumption of international negotiations for disarmament.

Meanwhile My Armed Forces have continued to contribute to peace and order throughout the world.

By the signing of the Antarctic Treaty last December, the twelve Governments concerned, which include My own and those of the United States and the Soviet Union, have agreed to co-operate in the peaceful use of the Continent in the interests of science.

I was most happy to meet, in May, the Prime Ministers and other representatives of Commonwealth countries. Their meeting revealed a wide measure of agreement on international problems, notably on the need to lessen world tensions and to promote the economic and cultural progress of the less-developed countries.

I have given My Assent to an Act which established the independent Republic of Cyprus. Certain Sovereign Base Areas and other military facilities in the island are retained for the United Kingdom and My Government look forward to a long friendship with the new Republic.

Two other countries for which My Government in the United Kingdom have hitherto been responsible have achieved independence. In June I withdrew My protection from the Somaliland Protectorate, confident that the long tradition of friendship between the British and Somali peoples will continue and flourish.

This month Nigeria became the eleventh Member of the Commonwealth. I have shared in the joy with which that great country then received My Cousin, the Princess Alexandra. My Husband and I have very happy memories of our own visit to Nigeria five years ago and we, together with My Government and all My People in the United Kingdom, extend to My People there our warmest good wishes for the future.

I have given My Assent to an Act which reflects the decision of the Government of Ghana to adopt a Republican Constitution.

My Government in the United Kingdom have continued to give financial help to the less-developed countries, and in particular to Commonwealth countries, including loans and grants for development, welfare and reconstruction.

Acts have been passed enabling the United Kingdom to take part in the Commonwealth Scholarship and Fellowship Plan and making possible a freer movement of students and teachers between this country and the rest of the Commonwealth.

The Commonwealth Economic Consultative Council, which met in London in September, agreed to initiate a Special Commonwealth African Assistance Plan in order to give further help in raising the standards of life in less-developed Commonwealth countries in Africa.

My Government have published their plan for My Overseas Civil Service, providing greater security for its members and making it easier for territories which achieve self-government to retain them in their employment.

Members of the House of Commons:
I thank you for the provision which you have made for the public services.

My Lords and Members of the House of Commons:
As part of their policy to assist the development of overseas countries, My Government have joined the new International Development Association and are contributing substantially to its resources.

They have ratified the Convention establishing the European Free Trade Association, and have taken part in negotiations for remodelling the Organisation for European Economic Co-operation with the United States and Canada as full members.

Support for home agriculture and for the fishing industry has been maintained. My Government have introduced improvement grants for horticultural producers and their co-operative marketing associations. They have brought to a successful conclusion the long campaign for the eradication of tuberculosis in cattle in this country.

An Act has been passed to help to provide additional opportunities for employment in those areas where high and persistent unemployment exists or is threatened.

My Government have announced a substantial increase in the road programme. An Act has been passed to facilitate enforcement of the law on road traffic and to amend the law on parking and traffic regulation.

An Act has been passed to improve the arrangements for licensing air services and to ensure that all airline operators maintain high standards of safety.

Effect has been given to the main recommendations of the Royal Commission on Betting, Lotteries and Gaming, by legislation providing for the registration of bookmakers, permitting the establishment of licensed betting offices, and replacing the outmoded law on gaming by provisions more acceptable to modern opinion.

An Act has been passed which will give added protection to those who invest their savings in building societies.

An Act has been passed to control the location and conditions of caravan sites and to strengthen the procedure for enforcing planning control in England and Wales.

In Scotland the law on mental health has been modernised and new provision made for the care of those who are sick in mind.

Measures have been taken to make legal aid and advice more widely available. The right of appeal to the House of Lords in criminal cases has been extended and the law relating to contempt of court has been amended.

The law relating to charities in England and Wales has been consolidated and reformed, to enable the best use to be made of charitable resources for the benefit of the community.

SECOND SESSION OF THE FORTY-SECOND PARLIAMENT

1960–1961

OPENING (1 November 1960)

My Lords and Members of the House of Commons:

My Husband and I look forward eagerly to the series of visits we shall make next year in the Commonwealth, where we shall renew and extend the friendships which we value so very highly.

In the early part of the year we shall visit India and Pakistan, on the invitation of the Presidents of those countries; and I welcome especially this opportunity of seeing for the first time something of these two great nations of the Commonwealth.

No less a pleasure is the prospect of our journey to Africa, where, later in the year, we shall visit the Republic of Ghana, Sierra Leone and the Gambia. We shall be happy to visit also the Republic of Liberia.

My Husband and I look forward with lively satisfaction to renewing our friendships with His Majesty the King of Nepal, His Imperial Majesty the Shahinshah and the President of the Italian Republic when we visit their countries next year.

Throughout the coming session, My Government will continue to give resolute support to the work of the United Nations. The improvement of relations between East and West remains a primary object of their policy. In particular, they will go on working for the success of the Geneva Conference on the Discontinuance of Nuclear Weapons Tests and will do their utmost to achieve comprehensive disarmament under effective international control.

My Government will play their full part in maintaining the North Atlantic Alliance and the other regional pacts to which they belong. My Armed Forces will continue to make their contribution to the safeguarding of world peace.

The friendship which links us to our great ally, the United States of America, is a powerful element in the defence of peace.

My Government will convene a conference to review the Constitution of the Federation of Rhodesia and Nyasaland in accordance with the provisions of that Constitution.

A Bill will be brought before you to enable Sierra Leone to achieve its independence within the Commonwealth.

My Government hope that in Malta self-government can be restored on firm foundations and that, with the co-operation of a Maltese Government, their efforts to expand the island's economy will be successful.

Members of the House of Commons:

Estimates for the public services will be laid before you in due course.

My Lords and Members of the House of Commons:

My Government will seek to maintain a sound economy and to ensure a well-balanced growth of production in conditions of high and stable employment. Their aim will be to preserve stability of the general level of prices and to further the expansion of overseas trade and strengthen the balance of payments.

They have entered into negotiations under the General Agreement on Tariffs and Trade, which they hope will result in a significant reduction in trade barriers. They will continue to co-operate with their partners in consolidating the European Free Trade Association. At the same time, they will work towards the political and economic unity of Western Europe, on a basis satisfactory to all the Governments concerned.

My Government will introduce legislation to enable to United Kingdom, in common with others of our friends, to help the Governments of India and Pakistan to finance the construction of important works in the Indus River Basin.

At home My Ministers are resolved to maintain a stable, efficient and prosperous agriculture. They will introduce legislation to reorganise and improve Covent Garden Market and to amend the law relating to land drainage in England and Wales.

They will continue to support and encourage our fishing industry and to seek a solution of the delicate problems of fishery limits, especially with those countries off whose coasts our fishermen have traditionally fished.

My Government will follow out their policy of advancing the social welfare of My People. War pensions will be increased and authority will be sought for increases in retirement pensions and other benefits, and in contributions under the National Insurance schemes.

My Government's concern for young people will be shown by the continued expansion of schools and colleges and by greatly increased efforts to train and recruit more teachers. They will continue to encourage the expansion of the Youth Service and will authorise an increasing level of expenditure on the physical recreation of the young. Awards for students at universities and for those taking comprable courses at other institutions of higher education will be granted on an improved basis.

A high rate of house-building will be maintained, and the slum clearance drive will continue. A Bill will be introduced to amend the law relating to the respective responsibility for repairs as between landlords and tenants on short-term tenancies. My Ministers will put forward proposals to amend the law of rating and valuation and to facilitate the 1963 revaluation.

My Government will endeavour to improve the protection of the community against crime. The strength, efficiency and well-being of the police will be their continuing concern; and they will seek to make more effective the various methods of penal treatment. They will introduce a Bill to provide in England and Wales, better means of dealing with young offenders; to extend compulsory aftercare to prisoners and so to discourage them from reverting to crime; and to improve the management of approved schools. Proposals for legislation in the same field in Scotland will be laid before you.

Legislation will be introduced to provide for a levy on horse-racing and, in England and Wales, to check abuses by registered clubs and to reform the licensing laws.

Authority will be sought for an increase in the number of judges in the Supreme Court.

My Government will persevere with measures to promote economic growth in the Highlands and Islands and to develop modern standards of living there; and they will put forward legislation to amend the Crofters (Scotland) Act.

A Bill will be introduced to extend the investment powers of trustees.

Legislation will be laid before you to amend the Weights and Measures Acts.

Legislation is being prepared to provide financial assistance towards the construction of a new Atlantic liner to replace the *Queen Mary*.

My Government will submit to you proposals for reforming the structure and functions of the British Transport Commission.

They are preparing legislation designed to promote greater safety on the roads and, in order to relieve traffic congestion in London, to make possible the construction of an underground garage under part of Hyde Park.

Other measures will be laid before you in due course.

PROROGATION (24 October 1961)

My Lords and Members of the House of Commons:

I was deeply moved by the enthusiastic welcome which My Husband and I received during our visits to India and Pakistan. We shall long treasure most vivid and warming memories of all that we saw in these great and growing countries, whose rich cultural heritage is now rivalled by their striking technical and industrial advance.

It gave us great pleasure to visit Iran as the guests of His Imperial Majesty the Shah-in-Shah and to renew our friendship with Their Majesties The King and Queen of Nepal. We were also glad to meet the Head of State of the Republic of Turkey.

I recall with pleasure the welcome given to us by the President and people of Italy and our reception by His Holiness Pope John XXIII.

I was happy to welcome the President of the United States and Mrs. Kennedy when they came to London in June.

My Government have worked for a resumption of negotiations on general disarmament. They have also striven for international agreement on the discontinuance, under effective control, of all tests of nuclear weapons. They deeply regret that the Soviet Government should have initiated the resumption of these tests.

My Government have maintained their support for the United Nations and participated fully in the work of its agencies. My Ministers share my sense of the great loss which the United Nations has sustained by the tragic death of the Secretary-General, Mr. Hammarskjoeld.

The North Atlantic Alliance and other regional associations for defence have continued to be the basis of My Government's defence policy, and My Armed Forces have contributed to peace and order throughout the world. Their ability to come to the aid of those threatened has been convincingly demonstrated by their swift response to the request from the Amir of Kuwait.

In March I was most happy to receive the Prime Ministers of all Commonwealth countries on the occasion of their meeting in London, when the discussions showed a wide measure of agreement on the question of disarmament and other world problems.

The Commonwealth Prime Ministers accepted the application from the Republic of Cyprus for Membership of the Commonwealth. In April Sierra Leone attained independence and was also admitted to Commonwealth Membership. I extend to both countries my warmest good wishes.

The Union of South Africa withdrew from the Commonwealth on 31st May, 1961, and has become a Republic.

Following on a plebiscite held last February United Kingdom Trusteeship in the Cameroons has been terminated. The Northern part has joined Nigeria and the Southern part has united in a Federation with the Cameroun Republic.

I was pleased to open the Seventh Conference of the Commonwealth Parliamentary Association, which met in London last month, and to welcome representatives of sixty-one different legislatures in all parts of the Commonwealth.

Further constitutional advances have been made

in many territories.

Negotiations have been opned by My Government with a view to joining the European Economic Community if satisfactory arrangements can be made to meet the special interests of the United Kingdom, the Commonwealth and the European Free Trade Association. My Government have ratified the Convention establishing the Organisation for European Co-operation and Development.

Members of the House of Commons:

I thank you for the provision you have made for the public services.

My Lords and Members of the House of Commons:

My Government have sought to deal with an unsatisfactory balance of payments in such a way as to increase the competitiveness and the efficiency of the national economy. The short-term steps taken have included a drawing on the International Monetary Fund. Since the end of July there has been a steady improvement in the strength of sterling.

A new Department of Technical Co-operation has been set up to co-ordinate and improve the administration of the technical assistance which My Government has continued to provide on a substantial scale to developing countries.

Support for home agriculture has been maintained. Acts have been passed to enable drainage charges to be levied on agricultural land and to provide for the reorganisation and improvement of Covent Garden Market.

My Government have continued to support the fishing industry and to seek a settlement of problems of fishery limits in those waters of importance to our fishermen. To this end, they have made agreements with the Governments of Iceland and of Norway.

Legislation has been passed to make fresh provision for the reorganisation and development of crofting in the Highlands and Islands.

Measures were taken to strengthen the finances of the National Health Service by increasing the National Health Services Contributions and certain charges.

Progress has been made with the building of schools and technical colleges and with the expansion of teacher training colleges. Improved financial assistance has been made available for students at universities, teacher training colleges and other similar institutions. Steps have been taken, in co-operation with the local education authorities and voluntary organisations, to develop the Youth Service.

My Government have continued to give special attention to the social welfare of My People. War pensions have been increased; retirement pensions and other benefits provided under the National Insurance and Industrial Injuries Schemes have been raised, and improvements have been made in the scales of national assistance. A system of graduated pensions and contributions has been brought into operation.

My Government have been concerned to improve the protection of the community against crime. An Act has been passed to provide better means of dealing with young offenders, to extend the scope of the compulsory supervision of persons released from custody and to give new powers in connection with the management of approved schools. A number of new detention centres has been completed.

Measures have been passed to reform the licensing laws and to strengthen the law relating to registered clubs in England and Wales.

Legislation has been enacted to provide in England and Wales for a better distribution of housing subsidies, and to assist the further improvement of housing conditions generally.

An Act has been passed to amend the law of rating and valuation and to facilitate the 1963 revaluation in England and Wales.

An Act has been passed to re-organise the financial arrangements of the Post Office in recognition of its commercial character.

Acts have been passed to amend the investment powers of trustees and to revise and simplify previous legislation for the management of the Crown Estate by the Crown Estate Commissioners.

THIRD SESSION OF THE FORTY-SECOND PARLIAMENT

1961–1962

OPENING (31 October 1961)

My Lords and Members of the House of Commons:

My Husband and I look forward to our coming journey to West Africa.

It gives Me much pleasure that My Husband is to visit the countries of Latin America next year and that Princess Alexandra is on her way to South-East Asia and the Far East.

I shall be glad to welcome President Sukarno of Indonesia on a State visit to this country.

My Government will continue to give resolute support to the United Nations. They believe it to be essential for the future of the world that the authority of this organisation should be sustained, and that it should be enabled to carry out the tasks assigned to it under its Charter.

The improvement of relations between East and West remains a primary object of My Government's policy, and they will continue to seek peaceful co-operation with all countries.

My Government will seek, in conjunction with their allies, to achieve by negotiation a settlement of the Berlin question which will preserve the security and freedom of the people of West Berlin.

The North Atlantic Alliance is now more than ever essential for the continued safety of Europe and the world. My Government will continue to play their part in keeping it and the other regional pacts to which we belong strong and united. The close friendship between this country and the United States will be maintained and, in co-operation with My allies, My armed forces will continue to contribute to the prevention of war. Legislation will be proposed giving power to retain for an additional six months certain National Servicemen who are serving full-time, and to recall for a similar period National Servicemen who have a liability to part-time service. In addition, the reserve organisation of My army will be reviewed.

My Government will continue to work for the success of the Geneva Conference on Laos and for the maintenance of peace in South-East Asia.

Guided by the principles agreed upon between the Prime Ministers of the Commonwealth countries at their last Meeting, My Government will do their utmost to achieve general and complete disarmament under effective international control. In spite of the action of the Soviet Union in continuing to conduct nuclear tests on a massive scale in defiance of world opinion. My Government will persevere in their endeavour to promote an international agreement on the discontinuance of tests of nuclear weapons.

A measure will be laid before you to amend the law to accord with the new status of South Africa.

Legislation will be introduced to enable Southern Rhodesia to be granted a new Constitution.

Bills will be introduced to provide for the independence of Tanganyika and of Uganda and for constitutional changes in the West Indies.

My Government will make every effort to bring to a successful conclusion the negotiations which they are undertaking with the European Economic Community and will at all times maintain close consultation with the interests involved in the United Kingdom and with the other members of the Commonwealth and of the European Free Trade Association.

Members of the House of Commons:

Estimates for the public services will be laid before you in due course.

My Lords and Members of the House of Commons:

My Ministers will continue to direct their policies towards maintaining the stability of sterling. They will seek to strengthen the balance of payments by the measures already announced, including especially the vigorous promotion of exports. Legislation will be laid before you to raise the limits of the liabilities to be assumed by the Export Credits Guarantee Department.

My Ministers will continue to seek the co-operation of both sides of industry in the better co-ordination of the national effort with a view to promoting faster economic growth, while maintaining stability in prices and a high and stable level of employment.

They will seek to keep public expenditure within limits justified by the national resources. Continuing efforts will be made to secure a better relationship between increases in incomes and in national productivity.

My Government will introduce a Bill to give effect to the proposals already submitted to you for the re-organisation of the undertakings under the control of the British Transport Commission.

A Bill will be introduced to ensure the orderly development of privately-owned industrial pipelines.

Proposals will be laid before you to amend the law relating to teachers' salaries, school-leaving dates and the award of grants to students.

My Government are resolved to maintain a stable, efficient and prosperous agricultural industry. They will lay before you a Bill to implement their proposals on the Report by the Committee on the Fishing Industry and on drift netting for salmon.

Legislation will be proposed to amend local

government financial arrangements in Scotland; to secure better distribution of Scottish housing subsidies and amend the law relating to housing in other respects; and to make certain amendments in the licensing law of Scotland.

Proposals will be laid before you for improving the machinery for administering criminal justice with a view to securing greater expedition and efficiency.

Legislation will be introduced to control the immigration to the United Kingdom of British subjects from other parts of the Commonwealth, and to give powers for the expulsion of immigrants convicted of criminal offences.

A Bill will be introduced to improve the provision for supplementing workmen's compensation and to make certain alterations in the administration of the schemes for family allowances, national insurance and industrial injuries.

Plans will be laid before you for the development of the hospitals over the next decade, within the framework of the National Health Service as a whole.

Authority will be sought for the establishment of national training councils for health visitors and social workers.

You will be invited to approve a measure designed to promote greater safety on the roads:

Other measures will be laid before you in due course.

PROROGATION (25 October 1962)

My Lords and Members of the House of Commons:

My Husband and I were touched by the memorable welcome given to us during our visit to Ghana, Sierra Leone and the Gambia. We also had great pleasure in visiting Liberia and later in welcoming the President of Liberia and Mrs. Tubman on a State Visit to this country.

I was very glad to welcome the King of Norway as My guest in Edinburgh last week. This was the first State Visit to be held in Scotland since the Union of the Crowns in 1603.

The bonds of friendship between My People and those of other countries have been strengthened through visits which have been paid by My Husband and by members of My Family.

My Government have continued their active support for the United Nations and its Agencies, and have worked to achieve the purposes to which the United Nations Charter gives expression. At the Conference in Geneva they have supported proposals for general and complete disarmament and jointly with the Government of the United States have brought forward proposals for the banning of tests of nuclear weapons. Unfortunately, owing to the

attitude adopted by the Soviet Union and its allies, agreement has not yet been reached on either of those issues.

My Government have continued to play a full part in the international organisations to which the United Kingdom belongs. The North Atlantic Alliance and other regional associations for defence have remained an integral part of My Government's defence policy.

My Government played a leading part in the negotiations on the Laotian question at the Geneva Conference in July. These resulted in the signature of an agreement to end the civil war in Laos and to provide international undertakings to respect the neutrality of that country. I extend to the Kingdom of Laos My good wishes for its future peace and prosperity.

My Government are in close consultation with the United States and My other allies about the dangerous situation created by the supply of offensive weapons to Cuba.

My Government have continued negotiations with a view to joining the European Economic Community if satisfactory arrangements can be made to meet the special needs of the United Kingdom, of other Commonwealth countries and of the European Free Trade Association. My Government have also initiated negotiations for membership of the European Coal and Steel Community and Euratom.

My Government have signed two Conventions establishing organisations which will enable this country to co-operate with other European countries in space projects.

During the present Session Tanganyika, Jamaica, Trainidad and Tobago and Uganda have become independent members of the Commonwealth. I extend My warmest good wishes to these countries.

I was pleased to welcome in London last month the Heads of Government of all member countries of the Commonwealth, or their representatives.

The Federation of the West Indies has been dissolved and plans have been made for preserving common services previously administered by the Federal Government.

I welcomed the holding of the second Commonwealth Education Conference in New Delhi in January. I believe that co-operation in education will help to strengthen the links between the countries of the Commonwealth.

My Government and the Government of the Federation of Malaya have reached a decision in principle that a Federation of Malaysia should be brought into being by 31st August, 1963.

My Government have continued to give financial help to the overseas territories for which they are responsible. An Act has been passed to raise the limit on the aggregate amount of loans from the International Bank to the Colonial Territories which may be guaranteed by My Treasury.

My Armed Forces have continued to play their part in the maintenance of peace and stability in the world. An Emergency Reserve has been created in My Territorial Army in which volunteers may be called out for service with the Regular Army for short periods. I pay tribute to the millions of men who since 1939 have been called upon to serve under the National Service Acts.

Members of the House of Commons:

I thank you for the provision which you have made for the public services.

My Lords and Members of the House of Commons:

My Government have set up the National Economic Development Council to consider ways of improving economic efficiency and promoting more rapid growth and have sought to keep the rise of incomes within the rate of increase of national production.

The strength of sterling has been maintained, and the substantial drawing obtained from the International Monetary Fund in 1961 has been repaid in full.

My Ministers have taken important steps to enrich the nation's cultural life especially by setting in train the establishment of a National Theatre.

My Government have continued their support for agriculture. Legislation has been passed providing further financial assistance for the fishing industry and additional powers for the regulation of sea fisheries, including salmon fishing.

An Act has been passed reducing the number of school-leaving dates and introducing more liberal arrangements for grants to full-time students in universities and elsewhere.

Legislation has been passed establishing Councils for the training of health visitors and for training in social work.

My Ministers have announced their intention of carrying through comprehensive plans for the development of our hospitals.

Powers have been taken to exercise control over the rate of immigration to the United Kingdom of Commonwealth citizens from other parts of the Commonwealth.

Measures have been enacted to improve the administration of criminal justice in England and Wales and to amend the law relating to the adminis- tration of justice in Northern Ireland and the legislative powers of the Parliament of Northern Ireland.

My Government have continued to give their attention to the housing conditions of My People and are increasing their efforts to clear the slums.

Alterations and improvements have been made in the schemes for family allowances, national insurance and industrial injuries. The scales of national assistance have been increased, and the provision for

supplementing workmen's compensation has been improved.

An Act has been passed to ensure the orderly development of industrial pipelines.

Legislation has been passed providing for a better distribution of housing subsidies in Scotland and amending in other respects the law relating to housing in that country. The liquor licensing law in Scotland has been amended.

Acts have been passed to provide for the reorganisation of the nationalised transport under- takings and to make further provision for safety on the roads.

FOURTH SESSION OF THE FORTY-SECOND PARLIAMENT

1962–1963

OPENING (30 October 1962)

My Lords and Members of the House of Commons:

My Husband and I greatly look forward to our coming visit to Australia and New Zealand. I have the happiest recollection of our visit in 1953 and 1954, and it is a source of deep pleasure to Me that we can renew our acquaintance with those great and growing members of the Commonwealth.

My Government have been shocked by the invasion of Indian territory by Chinese armies. They fully support India's decision to defend her rightful frontiers.

My Government regard the development and improvement of relations between East and West as one of the most important aims of their policy. They will maintain their support for the United Nations, and they will continue to work for international agreement on general and complete disarmament. They will persevere in their efforts to secure a treaty banning nuclear tests.

My Government were gravely concerned at the dangers of the recent introduction of offensive missiles into Cuba. They have played their full part in close consultation with My allies, in efforts to deal with the critical situation which arose. My Government were glad to learn that those missiles are to be dismantled under the supervision of the United Nations. They will co-operate with My Allies in seeking wider agreements in the field of controlled disarmament.

My Government will continue, in conjunction with My allies, to seek to achieve by negotiation a settlement of the Berlin question which will preserve the security and freedom of the people of West Berlin.

My Government will seek to strengthen the bonds which link the countries of the North Atlantic Alliance, which has a powerful contribution to make in maintaining the peace of the world. My Government will also take a full part in the work of other international bodies of which the United Kingdom is a member and will strive by all possible means to ensure the security and increase the prosperity of all countries in the free world.

In co-operation with My allies, My Armed Forces will maintain their contribution to the prevention of war.

My Government have welcomed the proposals put forward by the United Nations for conciliation in the Congo. It is their hope that the fair implementation of these proposals may lead to the co-operation of all elements in the Congo in the vital task of reconstructing that country.

My Ministers recognise the great political and economic importance of the development of the European Communities and the opportunities which British accession to these Communities would bring. In close consultation with the other members of the Commonwealth and of the European Free Trade Association, and having full regard for those interests in the United Kingdom which are particularly concerned, they will use every effort to bring the current negotiations to a conclusion acceptable to Parliament.

In pursuance of the plan for the proposed new Federation of Malaysia, detailed discussions are proceeding and in due course legislation will be laid before you.

You will be asked to make provision for extending the present powers of the Colonial Development Corporation.

My Ministers will encourage men and women from this country to offer their services for work in developing countries overseas, whether in the service of the other Governments concerned, as specialist advisers, or under schemes of voluntary recruitment.

Members of the House of Commons:

Estimates for the public services will be laid before you.

My Lords and Members of the House of Commons:

My Ministers will continue to promote efficient and sound expansion of the national economy, with a high and stable level of employment.

My Ministers will pursue their aim of improving the balance of oversea payments and maintaining the strength of sterling. In co-operation with other Governments they will give constant attention to means of sustaining a rising level of world trade.

My Government are resolved to maintain a stable, efficient and prosperous agricultural industry. They will lay before you proposals on certain miscellaneous questions affecting agriculture. The fishing industry will continue to receive help and support.

My Government will promote further improvements in the social conditions and in the housing, health and welfare of My People.

Plans will be laid before you for the development in England and Wales over the next decade of the health and welfare services of the local authorities, in parallel with the development of the hospitals.

A Bill will be introduced to extend the powers of local authorities in connection with the care of children, and to give effect to other recommendations which have been made by the Committee on Children and Young Persons.

Fresh provision will be made for securing the health, safety and welfare of persons employed in shops and offices.

A Bill will be introduced to increase the pensions of retired members of the public services and their dependants.

The position of war pensioners and those who are receiving national insurance benefits will be kept under close review.

My Government will continue to give attention to measures for the further protection of consumers. They will introduce legislation to bring up to date and extend the Weights and Measures Acts and they will establish a Consumer Council to represent and promote the interests of consumers.

My Government propose to introduce a Bill which will require employers to give their employees written statements about terms of employment and will prescribe minimum periods of notice.

Continued attention will be given to improving the supply of teachers for the schools. The expansion of university and technical education will continue.

Legislation will be proposed for the reorganisation of local government in Greater London.

Legislation will be required to amend and continue the operation of the Television Act, 1954.

A Bill will be introduced to provide for the conservation and development of water resources in England and Wales.

Bills will be laid before you to amend the criminal law of Scotland and make provision regarding legal aid in criminal cases, to revise the arrangements for paying grants to Scottish local authorities and to amend the law relating to education in Scotland.

Other measures will be laid before you.

PROROGATION (24 October 1963)

My Lords and Members of the House of Commons:

It was a great joy to My Husband and to Me to visit Australia and New Zealand again and to see the splendid progress made since our previous visit 10 years ago. On my outward journey I was able to spend a short time in Fiji.

My Husband and I were glad to welcome the King and Queen of the Belgians, the King and Queen of the Hellenes, and the President of India on their visits to this country.

My Government have maintained their support for the United Nations and its Agencies and have worked for the achievement of the aims expressed in the United Nations Charter. In the pursuit of general and complete disarmament they have been encouraged by the Treaty banning nuclear tests in the atmosphere, in outer space and under water, which has now entered into force. They hope that this agreement will be followed by others helping to reduce international tension.

My Government have continued to play an active part in the international organisations of which the United Kingdom is a member. My Armed Forces, and the regional defence organisations to which the United Kingdom belongs, have helped to maintain peace and stability in many parts of the world. My Government were quick to respond to India's request for assistance to help to meet Chinese attacks.

My Government deeply regretted the interruption of the negotiations for the accession of the United Kingdom to the Treaties of Paris and Rome. They have continued to work for a wider European unity. They have proposed that the work of the Western European Union and the Council of Europe should be further developed, and have continued their efforts to strengthen the European Free Trade Association.

My Government joined with the Government of the Federation of Rhodesia and Nyasaland, the Governments of Southern and Northern Rhodesia and observers from the Government of Nyasaland in a Conference on the dissolution of the Federation. There was full agreement that arrangements should be made for the orderly and speedy transfer of Federal responsibilities to the territorial Governments. The necessary enabling legislation has been passed. A date has been announced for the proposed independence of Nyasaland.

My Government welcomed the achievement of independence by North Borneo (now named Sabah), Sarawak and Singapore when they joined the States of the Federation of Malaya in Malaysia. My Government particularly welcomed the Report by the Secretary-General of the United Nations confirming that popular support for Malaysia existed in Sabah and Sarawak.

Agreements have been reached on constitutional advance in the Bahamas, British Honduras and the Gambia, and My Government have outlined the form which they consider the new Swaziland Constitution should take. Dates for the proposed independence of Kenya, Malta and Zanzibar have been announced. Aden has acceded to the Federation of South Arabia.

My Government have continued to work through the General Agreement on Tariffs and Trade for the freer flow of international trade with particular regard for the needs of the developing countries. The power of the Commonwealth Development Corporation to invest in some Commonwealth countries has been extended.

A Treaty of Commerce Establishment and Navigation between the United Kingdom and Japan has entered in force.

Members of the House of Commons:

I thank you for the provision which you have made for the public service.

My Lords and Members of the House of Commons:

Through their fiscal, monetary and other economic policies, My Government have laid the foundations for a faster rate of economic expansion and growth in real incomes. They have participated in the work of the National Economic Development Council and have welcomed the important contribution of the National Incomes Commission to this objective. A wide range of special measures has been taken to stimulate employment in Scotland, North-East England and in the development districts in other parts of the country. Steps have been taken to increase considerably the facilities for the retraining in building and engineering of workers displaced by industrial change.

The strength of sterling has been maintained and My Government have continued to play a leading part in the growing international co-operation on monetary affairs.

An Act has been passed enabling hereditary peerages to be disclaimed and admitting hereditary peeresses and all Scottish peers to the House of Lords.

My Government have announced their intention to adapt the agricultural support system to present needs within the principles of the Agricultural Acts of 1947 and 1957. They are engaged in consultations on measures to secure greater stability in the market for cereals and fatstock. Several forms of new or improved assistance to agriculture have been provided. My Government have taken steps to secure freedom to extend United Kingdom fishing limits.

A further large expansion of the teacher training colleges has been undertaken. Support for advanced study and scientific research in the universities is increasing substantially with the growth of Exchequer Grants through the University Grants Committee, and has been further increased by extra assistance from the Research Councils. An Act has been passed to provide means of determining teachers' salaries in England and Wales until 1965.

Plans for the development of the health and welfare services of local authorities in England and Wales have been laid before you. Measures have been enacted to promote the welfare of children and to secure the health, safety and welfare of persons employed in shops and offices.

Acts have been passed to re-organise local government in Greater London and to provide for the comprehensive management of the water resources of England and Wales.

Legislation has prescribed minimum periods of notice for the termination of employment and has required employers to provide written statements of terms of employment.

The period for which the Independent Television Authority provide television services has been extended to 1976 and the powers and duties of the Authority have been amended.

Legislation has been passed improving the law relating to criminal justice in Scotland, revising the arrangements for paying grants to Scottish local authorities and amending the law relating to education in Scotland.

A Consumer Council has been established, the Weights and Measures legislation has been modernised and extended, and an Act has been passed to regulate the soliciting of deposits from the public.

An Act has been passed increasing substantially the penalties for provoking disorder in public places or at public meetings.

War pensions and the pensions of retired public servants have been increased, pensions and other benefits under the National Insurance and Industrial Injuries Schemes have been raised and national assistance scales have been improved.

FIFTH SESSION OF THE FORTY-SECOND PARLIAMENT

1963–1964

OPENING (12 November 1963)

My Lords and Members of the House of Commons:

The Nuclear Test Ban Treaty signed last summer in Moscow was the result of many years of patient effort by My Government in co-operation with successive administrations in the United States, and has been welcomed throughout the world. Encouraged by this My Government will pursue the cause of peace with renewed confidence and vigour. They believe that by patience and persistence a steady increase of confidence can be achieved between the two great groups of Powers. They will continue to support the freedom of West Berlin and to seek solutions of the problems of European security and Germany.

They will continue their support for the United Nations in many spheres, both in its work for the preservation of peace and in its economic and social activities. At the same time, in accordance with the Charter, they will continue to play their part in the North Atlantic Alliance and other regional associations for the defence of freedom.

They belive that the Commonwealth has a significant part to play in ensuring stability and peace in the world, and they will continue to take all possible steps to strengthen the links between the Governments, and peoples, of the Commonwealth. In their efforts to expand world trade, My Government will continue to attach great importance to the maintenance and development of commerce between Commonwealth countries.

My Government will carry out loyally their obligations to various international organisations. In this spirit they will continue their efforts to reduce barriers to trade, both within and beyond Europe. They will sustain, to their best, the developing strength of the European Free Trade Association, and at the same time continue to seek harmonious relationships with the European Economic Community and its member States. They will work for the strength and unity of Europe, through the Council of Europe and the Western European Union.

My Government will continue their efforts to promote peace and stability in South and South-East Asia.

My Government attach great importance to the forthcoming tariff negotiations in the General Agreement on Tariffs and Trade and to the United Nations Conference on Trade and Development. Their success would make it possible to increase Commonwealth and international trade. This will particularly benefit the developing countries for which My Government will also be providing an expanding programme of financial and technical assistance.

As a result of the successful outcome of the Victoria Falls Conference proposals will be laid before you to transfer the responsibilities of the Government of the Federation of Rhodesia and Nyasaland to the territorial Governments. Bills will be introduced to provide for the independence of Kenya, Malta, Nyasaland and Zanzibar, and to provide a new Constitution for the Bahamas.

My Armed Forces will continue to play their part in maintaining order and security in the world.

Legislation will be laid before you to carry out the intentions that My Government declared in Parliament last summer with regard to the reform of the central organisation for Defence. My Government are confident that this modernisation of the whole defence system is in accordance with the needs and spirit of the time. Provision will also be made to improve the organisation of My Reserve Forces.

Members of the House of Commons:

Estimates for the public services will be laid before you.

My Lords and Members of the House of Commons:

My Ministers will bring forward further proposals for the modernisation of Britain, covering many of the economic and social aspects of our national life.

Plans for comprehensive regional development will be laid before you for central Scotland and North-East England. Plans appropriate to other regions will follow. A Bill will be introduced to make improved provision for industrial training. My Ministers are engaged in discussions with both sides of industry about severance payments to employees who become redundant.

My Ministers will encourage the provision of a modern transport system by all appropriate means, including planning investment and research. Legislation will be introduced to secure the ordered development of the major ports under the guidance of the National Ports Council.

My Government will ensure a proper balance between home-grown and imported food on the basis of an efficient and prosperous home agriculture. To this end they will lay before you proposals to prevent imports from undermining the market and intend to adapt the guarantee arrangements for cereals and fatstock. Legislation will be introduced to promote the well-being of horticulture. Proposals will also be made to enable rights to be conferred on breeders of new varities of plants.

My Government will continue to support the fishing industry and have invited Western European countries to discuss fishing problems, including access to fishing grounds and markets.

My Ministers are determined to maintain the expansion of the economy in all parts of the country based on a high and stable level of employment. They will continue to encourage growth without inflation, aided by the work of the National Economic Development Council and the National Incomes Commission and supported by a sustained export effort.

These developments at home must be matched by action designed to sustain our economic position overseas. With other Governments My Ministers will continue to promote arrangements for international payments on a scale adequate to maintain the growth of the world's economy. They will maintain the position of sterling and strengthen the balance of payments.

My Ministers will ensure that economic growth is matched by social advance. Great progress has already been made in the development of higher education. My Ministers recognise the importance of securing a substantial further expansion of the universities and of other institutions of higher education. They will, therefore, bring forward proposals based on the recommendations of the Committee on Higher Education. They will press forward the measures needed to provide for a rising school population and to improve the standards of school education. They will review and strengthen the organisation for supporting science and technology, and encouraging their application to industrial processes; will promote a further increase in the number of qualified scientists and engineers; and will encourage the growth of research.

The rate of house building will be increased. Measures will be laid before you to stimulate building by housing societies, to provide for the systematic improvement of many more houses each year and to strengthen and extend the powers of local authorities to secure better living conditions for the tenants of houses in multiple occupation. Steps will be taken to help the construction industries to increase productivity and to achieve larger building programmes.

Bills will be introduced to reorganise the arrangements for the administration of justice in Greater London, to alleviate hardship resulting from litigation between persons who receive legal aid and those who do not, and to empower the Court of Criminal Appeal to order a new trial of a convicted person on grounds of fresh evidence.

You will be invited to consider arrangements for the payment of compensation to the victims of crimes of violence.

A Bill will be introduced to implement recommendations of the Royal Commission on the Police and to bring up to date the law relating to police administration.

My Ministers will continue to give special attention to the development of the Highlands and Islands. Measures will be introduced to develop the tourist industry in Scotland and to improve the amenities of the countryside; and to amend the law of Scotland concerning succession.

A Bill will be laid before you providing relief to certain householders suffering hardship from increased rates as the result of revaluation of their houses.

Other measures will be laid before you.

Note: There was no Prorogation Speech. Parliament was Dissolved on September 25 during the Summer Recess.

FIRST SESSION OF THE FORTY-THIRD PARLIAMENT

1964–1965

OPENING (3 November 1964)

My Lords and Members of the House of Commons:

My Husband and I look forward with pleasure to our forthcoming visits to Ethiopia and the Sudan and to the Federal Republic of Germany. We were glad to be in Canada last month to attend the centennial celebrations commemorating the conferences held at Charlottetown and Quebec City in 1864 and to pay a further visit to Ottawa.

In international affairs it will be the principal purpose of My Ministers to seek to reduce East-West tension. To this end they will give renewed and more vigorous support to the United Nations in its vital role of freeing the world from the threat of war; and they will consider how this country can make a more effective contribution to the Organisation's peace-keeping capability. They will seek to encourage further progress towards disarmament and to contribute other steps which will permit the East-West conflict to be replaced by international co-operation in promoting peace and security throughout the world.

My Government reaffirm their support for the defence of the free world—the basic concept of the Atlantic Alliance; and they will continue to play their full part in the North Atlantic Treaty Organisation and in other organisations for collective defence. They will review defence policy to ensure, by relating our commitments and our resources, that My Armed Forces are able to discharge their many tasks overseas with the greatest effectiveness and economy. In particular, they will make constructive proposals for renewing the interdependence of the Atlantic Alliance in relation to nuclear weapons, in an endeavour to prevent duplication of effort and the dissemination of weapons of mass destruction.

New arrangements have been made to aid and encourage the economic and social advance of the developing nations, including the remaining dependent territories. My Ministers will also endeavour to promote the expansion of trade to this end, and they will seek, in co-operation with other countries and the United Nations and its agencies, to stimulate fresh action to reduce the growing disparities of wealth and opportunity between the peoples of the world.

My Ministers will have a special regard to the unique role of the Commonwealth, which itself reflects so many of the challenges and opportunities of the world. They will foster the Commonwealth connection on a basis of racial equality and close consultation between Member Governments and will promote Commonwealth collaboration in trade, economic development, educational, scientific and cultural contacts and in other ways.

My Government will continue to play a full part in the European organisations of which this country is a member and will seek to promote closer European co-operation.

A Bill will be introduced to provide for the independence of the Gambia.

Members of the House of Commons:

Estimates for the public services will be laid before you.

My Lords and Members of the House of Commons:

At home My Government's first concern will be to maintain the strength of sterling by dealing with the short-term balance of payments difficulties and by initiating the longer-term structural changes in our economy which will ensure purposeful expansion, rising exports and a healthy balance of payments.

Our industries will be helped to gain the full benefits of advances in scientific research and applied technology.

Central and regional plans to promote ecomonic development, with special reference to the needs of the under-employed areas of the country, are being prepared. New arrangements will ensure proper attention to the needs of Wales. Legislation will be introduced to provide for the appointment of a Highland Development Board.

My Government will initiate early action to re-establish the necessary public ownership and control of the iron and steel industry.

To foster the health and prosperity of agriculture, they will continue the system of guarantees under the existing Acts and will promote measures to secure better marketing arrangements for farm produce. They will encourage the development of the fishing industry and the steady expansion of forestry.

My Government will call on trade unions and employers' organisations to co-operate in eliminating those restrictive practices, on both sides of industry, which impair our competitive power and the development of the full potential of the economy. They will take steps to improve industrial efficiency by dealing more effectively with monopolies and with problems arising from mergers. They will also take action to improve the arrangements for industrial training and for the retraining of workers changing their employment. A Bill will be introduced to give workers and their representatives the protection necessary for freedom of industrial negotiation.

To the end that all may share the benefits of rising productivity, My Ministers will work for more stable prices and a closer relationship between the increase in productivity and the growth of incomes in all their forms; and they will promote reforms in taxation and better arrangements for local government finance. They will pay special attention to protecting the interests of consumers.

Action will be taken to require companies to disclose political contributions in their accounts.

My Government will have particular regard for those on whom age, sickness and personal misfortune impose special disabilities. They believe that radical changes in the national schemes of social security are essential to bring them into line with modern needs. They will therefore embark at once upon a major review of these schemes. Meanwhile, they will immediately introduce legislation to increase existing rates of National Insurance and associated benefits.

Action will be proposed to modernise and develop the health and welfare services. Steps will be taken to increase the number of doctors and other trained staff in the National Health Service. Prescription charges for medicines will be abolished.

My Ministers will enlarge educational opportunities and give particular priority to increasing the supply of teachers. Bills will be introduced to establish new machinery for determining teachers' pay in England and Wales and for the governance of the teaching profession in Scotland.

My Government will pursue a vigorous housing policy directed to producing more houses of better quality, and will promote the modernisation of the construction industry. They will restore control of rents; they will establish as rapidly as possible a Crown Lands Commission with wide powers to acquire land for the community; and they will provide for leasehold enfranchisement. In conjunction with a progressive transport policy and a system of comprehensive regional planning, these measures will be directed to providing a fresh social environment in keeping with the needs and aspirations of the time.

My Government will be actively concerned to build up the strength and efficiency of the police, to improve the penal system and the after-care of offenders, and to make more effective the means of sustaining the family and of preventing and treating delinquency. Facilities will be provided for a free decision by Parliament on the issue of capital punishment.

My Government are studying the report, which they have recently received, of the Committee appointed last year on the Remuneration of Ministers and Members of Parliament.

Other measures will be laid before you.

In all their policies My Government will be concerned to safeguard the liberties of My subjects. They will take action against racial discrimination and promote full integration into the community of immigrants who have come here from the Commonwealth. They will propose the appointment of Law Commissioners to advance reform of the law, and will propose new measures for the impartial investigation of individual grievances. In so doing they will be acting in the spirit which has always animated Parliament, whose seven hundredth anniversary will be recorded in this Session.

PROROGATION (8 November 1965)

My Lords and Members of the House of Commons:

My Husband and I were glad to welcome to this country the President of Chile and Senora de Frei.

We were touched by the warmth of our reception during our State Visit to the Federal Republic of Germany. We have also vivid memories of our friendly welcome in Ethiopia and the Sudan.

It was with great pleasure that I welcomed in London in June the Heads of Government or their representatives from all the member countries of the Commonwealth. This was the first Meeting of Commonwealth Prime Ministers to be attended by the President of Zambia and the Prime Ministers of Malta and of The Gambia. My Government welcomed the decisions to establish the Commonwealth Secretariat and the Commonwealth Foundation.

My Government have continued to work for peace and understanding in international relations. They have striven to promote the stability of South-East Asia, in particular, by seeking a peaceful settlement of the conflict in Vietnam. To this end the Commonwealth Prime Ministers at their Meeting in June appointed a Commonwealth Peace Mission.

My Government have taken practical steps to resolve difficulties at the United Nations and to support United Nations peace-keeping and economic and social work.

My Government were much concerned at the recent outbreak of hostilities between our two Commonwealth partners, India and Pakistan. They have throughout given full support to the efforts of the United Nations Secretary-General and the Security Council which, aided by the wise statesmanship of the leaders of both countries, have led to the achievement of a cease-fire.

My Ministers have played their full part in the North Atlantic Treaty Organisation and our other alliances for collective defence. They have been active in seeking progress towards disarmament and the non-dissemination of nuclear weapons.

My Government have continued to co-operate in strengthening the European Free Trade Association and have made proposals to bring about closer co-operation between the Association and the European

Economic Community.

My Government are happy that the new State of Singapore has become a member of the Commonwealth.

My Government have established a new Ministry to administer our technical aid and economic aid to the developing nations. The first Commonwealth Medical Conference has been held in Edinburgh.

My Government have continued their unremitting efforts to bring about through negotiation a peaceful and honourable solution in Rhodesia on a basis acceptable to the people of the country as a whole.

Members of the House of Commons:

I thank you for the provision which you have made for the public services.

My Lords and Members of the House of Commons:

My Government's first aim has been to restore the balance in our external payments and maintain the strength of sterling. New schemes to help exporters have been introduced. My Ministers have continued to play a full part in the discussions on international liquidity and an Act has been passed to enable the United Kingdom to give effect to the decision to raise members' quotas in the International Monetary Fund.

Important reforms have been effected in the taxation of companies and capital gains, and improvements have been made in the control of public expenditure.

My Government have prepared a National Plan to secure more rapid growth in the economy through the improvement of industrial productivity and a better use of our national resources. Regional Economic Planning Councils and Boards have been established to assist with this work.

In order to promote the development of the economy, the stability of prices and the faster growth of real incomes, My Government have agreed with management and unions a policy on productivity, prices and incomes, and set up the National Board for Prices and Incomes.

The Ministry of Technology has been formed and legislation passed to assist in the promotion of advanced technology: scientific research in universities and elsewhere has been strengthened, and the Science Research Council and Natural Environment Research Council have been established.

My Government have provided more help for small farmers and better facilities for agricultural credit. They have set up a Home Grown Cereals Marketing Authority to promote better marketing.

An Act has been passed to enlarge the Monopolies Commission, to extend its purview to services and mergers, and to strengthen My Government's powers to implement decisions taken

after consideration of its reports.

Pensions and other benefits under the national insurance, industrial injuries and war pensions schemes, and the scales of national assistance, have been substantially increased. The earnings rule for widows' benefits has been abolished and local authorities have been given power to provide free or cheap travel on municipal transport for the aged and disabled. A comprehensive review of the social security schemes has begun.

Provision has been made for redundancy payments and the retraining of adult workers has been vigorously extended.

A Royal Commission has been appointed to consider relations between management and employees and the role of trade unions and employers' associations in promoting the interests of their members and in accelerating the social and economic advance of the nation. Legislation has been passed to remove an uncertainty in the law affecting persons acting in contemplation or furtherance of a trade dispute.

Local education authorities have been asked to prepare plans for reorganising their schools on comprehensive lines and measures have been taken to improve the supply of teachers. New machinery has been created for determining teachers' pay in England and Wales, and power has been taken to establish a General Teaching Council for Scotland.

Support for the Arts has been increased and broadened; and a Sports Council has been set up.

A start has been made on my Government's plans for modernising the health and welfare services. Charges for National Health Service prescriptions have been abolished.

Legislation has been passed to restore security of tenure to tenants of decontrolled houses, to provide machinery for fixing fair rents for privately rented accommodation, and to make the harassment of tenants an offence.

My Government have taken steps to promote the integration into the community of immigrants from the Commonwealth. An Act has been passed to prohibit discrimination on racial grounds in places of public resort and to penalise incitement to racial hatred.

An Act has been passed strengthening the law regarding the possession and use of firearms and ammunition.

My Government have taken powers to control office development.

A Highlands and Islands Development Board has been established for the economic and social development of the area.

Permanent Law Commissions, for England and Wales and for Scotland, have been established for the systematic and continuous review of the law.

SECOND SESSION OF THE FORTY-THIRD PARLIAMENT

1965–1966

OPENING (9 November 1965)

My Lords and Members of the House of Commons:

My Husband and I look forward to our forth-coming Caribbean tour and to our visit to Belgium.

My Government will seek to promote peace and security throughout the world, to increase international confidence and co-operation and to strengthen the United Nations. They will promote disarmament, and in particular will seek the conclusion of a treaty to prevent the further spread of nuclear weapons. They will persevere in efforts to secure peace in Vietnam and to promote the stability of South-East Asia.

They will continue to support Britain's alliances for collective defence and will work for a generally satisfactory organisation of the nuclear resources of the allies.

My Government will continue to work for the greater unity of Europe. They will seek to strengthen the European Free Trade Association and to promote co-operation between the Association and the European Economic Community, and the establishment of a wider European market.

They will play a full part in promoting the success of the negotiations for tariff reductions under the General Agreement on Tariffs and Trade. They will seek a successful conclusion to their discussions with the Government of the Republic of Ireland on the establishment of a Free Trade Area between the two countries. They will continue to encourage Commonwealth trade.

My Ministers will continue to assist, in concert with other industrialised nations and the international institutions, the social and economic advance of the developing countries.

My Government will maintain their unremitting efforts to bring about through negotiation a peaceful and honourable solution in Rhodesia on a basis acceptable to the people of the country as a whole.

A measure will be laid before you to reorganise the Army Reserve and Auxiliary Forces.

Members of the House of Commons:

Estimates for the public services will be laid before you.

My Lords and Members of the House of Commons:

My Government's aim is to develop a soundly based economy. They will give priority to ensuring that balance in external payments is restored next year and that the strength of sterling is maintained. They will continue their efforts to increase exports. They will also further the international discussions of means of strengthening the world payments system.

In implementing the National Plan My Government will extend the range of the Economic Development Committees and encourage British industry to achieve greater competitive efficiency by reorganisation, the more general use of advanced technology, and better use of manpower. They will give special attention to ensuring balanced economic growth in all regions.

Steps will be taken to improve the arrangements for providing incentives for industrial investment with due regard to the development of the economy and the special needs of particular areas.

My Government will strengthen and develop the policy for productivity, prices and incomes for which they have agreed with management and union. They will introduce a Bill for this purpose, and will continue to develop the policy in co-operation with all concerned.

My Government consider the more efficient working of the ports, including a radical improvement in industrial relations and more efficient use of labour in the docks, to be of the highest importance and will introduce legislation and take other necessary action to further this objective.

My Ministers will pursue their policy for the selective expansion of agriculture, based on increasing productivity. They will introduce legislation for the longer term development of agriculture through better farm structure, co-operation, and improved hill farming and to establish a Meat and Livestock Commission. They will promote the economic development of the fishing industry.

For the protection of consumers, a Bill will be introduced to strengthen the law on misleading trade descriptions.

Legislation will be introduced to remove statutory limitations impeding the proper use of the manufacturing resources of the nationalised industries.

A Bill will be introduced to assist the financing of the coal industry and the redeployment of its manpower.

A Bill will be introduced to establish a Land Commission with power to acquire land for the community and to recover a part of the development value realised in land transactions. My Ministers will introduce legislation to reform the leasehold system for residential property in England and Wales, including provision for leasehold enfranchisement.

Legislation will be introduced to establish a new system of Exchequer subsidies for local authority housing.

A Bill will be introduced to regulate priorities in

privately sponsored construction.

Legislation will be introduced to lessen the injustices of the rating system and to limit the burden of rates.

My Ministers will continue to develop higher education. A Bill will be introduced to facilitate revision of the constitution of the older Scottish universities and to provide for separate universities at St. Andrews and Dundee.

My Government will take steps to provide more teachers and promote further advances in secondary education on comprehensive lines. A Public Schools Commission will be set up to advise on the best way of integrating the public schools with the State system.

Measures will be laid before you to provide supplementary national insurance benefits, related to earnings, in the early stages of sickness, unemployment and widowhood; to extend the supplementation of workmen's compensation; and to empower agricultural wages boards to fix minimum rates of sick pay for agricultural workers.

Other measures will increase the pensions of retired members of the public services and their dependents and provide a pensions scheme for teachers' widows in England and Wales.

My Government are studying with the medical profession ways of improving the family doctor service and will introduce the necessary legislation.

Measures will be introduced to improve the administration of justice and to reform and modernise the law.

My Government will promote the provision of improved services for the family, the development of new means of dealing with young persons who now come before the courts and the advancement of penal reform.

Further steps will be directed to the effective integration of immigrants into the community and to strengthening the control of Commonwealth immigration.

A measure will be introduced to provide for fuller disclosure of information by companies, including the disclosure of political contributions.

A Bill will be introduced for the appointment of a Parliamentary Commissioner for Administration with powers to investigate individual grievances.

My Ministers will bring forward proposals for the more effective co-ordination of inland transport. You will be invited to approve a measure designed to promote greater safety on the roads.

Provision for meeting the special needs of Scotland will be made in the various measures proposed by my Government.

Other measures will be laid before you.

PROROGATION (10 March 1966)

My Lords and Members of the House of Commons:
My Husband and I would like to thank the many peoples we visited in our delightful Caribbean tour for the warmth of their hospitality.

My Ministers have participated fully in the work of the United Nations and its specialised agencies. My Government have improved and increased financial and technical aid to developing countries and have joined in international efforts to relieve the current food shortage in India.

My Ministers have constantly sought means of bringing peace to Vietnam, and stability to South-East Asia.

In consultation with the Government of British Guiana My Government have concluded an Agreement with Venezuela which will promote good relations between Venezuela and the future independent Guyana.

My Ministers have sought to make progress towards disarmament, and in particular an international treaty to prevent the spread of nuclear weapons.

They have continued to support the North Atlantic Treaty Organisation and other alliances for collective defence, and to work for closer interdependence in the nuclear resources of the Atlantic alliance.

My Ministers have worked for closer co-operation between the European Free Trades Association and the European Economic Community. They have developed personal contacts with the leaders of the Soviet Union and other countries of Eastern Europe.

They have concluded an Agreement establishing a Free Trade Area with the Republic of Ireland. They have actively promoted the tariff negotiations under the General Agreement on Tariffs and Trade, and the development of trade within the Commonwealth.

My Government have vigorously pursued their policy of bringing the illegal regime in Rhodesia to an end so that a peaceful and lasting constitutional settlement, based on the rule of law and acceptable to the Rhodesian people as a whole, can be achieved. This policy received general endorsement at the Meeting of Commonwealth Prime Ministers at Lagos in January.

Progress has been made with negotiations on constitutional advances for several of our remaining dependent territories.

My Government have announced their plans for meeting the nation's defence needs in the next decade at lower cost, and for reorganising the Army Reserves.

Members of the House of Commons:
I thank you for the provision you have made for the public services.

My Lords and Members of the House of Commons:

My Government have been carrying through with success policies designed to strengthen sterling and restore the balance of payments. The country's export trade is now greater than ever before. They have put forward proposals for a more positive system of investment incentives designed to stimulate those sectors of the economy which contribute most directly to the balance of payments and to promote expansion in the under-developed regions of Britain. They have introduced new methods of planning and control of public expenditure. They have made proposals for the establishment of an Industrial Reorganisation Corporation and have continued to encourage the use of advanced technology in industry.

My Government have published plans for the expansion of the Scottish economy. The construction of the Prototype Fast Reactor in Caithness will help to sustain the economy in the Highlands.

My Government have strongly encouraged the development of industrial training and have announced improved arrangments for training workers in the development districts.

My Government have developed, in consultation with management and unions, their policy for productivity, prices and incomes. They have introduced a system for advance notification of increases in prices and incomes and put forward proposals for legislation to strengthen it.

My Government have introduced proposals for the establishment of a Meat and Livestock Commission, for the longer-term development of agriculture, and to empower agricultural wages boards to fix minimum rates of sick pay for agricultural workers. They have announced arrangements to provide investment incentives for agriculture, horticulture and fisheries.

An Act has been passed to assist the finances of the coal industry and the redeployment of its manpower.

With a view to ensuring regular employment for dock workers, My Government have put to the industry proposals for a revised statutory dock labour scheme.

Proposals have been put forward for the establishment of a Land Commission to acquire land for the community and to recover part of the development value realised in land transactions.

An Act has been passed providing for rate rebates for domestic occupiers of limited means and entitling householders to pay rates by instalments. A scheme has been put forward for progressively increasing Exchequer grants to local authorities to reduce the annual increase in rates on house property.

My Ministers have announced an enlarged housing programme and a substantial increase in housing subsidies and have further developed their plans to extend owner-occupation by bringing mortgages within the reach of more families. Proposals have been made for legislation to give greater security to occupying leaseholders in England and Wales of residential property with an original long lease and to enable them to acquire the freehold.

My Government have proposed a measure to strengthen the law protecting consumers by prohibiting mis-descriptions of goods and services and to confer power to require that consumers are given information about the goods they buy.

Proposals have been put before you for requiring the public disclosure of more information by companies, including the disclosure of political contributions.

Provision has been made for supplementary national insurance benefits, related to earnings, to be paid in the early stages of sickness, unemployment and widowhood, and for additional benefits to be paid to certain war and industrially disabled pensioners. Plans have been worked out for a Ministry of Social Security and a new scheme of benefits to replace national assistance. A reciprocal Agreement with the Government of the Republic of Ireland on social security has been signed.

In consultation with the médical profession, My Ministers have drawn up proposals for reshaping the family doctor service and legislation needed to implement them has been passed.

A Public Schools Commission has been set up to advise on the best way of integrating the public schools with the State system of education.

Provision has been made for a pension scheme for teachers' widows in England and Wales.

An Act has been passed to facilitate revision of the constitution of the older Scottish universities and to provide for separate universities at St. Andrews and Dundee.

My Government have announced an increase in financial support for the arts. They have put forward proposals for protecting the beauty of the countryside and promoting its enjoyment.

Legislative proposals have been put before you to promote safety on the roads.

Proposals have been put forward for reform in the treatment of adult offenders.

Progress has been made in the systematic reform of the law.

My Government have announced that decimal currency will be introduced in 1971.

FIRST SESSION OF THE FORTY-FOURTH PARLIAMENT

1966–1967

OPENING (21 April 1966)

My Lords and Members of the House of Commons:

My husband and I look forward with pleasure to our visit to Belgium, and to the State Visits which the Federal President of the Republic of Austria and His Majesty King Hussein of the Hashemite Kingdom of Jordan will pay to this country.

My Government, in co-operation with the other members of the Commonwealth and with our allies, will continue to work for peace and security in all parts of the world through support for the United Nations. They will sustain efforts to achieve disarmament, and, especially, agreements on the non-proliferation of nuclear weapons and on the extension of the Nuclear Test Ban Treaty.

A particular concern of My Ministers will be to use all available means to achieve a negotiated settlement of the conflict in Vietnam. They will continue to assist Malaysia and Singapore in their defence against Indonesia, and will not relax their efforts to bring peace to this whole area.

My Government will continue to give full support to the maintenance of the North Atlantic Treaty and its Organisation, which they regard as a necessary basis from which to promote greater stability in East-West relations. They will continue to work for nuclear interdependence in the West.

They will also support Britain's other alliances for collective defence, and press forward with policies designed to enable Britain to play her full part in the promotion of peace throughout the world without overstraining her military or economic resources. A Bill will be introduced to reorganise the Army Reserve and Auxiliary Forces.

My Government will continue to promote the economic unity of Europe and to strengthen the links between the European Free Trade Association and the European Economic Community. They would be ready to enter the European Economic Community provided essential British and Commonwealth interests were safeguarded. They will work for tariff reductions under the General Agreement on Tariffs and Trade and for an expansion of Commonwealth trade.

Further steps will be taken to assist My peoples in the remaining Colonial territories to reach independence or some other status which they have freely chosen.

My Government will pursue the policy of bringing the illegal regime in Rhodesia to an end, so that a peaceful and lasting constitutional settlement, based on the rule of law and acceptable to the Rhodesian people as a whole, can be achieved.

Members of the House of Commons:

Estimates for the public services will be laid before you.

My Lords and Members of the House of Commons:

A prime aim of My Government's policy will be to restore equilibrium in the external balance of payments. They are determined to maintain the strength of sterling. They will continue to work for increased liquidity for financing world trade.

In consultation with industry, the National Economic Development Council and the regional Economic Planning Councils, My Government will take action to stimulate progress in implementing the National Plan and in securing balanced growth in all parts of Great Britain. They will renew their efforts, in co-operation with trade unions and employers' organisations, to increase the productivity and competitive power of British industry.

To this same end, My Government will promote a more positive system of investment incentives to improve the efficiency of those parts of the economy which contribute most directly to the balance of payments and to encourage development where it is most needed. Legislation will be introduced to create an Industrial Reorganisation Corporation to promote greater efficiency in British industry and to develop projects of special importance.

My Government will continue to develop, in consultation with management and unions, the agreed policy for productivity, prices and incomes. Proposals for legislation to reinforce this policy, while preserving the voluntary principle on which it is based, will be laid before you.

My Government will continue to promote modernisation and increased productivity in farming, horticulture and fishing, and will introduce measures for the longer-term development of agriculture and the establishment of a Meat and Livestock Commission.

A Bill will be introduced to restore public ownership and control of the main part of the steel industry.

Legislation will be introduced and other measures taken to improve efficiency and industrial relations in the docks.

Bills will be introduced to relieve the domestic ratepayer and reorganise Exchequer grants to local authorities; to establish a new system of Exchequer subsidies for local authority housing, and to assist those of modest means in buying their homes.

Legislation will be brought before you to provide for the establishment of a Land Commission to acquire land for the community and recover part of the development value realised by land transactions. My Ministers will present a Bill on leasehold reform.

A Bill will be introduced to regulate privately-sponsored construction.

My Government will bring forward Bills to reorganise the arrangements for water supply in Scotland, and for the conservation of the Scottish countryside and the development of facilities for its enjoyment.

Legislation will be introduced to implement the agreed arrangements for increased grants to voluntary schools in England and Wales.

My Government will promote further progress in the development of comprehensive secondary education.

Further steps will be taken to increase the supply of teachers. New machinery will be proposed for settling the remuneration of teachers in Scotland.

Higher and further education will be expanded to meet increasing demand. The development of science will be continued. In the arts, My Ministers will pursue their aim of making our cultural heritage available to all.

My Ministers will complete further stages of their major review of social security. While continuing to ensure to pensioners and other beneficiaries a fair share of the country's rising living standards, they will seek further means of dealing with the poverty that still exists. Legislation will be introduced to create a Ministry of Social Security and to replace National Assistance by a new system of non-contributory benefits.

My Government will continue to develop the health and welfare services and will pay special attention to the development of the family doctor service.

You will be invited to approve a measure designed to promote greater safety on the roads.

My Government will carry forward, where necessary by introducing legislation, the process of reforming the criminal and civil law and modernising the administration of justice. They will introduce legislation to make further reforms in the penal system; and to amend the law relating to the return of fugitive offenders to other Commonwealth countries.

Other measures will be laid before you.

PROROGATION (27 October 1967)

My Lords and Members of the House of Commons:

My Husband and I were glad to welcome to this country the President of Pakistan. We also welcomed the State Visits paid by the Federal President of the Republic of Austria, by His Majesty King Hussein of the Hashemite Kingdom of Jordan and by His Majesty King Feisal of Saudi Arabia.

My Husband and I had the great pleasure of being present at the celebration of Canada's centenary in Ottawa and of visiting Canada's International Exhibition at Montreal.

My Government have played a full part in the varied activities of the United Nations.

My Ministers have continued to seek progress towards disarmament and in particular an international treaty to prevent the spread of nuclear weapons. My Government have signed the Treaty governing the exploration and use of Outer Space.

My Ministers welcomed the restoration of good relations between Indonesia and Malaysia. They have also constantly sought means of bringing peace to Vietnam.

My Government have applied for membership of the European Economic Community, European Coal and Steel Community and European Atomic Energy Community. The closest consultation has been maintained with the Governments of the Commonwealth, the European Free Trade Association and the Republic of Ireland.

My Government have continued to play their full part in the North Atlantic Alliance and are co-operating in the study of its future tasks. Contacts with the Eastern European countries have been further developed.

My Government made strenuous efforts to prevent the outbreak of war between the Arab States and Israel. When hostilities nevertheless began, they worked unceasingly at the United Nations to bring about a cease-fire; and they have been continuously active in seeking a lasting settlement.

The Award which I made for the arbitration of a frontier dispute between Argentina and Chile has strengthened My Government's friendly ties with both countries.

An Act has been passed to provide for the relinquishment of My sovereignty over Aden, Perim and the Kuria Muria Islands.

It was with great pleasure that I welcomed to London in September 1966 the Heads of Government or their representatives from the Member Countries of the Commonwealth.

Four of our overseas territories became independent within the Commonwealth in the last 18 months—British Guiana (as Guyana), Bechuanaland (as Botswana), Basutoland (as Lesotho) and Barbados. Five of our West Indian territories assumed a new status of association with the United

Kingdom. Constitutional discussions were held with others of our territories.

My Government have supported the people of Hong Kong, whose fortitude and steadfast spirit they have greatly admired in recent months.

My Government have continued to seek by all practicable means to bring about a return to constitutional rule in Rhodesia in accordance with the multiracial principles approved by Parliament.

My Government have concluded a supplementary Trade Agreement with New Zealand.

My Government have continued to provide a high level of aid to less developed countries.

My Ministers have played an important part in international discussions to strengthen the world monetary system. My Government warmly welcome the agreement on special drawing rights which was reached by the International Monetary Fund.

My Government played a full part in achieving a successful conclusion of the Kennedy Round of trade negotiations, which will bring about a greater reduction in tariffs and other barriers to trade than any previous negotiations.

Acts have been passed to continue and modernise the legislation relating to the regular, reserve and auxiliary forces. My Government have completed the far-reaching examination begun in 1964 of the nation's defence needs in the next decade.

Members of the House of Commons:
    I thank you for the provision which you have made for the public services.

My Lords and Members of the House of Commons:
    In spite of a slackening in the growth of world trade and disturbances in the Middle East and elsewhere, My Government have made progress in restoring the balance of payments.

In pursuit of their endeavours to promote efficiency and high productivity in all parts of the country, My Government have introduced more positive incentives for investment and have set up an Industrial Re-organisation Corporation. My Government have introduced a Selective Employment Tax designed to redress the balance of taxation between services and manufacturing industry.

A Regional Employment Premium has been introduced to help manufacturing industry in development areas. This constitutes a major addition to My Government's other measures to improve the economic strength of these areas.

Acts have been passed to reinforce the voluntary observance of the prices and incomes policy. My Government welcome the increasing participation of management and unions in the operation of the policy.

Legislation has been enacted providing for the introduction of a decimal currency system in 1971.

Legislation has been passed to assist the shipbuilding industry to reorganise itself so as to become more competitive in world markets.

Public ownership of the main part of the steel industry has been restored.

The Docks and Harbours Act, and measures to end the system of casual employment, have provided the basis for greater efficiency in the docks.

An Act has been passed to require the public disclosure of more information by companies, including the disclosure of political contributions, and to strengthen the supervisory powers of the Board of Trade over insurance companies.

An Act has been passed to enable data-processing services and facilities to be provided by the Post Office.

My Government have set up a Meat and Live-stock Commission and a Central Council for Agricultural and Horticultural Co-operation.

Legislation has been passed dealing with the safety of goods vehicles, and with persons driving while affected by alcohol or drugs or while disqualified.

Improvements have been completed in the arrangements under which family doctors practise in the National Health Service.

Legislation has been passed to improve control over drug addiction.

Continued progress has been made with the reorganisation of secondary education on comprehensive lines, and practical measures taken to prepare for the raising of the school-leaving age.

New and vigorous steps have been taken to increase the output of teachers; and new machinery has been enacted for settling the remuneration of teachers in Scotland.

An Act has been passed to create a new Ministry of Social Security and to replace national assistance with a scheme of supplementary benefits. Provision has been made for improvements in pensions and benefits.

Legislation has been passed to establish a more generous system of Exchequer subsidies for certain housing; to assist persons of modest means in buying their homes; to provide for leasehold reforms; and to establish a Land Commission.

An Act has been passed to reorganise and increase Exchequer assistance to local authorities and to relieve the domestic ratepayers.

Legislation has been passed to reorganise water supply in Scotland and to establish a Countryside Commission for Scotland.

An Act has been passed providing for the appointment of a Parliamentary Commissioner for Administration.

I have appointed Royal Commissions to carry out reviews of local government in England, outside Greater London, and in Scotland, and another to review the system of Assizes and Quarter Sessions. My Government have made proposals for the reorganisation of local government in Wales.

An Act has been passed making further provision for the free use of the Welsh language in public business in Wales and Monmouthshire.

In fulfilment of an agreement entered into with other European countries, an Act has been passed to deal with unauthorised broadcasting at sea.

An Act has been passed which makes substantial reforms in the penal system and the procedure of the criminal courts in England and Wales.

Further progress has been made in the systematic reform of the law; under the impetus given by the creation of the Law Commissions 15 Acts consolidating sections of our statute law, and an Act repealing many obsolete statutes, have been passed.

SECOND SESSION OF THE FORTY-FOURTH PARLIAMENT

1967–1968

OPENING (31 October 1967)

My Lords and Members of the House of Commons:

My Husband and I look forward with pleasure to the State Visit of the President of the Republic of Turkey to this country and to our own approaching visit to Malta.

My Government will continue to play an active part in the constructive efforts of the United Nations to assure a peaceful and stable world.

My Ministers will continue their efforts to achieve progress on arms control and disarmament, and especially on an agreement for the non-proliferation of nuclear weapons.

My Ministers will seek to use all available means to achieve a negotiated settlement of the conflict in Vietnam.

My Government will continue to work through the United Nations for a just and lasting settlement in the Middle East.

My Government look forward to the early opening of negotiations to provide for Britain's entry into the European Communities. The closest consultation will be maintained with Commonwealth Governments, the Governments of the European Free Trade Association and the Republic of Ireland.

My Government will continue to participate actively in the North Atlantic Alliance as an essential factor for European security. At the same time they will work for improved East-West relations. They will also continue to support Britain's other alliances for collective defence.

During the coming Session, My Government intend to bring the peoples of South Arabia to independence.

My peoples in the remaining dependent territories will continue to be helped to achieve further constitutional advance.

The people of Hong Kong will continue to receive the full support of My Government.

My Government will continue to seek by all practicable means to bring about a return to constitutional rule in Rhodesia in accordance with the multi-racial principles approved by Parliament.

Members of the House of Commons:

Estimates for the public service will be laid before you.

My Lords and Members of the House of Commons:

The principal aim of My Government's policy is the achievement of a strong economy. This should combine a continuing surplus on the balance of payments sufficient to meet our international obligations and to maintain the strength of sterling with a satisfactory growth of output and with full employment.

Further measures will be taken to stimulate economic advance in the development areas and to promote a more even distribution of employment in all regions, as a means to national expansion.

Legislation will be introduced to extend My Government's powers to assist financially in the modernisation and technological advance of industry and in the expansion of its capacity.

My Government will continue to work with management and unions to promote an effective policy for productivity, prices and incomes.

As soon as they receive the report of the Royal Commission on Trade Unions and Employers' Associations, My Government will give consideration to the system of industrial relations and will then put their conclusions before Parliament.

A Bill will be introduced to establish a National Loans Fund and to amend the law relating to Government borrowing and lending and to Exchequer Accounts.

Legislation will be introduced to implement recommendations of the Tribunal appointed to enquire into the tragic disaster at Aberfan.

Legislation will be brought before you to provide for the better integration of rail and road transport within a reorganised framework of public control, to promote safety and high standards in the road transport industry, to strengthen the powers of local authorities to manage traffic, and to reorganise the nationalised inland waterways with special emphasis on their use for recreation and amenity.

A Bill will be introduced to establish a central system of vehicle registration and licensing.

Legislation will be brought before you to convert the Post Office from a Department of State to a public corporation.

My Government will continue to develop policies to secure a rising programme of housebuilding and better housing conditions for the people. For England and Wales a Bill will be introduced to modernise the town and country planning system and another to establish a Countryside Commission, and to provide for greater opportunities for leisure and recreation in the countryside.

My Government will introduce legislation to enable increased compensation to be paid to tenant farmers whose land is needed for development, to safeguard the welfare of farm animals, especially those reared by intensive methods, and on other agricultural matters.

My Government will seek powers to take provisional action against dumping in accordance with the code which was agreed in the Kennedy Round of trade negotiations at Geneva.

Legislation will be introduced to strengthen and amend the law on misleading trade descriptions.

A Bill will be introduced to provide comprehensive new arrangements in Great Britain for ensuring the safety and quality of medicines, whether for human or animal use; and another to enable improvements to be made in the country's public health and welfare services.

A Bill will be put before you to increase the level of family allowances.

Legislation will be introduced to reorganise the social services in Scotland.

Steps will be taken through the Council for Scientific Policy to expand and improve arrangements for scientific research and to encourage the international exchange of scientists in Europe.

Further progress will be made in the development of comprehensive secondary education, in the expansion of higher education, including the establishment of polytechnics, and in developing further education to meet the needs arising from the Industrial Training Act.

Measures will be taken to accelerate the improvement of schools in socially deprived areas.

My Ministers will continue to accord a high priority to the supply of teachers.

Legislation will be introduced to reduce the powers of the House of Lords and to eliminate its present hereditary basis, thereby enabling it to develop within the framework of a modern Parliamentary system. My Government are prepared to enter into consultations appropriate to a constitutional change of such importance.

Legislation will be introduced to extend the scope of the Race Relations Act.

Legislation will be introduced to reform the law on gaming.

My Government will carry forward their comprehensive programme of reforming the law particularly in the fields of family law, and the position of Justices of the Peace. They will also submit for consideration proposals on the law of property, of evidence and of theft.

Other measures will be laid before you.

PROROGATION (25 October 1968)

My Lords and Members of the House of Commons:

My Husband and I were glad to welcome to this country the President of the Republic of Turkey.

My Government have contributed positively to the wide-ranging work of the United Nations. They have been active in seeking a settlement to the dispute between the Arab States and Israel. They tabled the Security Council Resolution on the Middle East which was unanimously adopted in November 1967.

My Ministers have welcomed the opening of discussions in Paris which they hope will lead to the end of the Vietnam conflict.

My Ministers played a leading part in negotiations which led to the successful conclusion of the Treaty on the Non-Proliferation of Nuclear Weapons, and have made proposals for further measures of disarmament.

My Government have maintained their application for membership of the European Communities and regret that the attitude adopted by one of the present members of the Communities has so far prevented the opening of negotiations.

My Government have announced their intention of withdrawing British forces from Malaysia, Singapore and the Persian Gulf by the end of 1971. They intend that over the next few years there should be a measure of re-deployment of national resources and that Britain's defence effort should in future be concentrated mainly in Europe and the North Atlantic area. My Ministers took part in a successful conference with Ministers of Australia, New Zealand, Malaysia and Singapore in Kuala Lumpur, where the problems arising from that decision were considered.

My Government have continued to play their full part in the North Atlantic Alliance. They expressed their condemnation of the invasion of Czechoslovakia by the Soviet Union and some of its allies in violation of international law and the Charter of the United Nations.

My Government worked for and welcomed the restoration of diplomatic relations with the United Arab Republic, the Somali Republic, Sudan, Guinea, Algeria, Mali, Mauritania, the Democratic Republic of the Congo (Brazzaville), Iraq and Tanzania.

My Government have continued to seek to bring about a return to constitutional rule in Rhodesia in accordance with the multi-racial principles approved by Parliament. To this end they have co-operated with other members of the United Nations in giving effect to the Security Council Resolution of 29th May. Proposals for a settlement were communicated to Mr. Smith during the recent discussions at Gibraltar, and his reply is now being studied.

Three of our overseas territories became independent in the last 12 months—Mauritius, Swaziland, and Aden (as part of the People's Republic of Southern Yemen). Both Mauritius and Swaziland remained in the Commonwealth. A revised Constitution was introduced in Seychelles.

Last November, at the invitation of My Government in Malta, My Husband and I visited Malta and renewed our happy memories of My People in

Malta and Gozo. In April of this year My Government
in the United Kingdom welcomed the successful
settlement, to which they made an important
contribution, of the Malta Dockyard ownership problem.

My Government welcome the improvement in
relations between the parties to the Cyprus dispute.

Despite economic difficulties, My Government
have sustained their programme of aid to less
developed countries.

The announced reductions in the size of the
Services will mean the retirement of some officers and
men and lead to the disappearance of some famous
regiments. I am deeply grateful to all those concerned
for their distinguished and selfless service. The need
for recruits for the Forces, however, remains as
pressing as ever, and My Government will not relax
their efforts in this field.

Members of the House of Commons:
I thank you for the provision which you have
made for the public services.

My Lords and Members of the House of Commons:
Following the devaluation of sterling in November
1967, My Government have taken the measures
necessary to ensure a progressive improvement in the
balance of payments and to maintain the strength of
sterling at its new parity.

My Government have taken an active part in
international discussions about reform of the
international monetary system. Agreement has been
reached with members of the sterling area and
members of the Bank for International Settlements
on arrangements to consolidate the stability of
sterling.

A further Act has been passed to provide support
for the productivity, prices and incomes policy.

The growth of industry in the development
areas has been encouraged and special measures have
been taken to reduce the impact of colliery closures
in these areas.

An Act has been passed to provide for a better
integration of road and rail transport and to promote
higher standards in the road transport industry. The
Act will also enable improvements to be made in
traffic management and the financial and other
arrangements for the railways and nationalised inland
waterways.

An Act has been passed to promote industrial
expansion by enabling My Government to assist
projects likely to benefit the economy.

Legislation has been passed to assist the
exploitation of natural gas from the North Sea.

Major new developments have been promoted
in the production in the United Kingdom of primary
aluminium.

Legislation has been passed to strengthen the
law on misleading trade descriptions and on restrictive
trade practices.

Legislation has been passed to clarify the law in its
application to hovercraft; and to enable further
measures to be taken to control aircraft noise and
supersonic flight.

An Act has been passed enabling provisional
action in accordance with international agreement
to be taken against dumping.

My Government took steps to stamp out the
very serious epidemic of foot and mouth disease and
to ensure that the farms affected could resume
production on a sound basis.

An Act has been passed to enable additional
payments to be made to tenant farmers whose land
is needed for development, to safeguard the welfare
of farm animals, and for other agricultural purposes.

My Government have taken steps to protect
the most vulnerable members of the community from
the effects of price increases by improving
supplementary benefits, rate rebates and family
allowances.

Legislation has been passed to promote the
better provision and development of health and
welfare services; and to make new comprehensive
arrangments for controlling the safety, quality and
description of medicines.

Legislation has been passed to establish a
comprehensive social work service in Scotland; and
appropriate provision has been made wherever
necessary in other Acts to meet distinctive Scottish
needs.

An Act has been passed to improve the
government of colleges and special schools.

My Ministers have continued the revision of the
machinery of government to meet the changing
requirements which are placed upon it. The Foreign
Office and Commonwealth Office have been merged.
An Order has been made for the amalgamation of the
Ministry of Health and the Ministry of Social Security.
My Government have welcomed the report of the
Fulton Committee on the Civil Service; and an Order
has been laid before you for the transfer of the
necessary functions to a new Civil Service Department
which will be closely engaged in the reshaping of the
Civil Service following the recommendation of the
Committee.

An Act has been passed providing for more
effective planning control of development in
England and Wales and for increased public participation
in local planning.

Legislation has been passed to establish a
Countryside Commission, to provide for the
conservation of the countryside and for greater
opportunities for leisure and recreation there; and for
the appointment of a Welsh Committee of the
Commission.

An Act has been passed strengthening control
over immigration from other parts of the Commonwealth.

An Act has been passed to make discrimination

on racial grounds unlawful in employment, housing
and the provision of goods, facilities and services, and
to encourage the development of harmonious
community relations.

An Act has been passed to reform the law on
gaming and to strengthen control over commercial
gaming clubs and gaming machines.

Further progress has been made in the systematic
reform of the law, including that relating to theft,
evidence and justices of the peace in England and
Wales and to succession and evidence in Scotland.

THIRD SESSION OF THE FORTY-FOURTH PARLIAMENT

1968–1969

OPENING (30 October 1968)

My Lords and Members of the House of Commons:

My Husband and I look forward with pleasure to the State Visit of the President of the Republic of Italy and to our own visit to Brazil and Chile.

My Government will continue to play an active part in the efforts of the United Nations to ensure peace and to assist the advancement of the developing world.

My Government will continue to work through the United Nations for a just and lasting peace in the Middle East. They will take every opportunity open to them to help the two sides achieve a negotiated settlement of the Vietnam conflict.

I look forward to welcoming to London in January the Heads of Government of other member countries of the Commonwealth.

My Government intend to ratify the Treaty on the Non-Proliferation of Nuclear Weapons. They will continue to work actively for further progress on measures of arms control and disarmament in both the nuclear and non-nuclear fields. To this end they will vigorously pursue the proposals they have put forward to advance the negotiations.

My Government will maintain their application for membership of the European Communities and will promote other measures of co-operation in Europe in keeping with this.

My Government will continue to support Britain's alliances for collective defence and will play an active part in the North Atlantic Alliance as an essential factor for European security. The development of My Government's relations with the countries of Eastern Europe which took part in the invasion of Czechoslovakia has necessarily been set back, but it remains their aim to work for genuine East-West understanding.

My Government will continue to take the necessary steps to withdraw British forces from Malaysia, Singapore and the Persian Gulf by the end of 1971. Furthermore, in consultation with the Governments concerned, My Ministers will maintain their efforts to promote conditions favourable to peace and security in the areas concerned.

My Government will continue to seek to bring about a return to constitutional rule in Rhodesia in accordance with the multi-racial principles approved by Parliament.

Members of the House of Commons:

Estimates for the public services will be laid before you.

My Lords and Members of the House of Commons:

My Government will press forward their policies for strengthening the economy so as to achieve a continuing and substantial balance of payments surplus. This will enable us to meet our international obligations, rebuild the reserves, develop industry and safeguard employment.

My Government will work closely with other Governments to maintain the smooth working of the international monetary system. They look forward to the early entry into force of the Special Drawing Rights Scheme.

My Government will develop policies to encourage a better distribution of resources in industry and employment and to make fuller use of resources in the Regions.

Legislation will be brought before you to convert the Post Office from a Department of State to a public corporation.

Legislation will be introduced to integrate transport in London under local government control; and to establish a central system of vehicle registration and licensing.

Legislation will be introduced to help the development of tourism in Great Britain.

A Bill will be introduced to effect the change to a decimal currency.

My Government will continue to promote the development of agriculture's important contribution to the national economy.

Legislation will be introduced for assistance to the deep sea fishing industry and for the policing and conservation of fisheries.

My Government will lay before you proposals for action on the Report of the Royal Commission on Trade Unions and Employers' Associations. They will also bring forward proposals for amending the Merchant Shipping Acts in accordance with the recommendations of the Court of Inquiry on the Shipping Industry.

My Ministers will submit for consideration a proposal to enable the United Kingdom to give effect to the United Nations Convention on Genocide.

Legislation will be introduced on the composition and powers of the House of Lords.

My Government will begin consultations on the appointment of a Commission on the constitution. The Commission would consider what changes may be needed in the central institutions of Government in relation to the several countries, nations and regions of the United Kingdom. It would also examine relationships with the Channel Islands and the Isle of Man.

A Bill will be brought before you to reduce to eighteen the age for voting and to make other reforms in electoral law.

Legislation will be laid before you to reduce the age of majority to eighteen.

A Bill will be introduced to reform the law for England and Wales relating to children and young persons.

Our social security schemes will be kept under close review. My Government will publish for public discussion proposals for a new scheme of national insurance founded on earnings-related benefits and contributions.

Legislation will be brought before you to increase the pensions of retired members of the public services and their dependants.

My Government will give special attention to the form of administration of the health and welfare services.

Measures will be introduced to modernise the town and country planning system in Scotland; and to bring the law relating to education in Scotland into line with current developments.

Legislation will be introduced to give rights of appeal against decisions taken in the administration of immigration control.

A measure will be laid before you to provide for a specific grant towards a programme of additional local authority expenditure in urban areas of special social need. This will include additional provision for children below school age.

Proposals will be brought forward for implementing the recommendations of the Tribunal appointed to inquire into the tragic disaster at Aberfan.

Legislation will be introduced to give greater encouragement to the repair and improvement of older houses and their environment.

My Ministers will submit for consideration a proposal to raise the existing legislative limit on Government expenditure on the construction of the National Theatre.

Legislation will be introduced to make reforms in the administration of justice. My Government will carry forward their comprehensive programme for the reform of the law. In particular, Bills will be laid before you to extend in England and Wales the rights of succession to property by persons who are illegitimate and to amend the law of heritable securities in Scotland.

Other measures will be laid before you.

PROROGATION (22 October 1969)

My Lords and Members of the House of Commons:

My Husband and I were glad to welcome to this country the President of the Italian Republic and the President of the Republic of Finland. We had the great pleasure of visiting Brazil, Chile and Austria.

My Government have pursued their efforts to promote through the United Nations a settlement to the dispute between the Arab States and Israel.

My Ministers have contributed fully to the tasks of the North Atlantic Alliance. They have continued to work for the relaxation of tension with the countries of Eastern Europe and to seek their co-operation in trade and other practical matters.

My Government have maintained their application for membership of the European Communities.

My Ministers have welcomed the talks in Paris between all the major parties involved in the Vietnam conflict and hope that they will soon make real progress towards peace.

My Government have ratified the Treaty on the Non-Proliferation of Nuclear Weapons and have striven for further progress on arms control and disarmament. In particular they have put forward proposals for a complete ban on biological methods of warfare.

My Husband and I were pleased to welcome to this country Heads and Representatives of Commonwealth Governments for the Commonwealth Prime Ministers' Meeting. The Meeting recognised the spcial ties of co-operation and understanding that link member countries of the Commonwealth and which My Government in the United Kingdom have continued to further.

New constitutions have been introduced in the Commonwealth of the Bahama Islands and in the Turks and Caicos Islands.

My Ministers have again sought a return of constitutional rule in Rhodesia in accordance with the multiracial principles approved by Parliament. To that end they have maintained political and economic sanctions under the terms of the United Nations Security Council Resolution of 29th May, 1968. The Governor of Southern Rhodesia announced his resignation on 24th June after receiving My permission to do so. My Government subsequently ordered the closure of the British Residual Mission in Salisbury and Rhodesia House in London.

My Government have been much concerned by the continuing conflict in Nigeria. They have helped with the relief of suffering and starvation and they have contributed to the search for a peaceful settlement.

Further progress was made towards co-operative defence arrangements between our Commonwealth partners in South-East Asia, following upon My Government's decision to withdraw British forces from Malaysia and Singapore by the end of 1971.

The situation in Northern Ireland has caused My Ministers deep concern. My Forces have carried out their duties there with exemplary steadiness. My Ministers are doing all in their power in co-operation with the Northern Ireland Government to bring peace and reconciliation to the Province.

Members of the House of Commons:

I thank you for the provision which you have made for the public services.

My Lords and Members of the House of Commons:

My Government's first aim has been to strengthen the economy so as to achieve a continuing surplus in the balance of payments. The policies which they have pursued have brought about a great improvement in the past year.

My Ministers have taken part in international discussions leading to the decision last month to activate the scheme for Special Drawing Rights.

An Act was passed to make further provision for the introduction of decimal currency in 1971.

A Commission on Industrial Relations has been appointed to examine and promote improvements in the machinery for collective bargaining.

Further progress has been made in regional economic development, and measures have been announced for assistance to industry in selected intermediate areas.

My Government have put forward proposals to help the Lancashire textile industry take its place once again in the forefront of British industry.

An Act has been passed to assist and encourage the development of tourism in Great Britain.

Legislation has been passed to integrate public transport in London under local government control.

An Act has been passed to establish a central system of driver licensing and of vehicle registration and licensing.

Legislation has given My Inspectors of Mines and Quarries and the appropriate local authorities new powers to ensure the safety of tips of mine or quarry refuse.

An Act has been passed to convert the Post Office from a Department of State to a public corporation.

My Government have reviewed the contribution of agriculture to the national economy and have announced an extended programme of selective expansion in the interests of import saving.

Action has been taken to implement the recommendations of the Committee of Inquiry on Foot and Mouth Disease, and codes of practice for the welfare of farm animals have been approved.

An Act has been passed for assisting the deep-sea fishing industry and for the policing and conservation of fisheries.

Provision has been made for improvements in the pensions and benefits of the national insurance and supplementary benefits scheme and in war pensions. Legislation has provided for contributions to the national insurance scheme to be increased and to be related more closely to earnings, and proposals have been published for new schemes of national superannuation and social insurance based on contributions related to earnings.

An Act has been passed amending the law in England and Wales relating to children and young persons.

Legislation has been passed to enable the United Kingdom to accede to the United Nations Convention on genocide.

Provision has been made for appeals by Commonwealth citizens and aliens against decisions taken in the exercise of immigration control.

An Act has been passed to raise the limit of Government expenditure on building the National Theatre.

I was pleased to grant a Charter of Incorporation to the Open University and thereby to launch a significant and original venture in higher education.

Legislation has been passed to give greater encouragement for the repair and improvement of older houses and their environment.

An Act has been passed to provide financial assistance for urban areas of special social need.

Legislation has been passed to modernise the Scottish Town and Country Planning system, and to bring up to date the law relating to housing and education in Scotland.

I have appointed a Commission on the Constitution.

The Civil Service Department has been established and steps have been taken to set up a Civil Service College.

Legislation has provided for increased pensions for retired members of the public service and their dependants.

Legislation has reduced the age of majority to 18. The voting age has also been reduced to 18, and other reforms have been made in electoral law.

Further progress has been made in the systematic reform of the law, including that relating to the succession rights of illegitimate children, the jurisdiction of the county court, the trial of personal injury cases, and real property. Steps have been taken to repeal obsolete statutes and improve the form of the Statute Book.

FOURTH SESSION OF THE FORTY-FOURTH PARLIAMENT

1969–1970

OPENING (28 October 1969)

My Lords and Members of the House of Commons:

My Husband and I look forward to our visits to New Zealand and Australia, and to attending the Cook Bicentenary Celebrations in both countries.

With the coming 25th Anniversary year of the United Nations, My Government reaffirm their support for the efforts to ensure peace and to assist the advancement of less developed countries. They will pursue their work through the United Nations for a just and lasting peace in the Middle East, and towards an international agreement on tariff preferences for the developing countries.

My Ministers will continue to play an active part in the North Atlantic Alliance as the foundation of our security and thereon to build better understanding between East and West.

My Government will maintain their application to become full Members of the European Communities and desire an early commencement of negotiations. They will take a full part in promoting other measures contributing to European unity.

My Government will strive for further progress on nuclear and non-nuclear arms control and disarmament. They will be particularly concerned with chemical and biological weapons, and will follow up with vigour the proposals they have put forward for a complete ban on biological methods of warfare.

My Ministers will remain ready to assist in any way they can to bring peace to Nigeria and Vietnam.

My Government will continue working for an eventual return to constitutional rule in Rhodesia, in accordance with the principles approved by Parliament. They will steadfastly pursue their policy of economic sanctions and of maintaining isolation of the illegal regime until the conditions for an honourable settlement exist.

My Ministers will continue their efforts to ensure justice and to promote peace and harmony between all communities in Northern Ireland. They will bring forward proposals to facilitate the reorganisation of the Royal Ulster Constabulary and to establish a local defence force for security duties in Northern Ireland.

Members of the House of Commons:

Estimates for the public services will be laid before you.

My Lords and Members of the House of Commons:

My Government will press forward their policies for attaining a substantial and continuing balance of payments surplus in order to meet our international obligations and rebuild our reserves, achieve a more rapid rate of economic growth, and safeguard employment. To this end they will continue to develop policies for promoting the efficiency and competitiveness of industry.

My Government will continue to work with other Governments to improve the international monetary system.

A statement will be presented to you of My Government's future plans for public expenditure.

My Government will continue to foster the fullest use of resources in all regions and will lay before you measures to provide for assistance to industry in intermediate areas.

Legislation will be introduced to secure the safety, health and welfare of persons on offshore drilling installations.

Bills will be brought before you to promote improved industrial relations and to provide for equal pay for men and·women. Provision will also be made for certain reforms relating to industrial safety and health.

Legislation will be introduced to rationalise the work of the Monopolies Commission and the National Board for Prices and Incomes, and to combine them in a new body.

Proposals will be·submitted to you for controlling the development of labour-only subcontracting in the construction industry.

Bills will be introduced to amend the Merchant Shipping Acts and to make provision for the safety of fishermen.

Proposals will be brought before you to give effect to certain recommendations of the Committee of Inquiry into Civil Air Transport.

A Bill will be introduced to assist the film industry.

Legislation for the reorganisation of the ports will be presented to you.

Bills will be introduced to reorganise the electricity supply and gas industries and to enable the Gas Council to search for, refine and market petroleum.

Proposals will be brought before you to establish the nuclear fuel business of the United Kingdom Atomic Energy Authority as a separate Government-controlled company.

A Bill will be introduced to continue the Government's powers under the Coal Industry Act 1967 to help the coal industry.

My Government will continue to encourage the selective expansion of home agriculture. Legislation will be introduced to implement the Government's proposals on the marketing of eggs; to rationalise the grants payable to assist fixed capital investment in agriculture; to reorganise smallholdings; and to modernise the law relating to sales of fertilisers and feedingstuffs.

A Bill will be introduced requiring local education authorities to prepare plans for reorganising secondary education on comprehensive lines.

A Bill will be brought before you for establishing a more effective system of control over dangerous drugs.

A Bill will be brought before you to introduce new schemes of national superannuation and social insurance and to protect occupational pension rights on change of employment.

Legislation will be introduced arising out of the recommendations of the Seebohm Committee on Local Authority and Allied Personal Social Services; and fresh proposals will be made about the future administration of the National Health Service.

Proposals will be put forward for the reorganisation of local government in England, Scotland and Wales.

Legislation will be introduced to continue in modified form powers to limit increases in house rents.

A Bill will be introduced to modernise the law relating to the construction of highways in Scotland.

Legislation will be brought in to reform certain features of the feudal system of land tenure in Scotland and the Scottish law of heritable conveyancing, and to improve the organisation of the Sheriff Courts in Scotland.

My Government will carry forward their comprehensive programmes of law reform.

A Bill will be laid before you to make better arrangements for the recovery of civil debts and to enable the Courts to avoid causing hardship when making orders for possession of mortgaged property.

Legislation will be introduced to enlarge the powers of the Courts with regard to financial provision for parties to marriages which have broken down.

Other measures will be laid before you.

PROROGATION (29 May 1970)

My Lords and Members of the House of Commons:
My Husband and I and The Princess Anne had the great pleasure of visiting New Zealand and Australia and of attending the Cook Bicentenary Celebrations in both countries. We were also very pleased to visit Fiji and Tonga. The Prince of Wales was able to accompany us to New Zealand and on part of our tour to Australia.

My Government have maintained their application for membership of the European Communities, and negotiations to this end are likely to open shortly.

My Ministers have made a full contribution to the North Atlantic Alliance, which is the foundation of our security, and have sought to develop better understanding between East and West.

My Government have continued to play an active part in the disarmament negotiations and have followed up with vigour their proposals for a complete ban on biological methods of warfare. They welcome the entry into force of the Treaty on the Non-Proliferation of Nuclear Weapons.

My Government have urgently pursued their efforts to promote through the United Nations a settlement to the dispute between the Arab States and Israel, and have continued their efforts to help bring peace to the countries of Indo-China.

My Government welcomed the end of hostilities in Nigeria, and have made a substantial contribution to post-war relief and rehabilitation.

My Government have welcomed the condemnation by the Security Council of the latest racialist policies of the illegal regime in Southern Rhodesia. They have worked to make existing economic sanctions more effective.

My Government welcomed the peaceful settlement, through the good offices of the Secretary-General of the United Nations, of the long-standing difference with the Imperial Iranian Government over Bahrain.

New Constitutions have been introduced in the British Solomon Islands Protectorate and the Seychelles. Tonga will cease to be a Protected State on 4th June and My Government look forward to welcoming her as a Commonwealth partner.

In this 25th Anniversary Year of the United Nations My Government is taking a leading part in promoting its work.

My Government have announced substantial increases in overseas aid for the next three years.

My Ministers have continued their efforts to promote peace and harmony in Northern Ireland. Acts have been passed to establish the Ulster Defence Regiment and to enable police forces in Great Britain to be more closely associated with the Royal Ulster Constabulary.

Members of the House of Commons:
I thank you for the provision which you have made for the public service.

My Lords and Members of the House of Commons:
My Government have pursued successful policies to strengthen the economy and the balance of payments so as to provide the basis for sustained and accelerating growth in conditions of high employment. A large surplus in the balance of payments has been achieved, and external indebtedness has been greatly

reduced.

My Government have continued to work with other Governments to improve the international monetary system.

A statement has been presented to you on My Government's future plans for public expenditure.

The pay structure of My Armed Forces has been radically revised to give proper recognition to their qualifications and responsibilities.

An Act has been passed providing for equal pay for men and women.

My Government have proposed major reforms to modernise industrial relations.

Legislation was introduced to establish a Commission for Industry and Manpower to take over and develop the work of the National Board for Prices and Incomes and the Monopolies Commission.

A Bill was introduced to make certain reforms relating to industrial safety and health and an inquiry into all aspects of the subject has been set up.

Acts have been passed to promote greater safety and improved living conditions for those serving in the Merchant Navy and fishing fleets.

An Act has been passed to assist the film industry.

Regional economic development has been further encouraged, especially in the development areas, and legislation has been passed to assist intermediate areas and to encourage the speedy clearance of derelict land.

Bills were introduced to reorganise the electricity supply industry and the gas industry, and to enable the Gas Council to search for, market and refine petroleum.

A Bill was introduced to continue the Government's powers to assist the coal industry.

Legislation was brought forward to raise the limit on guarantees under the Shipbuilding Credit Scheme.

A Bill was introduced to transfer the nuclear fuel and radio-chemical business of the United Kingdom Atomic Energy Authority to Government-controlled companies.

A Bill to reorganise the ports was presented to you.

My Government have published plans for the future strategy for inter-urban roads in England.

My Government have continued to encourage the selective expansion of home agriculture. An Act has been passed introducing new arrangements for the marketing of eggs and rationalising the grants payable to assist fixed capital investment in agriculture.

My Government have continued to take steps to restrain increases in food prices and to promote the safety of food for the consumer.

My Government have brought forward a measure to provide strong, comprehensive and flexible powers to control the availability of dangerous drugs and to check their misuse.

A Bill was presented to advance further the reorganisation of secondary education on comprehensive lines. Progress has been made in replacing old schools, increasing the numbers of qualified teachers and reducing oversized classes.

The expansion of higher education has continued, and student places provided have far exceeded the forecasts of the Robbins Committee on Higher Education.

My Government have announced further proposals to intensify the fight against the pollution of the environment, and measures were introduced to reduce aircraft noise and to discourage pollution of the sea by oil. I have appointed a Commission on Environmental Pollution.

My Government have put forward proposals to reform local government in England and Wales.

An Act has been passed to limit increases in rents of local authority and private tenants. Assistance to home buyers under the option mortage scheme have been taken to provide more and better homes. Orders have been made to raise the income limits which govern the entitlement to rate rebate.

Proposals for controlling labour-only sub-contracting in the construction industry were laid before you.

An Act has been passed to reorganise local authority personal social services. New proposals have been made for the future administration of the National Health Service in England and in Wales.

Improvements in existing health and welfare services have continued, with special emphasis on hospitals for the mentally handicapped and other long-stay patients.

Proposals have been put before you for new schemes of national superannuation and social insurance based on earnings-related contributions.

My Government have taken steps to make further improvements in the levels of benefits provided under the Supplementary Benefits Scheme.

Legislation has been passed to reform the fuedal system in Scotland and the Scottish law of heritable conveyancing.

An Act has been passed to modernise the law relating to the construction of highways in Scotland.

An Act has been passed to reconstitute the High Court with a Family Division; to extend the power to dispense with the holding of assizes and to improve the arrangements for the recovery of civil debts.

Further advances have been made in the reform of the law. Legislation has been passed to extend the powers of the courts to make financial provision in matrimonial disputes and to give effect to various proposals of the Law Commission.

FIRST SESSION OF THE FORTY-FIFTH PARLIAMENT

1970–1971

OPENING (2 July 1970)
My Lords and Members of the House of Commons:

My husband and I look forward to our visit to Canada on the occasion of the centenaries of the Northwest Territories and of the Province of Manitoba.

The major international interests of Britain are the maintenance of peace, the promotion of prosperity, the settlement of disputes by conciliation and agreement, and the encouragement of trade and peaceful exchanges between nations.

My Government have welcomed the opening on the 30th of June of negotiations for membership of the European Communities. In these negotiations they will seek to reach agreement on terms fair to all concerned and will remain in close consultation with our Commonwealth and EFTA partners and with the Irish Republic.

My Government will work for the maintenance of the defensive strength of the North Atlantic Alliance and for a genuine reduction of tension in relations between East and West in Europe.

My Ministers will take a full part in the meeting of Commonwealth Heads of Government in Singapore in January 1971. They will co-operate with our Commonwealth friends in measures aimed at maintaining peace and stability in Commonwealth countries in South-East Asia.

My Government will work for a fair and lasting peace in the Middle East and for a settlement of the conflict in Indo-China. They will consult with leaders in the Gulf on how our common interests in that area may best be served.

My Government will make a further effort to find a sensible and just solution of the Rhodesian problem in accordance with the five principles.

In this 25th Anniversary year of the United Nations, which opens the Second Development Decade, My Government will lend their full support to international efforts to strengthen peace, to promote disarmament and to further world economic development. They will pursue an expanding aid programme and will seek agreement on tariff preferences for developing countries.

My Government will work for the development and progress of Britain's dependent territories.

A Bill will be placed before you to provide for the independence of Fiji.

My Government will review the role and size of the Territorial and Army Volunteer Reserve.

My Ministers will support the Northern Ireland Government in their efforts to promote peace and harmony among all communities on the basis of equality and freedom from discrimination, and to further the prosperity of the Province. I have noted with pride the patience, skill and fortitude with which My Armed Forces are carrying out their difficult task.

Members of the House of Commons:

Estimates for the public services will be laid before you.

My Lords and Members of the House of Commons:

At home My Government's first concern will be to strengthen the economy and curb the inflation. Rising production and a steadily growing national income must provide the resources for improving the social services and the environment in which we live. The energy and enterprise needed to achieve this will be encouraged by reforming and reducing the burden of taxation, providing new incentives to saving and liberating industry from unnecessary intervention by Government.

My Ministers attach the greatest importance to promoting full employment and an effective regional development policy. They will stimulate long-term growth in the less prosperous areas by increasing their economic attractions and improving their amenities.

My Ministers will start discussions with a view to encouraging agricultural expansion by changes in the present system of financial support. They will promote the efficient development of the fishing industry.

The work of the Industrial Training Boards will be reviewed and the facilities for re-training and for management training improved and extended.

A Bill will be introduced to establish a framework of law within which improved industrial relations can develop and a code of practice will be prepared laying down standards for good management and trade union practice.

My Government believe that vigorous competition is the best safeguard for the consumer. They will carry out a review of company law.

My Ministers will pursue a vigorous housing policy with the principal aim of improving the position of the homeless and the badly housed. After consultations with local authorities, housing subsidies will be refashioned so as to give more help to those in greatest need. Home ownership will be encouraged.

My Government will expand educational opportunities as growing resources make this possible, with priority for the improvement of primary schools. An inquiry will be instituted into teacher training. Local authorities in Scotland, as in England and Wales, will be set free to take effective decisions on the organisation of their schools.

Responsibility for primary and secondary education in Wales will be assumed by the Secretary of State for Wales.

Legislation will be brought forward to provide pensions for persons now over 80 who were too old to enter the present insurance scheme and for certain younger widows and to provide a constant attendance allowance for the very seriously disabled.

Legislation will be introduced on Commonwealth immigration. More assistance will be provided for areas of special social need, especially those in which large numbers of immigrants have settled.

Effect will be given to the recommendations of the Boundary Commissions for the redistribution of Parliamentary seats.

Proposals will be worked out in full consultation with all concerned, for local government reform in England, Scotland and Wales, associated with a general devolution of power from the central Government. At a later stage plans will be laid before you for giving the Scottish people a greater say in the own affairs.

Proposals will be put forward for permitting commercial local radio stations under the general supervision of an independent broadcasting authority.

A Bill will be brought before you to abolish the Land Commission.

My Ministers will intensify the drive to remedy past damage to the environment and will seek to safeguard the beauty of the British countryside and seashore for the future.

Bills will be laid before you to improve the arrangements for the administration of justice in England and Wales in accordance with the recommendations of the Royal Commission on Assizes and Quarter Sessions and to improve the organisation of the Sheriff Courts in Scotland.

My Government will make it their special duty to protect the freedom of the individual under the law and will examine ways in which this may be more effectively safeguarded.

Other measures will be laid before you.

PROROGATION (28 October 1971)

My Lords and Members of the House of Commons:

My Husband and I and the Prince of Wales and The Princess Anne recall with pleasure our visits to Canada. We also had the pleasure of visiting Turkey this month and of welcoming to this country Their Imperial Majesties the Emperor and Empress of Japan.

My Government have virtually completed negotiations for British membership of the European Communities and are confident that the outstanding issues can be satisfactorily settled in the near future.

My Government welcome as Commonwealth partners Tonga, Western Samoa and Fiji.

My Ministers have contributed fully to the work of the North Atlantic Alliance, and have sought to improve relations between East and West. They welcome the progress which has been made towards more normal relations with the People's Republic of China.

The decision has been taken to retain certain British forces in South-East Asia as part of Five-Power Defence arrangements relating to Malaysia and Singapore.

My Government welcome the establishment of a new relationship with the States of Bahrain and Qatar and the progress made towards establishing the United Arab Emirates.

My Government played an active part in cyclone relief work in East Pakistan. They have since contributed generously to international relief measures for refugees in India and to the United Nations' relief efforts in East Pakistan.

My Government have played an active role in the international disarmament negotiations. They have signed the Seabed Arms Control Treaty and welcome the agreement reached in the Conference of the Committee on Disarmament on a draft convention banning biological weapons.

My Ministers have been actively seeking to find an acceptable basis for the negotiation of a just settlement of the Rhodesian problem in accordance with the Five Principles.

Measures have been announced to encourage British private investment in developing countries and the necessary steps taken to enable My Government to continue to play their full part in the work of the International Development Association.

My Ministers have begun discussions with representative groups in Northern Ireland to seek agreed ways and means within the constitutional and democratic framework of giving the minority as well as the majority community an active, permanent and guaranteed role in the life and public affairs of the Province. They have endeavoured through meetings with the Prime Minister of Northern Ireland and the Prime Minister of the Irish Republic to create an atmosphere of greater understanding so that the process of political reconciliation may go forward to a successful outcome. I take a special pride in the skill, perseverance and restraint with which my Armed Forces are carrying out their onerous tasks in Northern Ireland.

Members of the House of Commons:

I thank you for the provision which you have made for the public services.

My Lords and Members of the House of Commons:

A substantial surplus has been maintained on the current account of the balance of payments; confidence in sterling has remained high; there have been substantial increases in the official reserves since June 1970 and over one thousand million pounds of official overseas debt has been repaid.

My Government have taken an active part in discussions to resolve problems of the international monetary system.

The burden of taxation has been significantly reduced, and provision has been made for a major reform of the structure of personal direct taxation. A simplified and improved system of tax allowances has been introduced for capital expenditure on plant and machinery with special treatment for the development areas. These are the first stages of a far-reaching programme to reform the tax system.

A major reorganisation of the structure of Central Government has been carried through. Special attention has been paid to improving the effectiveness of Departments and other public bodies. A Defence Procurement Executive has been established to unify defence research, development and procurement activities. Acts have been passed to establish a Civil Aviation Authority and a British Airways Board and to transfer the United Kingdom Atomic Energy Authority's nuclear fuel and radio-chemical production business to companies set up under the Companies Acts.

Provision has been made for further assistance to the coal industry and for a fresh look at the National Coal Board's non-colliery activities.

Steps have been taken to encourage effective competition in the interests of the consumer and of industrial efficiency. A far-reaching reform of credit control techniques has been introduced.

My Government have established Rolls-Royce (1971) Limited to continue essential activities of Rolls-Royce Limited and, with the United States Government's support for the Lockheed TriStar aircraft, are assisting the new company to produce the RB.211 engine for that aircraft.

Legislation has been passed to raise the limit on guarantees under the Shipbuilding Credit Scheme. Special attention has been given to helping the development and intermediate areas. Further expenditure has been authorised to improve economic and social opportunities in these areas and provision has been made for higher grants to be paid to assist the improvement during the next two years of older houses and their surroundings.

Action has been taken to encourage the expansion of agriculture and changes have been made in support arrangements to strengthen the market for agricultural products and to limit the commitment of public funds.

An Act has been passed to reform and modernise the system of industrial relations. Urgent steps have been taken to improve facilities for industrial retraining and to increase the number under training.

My Government have taken active steps to improve the quality of the environment in our towns and countryside and on the coast.

Acts have been passed to protect our shores from oil pollution and to make it easier for victims of pollution to claim compensation.

Plans have been announced for a primary trunk road network built to high standards and achieving substantial environmental improvements.

The decision has been taken to build a third London Airport at Foulness.

An Act has been passed to strengthen the law relating to fire precautions in residential establishments and places of amusement and public resort.

Legislation has been passed to abolish State management for the sale and supply of intoxicating liquor in Carlisle and certain districts of Scotland.

The law on the misuse of drugs has been strengthened.

My Ministers have made important improvements in the system of social security, giving priority to those most in need. They have provided pensions for those over 80 who were not previously entitled to them and for younger widows. They have introduced a new attendance allowance for the very severly disabled and better benefits for the chronically sick and their families. Legislation has been passed to introduce family income supplements for poor families with children and to remove obsolete provisions from the social security system and prevent its exploitation.

Substantial increases in national insurance retirement pensions and related benefits took effect in September, 1971. At the same time the occupational pensions of retired members of the public services and armed forces and their dependants were increased under new arrangements designed to maintain purchasing power.

A very substantial primary school improvement programme has been launched. Acts have been passed concerning school milk and the education of mentally handicapped children previously considered unsuitable for education in school.

The recommendations for redistribution of seats made by the Boundary Commissions for England, Scotland, Wales and Northern Ireland in their reports in 1969 have been implemented without modification.

An Act has been passed to extend the field from which candidates for election to local authorities may be chosen.

Legislation has been passed providing for a unified system of immigration control.

Acts have been passed to implement the recommendations of the Royal Commission on Assizes and Quarter Sessions and to improve the organisation of the sheriff court system in Scotland.

Further progress has been made in the systematic reform of the law and in the consolidation of enactments and repeal of obsolete statutes.

SECOND SESSION OF THE FORTY-FIFTH PARLIAMENT

1971–1972

OPENING (2 November 1971)

My Lords and Members of the House of Commons:

My Husband and I look forward to our visits to Thailand, Singapore, Malaysia, Brunei, Maldives and the Seychelles.

In their external policies My Government will protect and advance the nation's interests. They hope, following the successful conclusion of negotiations, shortly to sign an Instrument of Accession to the European Communities after which legislation will be laid before you. It will be their purpose to maintain the North Atlantic Alliance, sustain the Commonwealth association and uphold our other friendships and alliances throughout the world, while continuing their efforts to achieve international agreement on arms control and disarmament.

My Ministers will work for good relations with the Soviet Union and the countries of Eastern Europe; for peace in the Middle East; and for improved relations with the People's Republic of China. They will co-operate in the new arrangements concerning the defence of Malaysia and Singapore and will seek to promote stability in the Gulf. They will continue to work towards a solution of the problems of East Pakistan and the refugees; an end to the conflict in Indo-China; and a settlement of the Rhodesian problem in accordance with the Five Principles.

My Government intend to increase aid to the developing countries. They will continue to promote the development of the dependent territories and the well-being of their peoples.

My Government will continue to co-operate with other Governments to resolve the current difficulties in international payments and bring about lasting improvements in the international monetary system in the interests of expanding world trade.

My Ministers are determined that violence in Northern Ireland shall be brought to an end. They are no less determined to continue their efforts to establish political conditions in Northern Ireland which ensure for the communities there an active, permanent and guaranteed role in the life and public affairs of the Province.

Members of the House of Commons:

Estimates for the public services will be laid before you.

My Lords and Members of the House of Commons:

At home my Government's first care will be to increase employment by strengthening the economy and promoting the sound growth of output. Their aim will be to curb inflation, encourage increased efficiency, and maintain a strong balance of payments. In developing their regional policies they will pay close attention to the economic needs of particular areas.

Legislation will be brought before you to promote active competition and fair trading and to extend customers' protection in the sale of goods. Other measures will provide for extending the Shipbuilding Credit Scheme, for re-organising the structure of the gas industry, for assisting the exploration of our mineral resources, and for encouraging British investment overseas through the establishment of an insurance scheme.

My Ministers will pursue their proposals for reforming the tax system and will bring forward legislation to establish a value-added tax and to reform company taxation.

My Ministers will continue to encourage the efficient expansion of agriculture and will introduce legislation to simplify administrative procedures and improve agricultural services. They will support the United Nations in preparing for a Conference on the Law of the Sea in 1973.

A Code of Industrial Relations Practice will be presented for your approval and proposals will be made for developing training facilities to meet future manpower needs.

Bills will be brought before you to reform the finance of rented housing and to provide more help for public and private tenants in need.

Powers will be sought to facilitate the reform of pensions schemes in the public services.

The substantial programme of replacement and improvement of primary school buildings will be continued. Steps will be taken to raise the school-leaving age to 16. Grants to direct grant schools will be increased. Provision for higher and further education will be improved and expanded.

Legislation will be introduced to give effect to My Government's proposals for the reorganisation of local government in England (outside Greater London) and in Wales.

A Bill will be laid before you to reorganise the health services in Scotland.

My Government will pursue with vigour their policies for improving the environment. Legislation will be proposed to increase protection for ancient monuments and to extend the powers of local authorities to protect buildings in conservation areas.

Legislation will be introduced to provide for an alternative service of local radio broadcasting.

My Government acknowledge and share public

concern at the growth of violent crime. They will lay before you provisions to strengthen the administration of criminal justice. In particular, provision will be made to enlarge the powers of the courts to award alternative penalties to custodial sentences and to require offenders to make reparation to their victims.

Further measurers of law reform will be brought forward and a Bill will be introduced to improve the facilities for giving legal advice and assistance to persons of moderate means.

Other measures will be laid before you.

PROROGATION (26 October 1972)

My Lords and Members of the House of Commons:
My Husband and I recall with pleasure our visits to Thailand, Singapore, Malaysia, Brunei, Maldives, the Seychelles, Mauritius and Kenya, to France, and to Yugoslavia. We also had the pleasure of welcoming to this country Queen Juliana and Prince Bernhard of the Netherlands, the Grand Duke and Duchess of Luxembourg and the President of the Federal Republic of Germany and Frau Heinemann.

Negotiations for British membership of the European Communities were successfully concluded by My Ministers. Following the passage of legislation making the requisite changes in United Kingdom law an Instrument of Ratification of the Treaty of Assession has been deposited to provide for accession to the Communities on 1st January, 1973. At the European Summit My Government joined with the other Governments in formulating constructive policies for the future development of the Communities.

My Ministers have played a full part in the North Atlantic Alliance and have striven to improve relations between East and West. Ambassadors have been exchanged with the People's Republic of China. My Government have continued their efforts to achieve international agreement on arms control and disarmament and have signed the Biological Weapons Convention.

My Government regret the decision of Pakistan to withdraw from the Commonwealth. They welcome as a Commonwealth partner the People's Republic of Bangladesh and are making a substantial contribution to relief and rehabilitation in Bangladesh.

My Ministers welcomed the opportunity for discussions with the Shah of Iran during his private visit to this country in June. My Government re-affirmed their support for the Central Treaty Organisation at the Ministerial Meeting in London in June.

My Government deplore the action of the Government of Uganda in expelling residents of Asian descent. They have made strong representations to the Ugandan Government and have sought the support of many Commonwealth and foreign Governments in offering to those expelled a choice of countries in which to live. My Ministers accept the responsibility to admit to this country any citizens of the United Kingdom and Colonies who are expelled from Uganda and wish to make their homes here. The Uganda Resettlement Board has been established to ensure the orderly reception and resettlement of these unfortunate people.

I have been deeply grieved at the loss of innocent lives in Northern Ireland as a result of terrorism.

The Parliament of Northern Ireland has been prorogued and provision made for direct rule for one year. My Ministers have striven for peace and understanding in the Province and a just share in its government for all its citizens. A conference has been held as part of the process of consulting people and organisations on the future constitutional framework for Northern Ireland.

My Armed Forces are carrying out with skill and determination their difficult and dangerous duties in Northern Ireland. Their courage deserves the greatest admiration and they will continue to act with vigour against lawlessness from any quarter.

Members of the House of Commons:
I thank you for the provision which you have made for the honour and dignity of the Crown and for the public services.

My Lords and Members of the House of Commons:
My Government have taken vigorous steps to encourage economic growth and industrial modernisation and to increase employment. Special attention has been paid to the problems of the assisted areas. Legislation has been passed to make regional development grants, to give selective financial assistance to industry and to provide special help for shipbuilding.

All remaining short and medium-term official overseas debt has been repaid. The reserves are at a satisfactory level. In June My Government decided that for the time being the sterling exchange rate should not be maintained within the normal dealing margins. My Government welcome the establishment of a new Committee of Twenty in the International Monetary Fund which will meet at Ministerial level to press forward the study of international monetary reform.

The burden of taxation has again been significantly reduced. Tax reform has been carried forward by providing for a new system of company taxation, for the abolition of purchase tax and selective employment tax, and for the introduction of a value-added tax. My Ministers have published Green Papers containing proposals for a new tax credit system and for a different death duty system.

Under the Industrial Relations Act, 1971, a code

of industrial relations practice containing guidance
for management and trade unions has been approved.
Training opportunities for individuals have been
greatly improved. My Government have announced
proposals for the reform of industrial training
arrangements.

Acts have been passed to strengthen the finances
of the British Steel Corporation and to reorganise the
gas industry.

My Government have taken active steps to
promote a strong agricultural industry which will be
competitive within the enlarged European Economic
Community. Support is being given to the British
fishing fleet in the exercise of their right to fish on the
high seas off Iceland.

New arrangements covering Government-
financed research and development, the Research
Councils and the use of scientific manpower in the
Civil Service have been announced.

My Government have continued their policies
of protecting and improving the quality of the
environment. Legislation has been passed to prevent
the irresponsible disposal of poisonous wastes of land.
My Government played a leading part in the United
Nations Conference on the Human Environment.

Legislation has been passed to reform the finance
of rented housing, to give help to tenants who need it,
and to make improved financial arrangements for
slum clearance.

Legislation has been passed for the reorganisation
of local government in England (outside Greater
London) and Wales.

An Act has been passed to reorganise the health
services in Scotland and to establish a Health
Commissioner to deal with complaints.

Substantial increases have been made in national
retirement pensions and related benefits under the
first of the annual reviews introduced by My
Government.

Provision has been made for substantial extension
of the attendance allowance for the disabled; and
family income supplements have been increased.

Proposals have been published for the future
development of State and occupational pensions.

Pension schemes of the public services have been
reformed. An Act has been passed to improve and widen
the scope of the parliamentary pension scheme.

The School-leaving age has been raised to 16.

Grants to direct grant schools have been increased.

An Independent Broadcasting Authority has
been established.

An Act has been passed to widen the powers of
the courts to deal with offenders, strengthen the
administration of criminal justice and reform the
qualifications for jury service.

Legislation has been passed to improve the
facilities for giving legal advice and assistance to
persons of moderate means.

THIRD SESSION OF THE FORTY-FIFTH PARLIAMENT

1972–1973

OPENING (31 October 1972)

My Lords and Member of the House of Commons:

My Husband and I look forward to our visits to Canada and Australia.

My Government will play a full and constructive part in the enlarged European Communities. They look forward to the opportunities membership will bring, for developing the country's full economic and industrial potential, for working out social and environmental policies on a European scale, and for increasing the influence of the enlarged Community for the benefit of the world at large.

My Ministers will seek to maintain and strengthen the North Atlantic Alliance. They will continue to sustain the Commonwealth association. My Government seek a positive improvement in East-West relations and are preparing in co-operation with their allies for a conference on security and co-operation in Europe. They will work for peace in the Middle East and in Indo-China. They seek to build upon the improved relations with China and hope for a peaceful and lasting settlement in the South Asian Sub-Continent.

My Government will work for co-operation within the United Nations; will support the United Nations law of the sea negotiations; and will continue to pursue agreed measures of arms control and disarmament. They will co-operate with other Governments in combating international terrorism. A Bill will be introduced to enable My Government to give effect to the Montreal Convention for the suppresion of unlawful acts against the safety of civil aviation.

My Government are determined to protect the right of British fishermen to fish on the high seas off Iceland. They remain ready to reach an amicable interim agreement with the Government of Iceland.

My Government will continue their efforts to ensure that United Kingdom passport holders expelled from Uganda have the widest possible choice of countries in which to settle. Help will be given to those who settle here and to local authorities that need to make special provision for them.

My Ministers will continue to search resolutely for peaceful and just solutions to the political, social and economic problems of Northern Ireland. They are resolved that terrorism and violence shall be brought to an end. The reform of local government will be completed. Legislation will be introduced to provide for a poll on the question of the Border; and to make available additional grant and loan finance to the Northern Ireland Exchequer.

Members of the House of Commons:

Estimates for the public services will be laid before you.

My Lords and Members of the House of Commons:

At home, My Government's over-riding concern, as Britain enters the European Communities, will be to promote the high and sustained rate of economic growth which is essential for the achievement of their policies of providing increased employment and rising living standards, as well as for the provision of better houses, schools, and social services. To that end, they will continue their efforts to establish effective means of enabling a faster growth of national output and real incomes to be maintained consistently with a reduction in the rate of inflation.

It is My Government's intention to resume the maintenance of agreed margins round a fixed parity for sterling as soon as circumstances permit.

My Government will continue to pursue the reform of taxation, the burden of which they have already greatly reduced.

In developing their policies for economic growth My Government will pursue their measures to create confidence and stimulate employment in the assisted areas.

Legislation will be brought before you to establish an improved organisation for the Government's manpower services including a reform of the system of industrial training.

Specia help will continue to be given to those in need through the social security system and by means of rebates and allowances: and a Bill will be introduced to extend rent allowances to tenants of furnished accommodation.

Extra help will continue to be provided for areas of special social need.

Legislation will be introduced to promote fair trading and competition; and to improve the provisions of the law regarding insurance companies. Other measures to protect the consumer will be proposed.

A measure will be introduced to facilitate the building of a Third London Airport at Maplin.

My Government will continue to encourage, within the framework of the European Economic Community, a strong agricultural industry and the efficient production and marketing of food in this country.

My Government will take further positive action on the protection and improvement of the environment. A Bill will be laid before you to reorganise the management of water resources in England and Wales.

Legislation will be introduced to provide improved compensation for perons whose land is acquired by public authorities and for the injurious effects of public works schemes.

A Bill will be introduced to reform local government in Scotland. Legislation will be laid before you to reform certain aspects of local government finance in England and Wales; and to establish machinery for investigating complaints of maladministration in local government.

A Bill will be laid before you to reorganise the administration of the National Health Service in England and Wales and to establish a health service commissioner to deal with complaints.

Legislation will be introduced to reform the finances of the national insurance scheme and to encourage the more widespread development and improvement of occupational pension schemes.

My Ministers will carry out their announced annual review of retirement and public service pensions and related benefits.

My Ministers will present to Parliament proposals to extend the education service and to set new priorities.

My Government will vigorously pursue policies for the prevention of crime and the treatment of offenders. They are especially concerned at the continued growth in manifestations of violence. They will press forward plans for strengthening the police, prison and probation and aftercare services, developing the prison building programme and implementing the Criminal Justice Act.

Measures will be introduced to make further reforms in the law and improvements in the administration of justice.

Other measures will be laid before you.

PROROGATION (25 October 1973)

My Lords and Members of the House of Commons:

My Husband and I recall with pleasure our visits to Canada and Australia. We also had the pleasure of welcoming to this country the President of Mexico and Senora de Echeverria; and the Head of the Federal Military Government of Nigeria and Mrs. Gowon.

I was particularly glad to be present in Ottawa for the meeting of the Commonwealth Heads of Government. My Ministers actively participated in the very useful exchanges of views at this meeting,

They welcome the Bahamas as a new partner in the Commonwealth.

Following the accession of the United Kingdom to the European Community, My Government have played a full and constructive part in developing the policies and activities of the Community. Good progress has been made in carrying out the programme laid down at the European Summit in October 1972.

My Government have made a major contribution to the preparation of the Community's approach to the reform of the international monetary system, to the forthcoming multilateral trade negotiations and to the positive European response to the United States' Government initiative for the improvement of Transatlantic relations.

My Government have continued to place great value upon the North Atlantic Alliance. They have worked for an improvement in East/West relations and for a successful outcome to the conference on security and co-operation in Europe.

My Ministers have had fruitful contacts with their counterparts in Japan and were pleased to welcome Mr. Tanaka on his official visit to this country. My Government have built steadily on the improvement in relations with China. While My Government have maintained traditional diplomatic ties with the Government of the Republic of Viet-Nam at Saigon, diplomatic relations have been established with the Democratic Republic of Viet-Nam at Hanoi. Diplomatic relations were established with the German Democratic Republic. My Ministers have continued to work for the improvement of relations with the Union of Soviet Socialist Republics. For the first time two members of My Family have visited that country. The 600th Anniversary of the Anglo-Portuguese Alliance was celebrated.

My Government have supported the efforts of the international community to put an end to the hostilities in the Middle East. They profoundly hope that these efforts will open the way to the earliest possible achievement of a just and lasting peace in the area.

My Government have continued to seek an interim agreement on fisheries with the Government of Iceland and have recently considered new proposals.

The continued suffering in Northern Ireland has caused me deep distress.

The temporary arrangements for direct rule have been superseded by legislation creating a new constitution for Northern Ireland in which all citizens will have a share. A poll has been held under legislation enabling the people of Northern Ireland to express their views on the status of Northern Ireland within the United Kingdom. Legislation has also been passed to enable serious crime and terrorism to be dealt with effectively in an emergency.

My Armed Forces and the Royal Ulster Constabulary continue to carry out their appallingly difficult duties in Northern Ireland with fairness, courage and skill. Their sacrifices and success are contributing towards the eventual return to peaceful conditions in Northern Ireland and deserve the highest commendation.

Members of the House of Commons:

I thank you for the provision which you have made for the public services.

My Lords and Members of the House of Commons:

My Ministers have actively pursued policies to promote a high rate of economic expansion; and to bring inflation under control while providing help for the needy. They have published a consultative document on the next Stage of counter-inflation policy, together with proposals to help pensioners; and they have had discussions with the building socieities with a view to assisting those buying homes for the first time.

Tax reform has continued to be an important objective of My Government. Purchase Tax and Selective Employment Tax have been abolished and, following a period of thorough preparation and extensive consultation, a Value Added Tax has been introduced and new systems of personal and company taxation have been brought into operation.

The Employment and Training Act will enable a Manpower Services Commission to be established for the improvement of training and other manpower facilities in association with both sides of industry.

Steps have been taken to strengthen the nuclear design and construction industry.

Legislation has been enacted to promote competition and fair trading and to regulate pyramid selling; and to protect the consumer in the supply of goods. An Act has been passed to improve the protection given to insurance policy holders.

Legislation has been enacted to re-organise the water industry in England and Wales. An Act has been passed to establish a Nature Conservancy Council.

The scope of rent regulation has been extended; the scheme for rent rebates and allowances has been improved; and rent allowances for people living in furnished accommodation have been introduced. The availability of an exceptionally high rate of grant for house improvement in the development and intermediate areas has been extended for a further year.

An Act has been passed to confer new rights of compensation upon those whose property is affected by public works and to mitigate the effects of public works on their surroundings.

Legislation has been passed to facilitate the building of the Third London Airport at Maplin.

An Act has been passed to reform local government in Scotland.

Legislation has been enacted to re-organise the administration of the National Health Service in England and Wales and to establish Health Service

Commissioners to deal with complaints.

Provision was made for lump sums to be paid to national insurance retirement pensioners and other beneficiaries over pension age. Following the annual review substantial increases were also made in the rates of national insurance retirement pensions and related benefits. The levels of family income supplements were also raised.

An Act has been passed to reform the finances of the national insurance scheme and to encourage a more wide-spread development and improvement of occupational pension schemes.

Plans for the expansion and development of the education service up to 1981 have been announced.

Legislation has been passed to confer on both parents equal rights over the custody and upbringing of their legitimate children. Further progress has been made with the reform and consolidation of the law, and with the administration of justice.

FOURTH SESSION OF THE FORTY-FIFTH PARLIAMENT

1973–1974

OPENING (30 October 1973)

My Lords and Members of the House of Commons:

My Husband and I look forward to our visits to New Zealand, Norfolk Island, the New Hebrides, the British Solomon Islands, Papua, New Guinea, Australia and Indonesia.

In co-operation with other Member States My Government will play their full part in the further development of the European Community in accordance with the programme established at the European Summit in October 1972. This programme includes progress towards economic and monetary union; measures for the establishment of a regional development fund; and co-operation in foreign policy between Member States. My Government's objective throughout will be to promote the interests of the individual, whether as citizen or as consumer.

My Government will continue to work for a just and lasting peace in the Middle East.

My Government will continue their active role in Commonwealth Affairs. They will maintain their support for the North Atlantic Alliance.

My Government will continue to attach high importance to our relationship with the United States of America; will persist in the search for opportunities to develop our relationship with the Soviet Union; will work to promote the fullest co-operation with Japan; and will seek to consolidate good relations with China.

My Ministers will work for the success of the conference on security and co-operation in Europe and of the negotiations for force reductions in Central Europe.

Within the United Nations My Government will work for agreement on measures relating to arms control and disarmament; and will take an active part in the United Nations conference on the law of the sea. A measure will be introduced to enable the United Kingdom to ratify the United Nations convention on the prohibition of biological weapons.

My Ministers will continue to support the principle of peaceful change in Southern Africa; and in Rhodesia to encourage Africans and Europeans to reach agreement on a just and lasting solution to their differences.

My Government are continuing to seek an interim agreement on fisheries with the Government of Iceland.

My Ministers will continue to strive towards the ending of violence in Northern Ireland and an equitable resolution of the political, social and economic problems there. Legislation will be introduced to ensure that in seeking and holding employment My subjects in Northern Ireland are not discriminated against because of their religious or political beliefs or affiliations.

Members of the House of Commons:

Estimates for the public services will be laid before you.

My Lords and Members of the House of Commons:

At home, My Government's continuing aim will be to secure a prosperous, fair and orderly society; to maintain their policies for promoting employment and for raising standards of living; and to improve the health, welfare, educational and other social services. They will have particular regard to the requirements of the old, the sick and the needy.

As a condition of securing these objectives one of My Government's primary concerns will be to sustain the expansion of the economy while achieving the necessary improvement in the balance of payments. They will so contain public expenditure that the rise in productive investment and in exports is not put at risk. My Government will continue their efforts to counter inflation.

My Government will continue to play an active part in the development of a reformed international monetary system.

The reform of taxation will continue. Legislation will be brought forward to enable a tax credit scheme to be implemented in due course.

My Government will again review retirement and public service pensions and related benefits.

My Ministers will continue to give high priority to housing policies and in particular to improving living conditions in the worst housing areas, and to giving additional help to the voluntary housing movement.

My Government will lay before you measures providing for greater control over environmental pollution.

In pursuance of My Government's concern to encourage high standards throughout industry and commerce, major reforms in company law will be laid before you.

A Green Paper will be published containing proposals for promoting a greater degree of employee participation in industry.

Legislation to make better provision for the safety and health of workers and the public will be brought before you.

For the further protection of consumers a Bill will be introduced to reform and extend the law relating to credit.

Legislation will be introduced to provide for the licensing of sports grounds in the interests of the safety of spectators.

A Bill will be laid before you to help to remove unfair discrimination on grounds of sex in employment and training and to widen the range of opportunities open to women.

My Government will seek to encourage increased opportunities for voluntary service and to support activities organised by and for young people.

Legislation will be introduced to promote road safety, to improve the control of traffic and to permit greater flexibility in the provision of rural road transport. Legislation will be brought forward on the financing, construction and operation of the channel tunnel.

Measures relating to the extraction of petroleum from the United Kingdom Continental Shelf will be laid before you.

Legislation will be introduced to reform certain aspects of local government finance in England and Wales and to establish machinery for investigating complaints of maladministration in local government.

Measures will be brought before you on the reform of crofting and parts of the general law relating to land tenure in Scotland.

A Bill will be introduced to strengthen the laws against indecent public advertisement and display; and to extend the controls of cinematograph exhibitions.

My Ministers will continue to take action to ensure an efficient and soundly based agricultural industry.

Priority will continue to be given to programmes in support of law and order and law reform, to the improvement of community relations and to the problem of those suffering special disadvantages from the conditions of life in urban areas.

Other measures will be laid before you.

PROROGATION (8 February 1974)

My Lords and Members of the House of Commons:
My Husband and I had the pleasure of visiting New Zealand, where we attended the Commonwealth Games. I also had the pleasure of visiting the Cook Islands.

My Husband and I were pleased to welcome to this country the President of Zaire and Madame Mobutu.

My Ministers welcome Grenada as a new partner in the Commonwealth.

My Government have continued to make a strong contribution to the work of the European Economic Community. The meeting of Heads of State or Government at Copenhagen in December was the first of a planned series of meetings which will give a continuing impetus to the Community's progress.

Agreement has been reached between Member States on the content of a Social Action Programme designed to benefit very many people in the Community. Discussions on a Regional Development Fund are still in progress.

The Community has reached agreement on the measures to be included in a second stage of progress towards Economic and Monetary Union.

In this 25th year of the North Atlantic Alliance My Government have continued to work to strengthen the Alliance in discharging its vital role in the preservation of peace and security.

My Government have attached major importance to the development of closer understanding between East and West. They have played a full part in working for the success of the Conference on Security and Co-operation in Europe and in the opening stages of the negotiations for force reductions in Central Europe.

My Government have continued to attach the highest importance to the relations of the United Kingdom and of the European Community with the United States. Fruitful co-operation with Japan has continued to develop. My Ministers have had useful contacts with their counterparts in the Union of Soviet Socialist Republics. They have also had useful meetings with Ministers of governments of a number of East European countries. Relations with China have continued to develop favourably.

My Government have welcomed the opening of negotiations in Geneva on the disengagement of forces in the Middle East as a first step towards the establishment of a just and assured peace.

My Ministers have continued to play an active part in the development of a reformed international monetary system.

My Government have welcomed the proposal of the President of the United States for a conference of oil importing countries, to be followed by a conference with the oil producing countries.

My Government have concluded an interim agreement on fisheries with the Government of Iceland.

In Northern Ireland an Executive of the Assembly has entered into office and, in accordance with the constitutional arrangements, powers have been devolved upon the Assembly. After successful discussions between My Government, the Northern Ireland Executive and the Government of the Republic of Ireland, work has begun directed towards the development of mutual co-operation.

My Armed Forces and the Royal Ulster Constabulary continue to make their contribution towards the restoration of peace in Northern Ireland. They merit the highest praise.

Members of the House of Commons:

I thank you for the provision which you have made for the public services.

My Lords and Members of the House of Commons:

My Government have continued to pursue policies to counter the threat which inflation poses to the prosperity of the nation and to the maintenance of a fair and orderly society. They have sought to bring about settlement of industrial disputes in ways consistent with these objectives.

Measures have been announced to increase taxation on higher incomes and to reduce public expenditure, to help to meet the changed situation created by the higher prices of oil and the restricted supply of sources of energy.

My Ministers have acted promptly to minimise the disruption of industry and commerce due to shortages of energy. Legislation has been passed to provide additional powers of control over fuel and electricity.

Proposals have been announced for increases in the taxation of profits from land and property development and for ensuring that empty office blocks are brought into occupation.

Legislation has been introduced to give additional help to the voluntary housing movement and to improve living conditions in the worst housing areas.

A Bill has been introduced extending controls over waste disposal, water pollution, air pollution and noise. Measures have been tabled to control dumping at sea and to make provision concerning oil pollution by ships.

A Bill has been brought forward making better provision for the health and safety of workers and the public.

Legislation has been introduced providing for important reforms in company law.

As part of My Government's programme to ensure improved protection for consumers, measures have been laid before you to reform and extend the law relating to credit and to provide for unit pricing.

A Bill has been introduced to provide for the licensing of sports grounds in the interests of the safety of spectators.

Legislation has been brought forward to promote road safety, to improve the control of traffic and promote greater flexibility in the provision of rural road transport.

An Act has been passed to provide intitial finance for the channel tunnel and a further Bill has been introduced to provide for its construction and operation.

Legislation has been passed to reform certain aspects of local government finance in England and Wales and to establish machinery for investigating complaints of maladministration in local government.

Legislation has been brought forward on the reform of crofting and parts of the law relating to land tenure in Scotland.

A measure has been introduced to strengthen the laws against indecent public advertisement and display; and to extend the controls over cinematograph exhibitions.

Legislation has been passed to mitigate the effect on the pension entitlement of certain servants and other public service employees of the Counter-Inflation (Temporary Provisions) Act 1972.

FIRST SESSION OF THE FORTY-SIXTH PARLIAMENT

1974

OPENING (12 March 1974)

My Lords and Members of the House of Commons:

My Husband and I look forward with pleasure to our visits to Indonesia and Japan and to the State Visit which Her Majesty Queen Margrethe of Denmark will pay to this country.

My Government will work for the strengthening of international institutions and of co-operation between all countries concerned to promote peace and to achieve prosperity in the face of world-wide inflation and far-reaching monetary disturbance. They will attach particular importance to the work of the United Nations and its agencies and to co-operation within the Commonwealth.

My Government will seek a fundamental renegotiation of the terms of entry to the European Economic Community. After these negotiations have been completed, the results will be put to the British people.

Recognising the economic problems concerning the developing countries My Government will seek to increase the provision of aid and to establish a more liberal pattern of world trade.

My Government will give their support to the search for a just and lasting peace in the Middle East, based on the implementation of Security Council Resolutions 242 of 1967 and 338 of 1973.

Recognising that the availability and the price of oil is a problem for the whole world, My Government will co-operate with consumer and producer countries in seeking to establish arrangements which will be in the interests of all.

My Government will oppose all forms of racial discrimination at home and abroad. In Rhodesia they will agree to no settlement which is not supported by the African majority.

My Government will give full support to the maintenance of the North Atlantic Alliance. They will regard the North Atlantic Treaty Organisation as an instrument of *detente* no less than of defence. In consultation with their allies they will pursue a policy directed to maintaining a modern and effective defence system while reducing its cost as a proportion of our national resources.

My Ministers will contribute fully to the negotiations for force reductions in Central Europe and to the Conference on Security and Co-operation in Europe.

My Ministers will give their support to the constitutional arrangements which now offer to Northern Ireland the prospect of healings its political and social divisions and of achieving prosperity and security for all its people. They will play their part, together with the Northern Ireland Executive and the Government of the Republic of Ireland, in developing co-operation in matters of mutual interest and in bringing violence to an end.

Members of the House of Commons:

Estimates for the public service will be laid before you.

My Lords and Members of the House of Commons:

In home affairs, my Government will first seek to ensure a return to full-time working in industry. I have been able to end the State of Emergency, occasioned by the coal mining dispute, which had existed since 13 November 1973 and which I had renewed by Proclamation on 6 March 1974 before the dispute was settled.

My Government will give the highest priority to overcoming the economic difficulties created by rising prices, the balance of payments deficit and the recent dislocation of production.

Measures will be laid before you to establish fair prices for certain key foods, with the use of subsidies where appropriate; and to restrain price inflation.

Legislation will be introduced to reform and extend the law relating to consumer credit; and a measure will be laid before you to require goods, where appropriate, to be labelled with the price at which they are to be sold, and to provide for unit pricing.

My Government is taking immediate steps to halt the increases in rents due in 1974. They will bring forward comprehensive proposals, which will require the repeal of the Housing Finance Acts, to reform the law relating to rents and housing subsidies in England, Wales and Scotland. Urgent measures will be taken to reverse the fall in house-building, to protect furnished tenants from eviction and to encourage municipal ownership. Proposals will be prepared for bringing land required for development into public possession and for encouraging home ownership. Proposals will be brought forward to eliminate the abuses arising from the lump.

My Ministers will work for a greater measure of social justice as a pre-requisite of national unity at this difficult time. A Bill will be introduced to increase pensions and other social security benefits. Proposals will be put before you for the redistribution of wealth, the protection of the lower laid and the disadvantaged, and for better methods of meeting the needs of the disabled.

In the light of these measures, My Ministers will

discuss urgently with The Trades Union Congress, the Confederation of British Industry and the others concerned, methods of securing the orderly growth of incomes on a voluntary basis.

My Ministers will hold urgent consultations on measures to encourage the development and re-equipment of industry. A Bill will be laid before you to consolidate and develop existing legislation to promote national industrial expansion. High priority will be given to the stimulation of regional development and employment. They will develop an active manpower policy, and bring forward legislation for protecting the health and safety of people at work.

My Government will encourage the maximum economic production of food by the farming and fishing industries of the United Kingdom in the interests of the national economy.

My Ministers will set in hand urgent action to improve energy supplies, to secure their efficient use and to ensure that oil and gas from the Continental Shelf are exploited in ways and on terms which will confer maximum benefit on the community, and particularly in Scotland, and the regions elsewhere in need of development. An urgent examination will be carried out of the future of the coal industry.

Measures will be introduced to repeal the Industrial Relations Act and to replace it by new legislation which will include the establishment of a new conciliation and arbitration service.

Comprehensive proposals will be brought forward to reform the law relating to the adoption, guardianship and fostering of children on the basis of the recommendations of the Interdepartmental Committee on the Adoption of Children.

Within available resources, My Government will progressively improve and expand the National Health Service and the personal social services. They will review the working of the reorganised National Health Service.

My Government will give priority to improving educational facilities for children in need of special help, and will prepare plans for the nation-wide provision of nursery education and for the development of a fully comprehensive system of secondary education. A major review will be made of the particular needs of handicapped children.

The museum charges recently introduced will be abolished.

My Ministers will work for the protection and improvement of the environment including the improvement of public transport, and will reappraise accordingly the value of certain major development projects.

My Ministers will initiate discussions in Scotland and Wales on the Report of the Royal Commission on the Constitution, and will bring forward proposals for consideration.

My Ministers will make proposals for securing equal status for women.

My Ministers will consider the provision of financial assistance to enable Opposition parties more effectively to fulfil their Parliamentary functions.

Measures will be introduced to make further reforms in the law and improvements in the administration of justice.

Other measures will be laid before you.

Note: There was no Prorogation Speech. Parliament was Dissolved on September 20 during the Summer Recess.

FIRST SESSION OF THE FORTY-SEVENTH PARLIAMENT

1974–1975

OPENING (29 October 1974)

My Lords and Members of the House of Commons:

My Husband and I look forward with pleasure to our visits to Bermuda, Barbados, Bahamas, Mexico, Hong Kong, Japan; and to the meeting of Commonwealth heads of Government in Jamaica.

My Government will give their full support to international efforts to solve the world-wide problem of inflation and will play a full part in international discussions to solve the problems created by higher oil prices.

They will continue the policy of strengthening the United Nations, its agencies and other international institutions dedicated to the peaceful settlement of disputes, the promotion of human rights, the rule of law and the improvement of the quality of life. In the effort needed to deal with world problems, they attach high importance to the Commonwealth association.

My Government will energetically continue their renegotiation of the terms of the United Kingdom's membership of the European Economic Community. Within 12 months the British people will be given the opportunity to decide whether, in the light of the outcome of the negotiations, this country should retain its membership.

My Government recognise the economic problems confronting developing countries, and will seek to increase the provision of aid. They will promote international efforts to establish a more liberal pattern of trade.

My Ministers will continue to support the search for a just and lasting peace in the Middle East and to work for a satisfactory solution to the problems of Cyprus.

My Government will oppose racial discrimination at home and abroad. In Rhodesia, they will agree to no settlement which is not supported by the African people of that country.

My Government will continue to give full support to the maintenance of the North Atlantic Alliance. They will regard the North Atlantic Treaty Organisation as an instrument of *detente* as well as of defence. In consultation with their allies, and in the light of a searching review of our defence commitments and forces they will ensure the maintenance of a modern and effective defence system while reducing its cost as a proportion of our national resources.

My Ministers will support the policy of *detente* between East and West. They will continue to play a full part in international efforts to achieve general disarmament and to prevent the spread of nuclear weapons. They will participate fully in the negotiations for force reductions in Central Europe and in the Conference on Security and Co-operation in Europe.

My Ministers will continue to work for a political solution in Northern Ireland. The proposed Constitutional Convention will provide a means by which those elected to it can consider what provision for the government of Northern Ireland is likely to command the most widespread acceptance throughout the community; any solution must, if it is to work, provide for some form of genuine power sharing and participation by both communities in the direction of affairs in Northern Ireland. My Ministers will continue to act decisively against terrorism and lawlessness. They attach particular importance to co-operation with the Government of the Republic of Ireland in the field of security and in other matters of mutual interest.

Members of the House of Commons:

Estimates for the public service will be laid before you.

My Lords and Members of the House of Commons:

At Home, My Government, in view of the gravity of the economic situation, will as their most urgent task seek the fulfilment of the social contract as an essential element in their strategy for curbing inflation, reducing the balance of payments deficit, encouraging industrial investment, maintaining employment, particularly in the older industrial areas, and promoting social and economic justice.

The use of subsidies to keep down prices of certain foods will be continued. Further measures for the protection of consumers will be brought forward.

My Ministers will pursue their aim of achieving a fair redistribution of income and wealth. A measure will be brought before you for the introduction of a tax on capital transfers. My Ministers will propose the establishment of a Select Committee to examine the form which a wealth tax might take.

Measures will be placed before you to amend the Trade Union and Labour Relations Act 1974; and to establish the Conciliation and Arbitration Service on a statutory basis and to protect and improve working conditions generally. Proposals will be brought forward to tackle the abuses of "the lump" as a step towards creating a stable work force in the construction industry. My Ministers will publish proposals to ensure comprehensive safeguards for employment in the docks.

My Government attach major importance to a

general improvement in social security benefits in the interests of social justice. Measures will be introduced to increase existing social security benefits, including family allowances; to make additional provision for the disabled; to pay a Christmas bonus; and to set up a new earnings-related pension scheme.

Within available resources, My Government will continue to maintain and improve the National Health Service and, following consultations, will introduce proposals on democracy in the service.

My Government's education policy will continue to give priority to areas of greatest need and to children with special difficulties. Particular attention will be given to the development of a fully comprehensive system of secondary education and to nursery education. A Bill will be introduced to provide public lending rights for authors.

My Ministers will energetically pursue their policies for encouraging local authorities and housing associations to provide more homes to rent and to develop their programmes for improving existing homes, particularly in the areas of greatest stress. They will take action to secure a stable and adequate flow of mortgages. Bills will be laid before you to reform the law relating to rents and housing subsidies in England and Wales and in Scotland.

Legislation will be introduced to enable land required for development to be taken into community ownership and to tax realisations of development value.

My Ministers recognise the value to the nation of expanding domestic food production economically and efficiently, and will continue their discussions with the farming industry to this end.

My Government will continue to pursue a comprehensive energy policy which makes the fullest economic use of United Kingdom coal, oil and natural gas and experience in nuclear technology, and to encourage energy conservation. Legislation will be introduced to regulate further the development of offshore petroleum, to establish a British National Oil Corporation with rights to participate in this development; to ensure that the community receives a fair share of the profits; and to provide for the acquisition of oil sites in Scotland.

My Ministers wish to encourage industrial investment and expansion within vigorous and profitable public and private sectors of industry. For this purpose, legislation will be introduced to provide for the establishment of planning agreements and a National Enterprise Board; and to enable the shipbuilding and aircraft industries to be taken into public ownership.

Legislation will be introduced to provide additional protection for policy-holders of insurance companies, and for people booking overseas holidays and travel who suffer loss as a result of the failure of travel organisers.

My Government will urgently prepare for the implementation of the decision to set up directly-elected assemblies in Scotland and Wales.

Bills will be introduced to provide for the establishment of development agencies in Scotland and in Wales. Other proposals relating to Scotland will include measures on local government and summary jurisdiction.

Legislation will be brought before you with the aim of ending sex discrimination.

A Bill will be introduced to reform the law relating to the adoption, guardianship and fostering of children.

Measures will be introduced to improve the law and the administration of justice.

An early opportunity will be given for you to consider whether your proceedings should be broadcast.

Other measures will be laid before you.

Appendices

APPENDIX 1

BRITISH KINGS AND QUEENS SINCE 1900

Name	Accession
Victoria	20 June, 1837
Edward VII	22 January, 1901
George V	6 May, 1910
Edward VIII[1]	20 January, 1936
George VI	11 December, 1936
Elizabeth II	6 February, 1952

[1] Abdicated

APPENDIX 2

BRITISH GOVERNMENTS AND PRIME MINISTERS SINCE 1900

Date	Government	Prime Minister	Party
25 June, 1895	Conservative	Marquess of Salisbury	Conservative
12 July, 1902	Conservative	Arthur Balfour	Conservative
5 December, 1905	Liberal	Sir Henry Campbell-Bannerman	Liberal
8 April, 1908	Liberal[1]	Herbert Asquith	Liberal
7 December, 1916	Coalition	David Lloyd George	Liberal
23 October, 1922	Conservative	Andrew Bonar Law	Conservative
22 May, 1923	Conservative	Stanley Baldwin	Conservative
22 January, 1924	Labour	James Ramsay MacDonald	Labour
4 November, 1924	Conservative	Stanley Baldwin	Conservative
5 June, 1929	Labour[2]	James Ramsay MacDonald	Labour
7 June, 1935	National	Stanley Baldwin	Conservative
28 May, 1937	National	Neville Chamberlain	Conservative
10 May 1940	Coalition[3]	Winston Churchill	Conservative
26 July, 1945	Labour	Clement Attlee	Labour
26 October, 1951	Conservative	Sir Winston Churchill	Conservative
6 April, 1955	Conservative	Sir Anthony Eden	Conservative
10 January, 1957	Conservative	Harold Macmillan	Conservative
19 October, 1963	Conservative	Sir Alec Douglas-Home	Conservative
16 October, 1964	Labour	Harold Wilson	Labour
19 June, 1970	Conservative	Edward Heath	Conservative
4 March, 1974	Labour	Harold Wilson	Labour

[1] Coalition from 25 May, 1915
[2] National from 24 August, 1931
[3] National from 23 May, 1945

APPENDIX 3

PARLIAMENTARY SESSIONS SINCE 1900

Session	Met	Prorogued	Dissolved
TWENTY-SEVENTH PARLIAMENT			
1	3 December, 1900	15 December, 1900	
2	23 January, 1901	17 August, 1901	
3	16 January, 1902	18 December, 1902	
4	17 February, 1903	14 August, 1903	
5	2 February, 1904	15 August, 1904	
6	14 February, 1905	11 August, 1905	8 January, 1906
TWENTY-EIGHTH PARLIAMENT			
1	13 February, 1906	21 December, 1906	
2	12 February, 1907	28 August, 1907	
3	29 January, 1908	21 December, 1908	
4	16 February, 1909	3 December, 1909	10 January, 1910
TWENTY-NINTH PARLIAMENT			
1	15 February, 1910	28 November, 1910	28 November, 1910
THIRTIETH PARLIAMENT			
1	31 January, 1911	16 December, 1911	
2	14 February, 1912	7 March, 1913	
3	10 March, 1913	15 August, 1913	
4	10 February, 1914	18 September, 1914	
5	11 November, 1914	27 January, 1916	
6	15 February, 1916	22 December, 1916	
7	7 February, 1917	6 February, 1918	
8	12 February, 1918	21 November, 1918	25 November, 1918
THIRTY-FIRST PARLIAMENT			
1	4 February, 1919	23 December, 1919	
2	10 February, 1920	23 December, 1920	
3	15 February, 1921	10 November, 1921	
4	14 December, 1921	19 December, 1921	
5	7 February, 1922	4 August, 1922[1]	26 October, 1922
THIRTY-SECOND PARLIAMENT			
1	20 November, 1922	15 December, 1922	
2	13 February, 1923	16 November, 1923	16 November, 1923
THIRTY-THIRD PARLIAMENT			
1	8 January, 1924	9 October, 1924	9 October, 1924
THIRTY-FOURTH PARLIAMENT			
1	2 December, 1924	22 December, 1925	
2	2 February, 1926	15 December, 1926	
3	8 February, 1927	22 December, 1927	
4	7 February, 1928	3 August, 1928	
5	6 November, 1928	10 May, 1929	10 May, 1929
THIRTY-FIFTH PARLIAMENT			
1	25 June, 1929	1 August, 1930	
2	28 October, 1930	7 October, 1931	8 October, 1931

Session	Met	Prorogued	Dissolved
THIRTY-SIXTH PARLIAMENT			
1	3 November, 1931	17 November, 1932	
2	22 November, 1932	17 November, 1933	
3	21 November, 1933	16 November, 1934	
4	20 November, 1934	25 October, 1935	25 October, 1935
THIRTY-SEVENTH PARLIAMENT			
1	26 November, 1935	30 October, 1936	
2	3 November, 1936	22 October, 1937	
3	26 October, 1937	4 November, 1938	
4	8 November, 1938	23 November, 1939	
5	28 November, 1939	20 November, 1940	
6	21 November, 1940	11 November, 1941	
7	12 November, 1941	10 November, 1942	
8	11 November, 1942	23 November, 1943	
9	24 November, 1943	28 November, 1944	
10	29 November, 1944	15 June, 1945	15 June, 1945
THIRTY-EIGHTH PARLIAMENT			
1	1 August, 1945	6 November, 1946	
2	12 November, 1946	20 October, 1947	
3	21 October, 1947	13 September, 1948	
4	14 September, 1948	25 October, 1948	
5	26 October, 1948	16 December, 1949	3 February, 1950
THIRTY-NINTH PARLIAMENT			
1	1 March, 1950	26 October, 1950	
2	31 October, 1950	4 October, 1951	5 October, 1951
FORTIETH PARLIAMENT			
1	31 October, 1951	30 October, 1952	
2	4 November, 1952	29 October, 1953	
3	3 November, 1953	25 November, 1954	
4	30 November, 1954	6 May, 1955	6 May, 1955
FORTY-FIRST PARLIAMENT			
1	7 June, 1955	5 November, 1956	
2	6 November, 1956	1 November, 1957	
3	5 November, 1957	23 October, 1958	
4	28 October, 1958	18 September, 1959	18 September, 1959
FORTY-SECOND PARLIAMENT			
1	20 October, 1959	27 October, 1960	
2	1 November, 1960	24 October, 1961	
3	31 October, 1961	25 October, 1962	
4	30 October, 1962	24 October, 1963	
5	12 November, 1963	31 July, 1964[1]	25 September, 1964
FORTY-THIRD PARLIAMENT			
1	27 October, 1964	8 November, 1965	
2	9 November, 1965	10 March, 1966	10 March, 1966
FORTY-FOURTH PARLIAMENT			
1	18 April, 1966	27 October, 1967	
2	31 October, 1967	25 October, 1968	
3	30 October, 1968	22 October, 1969	
4	28 October, 1969	29 May, 1970	29 May, 1970

Session	Met	Prorogued	Dissolved
FORTY-FIFTH PARLIAMENT			
1	29 June, 1970	28 October, 1971	
2	2 November, 1971	26 October, 1972	
3	31 October, 1972	25 October, 1973	
4	30 October, 1973	8 February, 1974	8 February, 1974
FORTY-SIXTH PARLIAMENT			
1	6 March, 1974	31 July, 1974[1]	20 September, 1974
FORTY-SEVENTH PARLIAMENT			
1	22 October, 1974		

[1] Parliament was Dissolved during the summer adjournment and the date shown is that on which the House of Commons last met.

Index

INDEX

Throughout this index the attempt has been made to avoid referring to the more inconsequential statements on general topics.

References to visits by Heads of State to and from this country include those visits which were only proposed and never eventually undertaken.

No acronyms are used in this index.